FAIRNESS IN EMPLOYMENT TESTING

*Validity Generalization,
Minority Issues, and the
General Aptitude
Test Battery*

John A. Hartigan and Alexandra K. Wigdor,
Editors

Committee on the General Aptitude Test Battery
Commission on Behavioral and Social Sciences and Education
National Research Council

DISCARDED

NATIONAL ACADEMY PRESS
Washington, D.C.   1989

NATIONAL ACADEMY PRESS · 2101 Constitution Avenue, NW · Washington, DC 20418

NOTICE: The project that is the subject of this report was approved by the Governing Board of the National Research Council, whose members are drawn from the councils of the National Academy of Sciences, the National Academy of Engineering, and the Institute of Medicine. The members of the committee responsible for the report were chosen for their special competences and with regard for appropriate balance.

This report has been reviewed by a group other than the authors according to procedures approved by a Report Review Committee consisting of members of the National Academy of Sciences, the National Academy of Engineering, and the Institute of Medicine.

The National Academy of Sciences is a private, nonprofit, self-perpetuating society of distinguished scholars engaged in scientific and engineering research, dedicated to the furtherance of science and technology and to their use for the general welfare. Upon the authority of the charter granted to it by the Congress in 1863, the Academy has a mandate that requires it to advise the federal government on scientific and technical matters. Dr. Frank Press is president of the National Academy of Sciences.

The National Academy of Engineering was established in 1964, under the charter of the National Academy of Sciences, as a parallel organization of outstanding engineers. It is autonomous in its administration and in the selection of its members, sharing with the National Academy of Sciences the responsibility for advising the federal government. The National Academy of Engineering also sponsors engineering programs aimed at meeting national needs, encourages education and research, and recognizes the superior achievements of engineers. Dr. Robert M. White is president of the National Academy of Engineering.

The Institute of Medicine was established in 1970 by the National Academy of Sciences to secure the services of eminent members of appropriate professions in the examination of policy matters pertaining to the health of the public. The Institute acts under the responsibility given to the National Academy of Sciences by its congressional charter to be an adviser to the federal government and, upon its own initiative, to identify issues of medical care, research, and education. Dr. Samuel O. Thier is president of the Institute of Medicine.

The National Research Council was organized by the National Academy of Sciences in 1916 to associate the broad community of science and technology with the Academy's purposes of furthering knowledge and advising the federal government. Functioning in accordance with general policies determined by the Academy, the Council has become the principal operating agency of both the National Academy of Sciences and the National Academy of Engineering in providing services to the government, the public, and the scientific and engineering communities. The Council is administered jointly by both Academies and the Institute of Medicine. Dr. Frank Press and Dr. Robert M. White are chairman and vice chairman, respectively, of the National Research Council.

This project was supported by the Employment and Training Administration of the U.S. Department of Labor.

Library of Congress Cataloging-in-Publication Data

National Research Council (U.S.). Committee on the General Aptitude Test Battery.
    Final report: fairness in employment testing: validity generalization, minority issues, and the General Aptitude Test Battery/John A. Hartigan and Alexandra K. Wigdor, editors; Committee on the General Aptitude Test Battery, Commission on Behavioral and Social Sciences and Education, National Research Council.
        p. cm.
    Bibliography: p.
    Includes index.
    ISBN 0-309-04030-2 (paper); ISBN 0-309-04033-7 (cloth)
    1. General aptitude test battery—Evaluation. 2. Employment tests—United States—Evaluation. 3. Employment tests—Law and legislation—United States. I. Hartigan, John A., 1927–   . II. Wigdor, Alexandra K. III. Title.
HF 5549.5.E5N38   1989
153.9′4—dc20   89-32841
                                                                                                                      CIP

Printed in the United States of America

Committee on the General Aptitude Test Battery

JOHN A. HARTIGAN (*Chair*), Department of Statistics, Yale University
LORRIE A. SHEPARD (*Vice Chair*), School of Education, University of Colorado, Boulder
MARCUS ALEXIS, Dean, College of Business Administration, University of Illinois, Chicago
MANFRED EMMRICH, North Carolina State Employment Service, Raleigh
LARRY V. HEDGES, Department of Education, University of Chicago
IRA J. HIRSH, Department of Psychology, Washington University, and Central Institute for the Deaf, St. Louis, Mo.
RICHARD M. JAEGER, School of Education, University of North Carolina at Greensboro
STEPHEN P. KLEIN, The Rand Corporation, Santa Monica, Calif.
ROBERT L. LINN, School of Education, University of Colorado, Boulder
JOHN M. RAUSCHENBERGER, Employee Development Office, Ford Motor Company, Dearborn, Mich.
MICHAEL ROTHSCHILD, Department of Economics and Dean, Social Sciences, University of California, San Diego
PAUL R. SACKETT, Industrial Relations Center, University of Minnesota
O. PETER SHERWOOD, Solicitor General, New York State
HOWARD F. TAYLOR, Department of Sociology, Princeton University

ALEXANDRA K. WIGDOR, Study Director
HILDA WING, Research Associate
DIANE L. GOLDMAN, Administrative Secretary

Liaison Group, Members

ROBERT BOLDA, Personnel Research Division, General Motors Corporation, Detroit, Mich. (Retired)

RALPH G. CANTRELL, Virginia Employment Commission, Richmond

WAYNE F. CASCIO, Graduate School of Business Administration, University of Colorado, Denver

SUZAN CHASTAIN, Office of Civil Rights, Office of the Solicitor, U.S. Department of Labor

ROBERT DELAHUNTY, Office of the Assistant Attorney General (Civil Rights Division), U.S. Department of Justice

CONSTANCE L. DUPRE, U.S. Equal Employment Opportunity Commission (Retired)

PATRICIA J. DYER, IBM Corporate Employment and Placement, Armonk, N.Y.

KENNETH EDWARDS, Skill Improvement Department, International Brotherhood of Electrical Workers, Washington, D.C.

MANFRED EMMRICH, North Carolina State Employment Service, Raleigh

BOB FUNSTON, Oklahoma Employment Security Commission, Oklahoma City

JOHN E. HUNTER, Department of Psychology, Michigan State University

HENRY LEVIN, Departments of Education and Economics, Stanford University

PHILIP B. LYONS, U.S. Equal Employment Opportunity Commission

CHARLES F. NIELSON, Texas Instruments, Inc., Dallas, Tex.

EDWARD E. POTTER, McGuiness & Williams, Washington, D.C.; Equal Employment Advisory Council

MARJORIE RAGOSTA, Educational Testing Service, Princeton, N.J.; Committee on Disabilities and Handicaps, American Psychological Association

NAMBURY S. RAJU, Department of Psychology, Illinois Institute of Technology, Chicago

DENNIS K. RHOADES, National Economic Commission, American Legion, Washington, D.C.

WILLIAM L. ROBINSON, Lawyers' Committee for Civil Rights Under Law, Washington, D.C.

WILLIAM W. RUCH, Psychological Services, Inc., Glendale, Calif.

ROBERT A. SCHAERFL, U.S. Employment Service, U.S. Department of Labor

FRANK L. SCHMIDT, College of Business Administration, University of Iowa

NEAL W. SCHMITT, Department of Psychology, Michigan State University

DONALD J. SCHWARTZ, Office of Research and Analytic Services, U.S. Equal Employment Opportunity Commission

RICHARD T. SEYMOUR, Lawyers' Committee for Civil Rights Under Law, Washington, D.C.

JAMES C. SHARF, Career Entry Group, U.S. Office of Personnel Management

WILLIAM TRACEY, Employment Services, New Jersey Department of Labor, Trenton (Retired)

DENNIS L. WARMKE, Philip Morris U.S.A., Richmond, Va.

RAUL YZAGUIRRE, National Council of La Raza, Washington, D.C.

Preface

The Department of Labor is considering whether to promote the use of its General Aptitude Test Battery (GATB) throughout the U.S. Employment Service to screen many of the 19 million people who pass through the system annually in search of private- and public-sector jobs. This study was undertaken at the agency's request because system-wide use of the test battery for referral purposes raises important questions of public policy. In order to provide employers with the maximum benefits of testing, the Employment Service would need to refer applicants in order of test score. Such a policy, however, would severely reduce the employment opportunities of lower-scoring applicants, particularly of minority job seekers, who have lower average test scores as a group than the majority.

What is the appropriate balance between anticipated productivity gains from better employee selection and the well-being of individual job seekers? Can equal employment opportunity be said to exist if screening methods systematically filter out very large proportions of minority candidates? Such an outcome would leave employers—and the Employment Service—vulnerable to the charge of discrimination under Title VII of the Civil Rights Act of 1964.

In pilot projects of the test-based referral system, conducted since 1980, Department of Labor officials have adopted a score-adjustment strategy in which each applicant's test score is computed as a percentile score within his or her own racial or ethnic group (black, Hispanic, and other). By combining within-group percentile scores and top-down

vii

selection of the applicants to be referred, the Department of Labor sought a workable compromise between productivity goals and federal equal employment opportunity policy. However, the within-group scoring strategy created its own problem: the Department of Justice questioned its legality and constitutionality on grounds of reverse discrimination.

As a consequence of this challenge, the Department of Labor sought guidance from the National Academy of Sciences, which, through the National Research Council, has convened a committee of experts to conduct a thoroughgoing evaluation of the plan to use the GATB as the primary tool for deciding which applicants to refer to employers. The Department of Labor asked the committee to address a number of important technical questions to establish the appropriateness of using a single general aptitude test to predict performance in a large number of very different jobs. In addition, recognizing that these technical issues are surrounded by a complex web of governmental policies and legal requirements and have serious economic and social implications, the Department of Labor asked the committee to consider the possible effects of widespread adoption of testing in the Employment Service—effects on employers, on various categories of job seekers, and on the economic health of the country.

This study is intended to help policy makers decide whether the GATB should be given a primary role in the Employment Service referral system and, in that event, to offer guidance on methods for assembling the pool of job candidates and for reporting test scores. The policy context is described in Chapters 1 and 2. Chapter 3 presents an overview of the U.S. Employment Service and its activities. In Chapter 4 we look at the quality of the GATB, and in Chapter 5 discuss critical weaknesses in the test and in the GATB research program that must be overcome if it is to be used as a primary referral tool.

The principal scientific underpinnings of the Department of Labor's plan to use the GATB for referrals to all kinds of jobs, contained in the theory of validity generalization, are examined in Chapters 6 through 9. Chapter 8 looks at the accumulated body of GATB validity research and presents the committee's judgments about the degree of predictive accuracy that can reasonably be assumed for jobs not studied.

Chapter 10 describes the referral system—which we call the VG-GATB Referral System to signal its dependence on validity generalization—as it has been conceptualized by the research staff of the U.S. Employment Service. Chapter 11 discusses the potential effects of the system on the various Employment Service clients, and Chapter 12 analyzes the claims about economic benefits said to accrue from referring job candidates in order of test score.

Based on the technical findings presented earlier, Chapters 13 and 14 present the committee's recommendations to policy makers. In Chapter 13 the committee presents its conclusions about the fair use of employment tests and makes recommendations about adjusting the test scores of minority job seekers. Chapter 14 presents the committee's most important recommendations for the use of the GATB and the design of the VG-GATB Referral System.

In providing independent advice to the government on matters of science policy, the National Research Council depends on committees of volunteers chosen for their expertise, together with members of the permanent staff, to carry out its work. The members and staff of the Committee on the General Aptitude Test Battery include experts in statistics and meta-analysis, psychometrics, industrial and personnel psychology, economics, sociology, policy analysis, law, and the Employment Service—the expertise needed to address the broad range of technical and policy questions raised in this study. Brief biographies of committee and staff appear in Appendix C.

During the course of its study, the committee has called on a great many people, who gave generously of their time, their expertise, and their insights. Because the policy decisions ultimately made by the Department of Labor with regard to the GATB will have an impact, perhaps a great impact, on the interests of a variety of individuals, groups, and institutions, a carefully selected liaison group was appointed to ensure that the committee would be conversant with all relevant policy perspectives and areas of expertise. Our particular thanks go to the 28 members of this group who met with us on three occasions and provided needed information and position papers throughout. Individual members also presented occasional special briefings on specific issues before the committee.

We received assistance from other quarters as well. In response to questions from the committee about employers' reactions to the VG-GATB system and within-group scoring, the Employers' National Job Service Committee developed and circulated a questionnaire that elicited over 500 responses. Our work also benefited from the cooperation of the National Rehabilitation Association and the major veterans organizations.

We owe a great deal to John Hawk, personnel research psychologist in the test research division of the U.S. Employment Service, and his colleagues in the central and regional offices. In response to our sheer need to be educated about the Employment Service system and the GATB, they provided helpful briefing documents. As we came to grips with the very large undertaking required by our charge, they remained helpful and forthcoming in the face of frequent requests for data, documents long buried in the files, information about day-to-day operations, and myriad other questions that came up. Staff members of the

Northern Test Development Field Center provided the tapes of the GATB data base and arranged for the collection of a sample of item-level test data for our item-bias analysis. The Southern Test Development Field Center supplied useful information about the development of the GATB and the operations of the Employment Service system.

We would also like to recognize the contributions of several consultants who helped with our data analysis: Douglas Weeks assisted committee member Robert Linn in the differential validity and differential prediction analysis; Laura Burris and Victoria Crawshaw assisted Paul Sackett with the meta-analysis of the entire GATB data base; Robin Corley assisted Lorrie Shepard with a study of item bias; Anita Tesh assisted Richard Jaeger with a synthesis of the literature on GATB properties. Glen Sueyoshi contributed a background paper on the economic effects of improved employee selection as the question is addressed in the economics literature.

Our acknowledgments would not be complete without special thanks to staff members who worked with the committee: Hilda Wing, who assisted with the research and writing; Diane Goldman and Carolyn Sax, who provided administrative support and kept control of the evolving manuscript; and Christine McShane, whose graceful editing defied a hectic schedule.

JOHN A. HARTIGAN, *Chair*
ALEXANDRA K. WIGDOR, *Study Director*
Committee on the General Aptitude Test Battery

Contents

FAIRNESS IN

EMPLOYMENT TESTING

Summary

This volume is one of a number of studies conducted under the aegis of the National Research Council/National Academy of Sciences that deal with the use of standardized ability tests to make decisions about people in employment or educational settings. Because such tests have a sometimes important role in allocating opportunities in American society, their use is quite rightly subject to questioning and not infrequently to legal scrutiny. At issue in this report is the use of a federally sponsored employment test, the General Aptitude Test Battery (GATB), to match job seekers to requests for job applicants from private- and public-sector employers. Developed in the late 1940s by the U.S. Employment Service (USES), a division of the Department of Labor, the GATB is used for vocational counseling and job referral by state-administered Employment Service (also known as Job Service) offices located in some 1,800 communities around the country.

In recent years, the Department of Labor has begun to promote the use of the GATB throughout the Employment Service for referral to all jobs found in the U.S. economy. Spurred by the need to streamline operations because of severe staff reductions and budget cuts, and hoping as well to increase economic productivity by improving the person-job match, USES has encouraged the states to experiment with a test-based referral system that in this report is called the VG-GATB Referral System.[1] Although the

---

[1] "VG" stands for validity generalization, the theory used to extrapolate the empirically established validities of the GATB for predicting performance in some 500 jobs to all other jobs in the U.S. economy.

1

state pilot programs have tended to be a patchwork of old and new procedures, the major features of the experimental system as conceived by USES staff are as follows:

1. Virtually all registrants at Employment Service offices are to be administered the GATB.

2. Virtually all job orders are to be filled on the basis of GATB scores.

3. The group of job candidates referred to an employer are to be selected on the basis of rank-ordered test scores (plus any additional criteria such as educational or experience requirements imposed by the employer).

4. GATB scores are computed as percentile scores within each of three racial or ethnic groups: black, Hispanic, and other. The purpose of these score adjustments, which serve to erase group differences in test scores, is to mitigate the adverse effects that rank-ordering on the basis of test score would otherwise have on the employment opportunities of minority job seekers.

5. Given the dependence of this type of referral system on searching the registrant files to compile a list of job candidates from the highest score on down, computerization of the files to allow rapid data retrieval is encouraged to complement the VG-GATB Referral System.

ISSUES FOR STUDY

Faced with a Justice Department challenge on legal and constitutional grounds to one element in the VG-GATB Referral System—the use of within-group percentile scores—the Department of Labor sought the advice of the National Academy of Sciences on the future role of test-based referral in the Employment Service. A committee of experts established within the National Research Council was asked to study the issue of within-group scoring and further to undertake a thorough evaluation of validity generalization and its application to the GATB. The Department of Labor sought advice on whether the pivotal role envisioned for the General Aptitude Test Battery is technically justified, whether the anticipated economic benefits are realistic, and what the effects of widespread adoption of the VG-GATB Referral System might be on various constituencies of interest, including veterans, people with handicapping conditions, employers, and job seekers.

In seeking answers to these questions, the Committee on the General Aptitude Test Battery organized its work around nine topics, outlined briefly below. The text indicates the chapters of the report that contain the committee's complete statements. This overview concludes with a summary of the committee's central recommendations.

Issues in Policy, Equity, and Law
(Chapters 1, 2, and 13)

The VG-GATB Referral System raises important questions of social policy. The Department of Labor's adoption of within-group scoring and the subsequent legal challenge lodged by the former Assistant Attorney General for Civil Rights echo a deep-seated ambivalence in our society about the meaning of equality. At issue is the fairness of using race-conscious mechanisms to overcome the legacy of governmentally imposed discrimination that consigns most black Americans to the margins of social acceptance and economic well-being. Employment testing raises the issue in the public arena in a very concrete way: employee selection on the basis of rank-ordered test scores will screen out a large proportion of black and Hispanic candidates and thus expose employers (and the Employment Service) to legal action under the civil rights laws on grounds of discrimination; the use of score adjustments to mitigate these adverse effects on the employment chances of minority job seekers creates vulnerabilities to charges of reverse discrimination.

The claim of omnicompetence for the GATB—that it is a valid predictor for all 12,000 jobs in the U.S. economy—raises a different set of issues. It is based in part on the idea that the test measures some attribute that underlies performance in all jobs, an attribute that is usually identified as intelligence, or *g*. There are dangers in promoting intelligence testing to which policy makers should be sensitive. Data from intelligence testing were misused in the early twentieth century in a way that fed the racial and ethnic prejudices of the day, and the potential for generating feelings of superiority in some groups and inferiority in others is equally great today.

Findings and Conclusions

The committee is not in a position to make definitive statements about the legality of race-conscious scoring methods. Our aim is to explicate the issues that policy makers need to consider as they plan the future of the VG-GATB Referral System, and to offer advice on aspects of the problem that lend themselves to scientific analysis.

Is the Psychometric Quality of the GATB Adequate?
(Chapters 4 and 5)

The General Aptitude Test Battery is now some 45 years old. There have been four versions of the test: Forms A and B were introduced in 1947, and Forms C and D in 1983. A testing program of this sort always poses the danger of getting handcuffed to history; the issue is whether to make changes in the instruments as the technology advances. Altering a test can destroy its links to the research base; there is, therefore, a strong impulse toward preservation, which can ultimately result in an out-of-date test. Given the relatively advanced age of the GATB, we felt it important to look closely at the test's structure and content and its psychometric properties. We also wanted to see how it compares with other major test batteries.

Findings and Conclusions

Our study leads us to conclude that the GATB is adequate in psychometric quality, with the exception of two serious flaws that could significantly impair the usefulness of the test if it is made an important screening device throughout the Employment Service. The first flaw is weak test security due to the availability of only two current alternate forms of the test and due to administration of the test in a variety of protocols by a variety of organizations. It must be anticipated that the forms of the test will be available outside government channels once it becomes clear that getting a job through the Employment Service depends on doing well on the test.

The second flaw is the speededness of the test. Many of the subtests have such severe time limits that an average applicant can expect to complete only one-third of the test. Such tests are eminently coachable; that is, test takers can learn strategies to improve their performance. For example, scores can be substantially increased by randomly filling in the remaining blanks in the last minute of the test. The test will not retain its validity if such coaching becomes widespread.

We did not find the GATB markedly superior or inferior to other test batteries, such as the Armed Services Vocational Aptitude Battery (ASVAB), on two dimensions of central importance—predictive validity and test reliability. But the GATB does not compare well with the ASVAB in other ways, e.g., test security, the production of new forms, the strength of its normative data, and the severe time limits imposed even when speed of performance is not an essential aspect of the aptitude being measured.

How Well Does the GATB Predict Job Success?
(Chapter 8)

The question of greatest interest about any employment test is how accurate an estimate of future job performance it allows. No test provides anything close to perfect prediction; there are many characteristics of importance to actual job performance that tests do not assess, and others that tests do not assess very well. Nevertheless, tests can measure some relevant skills and abilities and are particularly good gauges of cognitive abilities. The GATB is supported by some 750 criterion-related validity studies. These show the degree of relationship between GATB scores and a measure of job performance (typically supervisor ratings of job incumbents, but in some cases grades in a training course) in about 500 jobs. The committee has reanalyzed the data from these 750 studies and looked closely at the adjustments for sampling error and restriction of range that appear in USES technical manuals reporting GATB validities.

Findings and Conclusions

Our findings speak directly to the question of how central a role in Employment Service job referrals the GATB could sustain technically. In the 750 studies, the correlations of GATB-based predictors with supervisor ratings, after correction for sampling error, are in the range of .2 to .4. The average validity (corrected for criterion unreliability) of GATB aptitude composites in studies conducted since 1972 is about .25, whereas corresponding adjustments for the older studies produce an average validity of .35. These correlations are modest. In the committee's judgment, they indicate that GATB scores can provide useful screening information, but that the predictive power of the test battery is not so strong that the GATB should become the sole means of filling all job orders.

The average values reported here are lower than those appearing in USES technical reports, which are .5 or higher. One reason for the discrepancy is that the committee had access to more data; the more recent (post-1972) studies tended to produce noticeably lower validities than did the older studies. In addition, although we acknowledge that the correlations are attenuated by criterion unreliability and range restriction, the committee does not accept the magnitude of the corrections that were made for these two factors in the USES technical reports. Since these corrections have the effect of substantially increasing the estimated correlations between test scores and ratings of job performance, the committee's estimate of GATB validities is substantially lower than that in the technical reports.

Does the GATB Predict Less Well for Minority Job Seekers?
(Chapter 9)

Because of the consistent differences in average group performance on standardized tests, a persistent concern about ability tests has been that they may be biased against minority group members. The 1970 Equal Employment Opportunity Commission (EEOC) *Guidelines on Employee Selection Procedures* required that data be generated and results be reported separately for minority and nonminority groups, and USES conducted about 200 validity studies during the 1970s and early 1980s to explore the question. We have looked carefully at the data reported by race to see if the GATB predicts differentially by race.

Findings and Conclusions

Our analysis of the 78 studies that had at least 50 black and 50 nonminority employees shows that there were differences in both the validities and the prediction equations for blacks and nonminorities. First, the average correlations between test score and supervisor ratings were .12 for blacks and .19 for nonminorities. Second, the formula that best predicts black performance is somewhat different from that predicting the performance of majority-group applicants. However, the use of a single formula for relating GATB scores to performance criteria would not be biased against black applicants; if anything, it would slightly overpredict their performance, particularly in the higher score ranges.

This finding needs to be treated with some caution. Differential prediction analysis takes the performance measure as a given. But there may be bias against blacks in the primary criterion measure used in the studies—supervisor ratings. Usually the supervisors were white. There is some empirical evidence, and it is plausible on historical and social grounds, that supervisors will favor employees of their own race. The size of the supervisor bias has not been determined, but its possible presence counsels caution in accepting supervisor ratings as an equally accurate estimate of job performance for both groups.

Are There Scientific Justifications for Adjusting Minority Test Scores? (Chapter 13)

In addition to the question of test bias, which is addressed by differential validity analysis (comparability of correlations) and differential prediction analysis (comparability of regression lines), there is a larger question of the evenhandedness of selection based on test scores. Our premise is that the inaccuracy of the test should not unduly affect the employment prospects of able minority workers. This premise led us to focus on the issue of selection error and specifically to ask whether there are differences among the majority and minority groups in false-acceptance and false-rejection rates.

Findings and Conclusions

Our analysis of the impact of selection error on minority and nonminority applicants demonstrates that in the absence of score adjustments, minority applicants who could perform successfully on the job will be screened out of the referral group in greater proportions than are equivalent majority-group applicants. Conversely, majority applicants who turn out not to perform successfully will be included in the referral group in greater proportions than equivalent minority applicants. This effect of selecting by rank order of scores is a function of prediction error and the existence of average group differences in test scores.

To explain: If applicants are placed by test scores alone, taking the applicants in order of test score produces workers with the highest expected supervisor ratings. Nonetheless, because prediction is imperfect, some high scorers will not perform well on the job and some low scorers could have done so. With no score adjustments, very low fractions of minority-group members will be referred for employment because minority-group members tend to score substantially lower on the GATB on average. For example, if 20 percent of the majority group were referred, only 3 percent of the minority group would be referred to a typical job handled by the Employment Service.

Yet, because the validities of test score for supervisor rating are modest, there is not so great a difference in average job performance between minority and majority applicants as there is in average test performance. Majority workers do comparatively better on the test than they do on the job, and so benefit from errors of false acceptance. Minority workers at a given level of job performance have much less chance of being selected than majority workers at the same level of job performance, and thus are burdened with higher false-rejection rates. (Note that these effects are a function of high and low test scores, not racial or ethnic identity.)

In sum, the modest validities of the GATB cause selection errors that weigh more heavily on minority workers than on majority workers. This outcome is at odds with the nation's express commitment to equal employment opportunity for minority workers. In the committee's judgment, the disproportionate impact of selection error provides scientific grounds for the adjustment of minority scores so that able minority workers have approximately the same chances of referral as able majority workers. Others will have to decide whether the scientific reasons are compelling in the realms of public policy and law.

The committee has analyzed two score-adjustment methods—the current USES system of within-group percentile scores and a performance-based method of computing scores. Both score adjustment strategies are race-conscious; both would virtually eliminate the adverse impact of the GATB on black and Hispanic subpopulations (at current validity levels); and both adjustments would be commensurate with the far less than perfect relation between the GATB test score and job performance.

Is the GATB Valid for Some, Most, or All Jobs?
(Chapters 6 and 7)

The VG-GATB Referral System was built on the claim that the GATB is a valid predictor of job performance for all 12,000 jobs in the U.S. economy. That is a big claim, and two chapters of the report are devoted to weighing its scientific merits.

Findings and Conclusions

In the committee's judgment, it is probable that the GATB has validities for supervisor ratings in the range of .2 to .4 for a wide variety of jobs similar to those served by the Employment Service, although we have seen no evidence to justify the claim that the test battery is a valid predictor for all 12,000 jobs in the economy. We accept the general thesis of validity generalization, that the results of validity studies can be generalized to many jobs not actually studied, but we urge a cautious approach of generalizing validities only to appropriately similar jobs.

Furthermore, the policy considerations do not end with a demonstration that the GATB has some predictive power for x numbers of jobs. The question that still must be asked is how much validity is enough to make a single fallible test the central means of referring workers to jobs throughout the Employment Service. Although exclusive use of the VG-GATB Referral System would make the matching of people to jobs slightly more efficient, it would do so at the cost of depriving the low scorers of any chance at jobs that many of them could have performed successfully. Policy makers will have to decide if such a cost is warranted. One would also want to consider whether it makes equally good sense to use a general test battery such as the GATB for jobs that do not require a great deal of prior training as well as for those that do. Should it be used for entry-level as well as experienced workers? For experienced workers or complicated jobs, other sources of information may be more valuable.

Will Increased Use of the GATB Result in Substantial Increases in Productivity? (Chapter 12)

Personnel psychologists have always made the logical assumption that matching people to jobs more effectively will increase productivity; this has been the underlying rationale for employment testing. In recent years, some researchers have attempted to put dollar values on the performance gains from testing. The proponents of validity generalization have been particularly notable on this count. The committee's analysis provides a critique of the specific claims of dollar gains that would result from use of the VG-GATB Referral System throughout the Employment Service, claims that have been developed in USES technical reports and repeated elsewhere.

Findings and Conclusions

The often-repeated claim that use of the GATB by the Employment Service will produce a gain of $79.36 billion is unfounded on close examination. It is based on overestimates of validities, of the variability of worker productivity, and of the selectivity of employers using the Employment Service. For example, it assumes that only 1 in 10 Employment Service applicants finds a job, an assumption that, if extended to the whole economy, would produce perhaps a very productive work force, but also 90 percent unemployment.

Potential Effects of the VG-GATB Referral System
(Chapters 10 and 11)

Although very little systematic information is available from the pilot studies, the committee gathered enough information to be able to suggest certain likely effects of the VG-GATB Referral System on Employment Service clients.

Findings and Conclusions

A universal testing program would have side effects whose economic and social consequences are not well established. Certain types of individual employers would benefit, although the benefits would tend to attenuate as more and more employers who compete in the same labor market adopt VG-GATB procedures. Certain types of job seekers would likewise benefit. However, were the VG-GATB system the only mode of referral through the Employment Service, the lowest-scoring applicants would be consigned to receiving little or no assistance in finding work, when in fact many such applicants could perform satisfactorily on many jobs.

If the VG-GATB Referral System did not include the kind of score adjustments currently made to the scores of black, Hispanic, and in some cases, Native American applicants, it would have a severe adverse impact on the employment opportunities of members of those demographic groups. In the committee's judgment, the VG-GATB Referral System is not viable without some sort of score adjustments so long as the government is committed to a policy of equal employment opportunity that looks to the effects of employment practices on racial and ethnic minority groups.

Veterans are accorded referral priority as a matter of statutory law. Because it would dramatically alter referral procedures in the Employment Service, the VG-GATB Referral System has been of some concern to veterans' organizations. The states have adopted a variety of mechanisms for incorporating veterans' preference in the VG-GATB system, the effects of which range from absolute preference to effectively no preference. The method of according veterans' preference in a test-based referral system that seems most compatible with the statutory grant of preference to "qualified veterans" would be the addition of some number of points before conversion of the scores to percentiles.

When Should the GATB Not Be Used?
(Chapter 11)

Any policy promoting greater use of the GATB for referral should be accompanied by clear guidelines outlining when its use is not appropriate. There are specific populations, such as people with certain handicapping conditions and people who do not have a command of the English language, for whom the GATB is simply not suitable as the main referral mechanism. There are also less clearly identifiable types of job seekers who will not be adequately served by the VG-GATB Referral System. For example, during the course of site visits to local Job Service offices, we learned that there are some communities that are extremely resistant to testing; one pilot test of the VG-GATB was discontinued because people in the area refused to use the Job Service if they had to take a test. Exclusive use of test-based referral would serve the interests of neither employers nor job seekers in such communities.

Findings and Conclusions

The GATB is not such a good predictor of job performance that traditional and alternative referral techniques should be abandoned. Its best use is to supplement current methods rather than replace them.

Forcing people to take the GATB as a condition for receiving job placement services serves no one's best interests. Filling job orders automatically and solely through the VG-GATB Referral System is not a prudent use of USES resources.

For people with disabilities, the GATB is appropriate primarily as a supplement to counseling rather than as the main referral instrument. Job counselors should continue to provide their main path of referral.

SUMMARY OF CENTRAL RECOMMENDATIONS

The committee's most important recommendations, summarized here, appear in full as Chapter 14 of this report. The findings and conclusions that provide the underlying rationale for these recommendations will be found at the end of Chapters 4 through 13, as will subsidiary recommendations.

Operational Use of the VG-GATB Referral System

1. Any expansion of the VG-GATB Referral System should be accompanied by a vigorous program of research and development. Two inadequacies in the testing program must be corrected:
   a. Test Security: It is essential that measures be taken to provide for test security to ensure fairness to examinees. Most important is the regular development of alternate forms of the test and frequent replacement of old forms. In addition, USES must produce, and the states must enforce, clearly specified security procedures of the kind used to maintain the confidentiality of other large-scale test batteries.
   b. Test Speededness: A research and development project should be put in place to reduce the speededness of the GATB. A highly speeded test, one that no one can hope to complete, is vulnerable to distortion from coaching. If this characteristic of the GATB is not altered, the test will not retain its validity when given a gatekeeping function that is widely recognized.

2. We recommend that no job seeker be obliged to take the GATB; every local office that uses VG-GATB referral should maintain an alternative referral path for those who choose not to take the test.

3. Because tests provide only partial information about future job performance, we recommend that Job Service offices that adopt the VG-GATB Referral System continue to use multiple criteria in choosing which applicants to refer.

Referral Methods

4. The committee recommends the continued use of score adjustments for black and Hispanic applicants in choosing which Employment Service registrants to refer to an employer, because the effects of imperfect prediction fall more heavily on minority applicants as a group due to their lower mean test scores. We endorse the adoption of score adjustments that give approximately equal chances of referral to *able* minority applicants and *able* majority applicants: for example, within-

group percentile scores, performance-based scores, or other adjustments.

    5. If the within-group score adjustment strategy is chosen:

        a. We recommend that USES undertake research to develop more adequate norming tables.

        b. An attempt should be made to develop norms for homogeneous groups of jobs, at the least by job family, but if possible by more cohesive clusters of jobs in Job Families IV and V.

        c. To correctly compute within-group percentiles, USES must estimate the average difference between the majority-group scores and the minority-group scores in applicants for homogeneous groups of jobs.

    6. We also recommend that USES study the feasibility of what we call a Combined Rules Referral Plan, under which the referral group is composed of all those who would have been referred either by the total-group or by the within-group ranking method.

Score Reporting

The decision concerning what kind of scores to report to employers and job applicants is separate from the choice of methods to use to create the referral pool. The uppermost concern in reporting GATB scores should be to provide the most accurate and informative estimate of future job performance possible.

    7. The committee recommends that two scores be reported to employers and applicants:

        a. a within-group percentile score with the corresponding norm group identified and

        b. an expectancy score (derived from the total-group percentile score) equal to the probability that an applicant's job performance will be better than average.

Promotion of the VG-GATB Referral Program

    8. Given the modest validities of the GATB for the 500 jobs actually studied, given our incomplete knowledge about the relationship between this sample and the remaining 11,500 jobs in the U.S. economy, given the Department of Justice challenge to the legality of within-group scoring and the larger philosophical debates about race-conscious mechanisms and the known problems of using a test with severe adverse impact, and given the primitive state of knowledge about the relationship of individual

performance and productivity of the firm, we recommend that the claims for the testing program be tempered and that employers as well as job seekers be given a balanced view of the strengths and weaknesses of the GATB and its likely contribution in matching people to jobs.

9. Given the primitive state of knowledge about the aggregate economic effects of better personnel selection, we recommend that Employment Service officials refrain from making any dollar estimates of the gains that would result from test-based selection.

10. The Employment Service should make clear to employers using the VG-GATB Referral System that responsibility for the relevance of selection criteria and the effects of selection on the composition of their work force lies directly with the employer. Use of tests approved by the U.S. Employment Service does not alter this allocation of responsibility under federal civil rights law.

Pilot Studies

There is too little evidence based on controlled, rigorous studies of the effects of using the VG-GATB Referral System for the committee to be able to assure policy makers at the Department of Labor that anticipated improvements have indeed occurred; this is not to say that they have not occurred.

11. If USES decides to continue the VG-GATB Referral System, it should undertake a series of carefully designed studies to establish more solidly the efficiencies that are believed to result.

12. This research should be a cooperative effort, involving federal and State Employment Service personnel and employers. USES should encourage state Employment Security Agencies that deal with large employers (e.g., Michigan) and states that have fully articulated VG systems in place (e.g., Virginia, Utah, Oklahoma) to take a leading role in conducting studies to demonstrate the efficacy of the VG-GATB Referral System.

13. We also recommend that the employer community, as a potentially major beneficiary of an improved referral system, take an active part in the effort to evaluate the VG-GATB Referral System.

Special Populations

Veterans

14. If government policy is to strike a balance between maximizing productivity and preference for veterans in employment referral through the VG-GATB Referral System, the Employment Service should adjust

veterans' VG-GATB scores by adding a veterans' bonus of some number of points before conversion to percentiles. Unadjusted expectancy scores should also be reported to employers and job seekers.

It should be noted on the referral slip that the percentile score has been adjusted for veterans' preference.

15. The Employment Service should continue to meet the needs of disabled veterans through individualized counseling and placement services.

People with Handicapping Conditions

16. For applicants with handicapping conditions, we recommend the continued use of job counselors to make referrals.

17. Measures should be taken to ensure that no job order is filled automatically and solely through the VG-GATB system. Job counselors who serve handicapped applicants, disabled veterans, or other populations with special needs must have regular access to the daily flow of job orders.

18. To ensure that handicapped applicants who can compete with tested applicants are given that opportunity, the GATB should be used when feasible to assess the abilities of handicapped applicants. But the test should be used to supplement decision making, not to take the place of counseling services.

19. Because special expertise in assessing the capabilities of people with handicaps is necessary and available, we recommend that the Department of Labor encourage closer coordination between state rehabilitation agencies and the state Employment Service agencies. States should consider placing state rehabilitation counselors in local employment service offices that serve a sizable population of handicapped people.

PART I

BACKGROUND AND CONTEXT

Part I provides the setting for the committee's study. Chapter 1 describes the difficult policy issues that officials need to consider as they decide on the future of the General Aptitude Test Battery and of the score adjustments used to mitigate the adverse effects of testing on minority job seekers. Chapter 2 focuses on the divergent conceptions of equity that have emerged as a product of the civil rights revolution of the 1960s and 1970s; it also traces the ambivalence present in American society, as it is reflected in government policy and law. Chapter 3 is an overview of the operations of the U.S. Employment Service, the federal-state system for bringing job seekers and employers together.

1

The Policy Context

Productivity has been one of the more worrisome public issues of this decade. Faltering American competitiveness vis-à-vis Japan, the deterioration of the steel industry and of manufacturing more generally, the decline in real income and the emergence of the two-earner family, the ballooning federal deficit and trade imbalances—such topics have become a staple of the popular press as well as the more rarified domain of economic analysis.

As part of the larger public discussion, the quality of the American work force has come under increasing scrutiny. Numerous articles and reports have described the decline in American public education and the failure of contemporary schools to prepare pupils to enter the labor market. There have been unflattering comparisons to the productivity of Japanese and Korean workers in the auto, electronics, and appliance industries. And there has been increased interest in finding better ways of selecting and using workers. There has been a resurgence of testing—testing to screen out applicants who are bad risks (drug testing, lie detector testing, honesty testing, health projections) and, to a lesser extent, ability or knowledge testing to identify the better prospects.

THE USES EMPLOYMENT TESTING PROGRAM

In response to the troubled state of the nation's economic health, the U.S. Employment Service (USES), a unit of the U.S. Department of Labor, developed a new role for its General Aptitude Test Battery

17

(GATB), a test of cognitive, perceptual, and motor skills used in state Job Service offices since 1947. Less than 8 percent of the approximately 9.5 million Job Service registrants who received some reportable service each year were given the GATB in the early 1980s, and then mainly for purposes of vocational counseling. It was felt that far more extensive use of the test battery to fill job orders might be justified. Recent developments in statistical methods—specifically, *meta-analysis*—seemed to hold out scientific promise that the GATB could be used to identify good workers for a wide range of jobs. From a policy perspective, the anticipated contributions to productivity were attractive.

The rationale for using general ability tests for employment screening is that ability tests can help employers identify good (more productive) workers. This proposition is based on a number of assumptions:

First, that there is a wide range of potential job performance in the people likely to be candidates for a particular type of job;

Second, that ability tests predict future job performance with a useful degree of accuracy;

Third, that higher scorers on the test are better performers in the long term (that is, if everyone could be trained to proficiency in a short period of time, the advantages of selecting high-ability workers would be fleeting).

If these things hold true, then selection of high-scoring applicants can be presumed to enhance work force efficiency and therefore contribute to the overall productivity of the firm. Although mental measurement specialists generally recognize that cognitive ability tests can measure only some of the attributes that contribute to successful job performance, they consider such tests to be, in the present state of the art, the most informative general predictor of proficiency for most jobs. (Note that we are talking about general employment screening, for which a single instrument is used to predict success in a range of jobs. For jobs that require extensive prior training and highly developed skills and knowledge, such as electronics specialist, jet engine mechanic, and lawyer, custom-designed instruments would be more informative than a general cognitive test.)

None of this was new in 1980 when the U.S. Employment Service began to envision a larger role for the GATB. But a catalytic innovation had occurred in one corner of the psychological measurement field during the 1970s. Traditional psychometric theory held that the validity of a given test is dependent on situational factors (the norming sample, geographic location, organizational climate) because the correlations between a test and the criterion of interest (e.g., job performance) were observed to vary from study to study. Thus, the theory went, a test valid in one setting might not be valid in another, and a new investigation of its validity would be required for each substantially new setting. This is the view that has informed federal equal employment opportunity policy and is officially recognized in the interagency *Uniform Guidelines on Employee Selection Procedures* (29 CFR Part 1607 [1985]).

In the mid-1970s, a number of analysts, preeminent among them Frank Schmidt and John Hunter, began to challenge this theory of situational specificity, arguing that the observed differences in a given test's validity from one setting to another were not real, but rather were artificial differences introduced by sampling error, unreliability in the criterion measures, and other weaknesses of the individual validity studies. The application of meta-analytic techniques for combining data from large numbers of studies, statistical techniques that had proved useful in many other scientific areas, led Hunter and Schmidt to conclude both that the results of individual validity studies substantially understate the predictive power of cognitive tests and that the validity of such tests can be generalized to new situations, even to new jobs. Convinced that this evidence establishes the importance of *g,* or general intelligence, to all types of job performance, some proponents of validity generalization, as this type of meta-analysis is called, have come to argue that a well-developed ability test can be used for selecting applicants for virtually all jobs. If this held true of the GATB, it would enable USES to encourage the states to start using the test much more widely in the Employment Service.

The Department of Labor contracted with John Hunter in 1980 to conduct validity generalization studies of the GATB, using the hundreds of individual validity studies that had been conducted since 1947. Hunter carried out four technical studies in 1981 in which he explicates his analysis of GATB validities and presents a dollar estimate of the economic gains that could accrue from using the GATB for personnel selection. The results were published as USES technical reports in 1983 (U.S. Department of Labor, 1983b,c,d,e). The reports advocate the generalizability of GATB validities to all 12,000 jobs in the U.S. economy. In the author's view, use of the GATB could be extended from the 500 jobs for which specific validation studies had been conducted to every job for which the Employment Service might be asked by employers to refer candidates. Moreover, Hunter maintains that substantial—one could say dramatic—economic gains would accrue from using test scores, from the highest score on down in rank-ordered fashion, to select the applicants to be referred to employers. By his calculations (U.S. Department of Labor, 1983e), optimal use of the GATB in 1980 (i.e., top-down selection) to refer the approximately 4 million people placed by the Employment Service that year would have yielded gains of $79.36 billion. In comparison, total corporate tax revenues at all levels were $59.2 billion in 1982 (Sueyoshi, 1988).

Not surprisingly, USES officials were encouraged by these findings. They decided to implement a new test-based referral system, which we call the VG-GATB Referral System in this report, on an experimental basis. With USES approval, North Carolina began a pilot project in fall 1981. By the end of 1986, some 38 states had experimented with VG-GATB referral in at least one local office. Six states (Maine, Michigan, New Hampshire, North Carolina, Utah, and Virginia) introduced the test-based referral plan in all local offices, although only Virginia replaced the earlier system of having placement counselors make referral decisions. Most states did not dramatically alter local office procedures, but simply supplemented existing procedures using the VG-GATB system, with its requirements for extra testing and file search, to fill job orders if requested by employers. Out of 1,800 local Job Service offices nationwide, approximately 400 introduced VG-GATB referral, typically in conjunction with the earlier system. Of these, 84 are located in North Carolina, 80 in Michigan, 38 in Virginia, 35 in Maine, and 25 in Utah.

Within-Group Scoring of the VG-GATB

An integral part of the VG-GATB Referral System, as USES presented it to state-level Job Service officials, was the conversion of scores on the test battery to percentile ranks within the population categories of "black," "Hispanic," and "other" (which includes all those not in the first two categories). This was a carefully considered policy decision.

Following the findings of the technical reports, USES designed the system to rank-order candidates by test score and to refer them from the top down in order to get the maximum economic benefit. There are, however, significant group differences in average test scores, which have been demonstrated with virtually all standardized tests. Blacks as a group score well below the majority group, and Hispanics fall roughly in between as a rule. As a consequence of these average group differences, strict top-down referral would adversely affect the employment chances of black and Hispanic applicants.

To counteract this effect, the experimental referral system stipulated that raw scores be converted into group-based percentile ranks. USES provided the conversion tables for making the score adjustments. The resulting percentile scores reflect an applicant's standing with reference to his or her own racial or ethnic group, thus effectively erasing average group differences in test scores. A black applicant with a percentile score of 50 has the same ranking for referral as a white candidate with a percentile score of 50, although their raw test scores (percentage correct) would be very different. For example, in the category of semiskilled jobs, blacks at the 50th percentile have raw scores of 276; Hispanics, 295; and others, 308. The meaning of these raw-score differences for estimated job performance is not self-evident. But to lend some perspective, a raw score of 308 within the black group is at the 84th percentile of that group.

By combining this method of scoring the GATB with top-down selection of the applicants to be referred to prospective employers, USES sought to further two policies that are considered very important by the federal government: the enhancement of national productivity (by serving the individual employer's interest in hiring the most able workers available) and the promotion of federal equal employment opportunity and affirmative action goals. Without some sort of compensatory scoring system, in the agency's view, referral of candidates on the basis of GATB test scores from the top down would reduce the employment opportunities of minority-group job candidates, thwarting the governmental interest in bringing minority workers into the economic mainstream and creating possible legal problems for both the Employment Service and the employers it serves. But if top-down selection were completely abandoned, in the agency's view, work-force efficiency would suffer.

The Justice Department Challenge to Within-Group Scoring

Some years into the experiment with the VG-GATB Referral System, the Justice Department challenged the program because of the way test scores are derived. In a letter to the Director of the U.S. Employment Service, dated November 10, 1986, Wm. Bradford Reynolds, then Assistant Attorney General for Civil Rights, strongly urged that all states that had adopted the validity generalization procedure be notified to cease and desist immediately. Mr. Reynolds adjudged the VG-GATB system to be an unlawful and unconstitutional violation of an applicant's rights to be free from racial discrimination because the within-group scoring procedure not only classifies Employment Service registrants by race or national origin, but also "requires job service offices to prefer some and disadvantage other individuals based on their membership in racial or ethnic groups. Such a procedure constitutes intentional racial discrimination."

The important point of difference between the two agencies was their judgment of the legality of extending race-conscious preferential treatment to some groups in society as a means of combating discrimination. Neither agency disputes the fact that there is a powerful legacy of discrimination to overcome. The question is means, not ends. The Department of Labor adopted a race-conscious scoring mechanism in order to avoid discrimination against minority-group members and to promote equal employment opportunity. Within-group scoring was thought of as an extension of a referral policy negotiated in 1972 among the Department of Labor, the Equal Employment Opportunity Commission, and the Department of Justice. The 1972 "referral ratio policy" stipulated that referrals of tested minority applicants should be in proportion to their presence in the applicant pool in all cases in which the tests had not been validated for minority applicants to the job in question (which in 1972 was virtually all 500 jobs for which testing was used).

The Department of Justice viewed preferential consideration for one racial group as discrimination against all others, on the grounds that it illegally advances the interests of one classification of people at the expense of others.

Officials of the Labor and Justice Departments agreed to a continuation of the status quo—no further extension of the VG-GATB Referral System and at the same time no cease-and-desist orders—until a thorough study of the GATB validity base, validity generalization, scoring and referral policy, and the potential impact of the referral system could be carried out by a body of experts. This volume reports the results of the agreed-upon study.

OTHER POLICY ISSUES

Although the immediate reason for this study stems from the divergent views of two federal agencies about the legality of score adjustments, there are more general questions that should also receive careful policy review, questions about the nature of cognitive tests and about the wisdom of allowing any one procedure to dominate federal and state efforts to promote economic well-being by bringing suitable workers and jobs together.

Validity Generalization and the Reemergence of *g*

Development of the theory of validity generalization has coincided with, indeed encouraged, a revival of interest in the concept of *g,* or general intelligence. To make any sense, the idea that test validities observed for some jobs can be generalized to all other jobs depends on the complementary idea that the test measures some attribute that underlies performance in all jobs. This common underlying factor is usually thought of in terms of general intelligence, although some commentators, wary of the connotations of genetic determinism that surround the concept of intelligence, prefer to speak of a general mental factor or cognitive factor. (In his studies of the GATB, John Hunter identifies two such factors: general cognitive ability, which he describes as very similar to the classical concept of general intelligence, and psychomotor ability. The first general factor he finds linked to performance in all jobs, the correlation increasing with the cognitive complexity of the job; the psychomotor factor is principally associated with performance in one particular family of cognitively less complex jobs. A third factor, perceptual ability, he found to be almost perfectly predictable from and causally dependent on the first two [Department of Labor, 1983b].)

Early IQ Testing

The idea of intelligence is closely bound up with the history of psychological testing in this century. The American adaptation of Alfred Binet's intelligence scale and introduction of the intelligence quotient in 1911, followed closely by the introduction of group intelligence testing with the Army Alpha in World War I, forged the link. From the beginning, ambitious claims have been made for such tests by those who saw them as a grand device for sorting people into the appropriate slot in society. In addressing Section H (Education) of the American Association for the Advancement of Science in 1912, E.L. Thorndike (1913:141) predicted:

It will not be long before the members of this section will remember with amusement the time when education waited for the expensive test of actual trial to tell how well a boy or girl would succeed with a given trade, with the work of college and professional school, or with the general task of leading a decent, law-biding, humane life.

Like many who would follow him, Thorndike (p. 142) read very expansive meanings into psychological tests:

Tables of correlations seem dull, dry, unimpressive things beside the insights of poets and proverb makers—but only to those who miss their meaning. In the end they will contribute tenfold more to man's mastery of himself. History records no career, war, or revolution that can compare in significance with the fact that the correlation between intellect and morality is approximately .3, a fact to which perhaps a fourth of the world's progress is due.

Thorndike was not alone among the early testing enthusiasts, either in his grand expectations for mental measurement, in his readiness to measure morality, progress, and man's mastery of himself, or in his facile assumptions about the congruence of intellect and high moral character. In hindsight it is clear that many of the advocates of early testing allowed their scientific judgment to be influenced by contemporary racial and ethnic biases and by unexamined assumptions about the proper social order. Historian of science Daniel Kevles has documented the mutual attraction of the eugenics and mental measurement movements in the early twentieth century. Eugenicists, the early students of human genetics, asserted that the new science proved that mental defectiveness and criminality, immorality, and other deviant behaviors are fundamentally hereditary. Intelligence testing seemed a perfect tool for identifying those whose inferior genetic endowment would adulterate the gene pool. In this context, IQ tests could quickly turn into weapons of racial and class prejudice (Kevles, 1985).

But proponents of psychological testing were also responding to genuine social needs. Recall that the nation was undergoing massive growth at the turn of the century. In the three decades between 1890 and 1920, the population increased by some 68 percent and the high school population grew by more than 711 percent (Tyack, 1974). The need for new institutions of social organization was urgent. To many psychologists, educators, employers, and citizens in general, intelligence tests seemed to offer a scientific tool to bring order to the classroom and the workplace.

The Army Alpha

The Army experiment with group intelligence testing of recruits during World War I illustrates both the promise of the technology and its dark underside. Robert M. Yerkes led a team of prominent psychologists, among them Lewis Terman and Carl Brigham, in this first major effort to apply social science to the practical problems of taking the nation to war. As originally designed, the Binet and similar intelligence tests would have been of little use in situations in which large numbers of people were to be tested because they could be administered only to individuals and, theoretically, only by a psychologist. They were used primarily to assess mental retardation, not for mass screening. By redesigning a version of the Stanford Binet intelligence scale to allow its administration in a group setting, Yerkes and his colleagues put testing on the map.

The Army Alpha, a paper-and-pencil test of general intellectual skills, made up of multiple-choice and true/false questions, and its oral analog, the Beta, were administered to almost 2 million recruits from June 1917 until the war ended, a noteworthy bureaucratic and logistic feat. One of the ironies of the story is that the Army testing program was largely experimental; it produced massive amounts of data but had little actual effect on selection or placement of recruits. Nevertheless, by transforming the intelligence scale into a test that could be administered to groups of people, and by using it to assess the intellectual skills of normal adults, the Army testing project legitimized the use of standardized, group-administered tests as a tool for making selection and placement decisions about individuals in mass society. Through the diligent promotion by Yerkes and others who had been associated with the Army testing project, the myth was established in the postwar period that it had been a great practical success (Kevles, 1968; Reed, 1987).

After the war, Yerkes spent a number of years at the National Academy of Sciences analyzing the test data on a randomly drawn sample of 160,000 recruits. The massive study published by the Academy (Yerkes, 1921) provides, among other things, a stark example of the dangers inherent in group testing and group comparisons. One of the most prominent themes to come out of the study involved the correlation between ethnic background and test scores. Yerkes' analysis showed that native whites scored highest on the Army Alpha. Of the immigrants, the highest scores were found for groups from northern and western Europe and the lowest for those from southern and eastern Europe. These findings fed the nativist sentiment of the period. They were picked up by anti-immigrationists as scientific corroboration that southern and eastern European immigrants, being intellectually inferior, would bring with them crime, unemployment, and delinquency.

Yerkes' analysis also showed that test scores on the Army Alpha correlated highly with length of residence in the United States and with years of schooling. Yet these findings failed to impress. Yerkes, Carl Brigham, and other psychologists who had participated in the Army testing project supported eugenics and immigration restriction with hereditarian arguments based on the Academy study.

Critics of Intelligence Testing

The claims made for the Army Alpha and the hereditarian interpretation of test results did not go entirely unchallenged. Walter Lippmann published a trenchant series of articles in the *The New Republic* in 1922-1923, in which he mocked Yerkes' conclusion from the Army data that the average mental age of Americans is about 14. Lippmann, who had read widely in the social sciences, criticized both the technical and the social assumptions of intelligence testing. He objected particularly to the claim that the Army test or any other tests measured hereditary intelligence, comparing it to phrenology, palmistry, and "other Babu sciences." Intelligence, he pointed out, is not some concrete, readily measurable entity, but rather an extremely complex concept that no one had yet succeeded in defining (Lippmann, 1922). He summed up his discomfort with the psychometric vision of man by saying (Lippmann, 1923:146):

I admit it. I hate the impudence of a claim that in fifty minutes you can judge and classify a human being's predestined fitness for life. I hate the pretentiousness of that claim. I hate the abuse of scientific method which it involves. I hate the sense of superiority which it creates, and the sense of inferiority which it imposes.

By the end of the decade, and in a somewhat less public forum, Carl Brigham came to similar conclusions about the arrogance of testers in the first flush of excitement over the new technology and its social uses. Brigham's *Study of American Intelligence,* published in 1923, had been an extremely influential popular exposition of the hereditary and racially determined nature of intelligence. Time and further study allowed him to disentangle his science from his social prejudices. His recantation came in a scholarly review of the status of intelligence testing of immigrant groups (Brigham, 1930:165):

This review has summarized some of the more recent test findings which show that comparative studies of various national and racial groups may not be made with existing tests, and which show, in particular, that one of the most pretentious of these comparative racial studies—the writer's own—was without foundation.

Relevance to Current Policy

Sixty years and more have passed since the advent of group intelligence testing. The statistical underpinnings of psychometrics have become much more sophisticated. And in recent years there have been interesting advances in psychobiology and, to a lesser extent, in cognitive psychology that shed some light on intellective or cognitive functioning. But most specialists would still agree with Lippmann's assessment of the concept of intelligence: it is a very complicated notion that no one has been able to define very well. Even if we can show correlational relationships between a test of verbal and mathematical skills such as the GATB and supervisor ratings of job performance, we are still a very long way from being able to claim that what we are measuring is an unambiguous, unitary capacity that is the essential ingredient in successful job performance.

Moreover, we cannot escape the connotations that have surrounded the concept of intelligence since the early days. Most psychologists are much more circumspect about drawing causal relationships between test scores and such things as character, criminal tendencies, or degeneracy than they were in the 1920s. The more simplistic hereditarian notions have long since gone out of vogue, at least from the academic literature. The basic texts used to train recent generations of students in the intricacies of psychological testing—those of Cronbach (1984) and Anastasi (1976)—emphasize the contingent nature of what we call intelligence and the complex interplay of heredity and environment at all stages of human development. But in common usage such refinements can easily be lost, and there is very real danger that the renewed popularity of g and its promotion along with validity generalization could become a tool of racial and ethnic prejudice, generating feelings of superiority in some groups and inferiority in others.

The potential for social damage from overstating the claims of testing is as great today as it was in the 1920s, because the United States remains a country of many identifiable ethnic and racial subpopulations, some of which are relatively disadvantaged economically and educationally. The target groups have changed to some extent—southern and eastern European groups have long since been assimilated into the lingual and cultural majority group and have disappeared as objects of social disrespect. But blacks, Hispanics, and Native Americans, all groups of people who perform less well on average on written tests of verbal and mathematical abilities, and who are economically and socially disadvantaged, are vulnerable to being stereotyped as of inferior intelligence.

Hence an important policy concern raised by the VG-GATB Referral System is that it may foster social division by encouraging Employment Service staff and clients to draw improper inferences about the potential contribution of minority-group members—indeed of any low-scoring job seeker—in the workplace or to society as a whole.

Should There Be Diverse Routes to Employment?

A second question for policy makers to consider is whether governmental endorsement of a test-based referral system, to the exclusion of other procedures, would be in the best interests of Employment Service clients or of the economy. If the VG-GATB Referral System is found legally defensible, it is not unreasonable to anticipate that the GATB could come to dominate entry to many kinds of jobs. Many employers would be drawn to use the Employment Service as a way of reducing their legal vulnerability to equal employment opportunity suits; some would also be attracted by the savings resulting from shifting the costs of testing and test validation to the government (although small companies can afford neither in any case).

The implications of such a development need to be carefully weighed. There are, for example, possible social costs that should not be ignored. A universal system of referral based on GATB test scores implies that people with the lowest scores might well be perpetually unemployed. Although the number of people who are unemployed would not increase, the dominance of a single sorting device could have the effect of perpetually subjecting the same individuals to the ill effects of unemployment. Is the GATB of sufficient utility to justify such an effect? Are there ways to prevent that from happening?

Would the government's sponsorship of the VG-GATB system, with its promised legal umbrella, tend to cause employers to eliminate their own testing programs, which have been tailored to their own specific needs?

Would this overload the states' capacity to respond and place an unexpected burden on their treasuries?

We value pluralism in our society. Is it therefore wise for the government to focus on just one characteristic, even if it is what we know how to measure best, when we also know that successful person-job matches can be effected in other ways? Is a simple sorting mechanism fair to individuals of whatever color or ethnic derivation who do not do well on cognitive tests but are, nevertheless, capable of successful participation in the work force?

THE INTERSECTIONS OF POLICY AND SCIENCE

Whether within-group score adjustments can or should be any part of the system used by the Employment Service to bring employers and job seekers together will not be decided solely, or even primarily, on the basis of scientific evidence. Likewise, the question of government sponsorship of a particular test that could come to dominate certain segments of the labor market is not simply a matter of the quality of the test instrument. Nevertheless, there are important aspects of the question of appropriate and equitable use of standardized tests that can be clarified through scientific analysis. And many of the claims made about the VG-GATB Referral System in general lend themselves to scientific investigation.

In the remainder of this report, we evaluate the claims made for the General Aptitude Test Battery, for validity generalization, and for the economic benefits of employment testing. We assess the likely impact of widespread implementation of the VG-GATB Referral System with and without score adjustments. We discuss possible alternatives to the within-group scoring system, including the so-called Golden Rule procedure for reducing group differences in ability test scores. We offer to the Department of Labor recommendations for policy alternatives that seem justified by the scientific evidence. And finally, we propose a research agenda for the agency to consider should it, through the U.S. Employment Service, decide to continue to promote a more extensive role for the GATB.

2

Issues in Equity and Law

PERSPECTIVES ON EQUALITY, FAIRNESS, AND SOCIAL JUSTICE

One might wonder how the Department of Labor and the Department of Justice, both agencies of the federal government, could have come to such divergent conclusions about the legality and fairness of within-group score adjustments. One might be tempted to explain the difference by pointing to the sharply divergent view of the law adopted by the Department of Justice in 1981 at the beginning of a new administration. Previously the federal agencies having responsibility for implementing the federal fair employment practices laws, including the Department of Justice, had been more closely aligned on the general policy of governmental use of race-conscious employment practices. But on further reflection, that contradictory assessment of the use of a race-conscious procedure to promote equal employment opportunity for black and Hispanic Americans reflects the ambivalent vision of the larger society.

The civil rights movement of the past quarter century, although it has for the first time in the nation's history brought black Americans under the mantle of equal justice, has also caused fissures in the general consensus about the meaning of fairness and justice. From the beginning, notions of equality under the law, fair competition, and equal opportunity gave the movement its strong ethical appeal, providing a rationale for ending the legalized caste system that blacks in America had been subjected to since the abolition of slavery. The focus of government policy and public sentiment was on getting rid of the whole edifice of

29

discriminatory and segregationist laws and customs that denied blacks equal access to education, housing, and jobs; freedom of movement in public places; the right to participate in political life—the full prerogatives of citizenship.

But, as government policy went on to address the systemic problems that were the legacy of slavery and segregation, the earlier consensus began to erode. Programs designed to enhance the opportunities of minorities and women, for example, minority set-asides in federal contracting and the encouragement of affirmative action hiring programs, generated a good deal of ambivalence. Many who had supported equality and equal competition for society's goods found that the same principles made them strong opponents of policies of preferential treatment intended to bring some measure of equality of life chances.

Philosophical Foundations

The policies that the committee has been asked to examine unavoidably involve questions of equity. Whereas most people adhere to some strongly held convictions about rights and justice and what is fair in allotting educational or employment opportunities, and most look to the Founding Fathers and the Constitution as important sources of their convictions, relatively few of us could lay claim to a systematic, coherent theory of social justice. To put the policy decisions facing the U.S. Employment Service in context, we consider briefly the sources of some of the ideas that have fueled public debate over the government's civil rights policies.

When the United States was founded, it was widely considered a radical experiment with little chance of success. Although there were classical and contemporary examples, few observers in England or on the Continent were confident that a society could survive without a monarch placed atop a hierarchical social order. In contrast to the traditional European systems based on hierarchy and subordination, the American revolutionaries, drawing on the ideas of John Locke and other contract theorists, advanced the concept of the state as a contractual agreement among free and equal individuals, secular by definition, and entered into for the mutual benefit of the participants. In this liberal—that is to say, antimonarchical—view of political society, the state is in some sense the product of the free choice of individuals, who are its members, not its subjects. The powers of the state are limited, since they derive from the people. And the state exists for the benefit of its members.

These ideas exerted a powerful and enduring impact on American political thought. They found expression in the Declaration of Independence ("We hold these truths to be self-evident, that all men are created equal . . .'') and in the adoption of our Constitution, the fundamental contract on which the system of government rests. Ideas and reality are never perfectly matched; to modern eyes the words of the Declaration and the structure of the society that espoused them seem irreconcilable. Property requirements kept most white males from full political participation in the early years of nationhood; women had few political and limited property rights until well into this century. But the most egregious departure from the liberal ideal was the total exclusion of blacks and American Indians from the political community it described. Most blacks were in a condition of chattel slavery, with no legal status, no rights, and no protections. As the Kerner Commission reported (National Commission on Civil Disorders, 1968), by 1776 some 500,000 blacks, comprising nearly one of every six people in the country, were held in slavery and indentured servitude. Yet the idea of government of, by, and for the people was powerful and very gradually provided a motive force for change.

Economic Liberalism

The ideas of political liberalism were reinforced in the nineteenth century by the growing popularity of laissez-faire economics. The work of Adam Smith and the British school of political economy knit together the liberal idea of the state as a voluntary association of free and equal individuals and the idea of a free-market economy based on the fair competition of individuals. Just as the political ideal demanded liberation from the elaborate caste systems of the past that had defined a person's legal and political status, access to careers, and, in some European countries, even modes of dress, so did economic liberalism seek to get rid of the welter of feudal and mercantilistic restraints on commerce.

A fundamental premise of laissez-faire economics, or what we have come to call capitalism, was that the operation of free and competitive markets would make a productive economy. Put another way, the unfettered actions of each individual to promote his own welfare were thought to increase the overall wealth of society. The comfortable belief that private gain promotes the public good encouraged a value system in the United States that prized individualism, competitiveness, and entrepreneurial spirit and inculcated a strong suspicion of government interference with economic activity.

These values fit well a society that was simultaneously undergoing industrialization, expansion across a continent, and massive immigration. Filtered through these economic ideas, concepts such as equality and fairness and justice took on a new cast. Equality tended to be thought of as the right to compete on an equal basis with others for the economic and other rewards of life in society. Fairness had to do with the rules of the competition, not the distribution of wealth in society.

Meritocracy

The constellation of ideas described above—that society is made up of equal individuals; that these individuals deserve equal treatment under law; that careers should be open to all, not reserved to privileged groups; that equal competition for rewards in a free-market economy promotes the interests of individuals and of the society as a whole—found institutionalized expression in the mid-nineteenth century establishment of the professional civil service based on merit hiring.

Historians have suggested that the merit system in the United States was a by-product of the egalitarian impulses of Jacksonian democracy. Andrew Jackson and his supporters believed that any man could do the government's work and that no man should do it for very long. They pushed the spoils system beyond the limits of contemporary taste and, in response, the elite classes who had traditionally staffed the federal bureaucracy espoused the principle of hiring on the basis of merit, as demonstrated by competitive examination (Hoogenboom, 1961).

Whatever the motives of early proponents of merit hiring, ideas have a power beyond the circumstances of their origin. The concept of meritocracy has had great social approval over the years—to the extent that we tend to forget that it is a construct and not a description of objective reality. The basic tenets of meritocracy in its American guise are:

1. The goods of society should be awarded to individuals on the basis of merit.

2. The qualification that merits reward in the allocation of jobs is talent (ability, experience), not family connection, social class, political loyalty, virtue, need, or other criteria that are irrelevant to job performance.

3. Social, economic, and political structures should be designed to allow open competition for positions.

4. A system of open competition and selection on the basis of competence satisfies both fairness and efficiency because every individual has the same chance to realize his or her potential regardless of birth or wealth and because all individuals will end up in the positions most suited to their talents.

5. Such a system is just because everyone has an equal opportunity to compete for positions and is rewarded as he or she deserves.

Meritocracy Revisited

If, as Fishkin (1983) put it, the main position in the meritocratic construct is that there should be a "fair competition among individuals for unequal positions in society," there has also been some recognition, both in formal and popular thought, that equality of opportunity may involve not just the absence of irrelevant barriers, but also some manner of equality of life chances (equality of life chances, that is, beyond the formal equality of individuals in a society that has no caste system, and no aristocracy). A cautious expression of this position would be that those with similar talents should have similar life chances. One might choose these grounds for supporting universal free public education. Many college scholarship programs—the New York State Board of Regents and the National Merit scholarships, for example—are intended to extend the opportunity for higher education to deserving (i.e., very smart) but needy students. A much more radical interpretation of equal opportunity might call for equalizing the conditions for the development of talent throughout society so that all children enjoy the same material and cultural advantages. There is probably not much room for this sort of idea to flourish within the liberal framework as long as liberalism is wed to the idea of a free-market economy, but some of the child-rearing experiments in the Israeli kibbutzim were attempts to provide just this sort of equality of nurture.

A moderation of the meritocratic ideal was espoused by many during the 1960s and 1970s. Borrowing from the formal thought of John Rawls, whose *Theory of Justice* was published in 1971, they interpreted the goal of equal opportunity to be promoting the self-respect of all members of society rather than unleashing acquisitive energies. Although not necessarily rejecting meritocracy as an appropriate basis for distributing social advantages, they argued that it should not be the sole ground. Special measures should be taken to ensure that all members enjoy a share of the benefits of society.

The Contemporary Impasse on Preferential Treatment

Policies of preferential treatment for members of social groups defined by race, ethnicity, or gender are at the heart of the question of within-group scoring. Because they also represent the broad divide between the pertinent value systems, the discussion below focuses on the arguments that have been marshalled for and against preferential treatment in the past 25 years or so. For simplicity's sake, prototypical positions are sketched, although the actual course of public debate has been far more complex.

The Case Against Preferential Treatment

Those strong proponents of the liberal tradition who have spoken out against affirmative action and preferential treatment (many of whom now call themselves neoconservatives) tend to focus on the ideal of equality and not to address as intensely the matter of inequality of life chances.

The most frequent argument hinges on the idea of color-blind law. From this perspective, the essence of equity is that all individuals are treated equally under the law. Proponents point out that it was the failure to realize the ideal of color-blind law that allowed the oppression of blacks, first as slaves and then as second-class citizens. A policy of preferential hiring betrays the principle of equality under the law. As one critic (Newton, 1973:312) put it:

The practice of reverse discrimination undermines the foundation of the very ideal in whose name it is advocated; it destroys justice, law, equality, and citizenship itself, and replaces them with power struggles and popularity contests.

A correlate of this position is that all racial classifications are presumptively unconstitutional. It is argued that the equal protection clause of the Fourteenth Amendment to the Constitution was intended to prohibit "conduct discriminating on the basis of race" and that the principle must hold whether the intention is benign, as in the use of race as a criterion of selection, or invidious. This was the position taken by Wm. Bradford Reynolds, the former Assistant Attorney General for Civil Rights, when within-group scoring of the GATB was challenged in 1986. A representative statement of the view appeared in a law review article in 1966 (quoted in Perry, 1977:549, n.62):

Any legal classification by race weakens the government as an educative force . . . . [A] statute specifically granting Negroes a benefit tends to undermine the principle we are working so hard to establish . . . that a person is entitled to be judged on his individual merit alone, that race is irrelevant to the worth of the individual. Preference for Negroes can thus be expected to be a major factor in preventing the education we are trying to bring about through a host of other laws.

Among people who adhere to what is sometimes called the nondiscrimination principle, the idea of equal treatment under the law has remained closely associated with the liberal idea that society is made up of autonomous individuals and that the law regulates the affairs of individuals. This belief led many to oppose the change of emphasis in government policy in the late 1960s, when the regulatory agencies charged with implementing the Civil Rights Act of 1964 started encouraging class action suits and otherwise judging compliance issues in terms of groups or classes of people.

Preferential admissions policies at universities and professional schools caused an outpouring of prose on the fairness of racial preference in the 1970s. Indeed, the *Bakke* and *DeFunis* cases popularized the concept of reverse discrimination, with its pejorative undertones (*Regents of the University of California v. Bakke,* 438 U.S. 265 [1978]; *DeFunis v. Odegaard,* 416 U.S. 312 [1974]). Among the arguments brought against preferential admissions policies were these: there is no way to identify the individual victims of discrimination or to prove that those benefiting from the policy of racial preference were in fact victims of past discrimination; there is evidence that the beneficiaries of preferential policies in professional school admissions come from privileged backgrounds; preferential treatment for blacks as a group creates injustice for identifiable white individuals; some whites who are innocent of any acts of past discrimination will pay the price; many members of white and other ethnic groups have also suffered discrimination and will want preferential treatment too.

Clearly the most compelling of these arguments has been that preferential treatment for blacks creates injustice for whites who are thereby denied the advantage of, in this case, professional education and the wealth and position that would follow. The element that makes this argument hold together is, of course, the meritocratic ideal. None of the adherents of this position would argue for the preferment of a white candidate over a black with better qualifications. They simply deny that race is a relevant qualification and find counterarguments about redress, reparations, needs, benefits to the individual, the provision of role models for the community, or the enrichment of the intellectual atmosphere of the university simply beside the point. From this point of view, the only fair criterion for the allocation of scarce social resources is individual talent, which in this context means predicted academic success.

To summarize, three principles drawn from the constellation of political, economic, and meritocratic ideas described above have been particularly important in the literature of opposition to policies of preferential treatment based on racial identity: equality under the law, individualism, and merit. To those who find themselves on this side of the divide, these three principles provide the possibility of equal opportunity in the society and are the grounds of social justice.

The Case for Preferential Treatment

The arguments in favor of preferential treatment also draw heavily from the liberal pantheon. Many, like Rawls, hark back to a first assumption of the contract theorists—that individuals freely enter into society for their mutual advantage—but go on from there to say that it would be hard to make the claim on grounds of equity that the disadvantaged receive their fair share in contemporary American society.

People who espouse preferential policies, whether cautiously or with enthusiasm, tend to have as their point of departure a recognition of the enormous, systematic injustices to which black Americans were subjected over hundreds of years. They acknowledge that to a significant degree many whites have benefited as a result. This line of thought has led many to argue that justice requires compensation, that the long history of unequal treatment has left blacks as a group so educationally, economically, and psychologically disadvantaged that, without special preference, they will be condemned by our newly color-blind society to remain de facto second-class citizens.

Others add that racial and sexual discrimination are not ancient relics but are so deeply entrenched in our language, attitudes, and living patterns that they continue to warp selection and admissions decisions. So long as this atmosphere continues, preferential consideration will be necessary to ensure equal justice.

From this perspective, equality cannot be restored simply by doing away with the laws that supported segregation, or simply by telling people they must not discriminate. The problems are systemic, not individual, and can be overcome only at the level of structural change. Laurence Tribe (1988), author of an important treatise on constitutional law, proposes that the equal protection guarantees of the Constitution can be understood within the framework of what he calls an "antisubjugation principle," under which government actions would be judged not on the basis of the motives of identified bad actors, but rather by their impact on members of protected groups. Because the current condition of blacks, women, and other identified groups in the society is the legacy of official oppression, of a subordination that was created by law and reinforced by the whole power of the state, he proposes that the constitutionality of government actions can be judged by their impact on the victims of official subjugation.

In response to the argument that the law recognizes only individuals, not groups or classes of people, legal scholars such as Burke Marshall and Owen Fiss point out that discrimination works not against individuals, but against a people. And the remedy, therefore "has to correct and cure and compensate for the discrimination against the people and not just the discrimination against identifiable persons" (Marshall, 1984:1006). Marshall, who was Assistant Attorney General for Civil Rights during the Kennedy and Johnson administrations, contests the assertion that the equal protection clause is concerned only with the protection of individuals against discrimination, saying that it pertains to individuals only by reason of their membership in groups. He points out that the Court in

Brown v. Board, 347 U.S. 483 (1954), did not say that the state had failed to protect Ms. Brown from discrimination, but that it violated the equal protection clause by running a segregated school system that was part of a state-imposed caste system. The order to dismantle the dual system of schools cannot be understood in terms of relief to individual victims (Marshall, 1984).

A logical extension of this interpretation of the law is to avoid a blanket rejection of racial classifications. Several authors distinguish between invidious racial classifications intended to oppress and benign racial classifications—Marshall uses the terms exclusionary and inclusionary purposes. It is suggested that those policies that aim to bring groups into the mainstream society, as transitional compensation either for past wrongs or present disadvantage, would satisfy the requirements of the Constitution.

Perhaps the most widely used argument in support of preferences is that equal opportunity and fair competition require special programs. The argument does not reject meritocracy in an absolute sense, but stresses the need to equalize life chances to make the system equitable. In a well-known commencement speech delivered at Howard University in 1965, President Lyndon Johnson said:

You do not take a person who for years has been hobbled by chains and liberate him, bring him up to the starting line of a race and then say "you are free to compete with all the others," and still justly believe that you have been completely fair.

A strong theme running through the literature that supports special treatment for the victims of systematic discrimination is that each member of society is equally valuable and that a just society will be organized to protect each member's self-esteem. Some variation of the idea is found in the work of legal scholars, political theorists, and moral philosophers. And it provides a rationale for distinguishing between discrimination against blacks, which insults, and discrimination for blacks, females, and others who are considered at risk, which does not.

Beyond Philosophy

Two lines of argument seem to cut through the intellectualization of the issue of preferential consideration for blacks or other disadvantaged minorities. First is the proposition, voiced by Abraham Edel (1977) and others, that there is nothing novel in the fact of preferential treatment as it occurs in affirmative action programs. Almost any policy decision brings loss to some and gain to others. We are all the beneficiaries of overt preferential treatment, as a few examples show. There is very wide social acceptance of the income tax write-off of mortgage interest. Very powerful forces support preferential treatment for veterans, including hiring preference in the civil service and referral priority by the U.S. Employment Service. There are many other less obvious examples, such as water rights and agricultural subsidies. Preference is not novel; only the intended recipient is.

Second is a skeptical assessment of the liberal values of equality, color-blind law, merit, and fair competition seen from the perspective of those who were barred from enjoying these things until the passage of the Civil Rights Act of 1964. As one author put it (paraphrased in Bell, 1984), the domination of blacks was sanctioned by religion in the colonial period. It was sanctioned by Social Darwinism in the postslavery period. And now the myth of equality provides a veneer for further oppression.

FEDERAL POLICY AND PREFERENTIAL TREATMENT

Given the deep ambivalence of our society, it is not surprising that the policies of the federal government in its several branches have often appeared as contradictory as the philosophical positions sketched above. We have mentioned the example of two former Assistant Attorneys General for Civil Rights, both of them well-respected legal thinkers, coming to very different conclusions about the constitutional permissibility of benign racial classifications. Perhaps more telling, the government with its administrative hand has become an important presence in virtually every personnel office in the country, at the same time that the Supreme Court has shown great reluctance to find constitutional justification for highly intrusive structural remedies. Taken as a whole, federal policy has described a difficult and halting evolution that cannot be said to have yet reached a state of equilibrium.

Some of the ambiguities of the federal posture were built into the Civil Rights Act of 1964 itself. The explicit language of the act did not go beyond the principle of color-blind practices. But Title VII of the act, entitled Equal Employment Opportunity, adopts a group-centered definition of discrimination, outlawing "employment practices" that "adversely affect" an individual's status as an employee because of that employee's race, color, religion, sex, or national origin.

Sponsors of the bill, including Hubert Humphrey, who was floor manager of the bill in the Senate, repeatedly denied that the term discrimination would be read as mandating racial quotas. Moreover, Section 703(j) of Title VII states specifically that nothing written therein should be interpreted as requiring any employer to "grant preferential treatment to any individual or to any group . . . on account of an imbalance which may exist with respect to the total number or percentage of persons of any race, color, religion, sex, or national origin employed by any employer." Furthermore, an amendment allowing the use of professionally developed ability tests was offered successfully by Senators Clifford P. Case and Joseph S. Clark. In support of the amendment, they entered an interpretive memorandum into the record (110 *Cong. Rec.* 7231 [1964]), which explained congressional intent as follows:

There is no requirement in Title VII that employers abandon bona fide qualification tests where, because of differences in background and education, members of some groups are able to perform better on these tests than members of other groups. An employer may set his qualifications as high as he likes, he may test to determine which applicants have these qualifications, and he may hire, assign, and promote on the basis of test performance.

At the same time, the proponents of the act understood that discriminatory practices were deeply entrenched in American society. They had witnessed a widespread and sustained resistance to the Supreme Court's school desegregation order in *Brown v. Board,* and they were aware that massive resistance to integration of the work force might also occur. As a consequence, a new agency was created by the act to foster compliance with Title VII; in addition, the Department of Justice was given broad authority to bring suit against employers when there was evidence of such systematic resistance.

As we describe below, the position that the federal government has reached through a long process of administrative and judicial interpretation of the Civil Rights Act of 1964 is one of tending to promote de facto preferences for certain protected groups, the language of Title VII notwithstanding. But neither Congress nor the Supreme Court has provided a clear rationale, a legislative or constitutional mandate for such preferences. And even though Congress appeared to approve some uses of preferences when it amended Title VII in 1972, it failed to do so with sufficient clarity to convince all members of the Supreme Court that it intended to do so (*Local 93, International Association of Firefighters v. City of Cleveland*, 478 U.S. 501, 543 [1986] [Rhenquist, W., dissenting]). One unhappy irony is that these developments have left employers, because they control scarce employment opportunities, open to challenge from members of minority groups if they do not extend preferential consideration, and open to challenge from majority-group members if they do.

Individual Rights, Group Effects, and the Law

A persistent anomaly in federal civil rights policy has been the adherence, on one hand, to the principle that the Constitution and Title

VII protect the rights of *individuals,* and the adoption, on the other, of a definition of discrimination that looks to the effects of employment procedures on *groups*.

There is no doubt that American law, true to its common-law origins, has traditionally been understood to apply to individuals. Indeed, so strong was this predisposition in the law that, as the legal establishment responded in the late nineteenth century to industrialization and the emergence of new forms of business organization, the fiction was built into the law that corporations are individuals.

There is also little doubt that Title VII of the Civil Rights Act of 1964 — as originally written—was designed to protect individual rights. Essentially negative in character, Title VII is an enumeration of unlawful employment practices addressed to employers, employment agencies, and labor unions. The language consistently used has to do with individuals: it shall be an unlawful employment practice to "fail or refuse to hire . . . any individual" because of race, color, etc.; to "deprive any individual of employment opportunities"; and so on. By outlawing discriminatory practices, the act was intended to extend to all individuals, regardless of race, color, religion, sex, or national origin, equal opportunities to secure employment. It is understandable that many understood the Civil Rights Act to be based on the premise that outlawing discriminatory practices would ensure the conditions in which people could sort themselves out by interest and ability. The hope was that this would alter employment patterns in America, bringing blacks, certain ethnic minorities, and women into the economic mainstream. And to some extent it did.

However, the traditional conception of individual rights and the individual's access to the courts for remedy does not comport well with widespread and deeply entrenched discrimination against a whole race. Congress also recognized that there was a strong possibility of massive, systematic resistance to the Civil Rights Act. Title VII not only gave individuals the right to sue an employer, employment agency, or labor union on grounds of discrimination; it also empowered the Attorney General to bring civil suit if an employer appeared to engage in a "pattern or practice of resistance" that prevented the full enjoyment of the rights secured by the act. These "pattern or practice" suits soon made work-force statistics and group outcomes the medium of courtroom argument. From the late 1960s to 1981, the Department of Justice pursued strong remedies and routinely sought to include remedial "goals and timetables" in its court judgments.

At the same time, the Equal Employment Opportunity Commission (EEOC) lent its considerable weight to focusing government policy on the overall effects of an employer's selection procedures and the underrepresentation of minority-group members in the work force. EEOC was created by the Civil Rights Act to provide leadership and guidance on the meaning of Title VII, to promote compliance and conduct compliance reviews, to summon witnesses, and to conciliate employment discrimination conflicts (it was also empowered to bring suit by the 1972 amendments to the act).

In 1966 the new agency made what must be considered among its most influential policy decisions when it interpreted Title VII discrimination to consist not merely of employment practices *intended* to discriminate or to treat people of protected status differently from others, but also of any employment practices that had an "adverse impact" on members of protected groups (Robertson, 1976:1–2). The legislative basis for this policy is found in Section 703(a)(2) of Title VII, which makes it an unlawful employment practice for an employer

to limit, segregate, or classify his employees or applicants for employment in any way which would deprive or tend to deprive any individual of employment opportunities or otherwise adversely affect his status as an employee, because of such individual's race, color, religion, sex, or national origin.

Like pattern-or-practice litigation, the EEOC's decision on the meaning of Title VII discrimination focused the attention of the authorities on work-force statistics, particularly on rates of selection.

This conceptualization of discrimination was confirmed in 1971, when the Supreme Court handed down its now famous decision in *Griggs v. Duke Power Co.* (401 U.S. 424 [1971]). Saying that Title VII proscribes "not only overt discrimination but also practices that are fair in form, but discriminatory in operation," the *Griggs* decision moved judicial notice to the *effects* of employment practices on protected groups as these effects are manifested in the composition of the employer's work force. Henceforth the courts would permit a Title VII challenge to any employment practices that had a disparate impact on people in the protected groups; an employer's actions would be scrutinized not only on the basis of his or her treatment of the plaintiff, but also indirectly by consequences of his or her employment practices on racial or other relevant groups. The relative proportions of such groups in the employer's work force compared with the makeup of the (appropriately defined) applicant pool would become an important question in assessing the employer's compliance with Title VII.

Like Title VII itself, the *Griggs* opinion specifically states that there is no requirement that preferential treatment be accorded to minorities or other protected groups; rather, qualifications are to be the controlling factor in employee selection. The problem with this formula is that it fails to take seriously the overwhelming disadvantage visited upon most blacks in America over three centuries. There is, in other words, an important, usually unspoken assumption underlying federal policy that there exist, by and large, a uniform distribution of ability and a similarity of preparation and career interests throughout the groups comprising the larger society. Thus, any underrepresentation of females, blacks, or other minorities can be ascribed to discrimination, unless the employer can show otherwise. The assumption was verbalized in *Teamsters v. United States* (431 U.S. 324, 342 n.20 [1977]):

absent explanation, it is ordinarily to be expected that nondiscriminatory hiring practices will in time result in a work force more or less representative of the racial and ethnic composition of the population in the community from which employees are hired.

In fact, the evidence from studies of a wide variety of ability tests and measures of performance indicates that there are substantial group differences in attributes that are important to performance in many kinds of jobs; although there is considerable overlap between the two, blacks as a group consistently perform less well than the majority group. Those who take seriously the effects of the kind of extreme economic, educational, and cultural disadvantage experienced by most blacks even today do not find this information surprising. It would be naive to expect the cultural patterns built over hundreds of years to be transformed in a generation. But for a number of reasons, no doubt political as well as philosophical, there has been little inclination on the part of Congress or the courts to pronounce a straightforward policy of preference as, for example, India has done to break down the lingering effects of its caste system.

The ambiguity of government policy is evident in the 1972 amendments to the Civil Rights Act. Through them, Congress elevated the Equal Employment Opportunity Commission, giving it broad new powers to bring suit and, at least by implication, endorsing the agency's aggressive posture on promoting a work force representative of the community. This more active stance is also evident in the amendments extending the Civil Rights Act to federal hiring; Congress incorporated the requirement that each federal department and agency must develop an affirmative action plan. Each federal department must also comply with Executive Order 11,478, which grew out of President Johnson's use of executive decree to bring more minorities into the mainstream economy by requiring federal employers and government contractors to take affirmative action to hire members of minority groups. Affirmative action plans are by definition not color-blind. They fall in the category of what Burke Marshall termed "inclusive discrimination."

Despite these effects of the 1972 amendments, what Congress chose not to do was equally significant. It did not remove the earlier language of Title VII that denies any requirement that private employers grant preferential treatment because of an imbalance in their work force. Noting this fact, some members of the Supreme Court have opined that when it amended Title VII in 1972, Congress did not intend to authorize the granting of racial preferences (*Firefighters v. City of Cleveland*, 478 U.S. at 543 [Rhenquist, W., dissenting]). In other words, in the private sector, the force of government pressure to increase the economic opportunities of minorities and women remained largely indirect, through the contracting authority and the increased power of the EEOC.

As a consequence, the government has devoted a good deal of energy to scrutinizing the instruments, such as employment tests, that are the proximate cause of adverse impact. The implementing agencies (EEOC, the Department of Labor, the Office of Personnel Management) have published the *Uniform Guidelines on Employee Selection Procedures* (29 CFR Part 1607 [1985]), which lays out technical requirements for the validation of tests and other objective procedures used for selection or promotion of employees. As a representative of the Department of Justice (a member of the committee's liaison group) reminded the committee, the costs of a validation study can be prohibitive, running into many hundreds of thousands of dollars (Delahunty, 1988). Judges have found themselves wrestling with the arcana of psychometric validation studies to find out if tests are sufficiently related to job performance to overcome an inference of discrimination based on work-force statistics. Some courts and other compliance authorities, "laboring under the spell of the 'equality of results' doctrine," as Mr. Delahunty put it, have imposed such stringent requirements for defending tests that many employers have quietly instituted measures to make the numbers come out right in order to avoid costly litigation.

Equity and Equal Protection Jurisprudence

In addition to legislative efforts to wipe out employment discrimination, the Constitution itself provides important safeguards with respect to governmental action. Adopted as one of three Civil War amendments passed by a Radical Republican Congress intent on protecting the newly emancipated blacks, the Fourteenth Amendment embodies the ideal of equal justice under law and provides that no state "shall deny to any person within its jurisdiction the equal protection of the laws." It has been the major vehicle for developing substantive meaning for the concept of equality.

The equal protection clause was of paramount importance in the early stages of the civil rights movement, when the emphasis was on getting rid of the laws and conventions of segregation, for example, in establishing the rights of blacks to attend the same schools as whites or to patronize restaurants, hotels, movie theaters, or other public accommodations. And the equal protection clause has continued to be important in housing, voting rights, and redistricting cases. But in the area of economic equity, the Supreme Court has been very hesitant to establish broad new constitutional remedies.

The pivotal case in setting the orientation of the Court was *Washington v. Davis* (426 U.S. 229 [1976]), which involved a constitutional challenge to a cognitive test used by the District of Columbia police department to screen applicants (Title VII protections were not available to the plaintiffs because the case was brought before the 1972 amendments to that statute were made applicable to public employers). Because the failure rate of black applicants was significantly higher than that of white applicants, plaintiffs claimed that its use was a denial of equal protection of the law. The Court rejected plaintiffs' claim, holding that under the Constitution the racially disproportionate results of the practice must be traced to a racially discriminatory purpose. This holding was reaffirmed in *Village of Arlington Heights v. Metropolitan Housing Development Corp.* (429 U.S. 252 [1977]), which, while recognizing that statistics can be critically important evidence in equal protection cases, held that normally such evidence alone would be insufficient to establish a violation of the equal protection clause.

Laurence Tribe suggests that the decision in *Washington v. Davis* "symbolizes the Supreme Court's trepidation about embracing the highly intrusive structural remedies that may be required to root out the entrenched results of racial subjugation" (1988:1510). He points out that under the intent approach, lawsuits involving constitutional claims become a search for a bigoted decision maker. The "perpetrator perspective" views contemporary discrimination not as a social phenomenon—the historical legacy of centuries of slavery and subjugation—but as the misguided, retrograde behavior of individual actors in an otherwise enlightened society (1988:1509).

In contrast to the formula for Title VII discrimination cases established by *Griggs,* which places a burden on the employer to defend practices that are shown to have adverse effects on minorities, the primary burden in constitutional cases lies with the plaintiff, who must show that the injury suffered was a consequence of an act of intentional discrimination by the defendant. In other words, motive remains crucial under the Constitution, whereas under Title VII the outcome is paramount.

Tribe enumerates some very strong reasons why the Court might choose this cautious path. There is a long tradition that binds rights to remedies, discouraging displays of broad discretionary relief. Given the experiences of the Warren Court and massive resistance to the judgment in *Brown v. Board,* the justices were sensitive to the limits on what ad hoc judicial action can achieve in a reluctant society. Above all, he believes, the Court was wary of a more aggressive role for fear that the federal courts would become deeply enmeshed in the day-to-day actions of state and local governments, reviewing choices about the allocation of public funds, zoning of residential neighborhoods, and so on.

It is Tribe's assessment, nevertheless, that the Court should have faced the problem of inequality squarely: "either grit the teeth and get to work fixing the inequality, no matter what it takes, or swallow hard and acknowledge that the constitutional wrong cannot be judicially put right" (1988:1512). Instead, in the absence of proof of a racially motivated government actor, the actual circumstances of racial disadvantage—unemployment, inadequate education, poverty, and political powerlessness—become unfortunate conditions, not the consequences of racial discrimination.

Affirmative Action

In previous sections we have developed the theme that the federal government has been reluctant to embrace straightforward policies according preferential treatment to the victims of systemic discrimination. The pressure on employers to adopt procedures that will increase the proportions of women and minority-group members in their work force has been largely indirect, a product of the emphasis on work-force statistics in EEOC compliance reviews and in Title VII litigation. The primary exception to this generalization is in affirmative action remedies and programs.

Authority for judicial intervention to order race-conscious remedial measures is found in Section 706(g) of Title VII, which states:

If the [U.S. District Court] finds that the respondent has intentionally engaged in . . . an unlawful employment practice charged in the complaint, the court may . . . order such affirmative action as may be appropriate, which may include, but is not limited to, reinstatement or hiring of employees, . . . or any other equitable relief as the court deems appropriate.

Courts have ordered a wide variety of race-conscious remedies, including the imposition of numerical hiring goals and timetables, one-for-one promotion ratios, score adjustments, and alternative selection procedures. These court-ordered affirmative action plans are uniformly temporary and remedial; they are expedients to be used pending the development of nondiscriminatory hiring or promotion procedures, and they are imposed in response to a finding of discrimination.

A second type of affirmative action program was created by Executive Order 11,246, which addressed employers doing business with the federal government. The executive order placed federal contractors under two obligations: not to discriminate in any part of the work force while under government contract and to take "affirmative action" to ensure that employees and applicants are being treated in a nondiscriminatory manner. Compliance is administered by the Department of Labor Office of Federal Contract Compliance (OFCC), which monitors each contractor's affirmative action program and, in cases of extreme recalcitrance, can blacklist the firm. The affirmative action program must include a work-force analysis, an underutilization analysis for each minority and sex, and planned corrective action including specific goals and timetables. (Executive Order 11,246 and successor Executive Order 11,478 also regulated government employment practices until they were superseded by the 1972 amendments to the Civil Rights Act.)

In the private sector, it was not until 1978 that the Supreme Court recognized the legality of voluntary affirmative action programs. Such programs are not part of a court-ordered remedy or developed in compliance with Executive Order 11,246, but are voluntarily adopted by an organization to improve the competitive position of minority-group members. As Justice Stevens recalled in his concurring opinion in *Johnson v. Transportation Agency, Santa Clara County, California* (107 S. Ct. 1442 [1987]):

Prior to 1978 the Court construed the Civil Rights Act of 1964 as an absolute blanket prohibition against discrimination, which neither required nor permitted discriminatory preferences for any group, minority or majority. [But in *Bakke* (1978) and *Weber* (1979)] a majority of the Court interpreted the antidiscriminatory strategy of the statute in a fundamentally different way. . . . It remains clear that the Act does not *require* any employer to grant preferential treatment on the basis of race or gender, but since 1978 the Court has unambiguously interpreted the statute to *permit* the voluntary adoption of special programs to benefit members of the minority groups for whose protection the statute was enacted. [Emphasis in original.]

Admitting that this judicial construction of the act, so clearly at odds with the color-blind rhetoric used by the senators and representatives who enacted the bill, gave him pause, Justice Stevens nevertheless affirmed the position. He cited both the public interest in the stable, orderly development of the law and the stated interest of Congress in avoiding undue federal interference with managerial discretion as reasons to do so.

But the crux of the matter, as the Court had observed in a previous decision (*Firefighters v. City of Cleveland,* 478 U.S. 501 [1986]), was that it would be unreasonable for the law triggered by the nation's concern over centuries of racial injustice to be interpreted to prohibit "all private, race-conscious efforts to abolish traditional patterns of racial segregation and hierarchy."

As might be expected, the Supreme Court has not given a blanket endorsement of voluntary plans that involve preferential treatment. It has not, for example, endorsed quotas, but rather has authorized the consideration of race or gender as one factor in selection or promotion decisions. It has not altered the remedial nature of legally acceptable race-conscious practices; there must be evidence suggestive of a prior condition of discrimination, illustrated perhaps by a manifest imbalance in the work force, that the affirmative action plan is intended to cure. The Court has also been at pains to emphasize the temporary nature of acceptable plans, and it has shown concern about the degree of burden imposed on majority-group members. When the affirmative action involved layoffs of workers with greater seniority, race-conscious measures have been struck down on grounds of reverse discrimination. In *Wygant v. Jackson Board of Education* (476 U.S. 267 [1986]), the Court rejected a broad claim of "societal discrimination" as an acceptable justification for adopting hiring preferences or other affirmative action policies that place burdens on others.

As an illustration of the Supreme Court's cautious approach in the emerging case law, Tribe notes that the Court has seemingly regarded all racially explicit set-asides and other measures that force visible burdens on individuals because of their nonminority status as "constitutionally problematic to *some* degree." No Justice, he points out, has endorsed minimal scrutiny of race-based preferences (Tribe, 1988:1523). Although developments in the law permitting voluntary affirmative action programs may ease the contradictory impulses in federal policy in some circumstances, the Court's limited and cautious recognition of affirmative action programs does not provide any general mandate to pursue racial balance.

Furthermore, employment practices that are not part of a bona fide affirmative action plan continue to make the employer vulnerable to the conflicting claims of individual rights and pressure to show a balanced work force. Indeed, the situation may be further complicated by a recent decision that extends the *Griggs* formula for the first time to subjective employment criteria.

In *Watson v. Fort Worth Bank and Trust* (101 L. Ed. 2d 827 [1988]), the Supreme Court acknowledges the problem of the surreptitious quota systems that have been a result of government equal employment opportunity policy. "We agree," Justice O'Connor writes for the Court, "that the inevitable focus on statistics in disparate impact cases could put undue pressure on employers to adopt inappropriate prophylactic measures." Having conceded that the extension of the disparate impact principle to subjective selection practices could increase the incentives for employers to adopt quotas or to engage in preferential treatment, however, the opinion offers little more than an exhortation that this *should not* be the outcome, for it would be contrary to the express intent of Congress and could violate the Constitution.

Little wonder if employers feel a bit like Alice in Wonderland. The government's efforts to extend social justice to whole classes of people are at odds with other important conventional values, and neither Congress nor the Court has produced a rationale to make the new dispensation wholly acceptable. The contradiction between a surface adherence to color-blind law and the underlying government policy to bring about occupational redistribution illustrates as well as anything can the ambivalence of our society on the meaning of equity.

PERSPECTIVES ON WITHIN-GROUP SCORING

In the emerging case law, the Supreme Court has recognized the use of race- and gender-conscious employment practices in rather closely circumscribed situations for the purpose of remedying past or present unlawful discrimination or to foster appropriate affirmative action. Although the Supreme Court has not itself had occasion to address the subject of within-group scoring, a variety of score-adjustment mechanisms intended to reduce adverse impact have been upheld at the appellate level, particularly in the Second Circuit. In this still-evolving area of law, commentators disagree about the boundaries of acceptable and unacceptable race-conscious procedures in general and about the specific procedures that have been used in pilot studies of the VG-GATB Referral System.

As detailed above, the former Assistant Attorney General for Civil Rights took issue with the scoring system promoted by USES because it classifies job applicants on the basis of their race or national origin and because it requires Employment Service offices to prefer some individuals and disadvantage other individuals on the basis of their membership in racial or ethnic groups. The Justice Department in the last administration found the practice unconstitutional under *Wygant* and under *Local 28, Sheet Metal Workers' International Association v. EEOC* (478 U.S. 421 [1986]). The Justice Department's position was that these cases make clear that racial preferences are permissible "only as a last resort to remedy persistent and egregious discrimination by the specific employer" (letter from Wm. Bradford Reynolds to Richard Gilliland, Director, U.S.

Employment Service, November 10, 1986). The GATB referral program, however, requires government agencies to extend racial preferences regardless of whether an employer has engaged in any racial discrimination, and it does so outside a specific remedial context. The Justice Department also found the score conversions illegal under Title VII, citing Section 703(j), quoted above, which denies any requirement for preferential treatment.

Other commentators, including the Lawyers' Committee for Civil Rights Under Law, read the case law rather differently. They point out that both Title VII and the Constitution permit (and sometimes require) the use of race-conscious selection procedures in appropriate circumstances. For example, the Supreme Court has held that private (*United Steel Workers of America v. Weber*, 443 U.S. 193 [1979]) and public (*Johnson v. Transportation Agency*) employers may, independent of any judicial finding of past discrimination, adopt race-conscious hiring or promotion plans as part of a voluntary affirmative action program to address a "conspicuous . . . imbalance in traditionally segregated job categories." As Justice Stevens wrote in a concurring opinion in *Johnson* (p. 3):

since 1978 the Court has unambiguously interpreted the statute to *permit* the voluntary adoption of special programs to benefit members of minority groups for whose protection the statute was enacted. [Emphasis in original.]

In the *Weber* case, in which a white employee challenged race-conscious admission to a new program to train workers for high-paying skilled-crafts jobs, the opinion of the Court emphasized the temporary duration of the plan, its remedial purpose, the "voluntary" nature of the plan, and the fact that it did not abrogate preexisting rights since the whole training program was new. In *Johnson,* a woman was promoted in preference to a man who had received a slightly higher rating, although both were rated as well qualified for the job of road dispatcher. At the time, none of the 238 incumbents in the job category was female. The Court, guided by its decision in *Weber,* affirmed that voluntary employer action can play a crucial role in furthering Title VII's goal of eliminating the effects of discrimination in the workplace. In rejecting the district court's finding that the affirmative action plan was illegal because it was not temporary, the Supreme Court reasoned that: the plan was flexible and did not impose quotas; it did not authorize blind hiring by the numbers, but expressly directed that numerous factors be taken into account; and the employer's plan was to "attain" a balanced work force, not to "maintain" a permanent racial and sexual balance.

The determination of whether or not a given race-conscious procedure is lawful turns on the facts surrounding its use. Advocates of within-group scoring argue that since the procedure was adopted in order to comply with the requirements of Title VII and that, without the scoring adjustment, the GATB would result in significant adverse impact against minorities, judicial precedent supports the legality of the procedure as a reasonable measure to eliminate that impact.

Representatives of the Lawyers' Committee for Civil Rights Under Law pointed out to our committee that the courts have approved the use of a variety of score-adjustment mechanisms intended to reduce adverse impact. For example, an appellate court approved adding 250 points to the score of each minority candidate on the basis of evidence that the scores of minority candidates on the written portion of a promotional examination underpredicted their job performance (*Kirkland v. New York State Department of Correctional Services,* 628 F.2d 796 [2d Cir. 1980], *cert. denied,* 450 U.S. 980 [1981]). In another case, the same court upheld a consent decree that called for a variety of race-conscious scoring procedures simply on the basis of a showing that the existing scoring and rank-ordered selection procedure had an adverse racial impact (*Kirkland v. New York State Department of Correctional Services,* 711 F.2d 117 [2d Cir. 1983], *cert. denied,* 465 U.S. 1005 [1984]). The race-conscious scoring procedures that the court approved included: separate frequency distributions for minority and nonminority candidates; establishing score zones in which a group of final examination scores are deemed the same for purposes of certification and appointment; and elimination of particular items that resulted in statistically significant adverse impact among candidates of substantially equivalent ability.

In these and a number of other cases, courts have upheld methods of score adjustment that, if followed, would reduce or eliminate the adverse racial impact of the selection practice and avoid continued violation of Title VII. These cases may or may not apply to a race-conscious scoring system voluntarily adopted by the Employment Service outside a remedial context. In addition, the emerging case law does not seem entirely consistent. In *San Francisco Police Officers' Association v. San Francisco* (812 F.2d 1125 [9th Cir. 1987]), the court of appeals rejected reweighting of three selection tests to eliminate an adverse impact against women, on the grounds that the reweighting "unnecessarily trammeled the interests of nonminority police officers." The adjustment of scores, in the court's opinion, became the sifting device, rather than the examinations themselves (812 F.2d at 1125 n.5). And in *Hammon v. Barry* (813 F.2d 412 [D.C. Cir. 1987], *petition for reh'g denied,* 826 F.2d 73 [D.C. Cir. 1987]), the court of appeals rejected selection of firefighters from rank-ordered lists compiled separately by race, sex, and ethnic group in proportion to their representation among those who passed the test. In this case the court failed to find the necessary "predicate of discrimination."

In addition to legal precedents, proponents of the adjustment of GATB scores point out that Section 6(A) of the *Uniform Guidelines* encourages the use of alternative selection procedures, including race-conscious procedures, as a way of achieving compliance with Title VII or for affirmative action purposes (there is a caveat that the procedures must be legal). The signatories to the *Uniform Guidelines* joined in adopting a set of "Questions and Answers to Clarify and Provide a Common Interpretation of the Uniform Guidelines" (43 Fed. Reg. 12,001 [1979]) in March 1979. The explication provided in Questions 30 and 31 strongly suggests that no validation is required of alternative procedures adopted to eliminate adverse impact, because federal law does not require a demonstration of the job relatedness of selection procedures that do not have adverse impact. In fact, under the *Uniform Guidelines,* use of alternative selection procedures to eliminate adverse impact is an option that is available to employers in lieu of validation. It would seem, then, that a within-group scoring procedure that eliminates adverse impact could fall within the *Uniform Guidelines*.

This committee is obviously not in a position to make a definitive statement about these conflicting interpretations of the legality of within-group scoring of the GATB. The evolution of fair employment law since 1964 has produced two grounds for race-conscious employment practices: the mitigation of adverse impact and voluntary affirmative action. It would appear that the Employment Service may not be able to justify use of score adjustments as part of its lawful affirmative action efforts because it is not acting as an employer. And, since in Justice Stevens's words, Title VII permits but does not require an employer to grant preferential treatment on the basis of race or gender, score adjustments for affirmative action purposes by a governmental employment agency might be found to constitute undue governmental interference with managerial discretion. If the scoring system is not justifiable as part of an affirmative action plan, then its acceptability would seem to depend on whether the weight of legal opinion will recognize the adoption of a generalized score adjustment, designed to prevent adverse impact, as an appropriate compliance effort under Title VII.

3

The Public Employment Service

There are approximately 110 million people working for more than 5 million employers in the United States, and the nation's economy is expected to generate an additional 20 million jobs by the year 2000. In any given year, a substantial percentage of the work force turns over; median job tenure for workers at the end of their working life in 1978 was 14.9 years for men and 9.4 years for women (quoted in Ehrenberg and Smith, 1987). A good part of the movement in the labor force is due to the natural progress of people's lives—entry into the world of work, career development, retirement. Less obviously, structural changes in the economy are reflected in employers' personnel needs, even as changes in the nature and preparation of the work force affect the ways business is done.

In a labor market as large and complex as that of the United States, how do employers and workers find one another? Whatever the theoretical attractions of scientific selection, job seekers and employers tend to use informal methods more heavily than formal job-matching systems such as the Employment Service system, private employment agencies, or school placement offices. Table 3–1 summarizes a Department of Labor survey of the methods used by employers to recruit new staff. It is apparent that employers rely to a great extent on word-of-mouth methods including current employees, newspapers, and gate hires. People looking for work likewise depend to a great extent on informal methods, as illustrated in Table 3–2.

52

TABLE 3–1 Employers' Sources for Recruiting Personnel

Recruitment Source	Employers Citing This Source (%)
Employees	54.0
Newspapers	45.0
Gate hires	37.0
Applications	34.0
Business associates	27.5
Job Service	27.0
School placement	15.0
Private agency	9.0
Community/welfare organizations	8.2
Labor unions	4.6
All others	2.7

SOURCE: U.S. Department of Labor. 1977. R&D Monograph No. 43.

Employers and job seekers use more than one method to fill a job or find a job. The methods used vary widely according to occupation, location, condition of the economy, size of the employer, industry type, and skill level required. A "Help Wanted" sign in a store window may be adequate to attract a person qualified for the position of stock clerk. However, locating a petroleum engineer willing to work at a company's foreign site is far more complex.

Some recruiting methods, such as internal promotions, employee referrals, and newspaper advertisements, are used for filling all types of vacancies. Other methods are more specifically tailored to particular types of jobs: for example, firms seeking professional and technical employees are likely to seek job candidates at colleges, universities, high schools, and trade and technical schools; however, walk-in applicants may well provide many employers with an ample supply of office workers and production/service employees.

Through the Public Employment Service, government plays an active, though supplementary, matchmaking role in certain segments of the labor market. A Bureau of National Affairs survey (1988:7–8) indicates that the Employment Service is used more frequently to secure production or service workers (68 percent) and office or clerical workers (66 percent) than to fill vacancies in professional and technical (38 percent), commissioned sales (30 percent), or management (23 percent) work forces. This pattern of activity is replicated in the data provided to the committee by one state's Employment Service. Table 3–3 reports the percentage of job orders received by job category. In contrast, employers tend to turn to private employment agencies and other sources, according to the Bureau of National Affairs survey, to recruit professional, sales, and managerial candidates. Nationwide, the people who applied to the Employment

TABLE 3–2   Job Search Method Used by Job Seekers

Job Search Method	Percentage Using Each Method
Applied to employer without suggestions or referrals	66
Asked friends about:	
Jobs where they work	51
Jobs elsewhere	42
Asked relatives about:	
Jobs where they work	28
Jobs elsewhere	27
Answered newspaper ads:	
Local	46
Nonlocal	12
Checked with State Employment Service (Job Service)	34
Checked with private employment agency	21
Contacted school placement office	12
Took Civil Service test	15
Asked teacher or professor for job leads	10
Checked with union hiring hall	6
Contacted local organization	6
Answered ads in professional or trade journals/periodicals	5
Placed ads in newspapers:	
Local	2
Nonlocal	1
Went to place where employers pick up workers	1
Placed ads in professional or trade journals/periodicals	1
Other	12

SOURCE: Bureau of Labor Statistics. 1975. *Monthly Labor Review.*

TABLE 3–3   Percentage of Job Orders by Occupational Category for One State Employment Service

Occupational Category	Percentage
Professional, technical, and managerial	4
Secretarial and clerical	14
Sales	4
Domestic	1
Service	16
Agricultural	3
Processing	9
Machine trades	8
Bench work	11
Structural work	13
Miscellaneous occupations	17

TABLE 3–4 Characteristics of Applicants for Employment Service Assistance

Type of Applicant	Number (millions)	Percentage of Total
Men	10.8	56.0
Women	8.4	44.0
Unemployment insurance claimants	7.0	36.5
Veterans	2.5	13.0
Economically disadvantaged	2.2	11.5

SOURCE: U.S. Department of Labor. 1988. *Employment Service Program Letter,* February 23.

Service for assistance in finding work in program year 1987 numbered some 19.2 million. Table 3–4 provides detail on the nature of the applicants. Of the 19.2 million Job Service registrants, approximately 6.9 million were referred to employers and 3.2 million were placed in jobs. Total expenditures during the 12-month period were $749,931,143, which amounted to a program cost of about $205 per individual placed.

HISTORICAL DEVELOPMENT OF THE PUBLIC EMPLOYMENT SERVICE

Beginnings

New York City established the first effective public employment office in 1834, which was followed in subsequent years by the establishment of municipal employment offices in other large cities. Late in the nineteenth century, the states of Ohio, New York, Illinois, and Massachusetts passed laws providing for a state employment service, operating offices in major cities in those states.

Federal involvement in the employment process began in 1907, when the Bureau of Immigration and Naturalization established 50 local placement offices and a procedure for employers to post vacancies at immigration ports of entry to help find jobs for immigrants. In 1913 the Division of Information was organized in the Bureau of Immigration; its purpose was to find jobs for immigrants entering the country through Ellis Island. By 1914 there were 96 public employment offices in the country.

The U.S. Department of Labor was established in 1916 and incorporated the Immigration Service, including its Division of Information. In 1918 the need to recruit workers for war industries led to establishment of the U.S. Employment Service (USES) as a unit of the Department of Labor. During 1918 there were 773 local employment offices in operation.

Federal funds for the entire U.S. Employment Service were curtailed in 1920, and most of its local offices were closed. States and municipalities provided the few public employment services available during that period, and the U.S. Employment Service continued mostly in name until 1933.

In 1930, Congress voted appropriations to open and maintain about 30 employment offices exclusively for veterans. The Doan Reorganization Act in 1931 established 129 offices with Veterans Placement Offices.

In the depths of the Great Depression, the Wagner-Peyser Act of 1933 was passed, forging the present Employment Service system as a cooperative federal-state venture. The act reinstated a U.S. Employment Service in the Department of Labor, and the Veterans Placement Service became a division of the Labor Department. The Wagner-Peyser Act made funds available to match state appropriations to establish state employment services under federal supervision. The actual organization and operation of the state employment services were placed under the administration of the states. Initially, the role of the U.S. Employment Service was to screen and place millions of workers into federally funded public works and job creation projects.

The Social Security Act of 1935 established the nation's system of unemployment insurance. This was combined with the Employment Service in a system of state agencies and made registration with the Employment Service a condition of receiving unemployment benefits. The Federal Unemployment Tax Act (FUTA) provided for the funding for the system and also spelled out the Employment Service's role in its administration. An employer payroll tax was instituted to create a trust fund for the payment of unemployment compensation. This employer tax also supports the job referral activities of the Employment Service. Together with the Wagner-Peyser Act, FUTA defined the broad outlines of the federal-state partnership in the State Employment Security System.

During World War II, the Employment Service was administered federally to handle war labor needs, but in postwar years it was returned to the federal-state structure. During the 1940s and early 1950s, the Employment Service significantly enhanced its counseling and testing capabilities to improve its services to returning veterans and others.

In the 1960s the Employment Service was enlisted in the Johnson administration's War on Poverty. USES policy emphasis shifted away from the mainstream work force to focus on people having difficulty in the labor market. The Manpower Development and Training Act of 1962 and its successor, the Comprehensive Employment and Training Act of 1973, focused on providing training opportunities for disadvantaged applicants. Although many employers took advantage of these training programs, there was a significant loss of placement activity during these years. Many within the Employment Service system attribute this decline to a loss of credibility in the employer community due to the focus on the economically disadvantaged rather than the mainstream work force.

By the late 1970s the Employment Service had become a cornucopia of special programs, responsibilities, funding sources, and emphases that included labor exchange duties; gathering, analyzing, and disseminating labor-market information; and special programs designed for poor and disadvantaged people, employers, veterans, migrant and seasonal farmworkers, handicapped people, older workers, dislocated workers, and alien and migrant workers (including migrant housing inspection).

Beginning in the mid-1970s the Employment Service saw a need to upgrade its negative public image as the "Unemployment Office." It was during this period that the name "Job Service" became a new national symbol of identification.[1] The Job Service was no less committed to assisting disadvantaged workers, but policy makers sensed the need to be more responsive to the entire public.

The Job Service increased its efforts to improve working relationships with employers. State-level employer committees were established to help local Job Service offices respond more effectively to the needs of employers and job seekers. The number of these committees, now known as Job Service Employers Committees, has grown to 1,100 nationwide, involving some 30,000 employers at local, state, and national levels. The national organization, the Employers' National Job Service Committee (ENJSC), meets annually to address matters of national concern in employment and training, especially the Employment Security system. A steering committee of the ENJSC also conducts quarterly sessions to help guide and support local committees.

The New Federalism

The Job Training Partnership Act of 1982 marked a growing trend for decreasing federal control and increasing state and local involvement in determining the type of employment and training services needed for given locales. This act sought to strengthen the role of governors and of local Private Industry Councils, comprised largely of employers, in determining what employment and training services are needed and how, where, and by whom they will be provided. The act also made significant revisions to the Wagner-Peyser Act, expanding the role of governors and private employers in matters relating to unemployment and the development of a skilled work force. Under the amended Wagner-Peyser Act, the

---

[1] The terms Employment Service and Job Service are used interchangeably in this report.

federal role is no longer specific and prescriptive; the act now provides that funds allotted to the Employment Service may be used for a variety of programs. Within this flexible design, veterans continue to receive priority services, in accordance with federal statutes.

In summary, several major pieces of federal legislation significantly affect the employment security system. The Wagner-Peyser Act (as amended) provides for the national system of Employment Service offices and determines the distribution of funds for its administration. The Social Security Act (as amended) established the national system of unemployment insurance and set up the administrative funding mechanism for employment security, including the Employment Service, through the Federal Unemployment Tax Act. Title 38 of the *United States Code* (as amended) and supporting legislation mandate that eligible veterans be given preference in all employment services provided by the Job Service. The Job Training Partnership Act of 1982 provides for employment training for the economically disadvantaged and dislocated workers who become unemployed due to plant closing and mass layoffs. Other federal laws affecting the Employment Service include the Migrant and Seasonal Agricultural Worker Protection Act of 1983 and laws related to the Food Stamp Program, the Work Incentive Program, and Alien Certification. Recent federal legislation, including the Economic Dislocation Worker Adjustment and Assistance Act, the Worker Adjustment and Retraining Notification Act, and the Family Assistance Act of 1988 will clearly affect the Employment Service in the future.

Other federal legislation, although not directed primarily at the Employment Service, has an effect on its activities. Most important, the Civil Rights Act of 1964, discussed in Chapter 2, has very specific implications for the state Employment Service system. To fail or refuse to refer for employment or otherwise discriminate against any individual because of race, color, religion, sex, or national origin is a violation of Title VII of that act. To rectify past discriminatory practices, affirmative action may be required of employers who seek applicants through the Job Service, particularly applicants who are members of a specific group that, for reasons of past custom, historical practice, or other nonoccupationally valid purpose, have been discouraged from entering certain occupational fields. When the Job Service is requested by an employer to assist with recruitment in such cases, the job order is identified as an affirmative action order and the specific needs of the employer are stated on the job order. In addition, applicants are informed that it is an affirmative action job order.

Table 3–5 summarizes the federal laws affecting the U.S. Employment Service system.

TABLE 3-5   Federal Laws Affecting the U.S. Employment Service

Legislation	U.S. Employment Service Program
Wagner-Peyser Act of 1933, as amended	Employment Service (labor exchange); Occupational Analysis Field Centers; Test Development Field Centers; and State Test Research Units
Job Training Partnership Act of 1982	Special programs involving employment training; Dislocated Worker Program
Social Security Act of 1935 Federal Unemployment Tax Act (FUTA) Emergency Unemployment Insurance Compensation Act Federal Supplemental Compensation Act Special Unemployment Assistance Program	Unemployment Insurance (UI) system; Wagner-Peyser, and the Title 38 U.S.C. programs for veterans through the Federal Unemployment Tax Act
Trade Readjustment Act Omnibus Trade and Competitiveness Act of 1988	Services, including UI, to individuals who are unemployed due to imports
Civil Rights Act of 1964, as amended Fair Labor Standards Act	USES administration of services; Labor Exchange Administration; wages and child labor provisions
38 U.S.C., Chapters 41, 42, 43 Veterans Employment, Training and Counseling Act of 1987	USES involvement with the preferential treatment of military veterans in job training and placement
Immigration Reform and Control Act of 1986	ES involvement with alien certification, employment, and I-9 requirements
Revenue Act of 1978 Tax Reform Act of 1986	ES responsibility for administering the Targeted Jobs Tax Credit Program at the state and local levels
Farm Labor Contractor Registration Act of 1963 Fair Labor Standards Act Occupational Safety and Health Standards Act Migrant Seasonal Agricultural Worker Protection Act of 1983	ES services to migrant/seasonal farm workers (includes inspection of migrant workers' housing)
Rehabilitation Act of 1973 Older Americans Act·	USES involvement with handicapped and older workers
Food Stamp Act of 1977	USES involvement with employment and training of food stamp recipients

Funding Levels

Although the 1980s have brought many new responsibilities to the Employment Service system, during this same period massive cutbacks in funding have occurred. At the beginning of the decade, federally funded staffing for the U.S. Employment Service was 30,000, but current federally supported staffing nationwide is less than 17,000. These funding cuts put a premium on productivity and have led states to aggressively seek more efficient methods of operation for the Employment Service. Nevertheless, the system has been forced to close over 500 full-service offices and severely reduce its programs supporting counseling, testing, employer services, and related activities.

STRUCTURE OF THE SYSTEM

The Public Employment Service exists as a labor-market intermediary to help employers find workers and to help job seekers find work. It is a cooperative federal-state program that has grown over the years to include a network of 1,800 local employment offices administered by the states.

In essence, the Employment Service serves as a "no fee" employment agency, or what an earlier generation called a labor exchange. Although there is great variety in plans and procedures from state to state, and indeed from local office to local office, the basic function of the Employment Service system is to take job orders from employers, to take applications from job seekers, and to make referrals of applicants to employers. The Employment Service views itself in this role as an honest broker, providing employers with access to a larger pool of potential employees than might otherwise be available to them and providing job seekers access to information about many job openings at a single location.

USES: The Federal Partner

The federal part of the Employment Service system, the U.S. Employment Service, is a division of the Employment and Training Administration of the U.S. Department of Labor. It provides research and technical support to State Employment Service Agencies as well as program monitoring and fiscal oversight. USES has carried out a variety of research programs over the years. In 1939, USES produced the first *Dictionary of Occupational Titles* (DOT), the basic tool for matching workers with jobs that is now in its fourth edition. In 1947 it developed the General Aptitude Test Battery (GATB) and made the test available to the states for use in vocational counseling and employment screening. Ongoing research on the GATB is conducted through a series of Test Development Field Centers, and the *Dictionary of Occupational Titles* and occupational codes are maintained through several Occupational Analysis Field Centers. Although located at State Employment Service Agencies, these centers receive programmatic direction from the national USES office.

The Employment and Training Administration oversees the administration of the Employment Service system through the USES national office and 10 regional offices. Guidance is provided to the states by the regional offices, primarily by requiring an annual plan from each state and then monitoring the state's activity. There is no specific instruction given as to how to accomplish goals and objectives: each state develops its own strategies to accomplish its plan, and there is much resulting diversity.

State-Level Activities

At the state level, the Employment Service is considered a major part of the State Employment Security Agency, which also administers unemployment insurance and labor-market information programs. Each State Employment Security Agency has its own particular character. Some are independent departments within state government; others are housed under the administration of higher-level or umbrella departments. All are staffed by state employees, but the specific organizational designation and location are determined by individual state legislatures and governors. Even the names are different from state to state, as reflected in Table 3–6. These variations in organizational location of the Employment Service within state governments add complexity to the federal-state partnership.

The geographic and industrial makeup of the states further complicates the picture. Large population centers require different approaches to service delivery and mix than do rural or smaller urban areas. Agricultural employers require different services than manufacturing plants or government agencies. Agriculture itself is changing, as traditional family farms are replaced by agribusiness.

The relationship of the unemployment insurance and the employment referral functions is also viewed differently by different states, resulting in variations in office structure and location. Some states operate two autonomous programs housed in separate local offices; other states combine management and location of the programs. Whatever the specific structure, statute and regulations mandate that services be coordinated and state work test requirements be met by the Employment Service.

TABLE 3–6   State Employment Security/Employment Service Agencies

State	Agency Title
Alabama	Department of Industrial Relations
Alaska	Employment Security Division, Department of Labor
Arizona	Department of Economic Security
Arkansas	Employment Security Division
California	Employment Development Department
Colorado	Department of Labor & Employment
Connecticut	Connecticut Labor Department
Delaware	Department of Labor
District of Columbia	Department of Employment Services
Florida	Department of Labor & Employment Security
Georgia	Georgia Department of Labor
Hawaii	Department of Labor and Industrial Relations
Idaho	Department of Employment
Illinois	Department of Employment Security
Indiana	Department of Employment & Training Services
Iowa	Department of Employment Services
Kansas	Department of Human Resources
Kentucky	Department for Employment Services
Louisiana	Office of Employment Security
Maine	Bureau of Employment Security
Maryland	Department of Economic and Employment Development
Massachusetts	Division of Employment Security
Michigan	Employment Security Commission
Minnesota	Department of Jobs & Training
Mississippi	Employment Security Commission
Missouri	Department of Labor & Industrial Relations
Montana	Department of Labor & Industry

Resources are initially allocated to State Employment Service Agencies on the basis of civilian labor force and the unemployment rate. State administrators allocate those resources according to local conditions. Administrative costs vary from state to state as well as within each state.

Computer automation has begun to have an impact on organization and efficiency. The degree to which states have automated is variable, and there is no standardization in this endeavor, although USES has approved software packages geared to networking local offices and states together for the exchange of employment placement opportunities.

Local Offices

The 1,800 local Employment Service offices vary in size from one- or two-person operations to offices with dozens of employees. The locations vary from temporary trailers in remote areas to high-rise city offices, with each size and location attempting to be an efficient labor exchange,

TABLE 3-6 *Continued*

State	Agency Title
Nebraska	Department of Labor
Nevada	Employment Security Department
New Hampshire	Department of Employment Security
New Jersey	New Jersey Department of Labor
New Mexico	New Mexico Department of Labor
New York	New York State Department of Labor
North Carolina	Employment Security Commission of North Carolina
North Dakota	Job Service North Dakota
Ohio	Bureau of Employment Services
Oklahoma	Employment Security Commission
Oregon	Employment Division
Pennsylvania	Department of Labor & Industry
Puerto Rico	Bureau of Employment Security
Rhode Island	Department of Employment Security
South Carolina	Employment Security Commission
South Dakota	South Dakota Department of Labor
Tennessee	Department of Employment Security
Texas	Texas Employment Commission
Utah	Department of Employment Security
Vermont	Department of Employment & Training
Virginia	Virginia Employment Commission
Virgin Islands	Employment Security Agency
Washington	Employment Security Department
West Virginia	Department of Employment Security
Wisconsin	Department of Industry, Labor, and Human Relations
Wyoming	Employment Security Commission

serving the people and employers in that area as well as exchanging information with other offices and other states.

The basic function of the local office is to match workers to jobs. Employers send or phone in job orders to a local office of their state Employment Service, specifying the type of jobs they need to fill; any special requirements for the job, such as educational credentials, work experience, or test results; and, if they choose, the number of applicants they would like the Employment Service to refer for each position. Each job order is assigned an occupational code drawn from the Department of Labor's *Dictionary of Occupational Titles,* which classifies jobs according to a scheme of broadly defined performance requirements.

In day-to-day operations, it appears that the pool available to fill a particular job order is usually determined by the people who come into the office while the job order is current as well as any applicants who are in the office's active applicant file. But when an employer needs a large number of workers—for example, to put on an additional shift or to staff a new facility—one or perhaps several local offices in a region will compile a large referral pool through advertising and file searches.

People in search of work who register at a local Employment Service office are generally interviewed by staff who assess their qualifications, recording information about education, job experience, and preferences.[2] In addition to being interviewed, a small number of applicants are given aptitude tests. On the basis of this information, one or more DOT codes are assigned to each registrant to reflect job experience. These codes are the major means of matching people to jobs, although the Employment Service interviewer will also decide who to refer on the basis of an employer's special requirements. In order to identify the most qualified available workers, the interviewer may also make additional judgments about the suitability of the individual registrant for the job.

Local-office personnel may also provide a variety of other services in conjunction with state or federally mandated programs. This array can include providing a work test for claimants for unemployment insurance, Aid to Families with Dependent Children, food stamps, and other benefits. The work test is a process through which a registered applicant is offered employment (the criteria are specified by the regulations for each benefit paying agency). If employment is refused, loss of applicant benefits may result.

In addition, pursuant to Title 38 of the *United States Code,* the Employment Service extends preference to veterans, especially disabled and Vietnam-era veterans, in referrals for jobs and other services. Employment opportunities for veterans are enhanced through the Federal Contractor Job Listing Program, the Targeted Jobs Tax Credit, and the Veterans' Job Training Act.

The local office may also provide specialized services for youths, people with handicaps, minorities, women, older workers, released prisoners or parolees, and others who may be disadvantaged in the job market. This may include special drives promoting the hiring of Vietnam-era veterans, cooperative arrangements with schools to serve dropouts and high school seniors planning to enter the labor market, and cooperative efforts with military recruiters to try to interest young people in the various branches of the Armed Services.

There may also be occasional needs for special recruiting, such as recruiting workers with hard-to-find skills for employers who have vacancies and are unable to fill them. Recruiting can be done locally, within the state, and across states. The office may also recruit seasonal

---

[2] This report uses the generic term counselor to refer to the positions of interviewer and counselor in the Employment Service system.

and year-round farmworkers needed by farmers and food processors. To the extent that resources permit, local offices will provide specialized services for migrants and seasonal farmworkers. The Employment Service office may have to certify that employer-provided housing meets standards when workers from other states are recruited. A staff member may have to make random checks to determine if working conditions are as specified. The office may also recruit and select qualified job seekers for referral to openings in other areas when local offices in those areas are not able to fill the openings from the local labor supply.

A major activity of Employment Service offices is to provide occupational and labor-market information and data for myriad purposes: for unemployed workers for their job search purposes; for employers in planning recruitment, in considering a plant location, and in marketing plans; for employment and school counselors in assisting applicants in need of counseling and career guidance; for school administrators to assist in curriculum planning and for vocational schools in determining occupations with reasonable prospects of employment; for administrators in human resource program planning; for classification of service delivery areas according to level of unemployment; for economic development planning by regional commissions and other planning bodies; for development of affirmative action plans; and for Employment Service planning to help reduce the impact of mass layoffs.

An office may also engage in research. For testing, the task may be to participate in collecting information used in developing aptitude and performance tests that are valid for job seekers, including minority job seekers. For occupational analysis, the local office may complete on-site observation and job analysis in order to describe occupations not covered or covered by obsolete descriptions in the *Dictionary of Occupational Titles*. The more current information can then be made available nationwide for use with job seekers by employers, schools, government agencies, and other users of occupational information.

For specific federal programs, a local office may have to prepare preference certificates for and obtain new-hire reports from employers in areas with high unemployment who agree to hire a certain percentage of disadvantaged workers and meet other criteria for contract preference. The office may have to complete the preparation of appropriate forms under the Immigration Reform and Control Act, as well as process alien labor certification applications and forward them to the Department of Labor for final action. When required, a local office will establish prevailing rates of pay through salary surveys and/or testing of the labor market through job orders and advertisements. The office also may have to provide certification of applicant eligibility and vouchering under the Targeted Jobs Tax Credit Program.

As this brief description suggests, the activities that engage the local Employment Service offices cover a tremendous range. The constraints of limited resources, especially cutbacks in staffing during the past decade, have made the conduct of these activities extremely difficult.

OPERATIONS AT THE LOCAL LEVEL

Local Employment Service offices across the nation are as diverse as the communities they serve. The previous section listed services that *may* be available through local offices. Because of constraints in funding as well as conscious decisions related to labor-market needs, each office will differ in the mix and degree of services offered. Because each local office coordinates its plans with its Private Industry Council and local elected officials, this alone may cause wide variances in service mix and delivery from one local office to another. To provide a context for the issues discussed in this report, in this section we provide a common profile of the local Employment Service office and describe three prototype local offices. Our purpose is to give a general picture of what happens when a job seeker comes to an Employment Service office. Taken together, the three separate local office environments explored are a sampling of the various operational procedures used to provide the same basic service.

Activities Common to All Offices

Job seekers register with their local Employment Service office by providing information about their work history, skills, education, training, and employment interest. Employers list job openings by providing information to the local office about the job, including a detailed description of the work involved, minimum screening requirements, and referral instructions. This information is matched, using varying degrees of automation. Selected applicants are called in, and referrals of qualified applicants are made to the employer. The ratio of referrals made to openings received depends on employer specifications, or the available pool of qualified applicants, or both. The basic function of every local office (all other legislative responsibilities notwithstanding) is the recruitment, screening, selection, and referral of job applicants to employers. The Employment Service does not make the hiring decision.

Every local office maintains a Job Information System, which enables applicants to peruse the lists of open job orders, albeit without employer identification. The job openings are listed by DOT job category and are presented in a number of ways. In some offices the lists are compiled in loose-leaf binders; in some the system is automated; in some the lists are available over the telephone. Most state agencies still require that an interviewer conduct screening prior to making specific referral information available to the applicant. However, some states are beginning to provide nonsuppressed listings (employer's name and application information provided) for applicants' self-service use.

Employer relations are promoted at the community level by each local office. Depending on available resources, personal visits and promotional telephone contacts are made to employers to solicit job orders and to inform employers about the services available. Since the system is funded through employer taxes, and since service to applicants depends on employers' willingness to list openings, this is a crucial aspect of the local office operation. Marketing strategies are localized to match the activities available in the local office. In other words, if the GATB is emphasized, then the benefits of test selection are promoted to the employer community. Conversely, if relatively few applicants are tested, then the local office uses programs other than testing to promote the Employment Service. Job Service Employers Committees, developed over the past 16 years, assist by advising local offices on how they can better serve the community, as well as by promoting use of the system to other employers.

Every local Employment Service office has statutory responsibilities with regard to veterans. Preferential service to veterans is clearly defined by Title 38 of the *United States Code*. Furthermore, Public Law 100-323 increased the number of Local Veteran Employment Representatives and clarified the roles and relationships between federal and state personnel. The Employment Service's responsibility to veterans represents an exception to the flexibility with which local offices administer programs.

Within this common framework there is enormous diversity among the local offices—diversity in size, in program emphasis, and in the human and other resources available. The profiles of three local office operations that follow illustrate this point.

Profile One: A Traditional Office

Local office one is in a medium-sized metropolitan location. The work-force population is over 300,000 and the employer population is 13,000. A total of 84 percent of the employers have fewer than 10 employees. The employment makeup is varied, with a high number of service jobs as well as a good diversity of manufacturing and industrial jobs. There is also a great deal of white-collar employment in the immediate metropolitan area.

Due to the high volume of intake, applicants are received by appointment only and are scheduled for group orientation, or intake, usually within two to three days after the appointment is made. Veterans are given priority service. All applicants fill out an employment application, including personal and work-related information. Personal information is primarily collected for the identification of target groups (e.g., handicapped, economically disadvantaged, veterans) and for labor-market information reporting. Job registrants who wish to file for unemployment insurance are assigned to an unemployment insurance group session following registration for work. Veterans are assigned to separate intake groups for employment registration, but they file for unemployment compensation with the general applicant population.

During the group intake, applicants are identified for special services that may be available, including counseling, testing, or other programs deemed appropriate. Typically, each applicant completes the group intake process; speaks briefly with an employment interviewer for the assignment of DOT occupational codes and to determine if a job order is currently listed for which the applicant is interested and qualified; and then is released. Occasionally applicants are referred to jobs on the spot, but usually job referral comes in the form of a call once the applicant's DOT code is matched to an open job order that comes in after the applicant has registered and is in active status in the files. For applicants with special needs (e.g., applicants with handicapping conditions, disabled veterans), counselors will make job development contacts with likely employers.

Testing is conducted on a very limited basis in this office, due to the limited staff available for test administration. Employers who use GATB testing have all applicants tested before they are referred. Applicants considered for referral to these employers are scheduled to take the GATB. Testing is not actively marketed to the employer community. Applicants who demonstrate difficulty in making occupational choices, changes, or adjustment decisions are referred to the employment counselor, who uses the GATB for diagnostic and assessment purposes. Those tested represent a small percentage of the overall applicant flow through the local office.

Profile Two: A VG-GATB Office

Local office two has geared its entire operations around the administration of the GATB. This is referred to as the "full-blown" approach to testing. Group intake is conducted as in local office one. However, in this local office, which is located in a small town with a strong base of manufacturing employment, all applicants are encouraged to take the GATB. Similarly, activities involving employer relations center around the promotion of test-based job referrals. Local-office staff time is spent to a large extent on test administration. The GATB, which takes approximately two and a half hours to administer, is given twice daily, four days a week. Test scoring and job matching are automated.

About 75 percent of all applicants are given the GATB. The reasons applicants give for not taking the test range from handicap limitations or literacy problems to a simple refusal to take any test. These applicants receive normal services without benefit of test selection. With such a strong emphasis placed on testing, however, there are few resources left to serve these applicants.

Profile Three: The Single-Employer Office

The third office profiled is located in a rural area. There is one major manufacturing plant in the area, and the local office primarily serves that employer. The skill and education levels of the applicant population are generally low. Turnover is high in the area, particularly with the major employer served; entry-level job orders with this employer are virtually constant. The local office is highly automated. Applicants and job orders are placed in the computer and are automatically matched, using any number of variables, for referral.

The VG-GATB program was adopted statewide as the primary screening and selection tool to be used by local offices, but this local office requested to discontinue the full-blown approach due to the strain on staff time. The local office manager felt that it was not a significant tool, considering the labor-market and labor-force makeup of his service delivery area.

Unlike larger offices (such as local office one), where specialists serve different applicant needs, staff members in local office three are, by necessity, cross-trained to handle all applicant and employer needs, including unemployment insurance administration.

Implications of Local-Office Procedures

The offices briefly profiled above illustrate how heterogeneous the Employment Service system must be if it is to be responsive to local labor-market needs. Although the goal of all local Employment Service offices is essentially the same, each office works within the framework of the individual state's philosophy of employment service and the needs of the local economy it serves.

This report evaluates one particular plan for Employment Service operations, which we call the VG-GATB Referral System. No matter how attractive VG-GATB referral turns out to be in general, its suitability for any particular local office will necessarily depend on local conditions.

The decision on whether or not to adopt test-based procedures is made at the state and local levels. Although this report can help federal and state officials arrive at some basic decisions about the future of the VG-GATB Referral System, the ultimate determination will no doubt come from 1,800 local-office administrators concerned with the practical management of available resources.

PART II

ANALYSIS OF THE GENERAL APTITUDE TEST BATTERY

In order to answer the questions posed by the Department of Labor, the committee took as its first task a thorough examination of the General Aptitude Test Battery itself. Chapter 4 summarizes the development of the test, describes its component subtests, discusses its reliability and convergent validity, and compares it with other test batteries. Chapter 5 discusses in detail several shortcomings of the GATB that need immediate attention if the test is to become the centerpiece of the Employment Service system: problems with test administration, the highly speeded nature of the test and its consequent vulnerability to coaching, and the paucity of available test forms and the test's consequent vulnerability to compromise.

4

The GATB: Its Character and
Psychometric Properties

The General Aptitude Test Battery (GATB) has been in use for more than 40 years, and for most of that time it has remained virtually unchanged. Through the years it has been used in state Employment Service offices for vocational counseling and referral and in addition has been made available for testing and counseling to high schools and technical schools, labor union apprenticeship programs, public and private vocational rehabilitation services, and other authorized agencies. The obvious first task for the committee was to sift through the years of research and experience with the GATB to assess its suitability as the centerpiece of the proposed VG-GATB Referral System. We looked carefully at the development and norming of the instrument, its psychometric properties, and evidence that it actually measures the aptitudes it claims to measure. We also looked with some care at four other widely used tests of vocational aptitudes in order to get a sense of the relative quality of the GATB.

This chapter describes the test and summarizes our analysis of its psychometric properties (a more detailed discussion appears in Jaeger, Linn, and Tesh, Appendix A). Chapter 5 addresses the two shortcomings that the committee feels must be dealt with if the GATB is to assume a central role in the Employment Service system of matching people to jobs: namely, the highly speeded nature of the test, which makes it vulnerable to coaching, and the paucity of available test forms, which makes it vulnerable to compromise.

73

DEVELOPMENT OF THE GATB

In the period 1942–1945, the U.S. Employment Service (USES) decided to develop a "general" aptitude battery that could be used for screening for many occupations. Drawing on the approximately 100 occupation-specific tests developed since 1934, USES staff identified a small number of basic aptitudes that appeared to have relevance for many jobs (U.S. Department of Labor, 1970:17):

1. *Intelligence* (G), defined as general learning ability;
2. *Verbal aptitude* (V), the ability to understand the meanings of words and language;
3. *Numerical aptitude* (N), the ability to perform arithmetic operations quickly and accurately;
4. *Spatial aptitude* (S), the ability to think visually of geometric forms and to comprehend the two-dimensional representation of three-dimensional objects;
5. *Form perception* (P), the ability to perceive pertinent detail in objects or in pictorial or graphic material;
6. *Clerical perception* (Q), the ability to perceive pertinent detail in verbal or tabular material—a measure of speed of perception that is required in many industrial jobs even when the job does not have verbal or numerical content;
7. *Motor coordination* (K), the ability to coordinate eyes and hands or fingers rapidly and accurately in making precise movements;
8. *Finger dexterity* (F), the ability to move fingers and manipulate small objects with the fingers rapidly and accurately; and
9. *Manual dexterity* (M), the ability to move the hands easily and skillfully.

Four of the nine aptitudes—clerical perception, motor coordination, finger dexterity, and manual dexterity—involve speed of work as a major component.

From the USES inventory of job-specific tests, those providing the best measure of each of the nine basic aptitudes (based on several statistical criteria) were selected for inclusion in the new General Aptitude Test Battery, which became operational in 1947. The operational edition of the GATB, B-1002, was produced in two forms, A and B. Form A was reserved for the use of Employment Service offices; Form B was used for validation research and for retesting and was made available to other authorized users for vocational counseling and screening. It was not until 1983 that two additional forms, Forms C and D, of GATB edition B-1002 were introduced.

THE STRUCTURE OF THE GATB

The General Aptitude Test Battery consists of 12 separately timed subtests, which are combined to form nine aptitude scores. Eight of the subtests are paper-and-pencil tests, and the remainder are apparatus tests. Two of the paper-and-pencil subtests (name comparison and mark making), as well as all four subtests that require manipulation of objects, are intended to measure aptitudes that involve speed of work as a major component. Each subtest is scored as number correct, with no correction for guessing.

The following descriptions of the subtests in Forms A and B of the GATB are based on material in Section III of the *Manual for the USES GATB* (U.S. Department of Labor, 1970:15–16). Examples of various item types are drawn from a pamphlet published by the Utah Department of Employment Security.

Subtest 1: Name Comparison

This subtest contains two columns of 150 names. The examinee inspects each pair of names, one from each column, and indicates whether the names are the same or different. There is a time limit of 6 minutes, or 2.40 seconds per item. This is a measure of the aptitude of clerical perception, Q.

Sample Item:

Which pairs of names are the same (S) and which are different (D)?
1. W. W. Jason .... W. W. Jason
2. Johnson & Johnson .... Johnson & Johnscn
3. Harold Jones Co .... Harold Jones and Co.

Subtest 2: Computation

This subtest consists of arithmetic exercises requiring addition, subtraction, multiplication, or division of whole numbers. The items are presented in multiple-choice format with four alternative numerical answers and one "none of these." There are 50 items to be answered in 6 minutes, or 7.20 seconds per item. This is one of two measures of numerical aptitude, N.

Sample Item:

Add (+)	766	(A) 677	(C) 777
	11	(B) 755	(D) 656
			(E) none of these

Subtest 3: Three-Dimensional Space

This subtest consists of a series of exercises, each containing a stimulus figure and four drawings of three-dimensional objects. The stimulus figure is pictured as a flat piece of metal that is to be bent, rolled, or both. Dotted lines indicate where the stimulus figure is to be bent. The examinee indicates which one of the four drawings of three-dimensional objects can be made from the stimulus figure. There are 40 items with four options each, to be completed in 6 minutes, or 9.00 seconds per item. This subtest is one of three measures of intelligence, G, and the only measure of spatial aptitude, S.

Sample Item:

At the left in the drawing below is a flat piece of metal. Which object to the right can be made from this piece of metal?

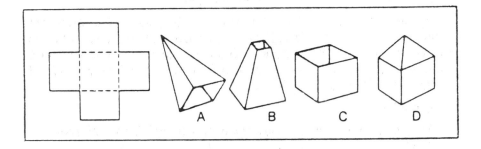

Subtest 4: Vocabulary

Each item in this subtest consists of four words. The examinee indicates which two of the four words have either the same or opposite meanings. There are 60 items, each having six response alternatives (all possible pairs from four). The time limit is 6 minutes, or 6.00 seconds each. This subtest is one of three measures of intelligence, G, and the only measure of verbal aptitude, V.

Sample Items:

1. Which two words have the same meaning?
   (a) open   (b) happy   (c) glad   (d) green

2. Which two words have the opposite meaning?
   (a) old   (b) dry   (c) cold   (d) young

Subtest 5: Tool Matching

This subtest consists of a series of exercises containing a stimulus drawing and four black-and-white drawings of simple shop tools. Different parts of the tools are black or white. The examinee indicates which of the four black-and-white drawings is the same as the stimulus drawing. There are 49 items with a time limit of 5 minutes, or 6.12 seconds per item. This is one of two measures of form perception, P.

Sample Item:

At the left in the drawing below is a tool. Which object to the right is identical? Variations exist only in the distribution of black and white in each drawing.

Subtest 6: Arithmetic Reasoning

This subtest consists of a number of arithmetic problems expressed verbally. There are five alternative answers for each item, with the fifth being "none of these." There are 25 items with a time limit of 7 minutes, or 16.80 seconds per item. This subtest is one of three measures of intelligence, G, and one of two measures of numerical aptitude, N.

Sample Item:

A man works 8 hours a day, 40 hours a week. He earns $1.40 an hour. How much does he earn each week?

(A) $40.00 (C) $50.60
(B) $44.60 (D) $56.00
(E) none of these

Subtest 7: Form Matching

This subtest presents two groups of variously shaped line drawings. The examinee indicates which figure in the second group is exactly the same size and shape as each figure in the first or stimulus group. Total test time is 6 minutes, or 6.00 seconds per item. This subtest is one of two measures of form perception, P.

Sample Item:

For questions 9 through 12 find the lettered figure exactly like the numbered figure.

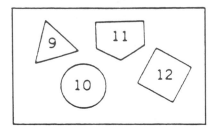 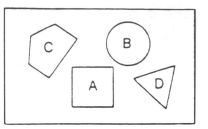

(The actual test would have 25 or more items within a group.)

Subtest 8: Mark Making

This subtest consists of a series of small empty boxes in which the examinee is to make the same three pencil marks, working as rapidly as possible. The marks to be made are short lines, two vertical and the third a horizontal line beneath them: ⊥⊥. There are 130 boxes to be completed in 60 seconds, or 0.46 seconds per item. This subtest is the only measure of motor coordination, K.

Subtest 9: Place

The equipment used for Subtests 9 and 10 consists of a rectangular pegboard divided into two sections, each containing 48 holes. The upper section contains 48 cylindrical pegs. In Subtest 9, the examinee moves the pegs from the holes in the upper part of the board and inserts them in the corresponding holes in the lower part of the board, moving two pegs simultaneously, one in each hand. This performance (moving 48 pegs) is done three times, with the examinee working rapidly to move as many of the pegs as possible during the time allowed for each of the three trials, 15 seconds or 0.31 second per peg. The score is the number of pegs moved, summed over the three trials. There is no correction for dropped pegs. This test is one of two measures of manual dexterity, M.

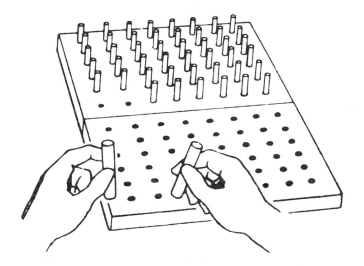

Subtest 10: Turn

For Subtest 10, the lower section of the board contains the 48 cylindrical pegs. The pegs, which are painted in two colors—one end red and the other end white—all show the same color. The examinee moves a wooden peg from a hole, turns the peg over so that the opposite end is up, and returns the peg to the hole from which it was taken, using only the

For Right-Handed Examinees

(Examinee stands here)

preferred hand. The examinee works rapidly to turn and replace as many of the 48 cylindrical pegs as possible during the time allowed, 30 seconds. Three trials are given for this test. The score is the number of pegs the test taker attempted to turn, summed over the three trials. The time allowed is 0.63 second per peg and there is no correction for errors. This subtest is one of two measures of manual dexterity, M.

Subtest 11: Assemble

The equipment used for Subtests 11 and 12 consists of a small rectangular board (finger dexterity board) containing 50 holes and a rod to one side, and a supply of small metal rivets and washers. In Subtest 11, the examinee takes a small metal rivet from a hole in the upper part of the board with the preferred hand and at the same time removes a small metal washer from a vertical rod with the other hand; the examinee puts the washer on the rivet and inserts the assembled piece into the corresponding hole in the lower part of the board using only the preferred hand. The examinee works rapidly to move and assemble as many rivets and washers as possible during the time allowed. There is one scored trial of 90 seconds, or 1.80 seconds per rivet. The score is the number of rivets moved; there is no correction for dropped rivets or for moving rivets without washers. This subtest is one of two measures of finger dexterity, F.

Subtest 12: Disassemble

The equipment for this subtest is the same as that described for Subtest 11. The examinee removes the small metal rivet of the assembly from a hole in the lower part of the board, slides the washer to the bottom of the board, puts the washer on the rod with one hand and the rivet into the corresponding hole in the upper part of the board with the other (preferred) hand. The examinee works rapidly to move and replace as many rivets and washers as possible during the time allowed. There is one timed trial of 60 seconds, or 1.20 seconds per rivet. The score is the number of rivets moved; there is no correction for dropped rivets or washers. This subtest is one of two measures of finger dexterity, F.

HOW GATB SCORES ARE DERIVED

There are more than 750 items on the GATB all together. But an applicant's score is not simply the sum of the correct answers on each subtest. The generation of GATB scores from subtest scores involves a number of conversion procedures intended to provide the scores with meaning and to suitably standardize and weight subtest scores in the

(Examinee sits here.)

Subtest 11.

(Examinee sits here.)

Subtest 12.

various forms of the test. This section describes the mechanics of producing GATB scores under traditional procedures and under the new VG-GATB Referral System (U.S. Department of Labor, 1970, 1984c). It also looks briefly at the development of GATB norms and the equating of test forms, both of which influence the conversions made.

Obtaining GATB Scores

There are three steps in obtaining GATB scores under the traditional procedures:

1. The first step is to calculate the number of items correct for each of the 12 subtests. There is no penalty for wrong answers.

2. The second step is to convert each raw score so that it is referenced to the norming population. The specific conversion depends on which aptitude the subtest score will be used for (arithmetic reasoning has a different value for G, intelligence, than for N, numerical aptitude), the form of the GATB that was administered, and the type of answer sheet used. There is a conversion table for each subtest for each form of the GATB. Three of the subtests are components of two different aptitudes and hence have two conversion tables for each form. Each raw score will go through two or three transformations in becoming an aptitude score.

3. The third step is to sum the converted scores into aptitude scores.

The conversion tables used to produce aptitude scores are designed to accomplish three things: first, to put all aptitude scores on a single measurement scale having a mean of 100 and a standard deviation of 20 in the norming population; second, to make scores on all operational forms of the test comparable with one another (so that a score of 109 on the verbal subtest in Form A means the same as a score of 109 on the verbal subtest in Form B); and third, to weight the components of an aptitude score when it consists of more than one subtest.

The new VG-GATB Referral System, in which all jobs are clustered into one of five job families, and in which percentile scores are computed on the basis of group identity (black, Hispanic, other), requires two further steps:

4. The conversion of aptitude scores to "B" scores. There are two aspects to the process: the aptitudes are reduced to three composites—a cognitive composite (G + V + N); a perceptual composite (S + P + Q); and a psychomotor composite (K + F + M)—and the composites are accorded different relative weights for each of the five job families according to their importance in predicting job performance in each family. There is a conversion table for each of the three composites, and each table has conversions for each of the five job families, for a total of

15 B scores. USES Test Research Report No. 45 (U.S. Department of Labor, 1983b) describes regression equations relating the three composite scores to job performance in each of the five job families. Regression coefficients were used to formulate relative weights for the aptitude composites in forming B scores.

5. The final step is to calculate percentile scores from the B scores. For each of the five job families, the three B (composite) scores are summed. Each of these five numbers is then converted into a percentile score for the appropriate population group (black, Hispanic, other).

Test batteries usually require score conversions of some sort—both to standardize the scale of measurement and to provide scores with meaning. However, the amount of manipulation that GATB scores undergo is of some concern to the committee. Each of the conversion tables is based on a set of judgments and analyses that we have not been able to fully reconstruct, despite a careful review of the GATB technical manuals. It is, therefore, difficult to comprehend the links between the raw scores and the within-group percentile scores. The several layers of computations have gradually accumulated over time. Exactly the same job family scores could be obtained by taking suitable linear combinations of the subtest scores. And indeed, predictors of almost the same validity as the job family scores would be obtained by an unweighted sum of the subtest scores.

GATB Norms

The purpose of norms is to show an individual's relative standing in some appropriate reference group. Norms for the GATB are based on what USES calls the General Working Population Sample, a subset of 4,000 of a total of 8,000 workers for whom complete GATB data were available in 1952. The sample of 4,000 was chosen to be representative of the work force as it appeared in the 1940 census, with one exception: the base population was restricted to employed workers ages 18 to 54 and included no farmers, foremen, proprietors, managers, or officials. The five occupational groups defined by the Bureau of the Census (professional and semiprofessional; clerical, sales; craftsmen; operatives; laborers, except farm and mine) were represented in the standardization sample in proportion to their presence in the census. The sample was also stratified on the basis of sex, age, and (less successfully) geographic location.

This General Working Population Sample is the reference population in which the GATB aptitudes are standardized to have a mean of 100 and a standard deviation of 20. A study conducted in 1966 with test data from

23,428 workers indicated that the norms had remained stable to that point. We have not seen more recent information on the General Working Population Sample norms; the significant structural changes in the economy since then, including the continued decline of manufacturing and emergence of new high-technology occupations, suggest the need for renewed attention to the GATB norming sample.

Norms for Within-Group Scoring

The GATB General Working Population Sample was not stratified by racial or ethnic group identity. As a consequence, implementation of the VG-GATB Referral System required additional normative data to permit within-group percentile scoring by job family (steps 4 and 5, above).

The current norms are based on the 8,310 blacks, 2,102 Hispanics, and 18,359 "others" in an expanded data base of 143 validity studies conducted since 1972. Native American norms were produced in 1986. The samples used were 472 Native American employed workers from GATB validity studies and 1,349 Native American applicants prior to 1985.

From the scant information available, the committee concludes that an improved normative base is required if group-based score adjustments continue to be used in the VG-GATB Referral System. The current norm groups are by no means nationally representative samples. Nor is it possible to evaluate how similar they might be to groups of applicants for particular jobs. Thus within-group percentile score conversions that produce the same distribution of percentile scores for all racial or ethnic groups in the norm group may provide quite different distributions among groups of applicants for particular jobs. Since most of the data are based on validity studies from only two job families (Job Families IV and V), special caution is appropriate for the remaining three job families.

Equating Alternate Forms of the GATB

As the *Standards for Educational and Psychological Testing* adopted by the major professional organizations point out (American Educational Research Association et al., 1985:31), alternate forms of a test would, in the ideal case, be interchangeable in use: "it should be a matter of indifference to anyone taking the test or to anyone using the results whether Form A or Form B of the test was used." However, even if considerable care is taken to make two forms of a test as similar as possible in terms of content and format, the forms cannot be expected to be precisely equal in difficulty. Consequently, the use of simple number-right scores without regard to form would place the people taking the more difficult of the two forms at a disadvantage. To take the unintended differences in difficulty into account, "it is usually necessary to convert the scores of one form to the units of the other, a process called test equating" (p. 31).

There are a number of data collection designs and analytical techniques that can be used to equate forms of a test. Detailed descriptions of the various approaches can be found in Angoff (1971) and in Petersen et al. (1989). Regardless of the approach, however, there are two major issues that need to be considered in judging the adequacy of the equating: (1) the degree to which the forms measure the same characteristic or construct and (2) the magnitude of the errors in the equating due to the procedure and sampling.

Our review of the evidence concerning the equating of GATB forms revealed a mixed picture (see Jaeger et al., Appendix A, for a detailed discussion; U.S. Department of Labor, 1984b). Alternate Forms A, C, and D of the first eight subtests of the GATB, which define all the aptitudes except finger dexterity and motor dexterity, have adequate intercorrelations and sufficiently similar patterns of correlations with the other subtest scores to treat the scores as interchangeable after equating. The procedures used to equate the alternate forms for the first eight subtests are reasonable and, if appropriately applied, should yield equated scores with relatively small standard errors of equating. Missing details concerning Form B preclude judgment at this time. In the future, better documentation of the details of the equating analyses needs to be provided to enable an independent check on the equating.

Forms C and D of Subtests 9 through 12 of the GATB do not correlate as highly with Form A as would be desirable to consider the forms to be interchangeable after equating. Furthermore, the pattern of intercorrelations among the subtests for Form D does not appear to be sufficiently similar to the pattern for Form C to conclude that the forms measure essentially the same characteristics. Finally, the equating procedures and sample sizes used for Subtests 9 through 12 produce results that are subject to larger errors of equating than the procedures and sample sizes used to equate Subtests 1 through 8. For these reasons, scores from the alternate forms that are based on Subtests 9 through 12 should not be considered to be interchangeable.

RELIABILITY OF THE GATB APTITUDE SCORES

Aptitude tests such as the GATB are intended to measure stable characteristics of individuals, rather than transient or ephemeral qualities. Such tests must measure these characteristics consistently, if they are to be useful. *Reliability* is the term used to describe the degree to which a test measures consistently. The psychometric literature includes a variety of methods for estimating test reliability. These methods differ in their sensitivity to various sources of measurement error, in their applicability to different types of tests, and in their usefulness for particular purposes. When tests are used to assess aptitudes or other traits that are expected to be stable across weeks, months, or years, the most appropriate reliability estimation procedures will reflect the stability of measurements across time.

The committee conducted a careful review of studies of the temporal stability of the GATB. The time period between test administrations ranged from one day to four years, and the studies have involved samples of examinees that varied widely in age and level of education. Estimates of the temporal stability of GATB aptitude scores have also been computed for examinees of different races.

Whether the stability coefficients of GATB aptitude scores are sufficiently large is a matter of interpretation. Certainly, the stabilities of the cognitive aptitudes (G, V, N) compare very well with those of corresponding aptitudes in other batteries and with those of many other tests used as a basis for selection and classification decisions concerning individuals. The gradualness of the degradation of these aptitudes' stability coefficients as a function of time interval is also impressive. Figure 4–1 is a scatter diagram that illustrates the stability coefficients as

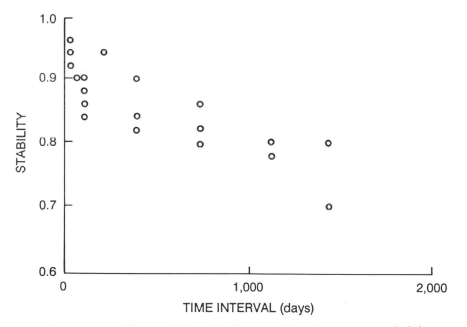

FIGURE 4–1 Stability coefficient for G versus time between test administrations.

a function of the time interval between test administrations for the G aptitude. The stability coefficients of the GATB perceptual aptitudes are somewhat smaller than those of the cognitive aptitudes, but again, compare well to those of corresponding aptitudes in other test batteries.

The stability coefficients of psychomotor aptitudes F and M are substantially smaller than those of other aptitudes assessed by the GATB and, if these aptitude scores were to be used individually for making selection or classification decisions, would be regarded as unacceptably small. However, this is probably not a problem for the VG-GATB system, since referral decisions are based on composites of aptitude scores. Although direct estimates of the stability of the operational GATB aptitude composites (such as KFM) are not available, the estimated stability coefficient over a time interval of two weeks or less for a unit-weighted composite of abilities K, F, and M is 0.81. This value is sufficiently large not to preclude interpretation of scores for individual examinees. (Additional information on the reliability of the GATB can be found in Appendix A.)

CONSTRUCT VALIDITY ISSUES

In this section we report on evidence that bears on USES claims that the subtests of the GATB measure the aptitudes with which they are identified in the GATB *Manual* (U.S. Department of Labor, 1970) and nothing more. In particular, the committee conducted an exhaustive review of the literature on convergent validity, which reports the strength of relationships between subtests of the GATB and corresponding subtests of other test batteries. Evidence of strong positive relationships between measures purportedly of the same construct is supportive of construct validity claims for all related measurement instruments. Thus the claim that the subtests of the GATB measure the aptitudes attributed to them (e.g., intelligence, verbal aptitude, spatial aptitude) would be enhanced by data of this sort and weakened if small to moderate correlations between corresponding subtests were to be found. (A detailed discussion of convergent validity findings can be found in Appendix A.)

Chapter 14 of Section III of the GATB *Manual* (U.S. Department of Labor, 1970), entitled "Correlations with Other Tests," is a primary source of convergent validity evidence. That chapter contains correlation matrices resulting from studies of the GATB and a variety of other aptitude tests and vocational interest measures. Results for 64 studies are reported. Since the publication of the GATB *Manual,* correlations between various GATB aptitudes or subtests and corresponding subtests

TABLE 4–1 Summary Statistics for Distributions of Convergent Validity Coefficients for the Cognitive GATB Aptitudes (G, V, and N), the Perceptual GATB Aptitudes (S, P, and Q), and the Psychomotor Aptitudes (K, F, and M)

Aptitude	Number of Studies	Minimum	First Quartile	Median	Third Quartile	Maximum
G	51	.45	.67	.75	.79	.89
V	59	.22	.69	.72	.78	.85
N	53	.43	.61	.68	.75	.85
S	19	.30	.58	.62	.70	.73
P	8	.38	.44	.47	.57	.65
Q	16	.24	.38	.50	.60	.76
K	1	.58	.58	.58	.58	.58
F	2	.37	.37	.39	.41	.41
M	1	.50	.50	.50	.50	.50

of other test batteries have been provided in studies by Briscoe et al. (1981), Cassel and Reier (1971), Cooley (1965), Dong et al. (1986), Hakstian and Bennett (1978), Howe (1975), Kettner (1976), Kish (1970), Knapp et al. (1977), Moore and Davies (1984), O'Malley and Bachman (1976), and Sakolosky (1970). The sizes and compositions of examinee samples used in these studies are diverse, as are the aptitude batteries with which GATB subtests and aptitudes were correlated. They range from 40 ninth-grade students who completed both the GATB and the Differential Aptitude Test Battery (DAT), to 1,355 Australian army enlistees who completed the GATB and the Australian Army General Classification Test. However, in 8 of 13 studies (many of which considered several independent samples of examinees), the samples consisted of high school students.

Distributions of convergent validity coefficients for the GATB cognitive and perceptual aptitudes are summarized in Table 4–1 and, for ease of visual comparison, are depicted in Figure 4–2. As can be seen, the distributions for the cognitive aptitudes of the GATB (G, V, and N) provide moderately strong support for claims that these aptitudes are appropriately named and measured, with median coefficients of .75, .72, and .68, respectively. The results are based on more than 50 studies of each aptitude. Corresponding results for the perceptual aptitudes of the GATB (S, P, and Q) are somewhat less convincing. Data for the psychomotor aptitudes are so meager (because the GATB is one of very few tests that attempts to measure them) that judgment on their convergent validity must be withheld.

Although the median convergent validity coefficient observed for the

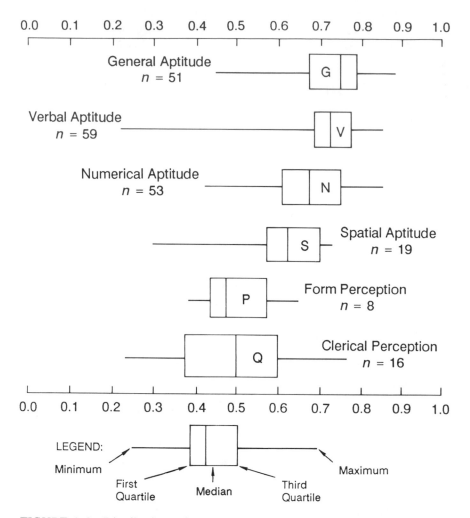

FIGURE 4–2   Distributions of convergent validity coefficients for GATB cognitive aptitudes (G, V, and N) and GATB perceptual aptitudes (S, P, and Q). The number of studies (n) on which the results are based are indicated for each aptitude.

spatial aptitude (S) was respectably large, the corresponding median values for the form perception (P) and clerical perception (Q) aptitudes were smaller than would be desired. The three-dimensional-space subtest is said to measure both intelligence and spatial aptitude and might therefore require greater reasoning ability and inferential skill than is typical of measures of spatial aptitude found in other batteries. The name comparison subtest of the GATB appears to tap only a subset of the skills typically associated with clerical perception.

COMPARISON WITH THE ASVAB AND OTHER TEST BATTERIES

The GATB is one of a number of test batteries used in this country for vocational counseling or employee selection and classification. In order to gauge the relative quality of the GATB, the committee reviewed four of the more widely used of these tests: the Armed Services Vocational Aptitude Battery (ASVAB), the Differential Aptitude Test, the Employee Aptitude Survey, and the Wonderlic Personnel Test. For purposes of this report, we limit our discussion largely to the ASVAB testing program, since it provides the closest parallel to the way the VG-GATB would function and might reasonably be considered an appropriate model should the Employment Service proceed with test-based referral as a major component of its employment program.

The ASVAB is the cognitive abilities test battery used to select and classify applicants for military service in the enlisted ranks. It is administered annually to approximately 1 million applicants for military service, as well as to an equal number of students in the tenth through twelfth grades and postsecondary students. (The latter administrations provide Service recruiters with the names of prospects and provide the schools with a vocational aptitude test battery for their students at no cost.)

The ASVAB is the most recent in a series of tests, beginning with the Army General Classification Test of the World War II era, used for initial screening of potential entrants into military service, for purposes of classification and assignment, or for both. Introduced in the late 1960s for use in the DOD Student Testing Program, the ASVAB was officially adopted in 1976 as the DOD enlistment screening and classification battery.

In the 13 years of its operational use, new forms of the ASVAB have been introduced at about four-year intervals. ASVAB Forms 5, 6, and 7 made up the first operational test battery; Form 5 was designated for use in the student testing program and the latter two in the Enlistment Testing Program. For enlistment processing, Forms 6 and 7 were replaced by Forms 8, 9, and 10 in 1980; by Forms 11, 12, and 13 in 1984; and by Forms 15, 16, and 17 in 1989. (In 1984, Form 14 replaced Form 5 as the current form for school administrations). The three forms introduced in 1980 included certain significant changes in the test battery, including the deletion of the spatial abilities subtest. The 1984 and 1989 batteries were developed to be parallel to their predecessor. Among the reasons for this cycle of new forms is the need to maintain the integrity of the test battery in the all-volunteer environment. The pressures on military recruiters to meet enlistment quotas must be balanced by close attention to test security.

ASVAB Test Parts

The ASVAB includes 10 separately timed subtests and takes about three hours to administer. There are eight power subtests (tests for which speed of work has no influence on an examinee's score) and two speeded subtests. The test parts are:

1. General science (GS);
2. Arithmetic reasoning (AR);
3. Word knowledge (WK);
4. Paragraph comprehension (PC);
5. Numerical operations (NO) (speeded);
6. Coding speed (CS) (speeded);
7. Auto and shop information (AS);
8. Mathematical knowledge (MK);
9. Mechanical comprehension (MC); and
10. Electronics information (EI).

Four of the subtests—AR, WK, PC, and MK—make up the Armed Forces Qualification Test (AFQT). The AFQT, which is considered a general measure of trainability, is used to determine eligibility for enlistment. In addition, each Service has developed its own set of aptitude composites from the ASVAB subtests, which are used to qualify applicants for various career fields. For example, the Army uses a selector composite termed "combat" which includes the ASVAB Subtests AR + CS + AS + MC.

Speededness of the ASVAB

The eight power subtests of the ASVAB appear not to be speeded. This is documented in the ASVAB Technical Supplement (U.S. Department of Defense, 1984b), which presents a study showing the proportions of eleventh- and twelfth-grade students omitting the last item for each of the eight ASVAB power subtests. Higher omit rates were generally shown by the younger students and for the arithmetic reasoning and word knowledge subtests. However, none of these omit rates was particularly high. On average, about 7 percent of twelfth-grade students omitted the last item of the eight subtests. This evidence permits the assertion that the ASVAB subtests so labeled are indeed predominantly power tests.

ASVAB Normative Data

Until 1980, the aptitude levels of military recruits were established with reference to a normative base representing all males serving in the Armed Services during 1944 (Uhlaner and Bolanovich, 1952). In 1980, the Department of Defense, in cooperation with the Department of Labor, undertook a study called *Profile of American Youth* to assess the vocational aptitudes of a nationally representative sample of youth and to develop current norms for the ASVAB. Subsequent forms of the ASVAB have been calibrated to this 1980 Youth Population, making it the only vocational aptitude battery with nationally representative norms.

The 1980 Youth Population norms were based on a sample of 9,173 people between the ages of 18 and 23 who were part of the nationally representative National Longitudinal Survey of Youth Labor Force Behavior. The sample included 4,550 men and 4,623 women and contained youth from rural as well as urban areas and from all major census regions. Certain groups—blacks, Hispanics, and economically disadvantaged whites—were oversampled to allow more precise analysis than would otherwise be possible (U.S. Department of Defense, 1982).

ASVAB Reliabilities

Reliability data are available for the form of the ASVAB administered to high school students both for the individual subtests and for the aptitude composites. The reliability estimates reported are alternate-form reliability coefficients. This approach combines the measure of temporal stability previously presented for the GATB with the administration of two forms of the same test so that the risk of distortion due to memory effects can be avoided.

The alternate-form reliabilities for subtests from ASVAB Forms 8, 9, and 10 range from .57 to .90 with a median of .79 (U.S. Department of Defense, 1984b). As would be expected, the reliabilities for the aptitude composites are higher; the academic composites ranged from .88 to .94, and the mechanical and crafts composites ranged from .84 to .95 (U.S. Department of Defense, 1984a).

In comparison, the alternate-form reliabilities for the GATB cognitive aptitudes are close to .90 and for the perceptual aptitudes are in the low .80s (U.S. Department of Labor, 1986).

ASVAB Validities

The ASVAB *Test Manual* (U.S. Department of Defense, 1984c) presents tables of validity coefficients for military training, separately by eight career fields. In all, 11 validity coefficients were provided by the Army, 47 by the Navy, 50 by the Marines, and 70 by the Air Force. Those Services reporting validities that were corrected for restriction of range computed the corrections using the 1980 Profile of American Youth Population. Validities were reported for both the AFQT and the aptitude or selector composite used to place recruits in each of the eight career fields.

There are difficulties in trying to interpret these data. The training criterion is problematic when self-paced instruction is used or when courses are graded pass/fail rather than along a numerical continuum. In addition, training criteria are dependent on the detail of records maintained by the particular training school, which differs by occupational specialty and by Service.

There are also difficulties in trying to summarize the data, largely because of differences in what each Service reported. Both the Army and the Navy reported uncorrected and corrected validities for the AFQT and the selector composites. The Air Force reported only selector validities, uncorrected, whereas the Marine Corps reported only corrected validities, but for both AFQT and the selector composites.

Nevertheless, enough data are presented to make an estimate of ASVAB validities. As is true of the GATB, there is a broad range of observed validities; there are examples of marginal predictive power and a few cases of dramatically high prediction—the Navy selector composite for cryptologic technician produces uncorrected validities of .60. Over all combinations, we estimate the weighted mean validity of the AFQT for training to be .33 (uncorrected) and for the selector composites to be .37 (uncorrected). These correlations are at the same general level of predictive efficiency as the mean validities we estimate for the GATB against a training criterion and, as might be expected, somewhat higher than the validities for a performance criterion (supervisor ratings) (see Chapter 8).

One trend in the military data that is pertinent in the context of this study of the GATB and validity generalization is that there is a tendency for the more job-specific selector composites to produce slightly higher validities than the AFQT. Of the studies that reported both AFQT and selector validities, the mean uncorrected selector validities were higher than the AFQT validities in 11 comparisons, were equal in 3 comparisons, and were lower in 5.

This pattern in the relative validities of selector composites and the AFQT is confirmed in more extensive reports of the Service data. Wilbourn and colleagues' report (1984) on the relationships of ASVAB Forms 8, 9, and 10 to Air Force technical school grades shows comparatively high mean validities for both AFQT and selector composites, with

TABLE 4-2 Uncorrected Weighted Validities for Training by Selector Composite and AFQT for Four Air Force Career Fields

Composite	Selector Composite Components	N	n	$\bar{r}_{Comp}$	$\bar{r}_{AFQT}$	$\bar{n}$
Mechanical	GS, AS, MC	19	9,185	.43	.39	483
Administrative	WK, PC, NO, CS	7	3,170	.21	.43	453
General	WK, AR, PC	16	9,183	.43	.41	574
Electronic	GS, AK, MK, EI	26	6,166	.48	.35	237

NOTE: N = number of studies; n = number of examinees; $\bar{n}$ = average number of examinees; $\bar{r}_{Comp}$ = uncorrected weighted validity of selector composite for training; $\bar{r}_{AFQT}$ = uncorrected weighted validity of the Armed Forces Qualification Test for training; GS = general science; AR = arithmetic reasoning; WK = word knowledge; PC = paragraph comprehension; NO = numerical operations (speeded); CS = coding speed (speeded); AS = auto and shop information; MK = mathematical knowledge; MC = mechanical comprehension; EI = electronics information.

SOURCE: Wilbourn, James M., Lonnie D. Valentine, Jr., and Malcolm J. Ree. 1984. Relationships of the Armed Services Vocational Aptitude Battery (ASVAB) Forms 8, 9, and 10 to Air Force Technical School Final Grades. AFHRL Technical Paper 84-08. Working paper. Manpower and Personnel Division, Brooks Air Force Base, Texas.

the selector composites producing slightly higher coefficients in three of the four aptitude areas (Table 4-2).

Army data are reported in McLaughlin et al. (1984). The Army reports validities for training and for Skill Qualification Tests (job knowledge tests), based on 92 school classes and 112 groups of test takers, each group with 100 cases or more. The uncorrected validities of the selector composite and the general composite (equivalent to the AFQT) in nine occupational areas are shown in Table 4-3. In six occupational areas, the selector composite validity was higher, in two areas the mean weighted AFQT validity was higher, and in the remaining occupational area, the values were the same.

There is some indication that the speeded nature of certain ASVAB subtests is what causes the break in the pattern of relative validities. According to McLaughlin et al. (1984), the reason lies in the lower validities of the two ASVAB speeded subtests (numerical operations, coding speed) compared with the higher validity of the two quantitative subtests (arithmetic reasoning, mathematics knowledge). As Tables 4-2 and 4-3 show, for both the Air Force and the Army, the administrative or clerical composite includes both speeded subtests but no test of mathematics. The AFQT, which then included a half-weighted numerical operations subtest plus a full weighted arithmetic reasoning subtest, has higher validity than composites with more of the speed factor and less of the quantitative factor.

TABLE 4–3 Uncorrected Weighted Validities for Training and SQT by Selector Composite and General Composite for Nine Army Career Fields

Composite	Selector Composite Components	N	n	$\bar{r}_{Comp}$	$\bar{r}_{General}$	$\bar{n}$
Clerical	CS, NO, WK, PC	16	10,368	.27	.39	648
Combat	CS, AR, MC, AS	8	14,266	.33	.31	1,783
Electronics	AR, EI, GS, MK	10	5,533	.29	.26	553
Field artillery	GS, AR, MC, MK	2	5,602	.36	.34	2,801
General maintenance	GS, AS, MK, EI	14	2,571	.26	.23	184
Mechanical maintenance	NO, EI, MC, AS	18	7,073	.30	.27	393
Operators/food	NO, WK, PL, MC, AS	11	8,704	.30	.30	791
Surveillance/communications	NO, CS, WK, PC, AS	5	3,729	.26	.34	746
Skilled technical	WK, PC, MK, MC, GS	14	7,061	.33	.32	504

NOTE: $r_{General}$ = Uncorrected weighted validity of the General Composite for Training and Skill Qualifying Test. See note in Table 4–2 for identification of other components.

SOURCE: Based on McLaughlin, Donald H., Paul G. Rossmeissl, Lauress L. Wise, David A. Brandt, and Ming-mei Wang. 1984. Validation of Current and Alternative Armed Services Vocational Aptitude Battery (ASVAB) Area Composites: Based on Training and Skill Qualification Test (SQT) Information on Fiscal Year 1981 and 1982 Enlisted Accessions. Technical Report 651. Alexandria, Va.: U.S. Army Research Institute for the Behavioral and Social Sciences.

The reason the Air Force validities are higher than those for the Army is not clear. McLaughlin et al. (1984) suggested that the Army's adoption in the 1970s of criterion-referenced assessment for technical training courses (i.e., pass/fail), and the simultaneous conversion of many courses into a self-paced mode, led to a large reduction in the psychometric quality of available training measures for validation purposes. However, despite any difference in overall validities for these two Services, the appropriate selector composite is a slightly but generally better predictor than the general composite, or AFQT.

CONCLUSIONS

GATB Properties

1. In terms of the stability of scores over time and stability between parallel forms of the test, the GATB exhibits acceptable reliabilities. The reliabilities of the cognitive aptitudes are particularly high and compare well with those of other tests used for selection and classification. The stability coefficients of the perceptual aptitudes are somewhat smaller, but well within the acceptable range. The reliabilities of the individual psychomotor subtests are low, although not so low for the psychomotor composite as to preclude its use.

2. Our review of a very large number of convergent validity studies provides moderately strong support for claims that the subtests of the GATB measure the cognitive constructs they purport to measure. The evidence for the perceptual aptitudes is mixed; the spatial aptitude test bears a respectably large relationship to similarly named subtests in other batteries, but evidence for the form perception and clerical perception subtests is less convincing. Since most aptitude test batteries do not have equivalent psychomotor subtests, this type of analysis is not useful in trying to establish that the K, F, and M subtests are appropriate measures of a psychomotor construct.

3. Only four operational forms of the GATB have been introduced in its 42-year history: Forms A and B were introduced in 1947 and were replaced by Forms C and D in 1983. So long as the GATB was used primarily as a counseling tool, this lack of new forms was probably no serious problem. If, however, the VG-GATB Referral System becomes a regular part of Employment Service operations and the GATB takes on an important gatekeeping function, then the frequent production of new forms, similar to the program for developing new forms of the Armed Services Vocational Aptitude Battery, will be essential to maintain the integrity of the GATB.

4. The scoring system for the VG-GATB seems unduly complex. It involves so many conversions, the exact nature of which is not fully documented, that the link between raw scores and the final within-group percentile scores is clouded.

5. The norms for the GATB are problematic. The General Working Population Sample, developed in the early 1950s to be representative of the work force as it appeared in the 1940 census, is at this point a very dated reference population. There have been enormous structural changes in the economy and the work force in the intervening years. The more recent norms, developed for the computation of within-group percentile scores, are based on convenience samples that can claim neither to be nationally representative nor scientifically drawn from populations of those who would be applicants for homogeneous clusters of jobs.

6. Our review of the available evidence regarding test equating indicates that Subtests 1 through 8 of GATB Forms A, C, and D (evidence is lacking on Form B) are sufficiently related to one another that the scores can be considered interchangeable after equating. The scores from the alternate forms of the psychomotor subtests (Subtests 9 through 12), however, should not be considered interchangeable.

Comparison with Other Test Batteries

7. On two dimensions of central importance—predictive validity for training criteria and test reliability—the GATB compares quite well with

the other test batteries we reviewed. For example, the mean uncorrected validities of the Armed Forces Qualifying Test for a training criterion we estimate to be about .33 across all Services (although some Services report substantially higher validities); for the GATB, the corresponding figure for predicting training criteria would be about .35 overall and .30 for studies since 1972. With the exception of one subtest (arithmetic reasoning), GATB reliabilities are also about the same as those of other test batteries.

8. However, if the GATB is to take on a much more important role in Employment Service operations—if, in other words, it takes on a major gatekeeping function like that exercised by the ASVAB—then it will need to be supported by a similar program of research and documentation. The areas in which the GATB program does not compare well with the best of the other batteries—test security, the production of new forms, equating procedures, the strength of its normative data, the integrity of its power tests—will take on heightened significance.

RECOMMENDATIONS

1. If the VG-GATB Referral System becomes a regular part of Employment Service operations, we recommend a research and development program that allows the introduction of new forms of the GATB at frequent intervals. The Department of Defense program of form development and equating research in support of the ASVAB provides an appropriate model.

2. Test equating will become far more important should the GATB become a central part of the Employment Service job referral system, because such use will necessitate the regular production of new forms of the test. The committee recommends both better documentation of equating procedures and special attention to creating psychometrically parallel forms of the apparatus-based subtests.

3. The USES long-term research agenda should include consideration of a simplified scoring system for the GATB.

4. The USES long-term research agenda should give attention to strengthening the normative basis of GATB scores. The General Working Population Sample should be updated to represent today's jobs and workers. In addition, more appropriate samples need to be drawn to support any score adjustment mechanisms adopted.

5. More reliable measurement of the psychomotor aptitudes deserves a place on the GATB research agenda.

5

Problematic Features of the GATB: Test Administration, Speededness, and Coachability

In this chapter we examine a number of characteristics of the GATB and the way it is administered that need immediate attention if the test is transformed from a counseling tool into the centerpiece of the U.S. Employment Service (USES) referral system. The difficulties we see range from easily cured problems with the current test administration procedures to some fundamental design features that must be revised if the General Aptitude Test Battery is to take on the ambitious role envisioned in the VG-GATB Referral System.

TEST ADMINISTRATION PRACTICES

Several features of USES-prescribed test administration procedures and the use of the National Computer Systems (NCS) answer sheet appear to be potential threats to the construct validity of the test. If these features affect members of various racial or ethnic groups to differing degrees, they could also be sources of test bias. Each of these issues warrants further investigation.

Instructions to Examinees

The GATB test booklet for each pencil-and-paper subtest instructs examinees to "work as quickly as you can without making mistakes." This instruction implies that examinees will be penalized for making errors when the subtests are scored. In fact, number-right scoring is used

99

for all pencil-and-paper GATB subtests, with no penalties for incorrect guessing or other sources of incorrect answers.

When asked how test administrators responded to questions concerning the type of scoring used with the GATB, the committee was told by USES representatives that honest answers were given. Thus, test-wise examinees who ask about scoring rules have an advantage that is not shared by examinees who do not raise this question. Use of an instruction that misleads examinees about the scoring procedures employed is inconsistent with the *Standards for Educational and Psychological Testing* (American Educational Research Association et al., 1985). It unnecessarily adds a source of error variance to observed test scores that will reduce measurement reliability. In addition, to the extent that test-wise examinees are differentially distributed across racial and ethnic groups, the inconsistency between test instructions and scoring procedures is a source of test bias that could be readily eliminated.

Our review of the GATB *Manual* (U.S. Department of Labor, 1970) and the contents of the GATB subtests has raised additional concerns about the vulnerability of the test battery to guessing. Consider Subtest 1, name comparison, a speeded test of clerical perception. Examinees are given 6 minutes to indicate whether the two names in each of 150 pairs of names are exactly the same or different. The GATB *Manual* indicates that the General Working Population Sample of 4,000 examinees was administered Form A with an IBM answer sheet. The mean score for name comparison was just under 47 items correct with a standard deviation of 17, meaning that it is a highly speeded test.

Let us hypothesize with the available statistics for Form A and an IBM answer sheet. If all scores were normally distributed, then scores at the 95th percentile for name comparison would be 75 items correct. On the basis of these statistics and assumptions, the optimal strategy for an examinee completing the name comparison subtest has two phases. The first would be to randomly mark one of the two bubbles for each of the 150 items as rapidly as possible, without reading the items in order to consider the stimulus names. Assuming an examinee could fill in 150 bubbles within 6 minutes, the second phase of the optimal strategy would then be to begin again with the first item, determine the correct answer, and change the answer already marked if necessary; the examinee would continue working through the subtest in this way until time was called.

On one form of the GATB, the actual proportion of items with a correct answer of "exactly the same" was 0.493 (74 of 150 items). Since for half the items on the subtest the correct answer was "exactly the same," an expected score of 75 items correct would result from marking all answers the same way. *This "chance" score is higher than the 98th percentile of the GATB General Working Population Sample on the name comparison*

TABLE 5-1 Worksheet on Chance Scores and Coaching for Power Subtests

	(1) Total Items	(2) Power Items[a]	(3) Remaining Items (1−2)	(4) Item Options	(5) Chance Score (1−2)/(4)	(6) Average Score on the Test	(7) Standard Deviation	(8) Effect Size (5)/(7)
Subtest 2 (computation)	50	18	32	5	6.4	20	4.8	1.33
Subtest 3 (three-dimensional space)	40	17	23	4	5.75	15.4	6	0.96
Subtest 4 (vocabulary)	60	18	42	6	7	21	8.3	0.84
Subtest 6 (arithmetic reasoning)	25	9	16	5	3.2	9.4	2.9	1.10

[a]Ninety percent of majority examinees would complete this many.

subtest. Scores could be improved further if the test taker were aware that short runs (3 to 4 items) on the name comparison subtest were identically scored (either "exactly the same" or "different"). In any case, this modified random marking strategy would yield a very high score simply because the subtest is very long and highly speeded.

Our analysis of individual item functioning demonstrates the potential effects of guessing in increasing GATB subtest scores. Table 5-1 presents a worksheet showing the score increase that could be expected for each of the would-be power tests, i.e., those where speed of work does not seem to be a defensible part of the construct (Subtests 2, 3, 4, and 6). The total number of items for each of the subtests can be compared with the number of items that would be included if the test were actually constructed as a power test. The power test limits were set such that 90 percent of the majority group would complete the test.

Column 5 shows the typical chance score (added to one's regular score) that could be earned by randomly marking the remaining items. The gain due to chance is also shown as an effect size in standard deviation units (column 8). The effects are large, roughly 1 standard deviation. Thus, assuming a normal distribution, a person scoring at the 50th percentile could increase his or her score to the 84th percentile by guessing on the unfinished portion of the test.

It is possible that the current test could be improved by using a penalty for guessing on the straight speed tests and a correction for guessing on the would-be power tests. As a matter of professional ethics it is essential that the examinees be informed of whatever scoring procedure is to be used and told clearly what test-taking strategies it is in their interests to use. The above analysis documents how vulnerable the current test is to attempts to beat the system. It is not clear what combination of shortened test and change in directions would be best to be fair to all examinees and to ensure the construct validity of each subtest. It would take both conceptual analysis and empirical work to arrive at the best solution. In considering alternatives, one would also have to ask how much the test could be changed without destroying the relevance of existing validity studies.

The National Computer Systems Answer Sheet

When USES first adapted the GATB to a separate, optically scanned answer sheet (the IBM 805 sheet), the test developers noted that "an attempt was made to devise answer sheets which would result in maximum clarity for the examinees and would facilitate the administration of the tests" (U.S. Department of Labor, 1970:2). Unfortunately, this objective is far less evident in the design of the currently used NCS answer sheet. The NCS answer sheet is in the form of a folded 12-inch by 17-inch, two-sided sheet that contains an area for examinee identification, a section for basic demographic information on the examinee, and a section for listing the form of the GATB that the examinee is attempting. In addition, the sheet has separate areas for recording answers to seven of the eight GATB pencil-and-paper subtests.

Several features of the NCS answer sheet call on the test-wiseness of examinees. The bubbles on the NCS answer sheet are very large, and examinees are told to completely darken the bubbles that correspond to their answers to each question. Following this instruction precisely is a time-consuming task that is most likely to be interpreted literally by examinees with the least experience in using optically scannable test answer sheets. Since all of the GATB subtests are speeded (as described above and discussed below), this deficiency will affect the test scores of examinees who follow the instruction most closely. For some subtests, such as the name comparison test, the design of the NCS answer sheet might add a significant psychomotor component to the abilities required to perform well.

THE INFLUENCE OF SPEED OF WORK

Due in large part to the early work and influence of Charles Spearman (Hart and Spearman, 1914; Spearman, 1927:chap. 14), pioneers in the field of educational and psychological testing theorized that measures of speed of work and measures of quality of work were interchangeable indicators of a common construct. It was not until World War II, close to the time that the GATB was under development, that researchers such as Baxter (1941) and Davidson and Carroll (1945) reported the results of factor analytic studies showing different structures for the same tests administered under time-constrained and unlimited-time conditions. The distinctiveness of speed of work and accuracy of work has since been corroborated by Boag and Neild (1962), Daly and Stahmann (1968), Flaugher and Pike (1970), Kendall (1964), Mollenkopf (1960), Terranova (1972), and Wesman (1960), among others.

A test for which speed of work has no influence on an examinee's score (i.e., a test in which every examinee is given all the time needed to attempt every test item) is called a pure "power" test. According to Gulliksen (1950a:230) a pure "speed" test is one that is so easy that no examinee makes an error and one so long that no examinee finishes the test in the time allowed. Commonly used aptitude tests rarely, if ever, fit the definition of a pure power test or a pure speed test. Many such tests, including the subtests of the GATB, combine elements of speed of work and quality of work to a largely unknown degree. However, scores on the GATB appear to depend on speed of work to a far greater extent than is true of more modern aptitude batteries.

All of the GATB subtests, whether intended to be tests of speed of work or power tests, have time limits that are extremely short. It is therefore likely that most examinees' scores on these subtests are influenced substantially by the speed at which they work. The subtests were initially designed "to insure that very few, if any, examinees would complete each test . . . ." The speed requirements of the tests have been increased since their initial design through the use of separate answer sheets and, more recently, through use of the NCS answer sheet. The NCS answer sheet imposes sufficient additional burden on examinees that the 1970 *Manual* contains a table of positive scoring adjustments to accommodate its use (see U.S. Department of Labor, 1970:43, Table 7–7).

Figures 5–1 and 5–2 illustrate the speeded nature of the GATB subtests. Subtest 5, tool matching, shown in Figure 5–1, was selected as an example of a speeded test, for which the ability to work quickly is logically a part of the intended construct. In contrast, Subtest 6, arithmetic reasoning, represents a construct that might be more accurately measured in an untimed or power test situation. (A *power test* is defined operationally as one where 90 percent of examinees have sufficient time to complete all of the test items.) The data were obtained for 7,418 white applicants, 6,827 black applicants, and 1,466 Hispanic applicants from

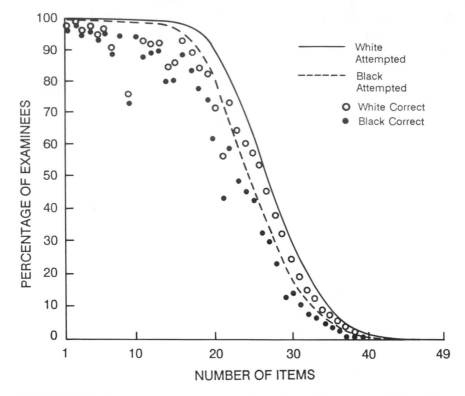

FIGURE 5–1   Percentages attempting and number of items correct for whites and blacks on Subtest 5, tool matching (speeded).

two test centers in 1988. The percentage of test takers attempting each item and getting each item right is plotted.

The steeply declining curves, drawn for whites and blacks only, demonstrate the speeded nature of the tests. For example in Figure 5–1, nearly 100 percent of both groups attempted the first 16 questions; then there is a sharp decrease in the number of examinees reaching each subsequent question such that by the midpoint of the test only 66 percent of whites and 53 percent of blacks are still taking the test. In pure speed tests the content of test questions is relatively easy, making it only a matter of how fast one works whether an item will be correct or incorrect. As would be expected in such a test, the percentage-correct curves in Figure 5–1 closely parallel the percentage-attempted curves, with some unaccounted-for difficulty at items 9 and 21.

Figure 5–2 also shows a strong overriding influence of speed. To satisfy the definition of a power test for the white group, the test would end at item 8. By the midpoint of the test, only 50 percent of whites and 27 percent of blacks are still taking the test. Although items 6 and 8 are relatively difficult even for examinees who reach them, the percentage correct on the majority of items follows the pattern delimited by the speeded nature of the test.

The use of speeded subtests to measure constructs that do not include speed as an attribute is a potentially serious construct validity issue. First, the meaning of the constructs measured is likely to be different from the conventional meaning attached to those constructs. For example, do two tests that require correct interpretation of arithmetic problems stated in words and correct application of basic arithmetic operations to the solution of those problems measure the same aptitude, if one is highly speeded and the other is not? The research cited above suggests that the two tests would measure different constructs.

Second, if the speed component of the tests does not assess the abilities of members of different racial or ethnic groups in the same way, the tests might be differentially valid for members of these groups. Helmstadter and Ortmeyer (1953:280) noted:

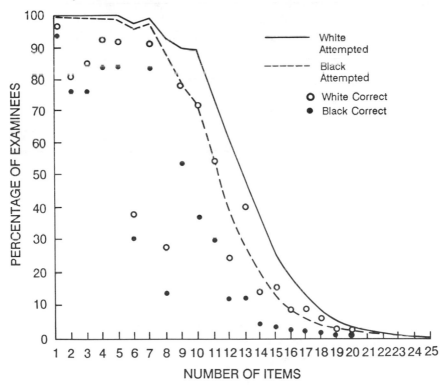

FIGURE 5–2 Percentages attempting and number of items correct for whites and blacks on Subtest 6, arithmetic reasoning (power test).

Although any test may rationally be considered as largely speed or largely power, the relative importance of these two components is not independent of the group being measured, and a test which samples depth of ability for one group may be measuring only a speed component for a second . . . .

As an example of the way this problem might be evidenced for the GATB, Subtest 7, form matching, requires examinees to pair elements of two large sets of variously shaped two-dimensional line drawings. A total of 60 items is to be completed in 6 minutes. Within this time, examinees must not only find pairs of line drawings that are identical in size and shape, but must then find and darken the correct answer bubble on the NCS answer sheet from a set of 10 answer bubbles with labels consisting of single or double capitalized letters (e.g., GG). The labeling of physically corresponding answer bubbles differs from one item to the next. Since the subtest is tightly timed, identification of the correct answer bubble from the relatively long list presented on the answer sheet might become a significant component of the skill assessed. One could, by inspection, confidently advance the argument that the subtest measures not only form perception, but also the speed of list processing and skill in decoding complex answer sheet formats. The latter skill is dependent on previous experience with tests. Since the extensiveness of such experience will differ for members of different racial or ethnic groups, the subtest might be differentially valid as a measure of form perception for white and black examinees.

Third, the severe time limits of the GATB subtests might produce an adverse psychological reaction in examinees as they progress through the examination and might thereby reduce the construct validity of the subtests. Having attempted a relatively small proportion of items on each subtest, examinees might well become progressively discouraged and thus progressively less able to exhibit their best performance. With the use of separate, optically scanned answer sheets, the most vulnerable examinees are those least experienced with standardized tests, a group in which minority examinees will be overrepresented.

These arguments on the racial or socioeconomic correlates of the effects of test speededness are admittedly speculative. Dubin and colleagues (1969) found few such correlates in a study with test-experienced high school students. However, they cited research by Boger (1952), Eagleson (1937), Katzenmeyer (1962), Klineberg (1928), and Vane and Kessler (1964) that indicated positive effects of extra practice and test familiarity in reducing test performance differences between blacks and whites.

ITEM-BIAS ANALYSES

Statistical procedures, referred to as item-bias indices, are used to evaluate whether items within a test are differentially more difficult for members of a particular subgroup taking the test.

Two caveats govern the interpretation of item-bias statistics. First, these indices are measures of *internal bias*. Bias is defined as differential validity whereby individuals of equal ability but from different groups have different success rates on test items. To establish that individuals have equal ability, the various item-bias methods rely on total test score (or some transformation of total score). Thus internal bias statistics are circular to some extent and cannot detect systematic bias. Systematic or pervasive bias could only be detected using an external criterion, as is done in predictive validity studies. What internal bias procedures are able to reveal are individual test questions that measure differently for one group compared with another. They provide information akin to factor analysis but at the item level. A large bias index signals that an item is relatively more difficult for one group.

The second caveat has to do with the meaning of bias as signaled by these statistics. The analytic procedures were designed to detect irrelevant difficulty, that is, some aspect of test questions that would prevent examinees who know the concept from demonstrating that they know it. An example of irrelevant difficulty would be a high level of reading skill required on a math test, thus obscuring perhaps the true level of mathematics achievement for one group compared with another. However, the statistics actually work by measuring multidimensionality in a test. For example, if physics and chemistry questions were combined into one science test, one subset of questions would probably produce many bias flags unless group differences in both subject areas were uniform. Thus many authors of item-bias procedures have cautioned that significant results are not automatically an indication of bias against a particular group. In fact, the statistical indices are often called measures of differential item functioning to prevent misinterpretation of the results. If each of the dimensions of the test is defensible and appropriate for the intended measurement, then the so-called bias indices have merely revealed differences in group performance.

In order to explore at least partially how the GATB functions and whether it functions differently for different racial or ethnic groups, the committee undertook an analysis of actual answer sheets for a sample of Employment Service applicants. Standard statistical procedures were used to examine characteristics of GATB items within each subtest. These analyses were conducted separately for 6,827 black and 7,418 white test takers from a Michigan test center and for 873 whites and 1,466 Hispanics from a Texas test center. The proportion answering each item correctly, the proportion attempting each item, and point-biserial correlations were calculated. The proportion attempted can index test speed whereas the proportion correct can index item and test difficulty. Point-biserial correlations show the degree of relationship between performance on an individual item and total score on the subtest, reflecting both speed and difficulty.

Proportion Attempted

Inspection of the proportion-attempted statistics shows the same pattern in all seven of the GATB paper-and-pencil subtests. Figures 5–1 and 5–2 give proportion attempted and proportion correct for tool matching and arithmetic reasoning, respectively. Virtually 100 percent of examinees attempt the first item and fewer than 1 percent finish each subtest. Subtests 1 (name comparison), 5 (tool matching), and 7 (form matching) are speeded tests; it is therefore not surprising that many examinees are unable to complete these tests. However, the number of items is far greater than is usual even for speeded tests. For example, Subtest 1 has 150 items, yet by item 75, only 9 percent of the Texas whites are still taking the test. Even smaller percentages of the other groups can be found at later items. Subtest 7 is 60 items long, but only 1 percent of the whites in the Texas sample make it to item 42.

The effect of unrealistic time limits is also apparent on the tests intended to be unspeeded. Power tests, for which examinees have sufficient time to show what they know, are ordinarily defined by a 90 percent completion rate. Subtest 2 (computation), comprised of 50 items, should be complete by item 17 to be a power test for the sample of Michigan whites. Subtest 3 (three-dimensional space) would have to finish with item 17 instead of 40, Subtest 4 (vocabulary) with item 16 instead of 60, and Subtest 6 (arithmetic reasoning) with item 9 rather than 25. Thus these subtests are more than twice as long for the given time limits than is appropriate for power tests.

The committee also conducted item-bias analyses using the Mantel-Haenszel procedure, whereby majority and minority examinees are matched on total score before examining differential performance on individual test items. In this case examinees were matched on total scores on a shortened test, defined as a power test or 90 percent completion test for the white group. These analyses consistently produced bias flags for a series of items in the middle of each test, suggesting that blacks were at a relative disadvantage in the range of the test at which the influence of time limits was most keenly felt.

Proportion Correct

Data on the proportion correct for each test item are difficult to interpret because of the pervasive effects of speed. For every group and test the proportion correct begins at item 1 with nearly 100 percent and trails off to 0 percent somewhere in the middle. Consistent with direct inspection of test content, this pattern in the statistics indicates that the items are arranged by difficulty, with very easy items first, then becoming increasingly more difficult. Even for the tests for which speed is not part of the construct, however, there is a very close correspondence between the proportion attempting an item and the proportion getting it correct. If examinees get to an item, they nearly always answer it correctly. Therefore, it is impossible to use these data to determine the actual difficulty of the items unconfounded by the effects of speed.

Point-Biserial Correlations

Point-biserial correlations have different meanings in speeded and unspeeded conditions. Subtest 1, name comparison, is primarily a speeded test. The items are all very similar in nature. The items in this test were inversely correlated with total test score on the basis of their location in the test rather than on the basis of their similarity-of-item content. That is, items at the beginning of the test correlated zero with total test score because all examinees got them right; these early items thus contribute nothing to the final ranking of examinees on total score. As an examinee progresses through this test, the effects of time limits begin to be felt and there is a gradual crescendo of point-biserial values. Examinees who work the fastest through the test (presuming they are not answering randomly) have higher test scores and get items right. There are, therefore, very high item-total correlations at the limits of good performance. These limits are somewhere in the middle of the test because it is so speeded. Eventually the peak in the point-biserial correlations trails off, presumably because some of the few remaining examinees are choosing speed rather than accuracy in order to answer more questions.

The pattern of point-biserial correlations in the so-called unspeeded GATB tests also reflects the influence of speed on total score. Examinees who get further in the test have higher test scores and are still doing well on the items they attempt. The highest point-biserial values tend to occur at the point at which half of the examinees are still attempting the items.

Available data are also pertinent to an entirely different topic. Earlier in the chapter we hypothesized possible strategies of random response to improve test scores. How test-wise are GATB test takers about the advantage of marking uncompleted items when time runs out? Although the rise and fall of point-biserial correlations suggests that a few examinees might be marking a few items randomly at the limit of their performance in order to obtain higher scores, the long strings of near-zero attempts for the later items suggest that the great majority of examinees are not following this strategy. These test-taking habits would be likely to change substantially if examinees were coached in such effective ways to improve their scores, a likely prospect if the VG-GATB Referral System becomes important.

Because the influence of speed so dominates all these GATB subtests, it is not possible to use point-biserial correlations to judge the homogeneity of items in measuring the intended construct. Hence, internal consistency estimates of reliability, based on point biserials, would be misleading.

PRACTICE EFFECTS AND COACHING EFFECTS

Because of the speededness of the GATB, the test is very vulnerable to practice effects and coaching. If the test comes to be widely used for referral, USES policy makers must be prepared for the growth of coaching schools of the kind that now provide coaching for the Scholastic Aptitude Test and tests for admission to professional schools. USES must also expect the publication of manuals to optimize GATB scores, such as those already available for the Armed Services Vocational Aptitude Battery (ASVAB).

Effects of Practice on GATB Scores

Practice effects are attributable to several influences. If examinees are retested with the same form of an examination, their scores might increase because they remember their initial responses to items and can therefore use the same answers without considering the items in detail, or because they become wiser and more efficient test takers as a result of completing the examination once. If examinees are retested with an alternate form of an examination, specific memory effects will not be present, and gains in score are attributable only to the effects of practice.

Data on the effects of practice on the GATB cognitive (G, V, and N), perceptual (S, P, and Q), and psychomotor (K, F, and M) aptitudes are reported in Figures 5–3 and 5–4, which are based on studies detailed in Appendix B, Tables B-1 to B-6. As the figures show, the estimated size of the effects of retesting on the GATB were greatest when the same form of the test was repeated.[1] Figure 5–3 summarizes the effects of retesting

---

[1]An *estimated effect size* is the difference between the mean score when examinees were tested initially and the mean score when examinees were retested, divided by the standard deviation of scores when examinees were tested initially. Thus an estimated effect size of 0.5 indicates that the mean score when examinees were retested was half a standard deviation unit higher than when the examinees were tested initially. With an effect size of 0.5, an examinee who outscored 50 percent of the other examinees when tested initially would, when retested, outscore 69 percent of the other examinees in the initial-testing normal-score distribution.

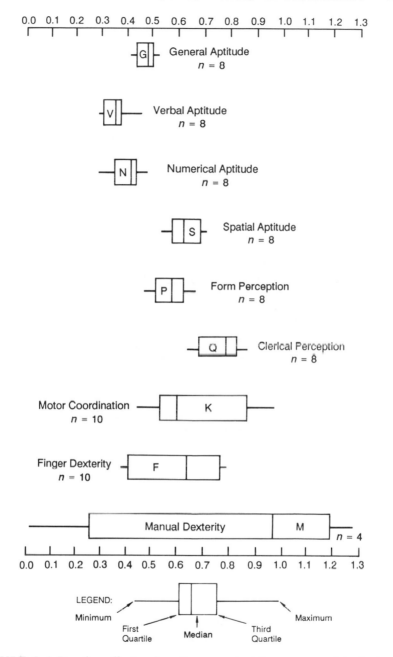

FIGURE 5–3 Practice effects when the same test form was used both times. Distributions of estimated effect sizes (initial testing to retesting) are expressed in standard deviations of initial aptitude distributions.

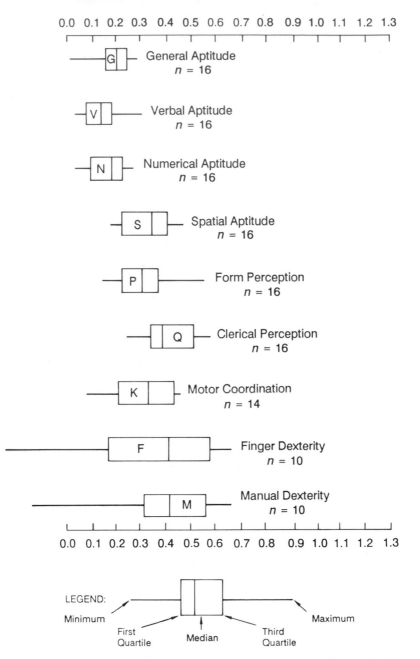

FIGURE 5–4 Practice effects when a different test form is used each time. Distributions of estimated effect sizes (initial testing to retesting) are expressed in standard deviations of initial aptitude distributions.

with the same form. For the cognitive aptitudes, mean scores increased by a third of a standard deviation from initial testing to retesting. Gains on the perceptual aptitudes averaged half a standard deviation to three-fourths of a standard deviation, and gains on the psychomotor aptitudes were even larger, approaching a whole standard deviation for the manual dexterity aptitude. As Figure 5–4 shows, however, a large component of these gains can be attributed to memory effects, since the corresponding gains were much smaller when an alternate form of the GATB was used for retesting. For the cognitive aptitudes, gains from practice alone averaged about a fifth of a standard deviation. For the perceptual and psychomotor aptitudes, gains due to practice were appreciably larger, averaging about a third of a standard deviation.

These results suggest that examinees should not be retested using the same form of the GATB, since their retest results are likely to be spuriously high due to memory effects. In addition, the results suggest that practice effects on the GATB are large enough, even when an alternate form of the battery is used for retesting, to conclude that many retested examinees will be advantaged substantially by the experience of having completed the GATB once. We do not know if these findings have changed over the 20 years since these studies were completed. These estimated effects of practice on the GATB can be regarded as lower bounds on gains that might be realized through intensive coaching.

Effects of Coaching on GATB Scores

If the use of the GATB were to be extended to the point that earning high scores on the GATB had a substantial relationship with employability, as would be the case if the VG-GATB Referral System were to be implemented widely, it is likely that commercial coaching schools, such as those presently in operation for the widely used higher education admissions tests, would be developed. The coachability of the GATB would then be a major equity issue, since those who could not afford to attend commercial coaching schools would be at a disadvantage.

Little direct information on the coachability of the GATB subtests is currently available. Rotman (1963) conducted a study with mentally retarded young adult males in which he provided an average of 4.55 days of instruction and practice on the GATB subtests that compose the psychomotor aptitudes K, F, and M. A group of 40 instructed subjects showed average gains in mean scores, expressed in units of estimated effect sizes, of 0.94 for K, 0.43 for F, and 1.23 for M. In comparison, a control group of 40 subjects who were retested with no intervening instruction showed average effect sizes of 0.52 for K, 0.04 for F, and 0.38 for M. Practice effects alone added substantially to the average scores of the control subjects on two of the three psychomotor aptitudes. Coaching added even more to mean scores for all three psychomotor aptitudes. Although the generalizability of these results to nonretarded examinees is questionable, the potential coachability of the GATB subtests that compose the psychomotor aptitudes is clearly indicated.

TEST SECURITY

If the Department of Labor decides to continue and expand the VG-GATB Referral System, USES will have to develop new test security procedures like those that surround the Scholastic Aptitude Test, the American College Testing Program, the Armed Services Vocational Aptitude Battery, and other major testing programs.

So long as the GATB was used primarily for vocational counseling, the issue of security was not pressing. But if it is to be used to make important decisions affecting the job prospects of large numbers of Americans, then it is essential that no applicants have access to the test questions ahead of time. This will require much tighter test administration procedures and strict control of every test booklet. State and local Employment Service personnel will require more extensive training in test administration procedures, and administrators will have to be selected with greater care.

The need for test security will make it imperative that no operational GATB forms be made available to private vocational counselors, labor union apprenticeship programs, or high school guidance counselors. With the development of additional forms on a regular cycle, the use of retired forms for these other purposes may be appropriate, although the demonstrated effects of practice with parallel forms (Figure 5–4) suggest the need for caution.

Most important, the new role envisioned for the VG-GATB will require a sustained test development program to produce more forms with greater frequency. The present GATB is administered from just two alternative forms, C and D, which replaced the 35- or 40-year-old Forms A and B. By contrast, three new forms of the ASVAB are introduced on a four-year cycle.

There is much accumulated wisdom on the subject of test security in the Department of Defense Directorate for Accession Policy and in the private companies that administer large test batteries. USES would benefit from reviewing their protocols as a preliminary to drawing up provisions for maintaining the security of the GATB.

CONCLUSIONS

Test Administration Practices

1. The instructions to examinees, if followed, do not allow them to maximize their GATB scores. No guidance is given about guessing on items the examinee does not know. This practice is inconsistent with accepted professional standards.

Speededness

2. Most of the GATB tests are highly speeded. This raises the issue of a potential distortion of the construct purportedly measured and could have effects on predictive validity.

To compound the problem, the test answer sheet bubbles are very large and examinees are told to darken them completely, penalizing the conscientious. When used with highly speeded tests such as the GATB, the combined effects of the instructions given to examinees and the answer sheet format add a validity-reducing, psychomotor component to tests of other constructs.

The excessive speededness of the GATB makes it very vulnerable to coaching.

Alternate Forms and Test Security

3. The paucity of new forms and insufficient attention to test security speak against any widespread operationalization of the VG-GATB without major changes in procedures.

At the present time, there are only two alternate forms of the GATB; there have been just four in its 40 years of existence, although two new forms are under development. In contrast, the major college testing programs develop new forms annually, and the Department of Defense develops three new forms of the Armed Services Vocational Aptitude Battery at about four-year intervals.

In addition, test security has not been a primary concern so long as the GATB was used largely as a counseling tool; it appears to be fairly easy for anyone to become a "certified GATB user" and obtain access to a copy of the test battery.

Item Bias

4. There is minimal evidence on which to decide whether the items in the GATB are biased against minorities. On the basis of internal analysis, there appears to be no idiosyncratic item functioning due to item content, although there could be bias overall.

There is a modicum of evidence that test speed affects black examinees differently from other examinees.

Practice Effects and Coaching

5. GATB scores will be significantly improved by practice. A major reason for this is the speededness of the test parts. Experience with other large-scale testing programs indicates that the GATB would be vulnerable to coaching. This is a severe impediment to widespread operationalization of the GATB.

The GATB's speededness, its consequent susceptibility to practice effects and coaching, the small number of alternate forms, and low test security in combination present a substantial obstacle to a broad expansion of the VG-GATB Referral System.

RECOMMENDATIONS

Test Security

If the GATB is to be used in a widespread, nationwide testing program, we recommend the adoption of formal test security procedures.

There are several components of test security to be considered in implementing a large testing program.

1. There are currently two alternate forms of the GATB operationally available and two under development. This is far too few for a nationwide testing program. Alternate forms need to be developed with the same care as the initial forms, and on a regular basis. Form-to-form equating will be necessary. This requires the attention to procedures and normative groups as described in the preceding chapter.

2. Access to operational test forms must be severely limited to only those Department of Labor and Employment Service personnel involved in the testing program and to those providing technical review. Strict test access procedures must be implemented.

3. Separate but parallel forms of the GATB should be made available for counseling and guidance purposes.

Test Speededness

4. A research and development project should be put in place to reduce the speededness of the GATB. A highly speeded test, one that no one can hope to complete, is eminently coachable. For example, scores can be improved by teaching test takers to fill in all remaining blanks in the last minute of the test period. If this characteristic of the GATB is not altered, the test will not retain its validity when given a widely recognized gatekeeping function.

PART III

VALIDITY GENERALIZATION AND GATB VALIDITIES

Part III is the heart of the committee's assessment of the scientific claims made to justify the Department of Labor's proposed plan for the widespread use of the General Aptitude Test Battery to screen applicants for private- and public-sector jobs. Chapter 6 is an overview of the theory of validity generalization, which is a type of meta-analysis that is proposed for extrapolating the estimated validities of a test for performance on jobs that have been studied to others that have not.

The committee then addresses the research supported by the Department of Labor to apply validity generalization to the GATB. Chapter 7 covers the first two parts of the analysis: reduction of the nine GATB aptitudes to (effectively) two general factors, cognitive and psychomotor ability, and the clustering of all jobs in the U.S. economy into five job families. Chapter 8 presents the department's validity generalization analysis of 515 GATB studies and compares those results with the committee's own analysis of a larger data set that includes 264 more recent studies.

Chapter 9 addresses the question of whether the GATB functions in the same way for different demographic groups. It looks at the possibility that correlations of GATB scores with on-the-job performance measures differ by racial or ethnic group or gender, and the possibility that predictions of criterion performance from GATB scores differ by group.

6

The Theory of Validity Generalization

META-ANALYSIS

Meta-analysis is the combination of empirical evidence from diverse studies. Although the term *meta-analysis* has emerged only in the past two decades, formal methods for combining observations have a long history. Astronomical observations at different sites and times have been combined in order to draw general conclusions since the 1800s (Stigler, 1986). Statistical techniques for combining significance tests and combining estimates of effects in agricultural experiments date from the 1930s (Hedges and Olkin, 1985).

Several major programs of quantitative synthesis of research have existed for decades in the physical sciences. For example, the Particle Data Group, headquartered jointly at Berkeley and Centre Européen de la Recherche Nucléaire in Switzerland, conducts meta-analyses of the results of experiments in elementary particle physics worldwide and publishes the results every two years as the *Review of Particle Properties*.

In medicine, meta-analyses are becoming increasingly important as a technique to systematize the results of clinical trials (*Proceedings of the Workshop on Methodological Issues in Overviews of Randomized Clinical Trials,* 1987), to collect research results in particular areas (the Oxford Database of Perinatal Medicine), and in public health (Louis et al., 1985).

In the social and behavioral sciences, meta-analysis has been used primarily in psychology and education, for such diverse purposes as to summarize research on the effectiveness of psychotherapy, the effects of class size on achievement and attitudes, experimental expectancy effects, and the social psychology of gender differences.

In studying a problem, every scientist must assimilate and assess the results of previous studies of the same problem. In the absence of a formal mechanism for combining the past results, it is always tempting to assume that the present experiment is of prime originality and to ignore or dismiss inconvenient or contradictory results from the past. Many superfluous data are collected because it is too difficult or confusing or unconvincing or unglamorous to assemble and examine what is known already.

Meta-analysis attempts to provide a formal mechanism for doing so. By combining information from different studies, meta-analysis increases the precision with which effects can be estimated (or increases the power of statistical tests of hypotheses). For example, many clinical trials in medicine are too small for treatment effects to be estimated with accuracy, but combining evidence across different studies can yield estimates that are precise enough to be useful. In addition, meta-analysis produces more robust evidence than any single study. The convergence of evidence produced under differing conditions helps to ensure that the effects observed are not the inadvertent result of some unrecognized aspect of context, procedure, or measurement. And finally, meta-analysis usually involves some explicit plan for sampling from the available body of research evidence. Without controls for selection, it is possible to obtain very different pictures of the evidence by selecting, perhaps inadvertently, studies that favor one position or another.

Although there is no general prescription for carrying out a meta-analysis, the procedure can be divided into four steps:

1. Identify relevant studies and collect results. It is important in this step to ensure the representativeness of the studies used. One particularly difficult source of bias to control for is called the file drawer problem, which alludes to the tendency for statistically insignificant results to repose unpublished and unknown in file drawers and thus not be available for collection.

2. Evaluate individual studies for quality and relevance to the problem of interest.

3. Identify relevant measurements, comparable across studies.

4. Combine relevant comparable measures across studies and project these values onto the problem of interest.

VALIDITY GENERALIZATION

Validity generalization is a branch of meta-analysis that draws on criterion-related validity evidence to extend the results of test research.[1] Our precise interest is the estimation of the validities of a test for performance on new jobs, based on meta-analysis of the validities of the test for studied jobs. There is a very substantial statistical and psychometric literature on estimating validities measured via correlation coefficients. This chapter presents in broad outline the statistical analyses used in validity generalization and focuses particularly on the work of John E. Hunter and his frequent collaborator, Frank L. Schmidt, because of Hunter's central role in applying validity generalization to the General Aptitude Test Battery (GATB) (Hunter, 1986; Schmidt and Hunter, 1977, 1981; Schmidt et al., 1982; U.S. Department of Labor, 1983b,c).

The Theoretical Framework

The fundamental problem addressed by validity generalization is how to characterize the generalizability of test validities across situations, populations of applicants, and jobs. The most prominent approach treats the problem as one of examining the variability across studies of validity coefficients. The theoretical framework is as follows.

One wants to estimate the "true" validity of a test for given jobs. (By *true validity,* we mean the validity that would obtain in studies conducted under ideal conditions, with job performance assessed with perfect accuracy by the criterion.) As a first proposition, it is assumed that there is some distribution of true validities across a population of jobs, and that this distribution of validities is then taken to apply to new jobs that have not undergone a criterion-related validity study. The conclusion will be in the form: the validity of the test for the new job lies between .3 and .5 with probability .9.

The questions remain: how are the observed validities to be used to estimate the distribution of true validities across a population of jobs, and thus what is the probable range of values that can be generalized to a new job? There are a number of ways in which the correlation coefficient obtained in any given study of the relation of test scores to job performance is affected by situational factors, so that the validity estimate differs from the true validity of the test for a new job:

---

[1]The *criterion-related validity* of a test is a measure of the relationship between the test score and a criterion of job performance (e.g., supervisor ratings). The relationship between test score and job performance is measured by the product moment correlation. Following standard practice, we refer to this correlation as validity, although this usage invites confusion with other psychometric and legal uses of the word validity.

Sampling error. The observed validities are based on a *sample* of workers; the true validities are based on a *population* of applicants. The difference between sample and population is adjusted for by taking into account sampling error of the observed validities. The major effect is that the variability of the observed validities over jobs is greater than the variability of true validities.

Restriction of range. The observed validities are based on a sample of *workers*, the true validities are based on a population of *applicants*. Because the worker group may be selected from the applicant group by criteria correlated with the test score, the distribution of test scores within the worker group may be different from that in the applicant group. There will be a corresponding difference between true validities for workers and applicants. For example, in a highly selective job, range restriction occurs so that nearly all workers will have a narrow high range of test scores, and the true validity will be lower than that for an unselected applicant group. If the applicant and worker distributions can be estimated, it is possible to correct for range restriction.

Reliability of supervisor ratings. The criterion of supervisor ratings is assumed to be perfectly measured in computing the true validities. Unreliable supervisor ratings will tend to make the observed validities smaller than the true validities; if the reliability of supervisor ratings can be estimated, an adjustment can be made for it in estimating the true validity.

Connecting the sample to the population. The new job is different from the jobs studied. If the jobs studied are assumed to be a random sample from the population of all jobs, then the sample distribution can be projected to the population distribution. This is the implicit assumption of the Schmidt-Hunter validity generalization analyses. If this assumption cannot be sustained, some other connection must be established between the jobs studied and the new job.

Each of these factors is considered below in some detail.

Sampling Error

The true validity for a given job, population of subjects, and criterion is the validity coefficient that would be obtained by conducting a validity study involving the entire population. Any actual validity study will use only a sample of subjects—typically a group of job incumbents chosen to participate in the study—and will yield an observed validity (a sample correlation), r, that differs from the true validity as a consequence of the choice of sample. The observed validity r will deviate from the true validity by a sampling error, e.

If several samples are taken from the same population, each would have a different observed validity. It is the variability of these observed validities about the true validity that tells us how confident to be in estimating the true validity by the observed validity r.

Suppose, for example, there is a population of 1,000 individuals for which the true validity of a test is .3. We draw a sample of 100 individuals and compute an observed validity of .41. Other samples of 100 individuals give validities of .22, .35, .42. The observed values vary around the true value by a range of about .1.

Now suppose there is another population of 1,000 individuals for which the true validity is unknown. We draw a sample of 100 individuals and compute an observed validity of .25. What is the true validity? We think that it lies somewhere in the range .15 to .35. Thus we use the distribution of sampling error to indicate how close the true validity is likely to be to the observed validity. (There may be other evidence such as prior information about the true validity.)

The average of the sampling error M is very close to zero for modest true validities. The variance of the sampling error, the average of $(e - M)^2$, is close to $1/(n - 1)$, where n is the sample size for modest true validities. Thus for sample sizes of 100, the variance is about .01 and the standard deviation is .1; we expect the observed validity to differ by .1 from the true validity.

Corrections for Sampling Error

To illustrate how corrections for sampling error fit into the estimation of the distribution of true validities in a population of jobs, we offer a hypothetical example. Assume, following Hunter and Schmidt, that the jobs actually studied form a random sample of the population of jobs. For each job studied a random sample of applicants is taken from the relevant population for that job, and an observed validity is computed for the random sample. Note that there are two levels of sampling, from the universe of jobs and from the universe of applicants for each job.

Provided that the different studies are independent, the expected variance of the observed validities is the sum of two components: the variance of the true validities plus the average variance of the sampling error.

Thus we estimate the mean true validity in the population of jobs by the average of the observed validities, but we must estimate the variance of true validities by the observed variance of observed validities less the average sampling variance. This is the correction for sampling error. A good practical estimate of the average sampling variance is the average value of $1/(n - 1)$ where n is the sample size (Schmidt et al., 1982).

An Example

We have 11 jobs with 1,000 applicants each. If all applicants were tested and evaluated on the job, the true validities would be (dropping the decimal point): 25, 26, 27, 28, 29, 30, 31, 32, 33, 34, 35.

We sample from the 11 jobs at random to get 4 jobs with true validities: 26, 28, 31, 32.

For each of the four jobs, we sample 101 from the 1,000 applicants. For the four samples we compute observed validities: 34, 16, 26, 40.

We use these observed validities to estimate properties of the original distribution of true validities. The mean true validity is estimated by the mean of the sample validities, 29. The sample variance is $(5^2 + 13^2 + 3^2 + 11^2)/3 = 108$, but this overestimates the variance of true validities because of sampling error. For each sample, the sampling error variance is $10,000/(n - 1) = 100$ approximately (remember that the decimal has been dropped, multiplying the scale by 100). Thus the average sampling error is 100, and the estimated variance of true validities is $108 - 100 = 8$.

The mean true validity is 30, estimated by 29, and the variance of true validities is 10 estimated by 8. These estimates are closer than we have a right to expect, but the important point is that a drastic overestimate in true validity variance may occur if the sampling error correction is not made.

Note that these procedures do not make assumptions about the form of the distribution from which the true validities are sampled (although distributional estimates derived from the procedures frequently do). However, the computation of an estimate of the sampling error variance does require weak assumptions about the distribution of test and criterion scores within studies. When the population validities are moderate, the estimate $1/(n - 1)$ is satisfactory.

The corrections for sampling error in the Hunter-Schmidt analyses, all in all, follow accepted statistical practice for estimating components of variance.

Restriction of Range

Observed validities are based on a sample of *workers,* whereas the true validities are based on a population of *applicants*. Since the worker group presumably has been selected from the applicant group by criteria correlated with the test score, the distribution of test scores within the worker group should be different from that in the applicant group. There will be a corresponding difference between "true" validities for workers and applicants.

It is necessary to develop a mechanism to relate the validities of workers and applicants. Since many applicants will never be employed on the job, it is impossible to assemble job performance data on a typical group of applicants. We must estimate, by some theoretical model, what the job performance would have been if the applicants had been selected for employment.

We make two assumptions. The first is that the linear function of test score that best predicts job performance, when computed separately for the population of applicants and the population of workers, has the same coefficient of test score in both groups. This means that a given increase in test score produces the same increase in predicted job performance in both groups. Some such assumption cannot be avoided, because we have data available only for the worker group but wish to use that data to make predictions about the applicant group.

The second assumption is that the error of the linear prediction of job performance by test score has the same variance in both groups. One might argue against this assumption on the grounds that workers' job performance will be predicted more accurately if the workers are rationally selected to maximize job performance. But methods of prediction of job performance are not so well developed that we would expect a very noticeable decrease in error variance in the worker group (see Linn et al., 1981).

Under these assumptions there is a remarkable formula connecting the theoretical validities in the two groups: the quantity $(1 - \text{validity}^{-2})$ multiplied by test score variance is the same in both groups. When the validities are moderate or small, this means that the ratio of the validities in the two groups is very nearly the same as the ratio of the standard deviations of test scores in the two groups. The ratio of the standard deviation in the worker group to the standard deviation in the applicant group will be called the *restriction ratio*. Thus if a worker group is thought to have a standard deviation only half that of the applicant group, then the restriction ratio is one-half, and the validity of the test for the applicant group is close to twice that of the worker group.

The main problem in determining the correction for restriction of range is identifying the appropriate population of applicants for a particular job and estimating the variance of test scores for those applicants. The validation study will use as subjects a set of workers on the job, but we wish to estimate the validity for a set of applicants for the job who will take the test through the Employment Service. Few data are available on the distribution of test scores of applicants for particular jobs. It is not even clear who should be regarded as applicants. Anyone who wishes to apply for the job? Anyone who wishes to apply for the job and is willing to take the test? Anyone who wishes to apply for the job and meets the employer's minimum qualifications?

The pool of applicants for jobs as laborers or as university professors may be considerably more restricted than the general population (because of self-selection or qualifications required). Consequently, the correlation between test score and job performance among the applicants to these jobs may not be as high as would be the case if the general population applied for and was employed in these occupations. Note also that the pool of potential job applicants is not necessarily fixed across localities and therefore across validity studies. For example, in localities with chronically high unemployment, the pool of potential applicants for low-paying jobs may include many people with high test scores who might not be available (because they are employed) in localities with low unemployment.

Corrections for Restrictions of Range

Suppose that the above assumptions about the relationship between test score and job performance are satisfied for worker and applicant groups. How can the observed validities be corrected for restriction of range? The standard procedure is as follows: for each job studied, the restriction ratio—the ratio of standard deviations of test scores for applicants and workers—is estimated. The sample validities computed on the sample of workers are adjusted to give estimated validities for the population of applicants for the job. The average of the true validities for the population of jobs, and the variance of the true validities for the population of jobs, with due adjustment for sampling error, are computed from the estimated validities adjusted for restriction of range.

The principal effect of the restriction-of-range correction is to increase or decrease the estimate of average true validity; for example, if the average restriction ratio is one-half, the effect is to double the estimate of mean true validity.

Let us trace the theoretical assumptions and the corresponding computations from applicant population to sample of workers on the hypothetical population considered previously.

We have 11 jobs with 1,000 applicants each. If all applicants were tested and evaluated on the job, the true validities would be (dropping the decimal point): 25, 26, 27, 28, 29, 30, 31, 32, 33, 34, 35.

We sample from the 11 jobs at random to get 4 jobs with true applicant validities: 26, 28, 31, 32.

The four jobs selected have restriction ratios of: 0.5, 0.5, 1, 1. Thus the true validities for populations of workers in the four jobs are 13, 14, 31, 32.

For each of the four jobs, we sample 101 from 500 workers on the job. For the four samples we compute observed validities: 21, 2, 26, 40.

The effect of the restriction of range is to lower the observed validities whenever the restriction ratio is less than 1. Thus the first two observed validities average 11 although the true validities average 27. When the ratio of standard deviations varies between jobs, a secondary effect is to increase the variance of the observed standard deviations.

In practice, only the observed validities are known, and one wants to infer properties of the true validities. To get from the worker sample back to the applicant population, we must undo the various operations in going from the population to the sample. The observed validities are corrected for restriction of range; the corrected observed validities are 42, 4, 26, 40. The new estimate of mean true validity is the corrected sample average 28; without the correction the estimate would be 22. The estimate of variance of true validity is the sample variance 307 less the average error variance in the four studies 300, yielding an estimated true variance of 7. Note that the adjusted validities are more variable than the unadjusted ones.

Estimating Restriction Ratios

In principle, it is possible to estimate the variances in test scores for different applicant groups—the variances necessary for correcting for restriction of range. However, in the GATB validity studies, which use workers on the job, no information is available about applicant groups for those jobs. It is not even clear how applicant groups should be defined for those jobs. It could be all people who applied for the job over a period of time, all people in the local labor market who met the requirements for the job, or all registrants in the local Employment Service office. The last definition might best fit the purpose of relating test scores to job performance for Employment Service registrants.

Methods have been developed to correct for restriction of range in a large sample of studies without knowing the restriction ratio for every individual study. It is assumed that the restriction ratios for the various studies have a known mean and variance, and that the distribution of restriction ratios is independent of the true validities (Callender and Osburn, 1980). The known mean and variance are sufficient to determine the correction. For example, if the restriction ratios have average value 0.5, the average true validity is estimated to be about twice the average observed validity. Similarly, if the restriction ratios have a large variance, a reduction will occur in estimating the variance of true validities compared with the observed variance of sample validities.

The model and calculations are as follows:

Sample validity = restriction ratio × true validity + error

Since the restriction ratio is assumed to have a distribution independent of the true validity:

average sample validity = average restriction ratio
× average true validity

variance of sample validity = average sampling variance
+ [restriction ratio variance
× (average true validity)^2]
+ [true validity variance
× (average restriction ratio)^2]

The variance calculation is only approximate, but the approximation is good whenever the restriction ratio has small percentage variation.

The same model may be used if multiplicative factors other than the restriction ratio are included; one need only know the mean and variance of the multiplicative factor.

Can GATB Restriction Ratios be Estimated?

The crucial question remains: What is the average restriction ratio? The simple option of using the variance derived from all workers who appeared in the studies (U.S. Department of Labor, 1983c) will lead to inflated corrections for restriction of range if this group is more variable in test scores than a typical applicant group for a particular job. This method of correction is also at odds with assertions made elsewhere by Hunter (U.S. Department of Labor, 1983e) that the selection methods of the Employment Service are "equivalent to random selection"; if indeed that were true, there would be no difference between applicant groups and worker groups in test score variance. In the absence of direct information for particular jobs, the conservative response is to apply *no correction* for restriction of range.

Lack of adequate reliable data about the variance of test scores in realistically defined applicant populations is a major problem in validity generalization from the GATB validity studies. The absence of direct data is so pronounced that the committee has chosen the conservative response of making no corrections for range restrictions in its analysis of GATB validities.

Reliability of Supervisor Ratings

In each validity study, a worker's job performance is measured by a supervisor rating. We distinguish between a *true rating,* done with exhaustive study of the worker's job performance, and an *observed rating,* performed under real conditions by the supervisor. We suppose that the observed rating differs from the true rating by some error that is uncorrelated with the true rating over the population of workers.

Reliability is measured by the ratio of the variance of the true ratings to the variance of the observed ratings. If there is no measurement error, the reliability would be 1; if the observed rating is unrelated to the true rating, the reliability would be zero.

The *reliability correction* is the ratio of the standard deviation of the true ratings to the standard deviation of the observed ratings. It is the square root of the reliability. Just as with the restriction ratio, the validity of test score with observed rating is divided by the reliability correction to become a validity of test score with true rating.

The main effect of the reliability correction is to increase the estimate of average true validity. A secondary effect, when reliabilities vary among studies, is to reduce the estimate of variance of true validities compared with the observed variance of sample validities.

Much the same things can be said about reliability corrections as for restriction of range corrections. It is a sensible correction if the required ratios of variances can be estimated, but in the GATB validity studies the reliability of the ratings is rarely available. In the Hunter and Schmidt validity generalization analysis, the mean and variance of the distribution of reliabilities across studies are assumed, and the mean and variance of true validities are corrected accordingly. If the reliabilities are underestimated, then the correction will be an overcorrection. The mean reliability of .60 assumed by Hunter and Schmidt causes a reliability correction of 0.78; the true validity estimate is increased by 30 percent. Given the dangers of overcorrecting, and given the observation of reliabilities higher than .60 in many studies, the more conservative figure of .80 seems more appropriate to the committee and is used in its calculations.

Connecting the Sample to the Population

The data available about validities of the GATB consist of some 750 studies, conducted by the USES, in collaboration with employers, over the period 1945–1985. We wish to draw conclusions about the validity of the GATB for jobs in new settings, as well as about the population of 12,000 job types in many different settings. In order to justify the extrapolation, we must establish a connection between the jobs studied and the targeted population of jobs.

In USES validity generalization studies (U.S. Department of Labor, 1983e), it is asserted that the jobs studied in each of five job families may be taken to be a sample from the set of all jobs in the corresponding job family. Inference about population characteristics is then based on the tacit assumption that the sample is random, that is, that all jobs in a job family have equal chance of appearing in job studies.

There are a number of reasons to be skeptical about the assertion that the jobs studied are representative of all jobs. The studies have been carried out over a long period of time, and it is fair to question whether a job study carried out in 1950 is as relevant in 1990 as it was then. Standard job conditions may have changed, the literacy of the work force may have changed, accepted selection procedures may have changed. There is indeed evidence of a general decline of validities over time in the USES data base.

Moreover, certain conditions must be met before a job appears in a validity study. An employer must be found who is willing to have workers spend time taking the GATB test and to have supervisors spend time rating the workers. The employer must be persuaded that the test is of some value in predicting job performance; why would the employer participate in a futile exercise? If the test is then more valid for some jobs and in some settings than others, and if we assume that either USES or employers are able to identify the more fruitful jobs and settings, then surely they would study such jobs first. The jobs thought to have low validity will have less chance of being studied. The net effect is that the average population validity will be lower than the observed sample validity, but we do not know enough about the selection rules for initiating and carrying out studies to estimate the size of the effect.

An example of such selection in GATB studies is provided by jobs classified as agricultural, fishery, forestry, and related occupations. They include 2 percent of the jobs in the *Dictionary of Occupational Titles,* but only 0.04 percent (3 studies of 777) of the jobs in the USES data base.

A related selection problem in publishing the results of studies is known as the file drawer problem. Results that show small validities may have less chance of being written up formally and being included in the available body of data. We do not have an estimate for the size of this effect for the GATB studies.

THE INTERPRETATION OF SMALL VARIANCES IN VALIDITY GENERALIZATION

Most writers in the area of validity generalization have argued that, if the variance of the validity parameters is estimated to be small, then validities are highly generalizable. Two justifications for this position are advanced. The first is that, if most of the variability in the observed validities can be accounted for by the artifacts of sampling error, unreliability of test and criterion, and restriction of range, then it is reasonable to assume that much of the rest can be accounted for by other artifacts. The second argument is that, if the variance in validity parameters is small, then the validities in all situations are quite similar.

There is little empirical evidence to aid in the evaluation of the first argument. Although it seems sensible to many, reasonable people might disagree on how much of the variation must be explained for the argument to be persuasive. For example, Schmidt and Hunter's (1977) "75 percent rule"—which suggests that, if the four artifact corrections explain 75 percent of the variation, then the remaining 25 percent is probably due to other artifacts (such as clerical errors)—is not universally accepted (see James et al., 1986, 1988; but see also Schmidt et al., 1988).

The argument that small variance among validity parameters implies that all validities are quite similar is more obviously problematic. Suppose that the sample of studies actually consists of two distinct groups (differing from one another in job or context), which have different distributions of validity parameters. If one of the groups in the sample has only a small number of studies and the other has a much larger number of studies, then between-group differences in validities need not greatly inflate the overall variance among validities.

Note also that, when studies in the sample are not representative of the universe of all jobs or contexts, the size of the two groups in the sample need not reflect their incidence in the universe. Thus jobs that might be associated with unusually high validities might occur infrequently in the sample of validity studies but occur with higher frequency in the universe of all jobs or contexts. Moreover, the existence of two groups of studies, each with a different distribution of validity parameters, cannot be detected from the estimate of the overall mean and variance of the validities alone. In general, omnibus procedures designed to estimate the variance of validity parameters (or to test the hypothesis that this variance is zero) are not well suited to detect the possibility that validities are influenced by moderator variables that may act on only a few studies in the sample. The reason is that because such omnibus procedures are sensitive to many kinds of departures from absolute consistency among studies, they are not optimal for detecting a specific pattern. To put this argument more precisely, the omnibus statistical test that tests for *any* difference among validities does not have as much power to detect a *particular* difference between groups of studies as does a test designed to detect that specific, between-group contrast.

CONCLUSIONS

1. The general thesis of the theory of validity generalization, that validities established for some jobs are generalizable to some unexamined jobs, is accepted by the committee.

Adjustments to Validity Coefficients

Sampling Error

The observed variance in validities is partly due to variance in the "true" validities computed for a very large number of workers in each job, and partly due to the differences between those true validities and the sample validities computed for the actual groups of workers available in each job.

2. For the GATB, the variance is justifiably adjusted by subtracting from the observed variance an estimate of the contribution due to sampling error.

Range Restriction

The adjustments of average validity are designed to correct for two deficiencies in the data. The first is that, although the correlation between test score and job performance is based on workers actually on the job, the prediction will be applied to applicants for the job. If workers have a narrower range of test scores than applicants, then the worker correlation will be lower than the applicant correlation; an adjustment for range restriction produces an adjusted correlation larger than the observed correlation.

3. Lack of adequate, reliable data about the variance of test scores in realistically defined applicant populations appears to be a major problem in validity generalization from the GATB validity studies. Appropriate corrections remain to be determined by comparisons between test score variability of workers and of applicants, and, in the meantime, caution suggests that no corrections for restriction of range be made.

Criterion Unreliability

A further deficiency in the data is that the criterion measure, usually supervisory ratings, is inaccurately measured and for this reason reduces the observed correlation. Thus an adjustment is used that produces a correlation between the test score and a theoretical criterion measured with perfect precision, which may reasonably be taken to be a better indicator of job performance than the observed criterion.

4. In the GATB validity studies, data on the reliability of the criterion are rarely available. Correction for criterion unreliability with too low a figure would inflate the adjusted validity. Given the observation of reliabilities higher than .60 in many studies, the committee finds that a conservative value of .80 would be more appropriate than the .60 value contained in USES technical reports on validity generalization.

Connecting the Sample to the Population

The generalization of validities computed for 500 jobs in some 750 USES studies to the population of 12,000 jobs in the *Dictionary of Occupational Titles* is justified only to the degree that these jobs are similar to the other jobs not studied. Thus a necessary component of validity generalization for the GATB is to establish links between the jobs studied and the remainder. One way to do so is to select the jobs at random from a general class. Failing randomness in selection, it is necessary to establish important similarities between the studied jobs and the target jobs.

5. The 500 jobs in the GATB data base were selected by unknown criteria. They cannot be considered a representative sample of all jobs in the U.S. economy. Nevertheless, the data suggest that a modest level of validity (greater than .15) will hold for a great many jobs in the U.S. economy.

7

Validity Generalization Applied to the GATB

CRITERION-RELATED VALIDITY RESEARCH AND VALIDITY GENERALIZATION

Since the 1940s the U.S. Employment Service (USES) has conducted some 750 criterion-related validity studies of the General Aptitude Test Battery (GATB). The great majority of the studies used supervisor ratings as the criterion, although a sizable minority of studies were conducted using training criteria. The purpose of these studies was to develop Specific Aptitude Test Batteries (SATBs) for specific jobs. SATBs consist of a subset (2 to 4 aptitudes) of the GATB with associated cutoff scores that best differentiate the good from the poor workers. Applicants whose scores on the chosen aptitudes exceeded the cutoff scores would be regarded as qualified to do the job.

Events following the passage of the Civil Rights Act in 1964 mandated increased emphasis on investigations of GATB test fairness for minorities. In 1967, USES initiated an effort to validate its tests for minorities. Jobs studied for SATB development tended to be those with large numbers of workers, in part because sufficiently large samples are easier to obtain in populous occupations. The minimum sample size acceptable was 50, small for the statistical task of validating prediction of performance from test scores, but large in light of the difficulty of finding cooperative employers who have 50 workers in a single job. Some SATB samples, particularly in apprenticeable occupations, were considerably larger, although they often came from multiple establishments. Although

134

the larger sample sizes were desirable, the comparability of the pooled establishments is not known.

As stated in a USES memorandum to the committee describing its testing program, by 1980, USES believed the GATB testing program to be at a crossroads. There were now over 450 SATBs covering over 500 occupations. But there are over 12,000 jobs in the *Dictionary of Occupational Titles* (DOT). The extraordinary difficulty of validating SATBs on minorities, because of small sample sizes, precluded increasing the number of occupations covered by more than two to five a year. Even with the best methods of sample search and data collection and analysis, it was clear that developing and validating test batteries for each of the 12,000 occupations was a practical impossibility. Moreover, the technology used in SATBs, requiring both selection of aptitudes and estimation of multiple cutoffs, had been identified as obsolete, technically deficient, and premised on incorrect assumptions by outside professional experts (see, e.g., Buros's *Seventh Mental Measurements Yearbook,* 1972).

At about the same time, the methodology of meta-analysis was receiving attention in mainstream psychology. USES staff saw possibilities in the work of John Hunter and Frank Schmidt, who were among the leaders in developing validity generalization, a variant of meta-analysis applied to validity coefficients, for use in personnel and industrial psychology.

The working assumption of industrial psychology prior to the late 1970s was that the sizable observed variation in validity coefficients from one criterion-related validity study to the next, even in apparently similar situations, was a reflection of reality. That is, validity was thought to be situation-specific, the sizes of validity coefficients being influenced by subtle, undetected differences across different workplaces. Schmidt and Hunter argued to the contrary, saying that most validation research has been done with small samples and most studies have inadequate statistical power to demonstrate the statistical significance of their results. The observed variation in validities, they proposed, is due to statistical artifacts, primarily sampling error, rather than to true differences in validity from one situation to another.

The VG-GATB Referral System is supported by a series of USES test research reports written by Hunter (U.S. Department of Labor, 1983b,c,d,e). Hunter analyzed the existing validity data base for the GATB, which at the time of his analysis consisted of reports of 515 validity studies carried out by the U.S. Employment Service and cooperating state employment services over the period 1945–1980.

His analysis may be divided into three parts. First, in *The Dimensionality of the General Aptitude Test Battery* (U.S. Department of Labor, 1983b), he argues that it is unnecessary to use all nine component aptitudes of the GATB in predicting job performance and that it is sufficient to use two composites, called cognitive ability and psychomotor ability, in making predictions. Second, *Test Validation for 12,000 Jobs* (U.S. Department of Labor, 1983c) constructs a classification of all jobs into five job families based on the data and things scale used in the DOT code for each job. A different weighting of cognitive and psychomotor ability, for prediction of job performance, is to be used within each job family. And finally, the same report generalizes the validities for the GATB studies within each job family to all jobs in the job family.

In this chapter we review the first two parts of Hunter's plan: dimension reduction and job classification. The next chapter presents Hunter's validity generalization analysis of the 515 GATB studies and compares his results with 264 more recent studies that suggest somewhat different ranges of validities than the earlier studies.

REDUCTION OF NINE APTITUDES TO COGNITIVE AND PSYCHOMOTOR FACTORS

The intention of the original GATB validity research program was to identify, for each job studied, a combination of specific aptitudes and minimum levels for those aptitudes, that an applicant should attain before being referred to a job; these are the so-called SATBs prepared for each job.

There are too many jobs in the U.S. economy, and too many new jobs being created, for the GATB research program ever to hope to cover more than a small fraction of them. Two kinds of problems stand in the way. First, it is not immediately clear that a validity study done for a particular job title in a particular plant is applicable to the same job title in another plant; the same duties in the job description may be performed in quite different working environments by different groups of workers. Thus some mechanism must be discovered for generalizing the validity results for jobs studied to jobs not studied, if the research is to be useful.

Second, the statistical base for a single job, consisting usually of a sample of fewer than 100 workers, is not by itself adequate to carry out the complex estimation involved in identifying three or four of the nine GATB aptitudes as relevant to the job and selecting minimum competency levels for the aptitudes. A good dose of job analyst's judgment must be used in selecting and calibrating the aptitudes, since the data available do not provide a sufficient basis for decision. Again, we wish to increase the statistical strength of conclusions by making some sensible combination of data for different jobs.

GATB Dimensions

Faced with the need to generalize validity results from the 491 jobs represented in the 515 studies to the other jobs in the economy, faced also with the problem of small sample sizes that plagues the SATB approach, Hunter's strategy (U.S. Department of Labor, 1983b) is both to reduce the number of variables relevant to predicting job performance, and to assume that the same prediction equations will apply across broad classes of jobs, so that all data for jobs in the same class may be combined in estimating the equation.

In developing his own position, Hunter describes two theories of job performance—the specific aptitude theory and the general ability theory. Traditional thinking in the GATB program was that job performance would be best predicted by the specific aptitude or aptitudes measured by the SATB and required by the job. For example, performance as a bookkeeper would be better predicted by the numerical aptitude than by general cognitive ability, and performance as an editor would be better predicted by the verbal aptitude than general cognitive ability. In this view, general intelligence has only an indirect relation to job performance; it is mediated by specific aptitudes.

The other position, which was the dominant view early in the twentieth century and is currently enjoying renewed popularity, is that one general cognitive ability, commonly called intelligence, underlies the specific abilities a person develops in school, at play, and on the job. In this view, the validities of the SATBs that were demonstrated in 40 years of research would be the effect of joint causation by a common prior variable, the underlying general cognitive ability. Hunter's analysis of the dimensionality of the GATB brings him to a variant of the general ability interpretation.

Hunter argues that, contrary to the SATB analyses, multiple regression techniques should be used in predicting job performance from the nine GATB aptitudes, because the nine are strongly intercorrelated (Table 7–1). However, the correlations between aptitudes, which must be known in order to apply multiple regression, are only poorly estimated in any one study, and a full multiple regression determining specific weights for each aptitude cannot estimate the weights accurately enough. On the basis of an analysis of the covariation of aptitudes across jobs, he proposes that the nine specific aptitudes fall into three categories of general abilities: cognitive, perceptual, and psychomotor. Although the cognitive and psychomotor abilities are only moderately correlated with one another, both are highly correlated with the perceptual composite (Table 7–2). As a consequence of this overlap, Hunter says that the perceptual composite will add little to the predictive power of the GATB; the nine GATB

TABLE 7-1 Correlations Between Aptitudes Based on 23,428 Worker and Aptitude Reliabilities (Decimals Omitted)

	G	V	N	S	P	Q	K	F	M
Intelligence (G)	100								
Verbal aptitude (V)	84	100							
Numerical aptitude (N)	86	67	100						
Spatial aptitude (S)	74	46	51	100					
Form perception (P)	61	47	58	59	100				
Clerical perception (Q)	64	62	66	39	65	100			
Motor coordination (K)	36	37	41	20	45	51	100		
Finger dexterity (F)	25	17	24	29	42	32	37	100	
Manual dexterity (M)	19	10	21	21	37	26	46	52	100
Reliability	88	85	83	81	79	75	86	76	77

SOURCE: U.S. Department of Labor. 1983. *The Dimensionality of the General Aptitude Test Battery (GATB) and the Dominance of General Factors Over Specific Factors in the Prediction of Job Performance for the U.S. Employment Service.* USES Test Research Report No. 44. Division of Counseling and Test Development, Employment and Training Administration. Washington, D.C.: U.S. Department of Labor, p. 18.

aptitudes may be satisfactorily replaced by just two composite aptitudes: *cognitive ability,* composed of general intelligence, verbal ability, and numerical ability; and *psychomotor ability,* composed of motor coordination, finger dexterity, and manual dexterity. (It should be noted that the general intelligence variable is the sum of verbal aptitude, spatial aptitude, and numerical aptitude with the computation test score removed; it is not measured independently of the others.) Predicting performance for a particular job thus can be reduced to appropriately weighting cognitive ability and psychomotor ability in a combined score for predicting performance, a much simpler task than assessing the relative weights of nine aptitudes.

TABLE 7-2 Correlations Between Composites (Decimals Omitted)

	GVN	SPQ	KFM
Cognitive composite (GVN)	100	76	35
Perceptual composite (SPQ)	76	100	51
Psychomotor composite (KFM)	35	51	100

SOURCE: U.S. Department of Labor. 1983. *The Dimensionality of the General Aptitude Test Battery (GATB) and the Dominance of General Factors Over Specific Factors in the Prediction of Job Performance for the U.S. Employment Service.* USES Test Research Report No. 44. Division of Counseling and Test Development, Employment and Training Administration. Washington, D.C.: U.S. Department of Labor, p. 22.

What Gets Lost in the Simplifying Process?

One obvious question to ask is whether the power of the GATB to predict for different kinds of jobs, that is, its usefulness in classifying applicants, is diminished by this broad-brush approach. A number of experts have commented to the committee (e.g., Lee J. Cronbach, letter dated July 6, 1988) on the exclusion of the perceptual composite. Hunter argues that the perceptual ability composite (S + P + Q) could be predicted essentially perfectly from the cognitive (G + V + N) and psychomotor composites (K + F + M)—if the composites were perfectly measured. With the actual composites, the multiple correlation for predicting SPQ from GVN and KFM is .80 and the perceptual composite is dropped from all but Job Family I. But part of the reason that GVN and SPQ are so highly correlated is that the spatial factor S is included in both G and SPQ.

A more general observation is that the composites do not predict the specific aptitudes very accurately, even after adjusting for less than perfect reliability.[1] The question remains whether the specific aptitudes need to be included with separate weights in the regression equations for job performance, or whether the effect of each specific aptitude is captured sufficiently well by including the corresponding composite in the equations predicting job performance. If the latter holds, the task of setting aptitude weights for jobs is much simplified.

In building the case, Hunter proposes that validities of aptitudes for jobs are constant for aptitudes in the same composite, so that it is appropriate to use only the composites and not the separate aptitudes in predicting performance. Thus the V and N aptitudes might have validities .25 .25 for one job, .20 .20 for another job, .30 .30 for another job. (The G aptitude must be treated differently.) If this is so, then the correlation between such validities over jobs would be 1. He therefore considers the correlations between aptitude validities over jobs (Table 7-3).

The reliability measure in Table 7-3 is based on the sampling error in estimating validities for individual studies. Since the average sample size is 75, a sample validity differs from a true validity by an error with variance approximately .013. The variance of sample validities over all studies is about .026. Thus the variance of true validities over studies is about .013. One way to compute reliability is the ratio of variance of true

---

[1]The reliability of a measurement is the correlation between repeated measurements of the same individual, so, for example, if the reliability were 1.0, repeated measurements would be exactly the same. If two variables are not reliably measured, the correlation between them will be lower than that between perfect measurements and may be increased by correcting for unreliability. Note that the same correction does not apply to correlations with intelligence, however, because it is not independently measured.

TABLE 7-3   Correlations Between Validities Over 515 Jobs (Decimals Omitted)

	G	V	N	S	P	Q	K	F	M
Intelligence (G)	100								
Verbal aptitude (V)	80	100							
Numerical aptitude (N)	81	61	100						
Spatial aptitude (S)	67	32	40	100					
Form perception (P)	45	30	48	53	100				
Clerical perception (Q)	57	54	63	30	57	100			
Motor coordination (K)	19	16	24	8	41	40	100		
Finger dexterity (F)	9	1	15	26	45	23	46	100	
Manual dexterity (M)	-2	-7	9	14	36	19	56	62	100
Reliability	54	47	47	47	46	44	45	53	52

SOURCE: U.S. Department of Labor. 1983. *The Dimensionality of the General Aptitude Test Battery (GATB) and the Dominance of General Factors Over Specific Factors in the Prediction of Job Performance for the U.S. Employment Service.* USES Test Research Report No. 44. Division of Counseling and Test Development, Employment and Training Administration. Washington, D.C.: U.S. Department of Labor, p. 32.

validities to the variance of measured validities, which would be about .5 here.

Hunter suggests that the above table of correlations between validities supports his "general ability theory," which would predict correlations of 1 between specific aptitudes in the same general ability group. He adjusts the given correlations by the reliability correction, which increases the within-block correlations to an average value of 1.09.

This is inaccurate, however. The standard reliability correction is inappropriate here because the errors in measuring different validity coefficients are correlated. Thus if the sample validity for form perception is higher than the true validity, then the sample validity for clerical perception is likely to be higher than the true validity for that sample. When the correlation between sample validities for form perception and clerical perception is computed across studies, it will tend to be positive simply because form perception and clerical perception are positively correlated.

Suppose for example that there were *no* variations in true validities between jobs. The true variance of validities would be zero. The correlation matrix of sample validities would then be approximately the same as the original correlation matrix between variables, because of correlated sampling errors.

At the other extreme, suppose the sample sizes were very large so that the sampling variance of validities was zero. Then the correlation matrix between sample validities would be the correlation matrix between true validities.

TABLE 7–4   Estimated Correlations Between True Job Validities
(Decimals Omitted)

	G	V	N	S	P	Q	K	F	M
Intelligence (G)	100								
Verbal aptitude (V)	76	100							
Numerical aptitude (N)	76	55	100						
Spatial aptitude (S)	60	18	29	100					
Form perception (P)	29	13	38	47	100				
Clerical perception (Q)	50	46	60	21	49	100			
Motor coordination (K)	2	−5	7	−12	37	29	100		
Finger dexterity (F)	−7	−15	6	23	48	14	54	100	
Manual dexterity (M)	−23	−24	−3	7	37	12	66	72	100

NOTE: Each entry is estimated by multiplying by 2 the corresponding entry in Table 7–3 and subtracting the corresponding entry in Table 7–1. A slightly more accurate estimate would subtract from each correlation the product of the average validities of the variables, which will be about .04.

In the present case, taking about half the variance in true validities and half the variance in the sampling error, as in the Hunter analysis, suggests (after complex computations) that the correlation of observed validities is about half the correlation of the true validities plus half the correlation between the variables. This produces an estimated matrix of correlations between true job validities (Table 7–4), which is quite different from Hunter's matrix using the standard correction for reliability.

If this is the way the true validities covary, then we can expect to find jobs with many different weightings appropriate for specific aptitudes. If cognitive ability and psychomotor ability were sufficient to predict job performance, then we would expect to be able to predict accurately the validities of all aptitudes for a given job by knowing the validities for these two composites. It is evident that the accepted composites do not predict the validity of individual aptitudes at all accurately. The perceptual aptitudes are not well predicted by the two composites, so that there must be many jobs in which they would have useful validities.

Since G is composed of a mixture of cognitive and perceptual aptitudes, let us look at the eight independently measured aptitudes. How should they be combined so that the combined aptitudes are sufficient for use in prediction equations? The highly correlated groups are VNQ, SP, and KFM. Composites based on these variables would predict validities for all variables reasonably well, and the correlations between the validities of the composites would be relatively small. These would be useful composites for classifying jobs into different groups within which different prediction equations might apply. It is interesting to note that GVN and KFM have negative correlations in Table 7–4, so that jobs for which GVN has high validity tend to be jobs for which KFM has low validity and vice versa.

Hunter and Schmidt (1982) consider models in which economic gains from job matching are obtained by using spatial aptitude and perceptual ability in addition to general cognitive ability. We offer this as further evidence that the SP composite might be of value.

Although it is convenient and simplifying to consider only cognitive and psychomotor ability in predicting job performance, the analysis supporting this reduction is flawed. The estimated correlations of true validities suggest that different relative weights for specific aptitudes might significantly improve prediction of job performance.

In developing prediction equations for a specific job, it is not at all necessary to use only the data available for that job. We know the overall correlations between specific aptitudes. We have an estimate of joint distribution of true validities. These collective data may be combined with specific data available for the job to develop regression equations predicting performance on the job. For jobs with no direct validity data, we would still need indicators of the specific aptitude validities for the job, such as provided by the five job families for Hunter's two-composite model.

The cognitive ability composite is defined as G + V + N, where G has already been defined as the sum of test scores on vocabulary, arithmetic reasoning, and three-dimensional space. Thus G already includes terms for verbal aptitude, numerical aptitude, and spatial aptitude. In terms of original standardized test scores, GVN is approximately

> three-dimensional space + 3 × vocabulary
> + 3 × arithmetic reasoning
> + 2 × computation.

These weights have developed as a historical accident, caused by the definition of G first and GVN second. Are these the correct variables to include in the cognitive factor? The correlations between aptitudes suggest that clerical perception, being highly correlated with verbal and numerical aptitude, might be sensibly included in a cognitive factor, and indeed this is suggested in the factor analyses of Fozard et al. (1972) and also by the pattern of estimated correlations of true validities (Table 7–4). If only two composites are to be used, one for cognitive ability and one for psychomotor ability, it is necessary to establish weights for the specific aptitudes in the composites. Since the aptitudes are highly correlated, it does not make too much difference which weights are used, but one would like to use weights that have some justification.

The case for rejecting the SPQ composite, because it is predicted by the other two composites with correlation .80, is weak. It is a mathematical truism that if several variables are highly correlated, then linear combinations of some of the variables will predict other linear combinations with high correlation. The question is whether the SPQ composite adds usefully to the prediction of job performance, and it is known that it does in some jobs. For the same reason, the case for rejecting specific aptitudes is weak. Not enough is known about predicting job performance to conclude quickly that two composites alone are sufficient, however convenient it is to work with only two variables in classifying jobs and constructing regression equations.

THE FIVE JOB FAMILIES

The question remains, what is the appropriate predictor for a job not previously studied? There would be no issue if cognitive ability alone were useful in predicting performance—validity might vary from one job to another, but, for every job, applicants would be referred in order of their cognitive score. But if two factors (or several factors) are to be used, their relative weight must be decided in each job.

Constructing the Five Job Families

Hunter divides all 12,000 jobs in the *Dictionary of Occupational Titles* into five job families (U.S. Department of Labor, 1983c), and a different weighting of the two abilities is proposed for predicting job performance within each job family. Before deciding on the specifics of the clustering techniques, he examined five different classification schemes for their effectiveness in predicting cognitive and psychomotor validities; each scheme uses attributes available for any job:

1. the test development analyst's judgments;
2. the mean aptitude requirements listed for each job in the *Dictionary of Occupational Titles*;
3. a five-level job complexity scale based on the DOT data-people-things scale, organized from 1 to 5 in descending order of complexity;
4. predictors from the Position Analysis Questionnaire (PAQ) (McCormick et al., 1972); and
5. the Occupational Analysis Pattern (OAP) structure developed by R.C. Droege and R. Boese (U.S. Department of Labor, 1979, 1980).

All five classification schemes were reported to perform about equally well in predicting observed validity with correlation .30, although Hunter notes that both PAQ and OAP offer some potential improvements over the data-people-things job complexity classification. However, since the data-people-things classification is available for all jobs through the

Dictionary of Occupational Titles, that classification was used in validity generalization from the GATB validity studies. The five job families used in the VG-GATB Referral System are therefore the five complexity-based families of the data-people-things classification, with one important difference: the order in which they are numbered does not reflect complexity.

Sample Jobs in the Job Families:
Family I—set-up/precision work: machinist; cabinet maker; metal fabricator; loom fixer
Family II—feeding/offbearing: shrimp picker; cornhusking machine operator; cannery worker; spot welder
Family III—synthesize/coordinate: retail food manager; fish and game warden; biologist; city circulation manager
Family IV—analyze/compile/compute: automobile mechanic; radiological technician; automotive parts counterman; high school teacher
Family V—copy/compare: assembler; insulating machine operator; forklift truck operator

For the mean observed validities for job complexity categories, see Table 7–5.

The final step in the classification system was the development of regression equations that predict job performance as a function of the cognitive, perceptual, and psychomotor composites within each job family (Table 7–6). (There are different recommended equations for training success, but these apply to a small fraction of jobs and applicants only.) It will be noted that the recommended regression equations differ somewhat from the equations computed for the observed validities. The

TABLE 7–5 Mean Observed Validities for Job Complexity Categories, and Beta-Weights of GVN, SPQ, and KFM in Predicting Job Performance for Jobs Within Each Category (Decimals Omitted)

Job Family	Complexity Levels	Validities GVN	SPQ	KFM	Beta-Weights GVN	SPQ	KFM	r	Number of Jobs
I	1. Setup	34	35	19	18	20	3	37	21
III	2. Synthesize/coordinate	30	21	13	34	−7	5	31	60
IV	3. Analyze/compile/compute	28	27	24	21	3	15	32	205
V	4. Copy/compare	22	24	30	9	5	25	33	209
II	5. Feeding/offbearing	13	15	35	5	−6	37	36	20

SOURCE: U.S. Department of Labor. 1983. *Test Validation for 12,000 Jobs: An Application of Job Classification and Validity Generalization Analysis to the General Aptitude Test Battery.* USES Test Research Report No. 45. Division of Counseling and Test Development, Employment and Training Administration. Washington, D.C.: U.S. Department of Labor, p. 21.

TABLE 7-6 Recommended Regression Equations for Predicting Job Performance (JP)

Job Family	Complexity Level	Regression Equation		Multiple Correlation
I	1	JP=.40 GVN + .19 SPQ + .07 KFM		.59
III	2	JP=.58 GVN		.58
IV	3	JP=.45 GVN	+ .16 KFM	.53
V	4	JP=.28 GVN	+ .33 KFM	.50
II	5	JP=.07 GVN	+ .46 KFM	.49

SOURCE: U.S. Department of Labor. 1983. *Test Validation for 12,000 Jobs: An Application of Job Classification and Validity Generalization Analysis to the General Aptitude Test Battery.* USES Test Research Report No. 45. Division of Counseling and Test Development, Employment and Training Administration. Washington, D.C.: U.S. Department of Labor, p. 39.

new equations are computed from validities corrected for restriction of range (in the worker populations studied compared with the applicant populations for whom the predictions will be made) and for reliability of supervisor ratings.

The effect of these corrections is to increase the multiple correlation that indicates the accuracy of the prediction by about 65 percent. Since GVN has greater restriction of range than KFM, the corrections tend to increase the estimated GVN validities more, and so give greater weight to GVN in the regression equations.

Do the Five Job Families Effectively Increase Predictability?

The majority of the GATB studies (84 percent of workers studied for job performance) fall into job complexity categories 3 and 4, which correspond to the Job Families IV and V in the eventual VG-GATB referral protocol. And indeed, about the same proportion of Job Service applicants apply for jobs in those categories. From Table 7-3, the correlation between GVN and KFM is .35. This means that the correlation between the predictor of success for Job Family IV and the predictor of success for Job Family V is .93. If we used a single predictor, say 2 GVN + KFM, it would have correlation greater than .96 with both these predictors. Thus the ordering of applicants by the score 2 GVN + KFM would be almost indistinguishable from the orderings by the different predictors for Job Families IV and V, and would have correlation at least .93 with the predictors in all job families except Job Family II (complexity level 5), which contains only 5 percent of the jobs.

We conclude that the job complexity classification based on data and things fails to yield classes of jobs within which prediction of job performance is usefully advanced by weighting the composites GVN and SPQ and KFM separately. The only class that justified different weighting was the small class of low-complexity jobs that included only 5 percent of the workers. For all the rest of the jobs we would have effectively the same predictive accuracy, and effectively the same order of referral of workers,[2] by using the single weighting 2 GVN + KFM.

Prediction of performance from a single factor would be expected by the proponents of Spearman's g, a single numerical measure of intelligence. A recent issue of the *Journal of Vocational Behavior* (vol. 31, 1986) is devoted to the role of g in predictions of all kinds. The general argument offered is that g does just as well as specialized test batteries developed, following Hull's (1928) prescription, by multiple regression. For example, Hunter (1986) argues that the specialized test batteries developed by the military for different groups of jobs (mechanical, electronic, skilled services, and clerical) predict performance no better in the category they were developed for than in other categories, and no better than g in any category. Thorndike (1986) argues that specialized batteries developed for optimal prediction on a set of people show marked drops in validity when cross-validated against other groups of people, and that a general predictor g is to be preferred unless the regression weights are based on large groups. Jensen (1986) asserts that "practical predictive validity of psychometric tests is mainly dependent on their g-loading," although he concedes that clerical speed and accuracy and spatial visualization "add a significant increment to the predictive validity of the GATB for certain clerical and skilled blue collar occupations."

We, for our part, remain unconvinced by the USES analysis that finer differentiation is not possible. We do acknowledge that the development of distinct aptitudes that allow differential prediction of success in various jobs has proven to be a thorny problem. The committee believes that the data reported in Army and Air Force studies (Chapter 4) did in fact tend to show slightly higher validities for the aptitude area composites (e.g., mechanical, electronic) than for the more general Armed Forces Qualification Test composite—but the operative word is *slightly*.

However, differential prediction (in this usage meaning the ability to predict that an individual would have greater chances of success in certain classes of jobs and lesser chances in others, depending on the aptitude

---

[2]Since the average differences between black and white examinees are higher for GVN than for KFM, there is an advantage in terms of reducing adverse impact to retaining Job Family V, which has a relatively higher loading on KFM. However, these advantages will not be significant if referral is in order of within-group percentiles, which have the same average for blacks and whites.

requirements of the jobs) is critical. It is precisely what is needed for a job counseling program to be of value for matching people more effectively to jobs.

Although the technical challenge of developing job area aptitude composites that provide differential prediction is great, the committee believes that the continued pursuit of more sophisticated occupational classification systems, such as that attempted in the OAP classification scheme, is worthwhile. The potential for very large data-gathering efforts exists if the use of the GATB is expanded. We suggest that USES make full use of such data to vigorously pursue the possibility of increased precision in the differential prediction of success in various kinds of jobs.

CONCLUSIONS

1. Although it is convenient and simplifying to reduce all nine GATB aptitudes to two composites—cognitive aptitude and psychomotor aptitude—for predicting job performance, the USES analysis supporting this reduction is flawed. Our analysis suggests that different relative weights for specific aptitudes might significantly improve prediction of job performance. And, as a matter of fairness, some individuals would look better if measured by the specific aptitudes for a class of jobs.

2. The case for rejecting the perceptual composite is weak. The two composites GVN and KFM do not predict the validity of the individual aptitudes accurately. The perceptual aptitudes are not well predicted by the two VG-GATB composites, which indicates that in some jobs the SPQ (perceptual) composite could add usefully to the prediction of job performance.

3. The categorization of all jobs into five job families on the basis of job complexity ratings derived from the DOT data-people-things job classification system fails to yield classes of jobs in which prediction of job performance is usefully advanced by weighting the composites GVN, SPQ, and KFM separately. Except for Job Family II, which has only 5 percent of Job Service jobs, a single weighting of 2 GVN + KFM would have the same predictive accuracy and, with the exception of black applicants in Job Family V, the same order of referral.

4. The present VG-GATB classification of jobs into five job families, since it has not identified job groups with useful differences in predictive composites, is of little value as a counseling tool. Since a given worker's performance is predicted by essentially the same formula for all jobs, it cannot be claimed that the worker is better suited to some jobs than to others.

RECOMMENDATIONS

1. Since the job classification scheme currently used in the VG-GATB Referral System has not identified job groups with useful differences in predictive composites and is therefore of little value as a counseling tool, we recommend that USES continue to work to develop a richer job classification that will more effectively match people to jobs.

Establishing an effective job-clustering system is a necessary prerequisite for the testing program to produce substantial system-wide gains (see Chapter 12).

8

GATB Validities

In Chapter 6 we described validity generalization as the prediction of validities of a test for new jobs, based on meta-analysis of the validities of the test on studied jobs. This chapter focuses on establishing the predicted validities of the General Aptitude Test Battery (GATB) for new jobs. The first step involves compiling the existing validity data, and the second is a matter of estimating the "true" validity of the test by correcting the observed validities to account for various kinds of weaknesses in existing research (e.g., small sample sizes). As part of its study of validity generalization for the GATB, the committee has conducted independent analyses of the existing GATB validity studies. The initial sections of the chapter compare the results of these analyses with the work done by John Hunter for the U.S. Employment Service (USES) based on a smaller and older set of studies (U.S. Department of Labor, 1983b,c,d). In addition, drawing on the discussion of corrections presented in Chapter 6, the second half of the chapter presents the committee's estimate of the generalizable validities of the GATB for the kinds of jobs handled by the Employment Service, an estimate that is rather more modest than that proposed in the U.S. Employment Service technical reports.

THE GATB VALIDITY STUDIES

Two sets of GATB validity studies are discussed in this chapter. The first is comprised of the original 515 validity studies analyzed by Hunter;

149

they were prepared in the period 1945–1980 with 10 percent 1940s data, 40 percent 1950s data, 40 percent 1960s data, and 10 percent 1970s data. A larger data tape consisting of 755 studies was made available to the committee by USES. It included these and an additional set of 264 studies carried out in the 1970s and 1980s. (The Hunter studies appear as 491 studies in this data tape, because some pairs of studies in the original 515 consisted of validity coefficients for the same set of workers using two different criteria for job performance; these pairs each appear in a single study on the data tape.) The original samples from the 515 studies summed to 38,620 workers, and the samples from the more recent 264 studies summed to 38,521 workers.

Written reports are available for the earlier 515 studies but not for the more recent 264. It is therefore possible to examine the earlier studies in some detail to determine their quality and comparability. An examination of 50 of the written reports selected at random showed very good agreement between the numbers in the report and the numbers coded into the data set. It is regrettable that no such reports are available for the more recent studies, since it leaves no good way to consider the characteristics of the samples that might explain the very different results of analysis for the two data sets.

An Illustration of Test Validities

Criterion-related validity is expressed as the product moment correlation between test score and a measure of job performance for a sample of workers. The degree of correlation is expressed as a coefficient that can range from −1.0, representing a perfect inverse relationship, to +1.0, representing a perfect positive relationship. A value of 0.0 indicates that there is no relationship between the predictor (the GATB) and the criterion. Figure 8–1 depicts this range of correlations with scatter diagrams showing the degree of linear relationship. In test validation research, the relationships between the test score and the performance measure are usually positive, if not necessarily strong. The lower the correlation, the less appropriate it is to make fine distinctions among test scores.

Basic Patterns of Validity Findings

The most striking finding from our analysis of the entire group of 755 validity studies is a distinct diminution of validities in the newer, post-1972 set. For all three composites, the 264 newer studies show lower mean validities, the decline being most striking for the perceptual and psychomotor composites (Table 8–1). (That the standard deviations are

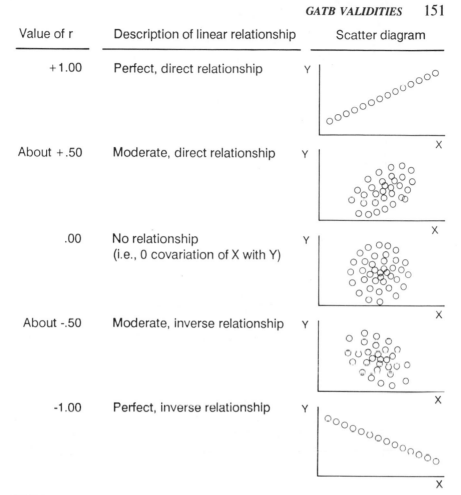

FIGURE 8–1   Interpretation of values of correlation (*r*).

TABLE 8–1   Mean and Standard Deviation of the Validity Coefficients, Weighted by Study Sample Sizes, Computed for Each Composite Across the 264 Studies, and Compared with Those Hunter Reported for the Original 515 Studies

	GVN		SPQ		KFM	
	515	264	515	264	515	264
Mean	.25	.21	.25	.17	.25	.13
Standard deviation	.15	.11	.15	.11	.17	.12

TABLE 8–2   Frequency Distribution of Validity Coefficients for Each GATB Composite Over All 755 Studies

Validity Category	Percentage of Studies		
	GVN	SPQ	KFM
−.40 – −.49			0.1
−.30 – −.39			0.1
−.20 – −.29	0.1	0.1	0.3
−.10 – −.19	1.0	1.1	1.2
.00 – −.09	3.7	4.1	6.6
.01 – .10	12.4	14.7	16.8
.11 – .20	24.7	22.9	24.0
.21 – .30	27.4	25.1	26.5
.31 – .40	18.1	18.7	12.7
.41 – .50	7.8	8.2	6.4
.51 – .60	3.9	2.5	3.6
.61 – .70	0.8	0.5	1.2
.71 – .80	0.1		0.1

also lower is readily explainable: the 264 additional studies have a much larger average sample size—146 as opposed to about 75 in the original set—resulting in less sampling error.)

To give a better sense of the validity data than is provided by means and variances, a frequency distribution of validity coefficients for each composite, over all 755 studies, is shown in Table 8–2. The values presented are the percentage of studies falling into each validity category.

Clearly, the range of observed validity coefficients is large. The question before us is to understand the meaning of this variability. In the next section we examine the effect of factors that might cause variation in the observed validity coefficients.

Potential Moderators of Validity

A number of study characteristics can be hypothesized as potentially affecting validity (and, therefore, contributing to the observed variability across studies). In our analysis of the 755 GATB validity studies, we looked at 10 characteristics:

1. sample size
2. job family
3. study type: predictive (i.e., tested at time of hire) versus concurrent (testing of current employees)
4. criterion type: performance on the job versus performance in training

5. age: mean age of individuals in the sample
6. experience: mean experience of individuals in the sample
7. education: mean education of individuals in the sample
8. race
9. sex
10. date of study

Each of these characteristics is discussed in turn.

Sample Size

Sampling error appears to be the single factor with the largest influence on variance in validity from study to study: removing the influence of sampling error is a major component of any validity generalization analysis. To get an intuitive feel for the effects of sampling error, GVN validities were examined separately for the entire sample, for samples with more than 100 subjects, for samples with more than 200 subjects, and for samples with more than 300 subjects. As N, the number of subjects, increases, random sampling error decreases. Thus we should see much less variation with large samples than with small samples. The distribution of GVN validity is presented in Table 8–3. It can clearly be seen that there is much more variation with small samples; as the mean N increases, validity values center much more closely on the mean.

TABLE 8–3 Percentage of Studies in Each Validity Category, Based on All 755 Studies

| Validity Category | Percentage of Studies | | | |
	All Studies (N = 755)	>100 (N = 192)	>200 (N = 81)	>300 (N = 33)
−.20 − .29	0.1			
−.10 − −.19	1.0			
.00 − −.09	3.7	2.6	1.2	
.01 − .10	12.4	10.9	8.7	6.1
.11 − .20	24.7	33.4	38.2	33.3
.21 − .30	27.4	33.3	40.8	51.5
.31 − .40	18.1	15.6	7.4	3.0
.41 − .50	7.8	4.2	3.7	6.0
.51 − .60	3.9			
.61 − .70	0.8			
.71 − .80	0.1			

TABLE 8–4   Variation of Validities Across Job Families in Old (515) and Recent (264) Studies

Job Family	GVN		SPQ		KFM	
	515	264	515	264	515	264
I (set-up/precision)	.34	.16	.35	.14	.19	.08
II (feeding/offbearing)	.13	.19	.15	.16	.35	.21
III (synthesizing)	.30	.27	.21	.21	.13	.12
IV (analyze/compile/ compute)	.28	.23	.27	.17	.24	.13
V (copy/compare)	.22	.18	.24	.18	.30	.16

Job Family

In both the original 515 studies and the recent 264 studies, validity clearly varies across job families. The mean observed validities (for both the data used by Hunter and the full data set) are presented in Table 8–4 for each of the three test composites.

A notable difference between the old and new studies is in the diminution of the KFM validities in Job Families IV and V.

Study Type: Predictive Versus Concurrent

Some studies are done using job applicants (predictive validation strategy), whereas others involve the testing of current employees (concurrent validation strategy). Some have argued for the superiority of the predictive strategy, based on the assumption that the full range of applicants will be included in the study and thus that range restriction will be reduced. This argument presumes that a very rare version of the predictive validation strategy is used, namely that *all* applicants are hired regardless of test score. More realistically, applicants are screened using either the GATB itself or some other predictor, and thus range restriction is likely in both predictive and concurrent studies. This point has been made in the testing literature; in 1968 the GATB data base was examined by Bemis (1968) and no differences in validity for predictive and concurrent studies were found. A comparison of predictive and concurrent studies was not reported for the original 515 studies.

No consistent difference in validities was found in the present study, as Table 8–5 shows. For some composite/family combinations, validity is higher for the predictive studies; for others validity is higher for the concurrent studies. The predictive/concurrent distinction is too crude to be of real value: for example, we do not know whether the GATB was or was not used as the basis for hiring in any or all of the studies labeled "predictive." Thus study type will not be tested further in this report;

TABLE 8–5 Variation of Validities by Study Type and Job Family, for All 755 Studies

Job Family	GVN		SPQ		KFM	
	Predictive	Concurrent	Predictive	Concurrent	Predictive	Concurrent
I	.14	.21	.10	.19	.00	.11
II	.15	—	.17	—	.33	—
III	.30	.29	.24	.20	.12	.17
IV	.29	.24	.26	.19	.21	.15
V	.20	.20	.26	.26	.27	.22

variation in validity due to study type will remain one unaccounted-for source of variance.

Criterion Type: On-the-Job Performance Versus Training Success

It has frequently been reported in the personnel testing literature that higher validity coefficients are obtained for ability tests when training success rather than job performance is used as the criterion. This makes conceptual sense, as there are probably fewer external factors influencing training success than job performance (e.g., job performance typically covers a longer time period and is probably more heavily influenced by supervision, work-group norms, variation in equipment, family problems, and so on). But it could also be a product of measurement technology— since training success is usually measured with a paper-and-pencil test, the similarity of measurement methods might artificially boost the correlation. Hunter reports substantially larger mean validities for GATB studies using training success. A summary based on the full data set is presented in Table 8–6.

Given the magnitude of these differences, the data set is broken down by both job family and criterion type for validity generalization analyses.

TABLE 8–6 Validities for Training Success and Supervisor Ratings, by Job Family, for All 755 Studies

Job Family	GVN		SPQ		KFM	
	Performance	Training	Performance	Training	Performance	Training
I	.19	.45	.18	.45	.11	.12
II	.15	—	.17	—	.33	—
III	.29	.30	.21	.20	.17	.10
IV	.23	.35	.19	.27	.16	.19
V	.20	.31	.21	.33	.22	.30

Age

Ideally, the effect of age would be examined by computing validity coefficients separately for individuals in different age categories. However, the present data base reports validity coefficients for entire samples and does not report findings by age. What is reported is the mean age for each sample. Thus we can determine whether validity varies by the mean age of the sample.

For the 755 studies, the mean "mean age" is 31.8 years, with a standard deviation of 6.3 years. Correlations (*r*) between mean age and test validity are as follows:

> *r* age/GVN validity = −.15
> *r* age/SPQ validity = −.06
> *r* age/KFM validity = .03

Thus the validity of the cognitive composite (GVN) tends to be somewhat lower for older workers, though not enough to require special consideration in validity generalization analysis. This finding does not seem to hold for SPQ and KFM.

Relationships between mean age and mean test score are also worthy of note:

> *r* age/GVN mean = −.28
> *r* age/SPQ mean = −.45
> *r* age/KFM mean = −.52

Thus studies in which the average age is higher tend to have composite scores that are notably lower, especially on SPQ and KFM.

Since the age-validity relationship is low, age is not treated as a moderator in the validity generalization analyses, though the age/mean-test-score relationship certainly merits consideration in examining the GATB program as a whole.

Experience

As with age, what is reported in the validity studies is the mean experience for each sample. In this data base, the mean is 5.5 years, with a standard deviation of 4 years. Note that what is coded is typically job experience rather than total work experience. Experience and age are highly related: the correlation between the two is .58.

Correlations (*r*) between mean experience and test validity are as follows:

> *r* experience/GVN validity = .03
> *r* experience/SPQ validity = .00
> *r* experience/KFM validity = −.16

The pattern is mixed, with less experienced samples producing higher KFM validities. This parallels the relationship between experience and test score means:

$$r \text{ experience/GVN mean} = .00$$
$$r \text{ experience/SPQ mean} = -.07$$
$$r \text{ experience/KFM mean} = -.32$$

Less-experienced samples score higher on KFM; in all likelihood this is age-related.

Experience is not treated as a moderator in the validity generalization analyses.

Education

The mean years of education across the 755 samples is 11.4 years, with a standard deviation of 1.5 years. The pattern of correlations between mean education and test validity is as follows:

$$r \text{ education/GVN validity} = .15$$
$$r \text{ education/SPQ validity} = -.10$$
$$r \text{ education/KFM validity} = .36$$

Thus GVN validity tends to be higher for more-educated samples, and KFM validity higher for less-educated samples. In all likelihood, this effect is caused by the relationship between job family and validity, namely, higher GVN validity for more complex jobs (requiring more education) and higher KFM validity for less complex jobs (requiring less education).

Validity Differences by Race

Validity differences by race are examined in detail in the following chapter. Suffice it to say here that most of the GATB validity studies do not report data by race, but analysis of the 72 studies with at least 50 black and 50 nonminority workers indicates that mean validities for nonminorities are higher than mean validities for blacks for all three composites.

Validity Differences by Sex

Many studies (345 of 755) are based on mixed-sex samples. However, 410 studies were done on single-sex samples (226 male, 184 female). Breaking studies down by job family and criterion type (performance criterion versus training criterion, the two important moderator variables identified in the earlier analyses), leaves few categories with enough studies for meaningful comparisons to be made. Nevertheless, in those

TABLE 8–7   Validities for Job Families by Sex: Comparison of the Mean Observed Validity Across Studies Split by Job Family, Type of Criterion Measure, and Sex of Sample (Mixed Samples Not Included in Analyses)

	GVN							
	Performance				Training			
	Male		Female		Male		Female	
Job Family	Mean	Number of Studies	Mean	Number of Studies	Mean	Number of Studies	Mean	Number of Studies
I	.28	21	—	—	.49	1	—	—
II	.23	1	.13	16	—	—	—	—
III	.36	12	.37	2	.32	7	.57	1
IV	.24	98	.23	31	.34	38	.38	14
V	.21	46	.20	118	.35	2	.37	2
	SPQ							
I	.29	21	—	—	.40	1	—	—
II	.22	1	.15	16	—	—	—	—
III	.24	12	.25	2	.19	7	.50	1
IV	.23	98	.22	31	.29	38	.29	14
V	.25	46	.23	118	.45	2	.40	2
	KFM							
I	.18	21	—	—	.03	1	—	—
II	.29	1	.34	16	—	—	—	—
III	.13	12	.19	2	.05	7	.48	1
IV	.19	98	.23	31	.21	38	.22	14
V	.25	46	.30	118	.32	2	.46	2

categories in which comparisons can be made (Job Families IV and V with a performance criterion and Job Family IV with a training criterion), the results suggest no effect due to sex. Results are summarized in Table 8–7.

Similar conclusions were reached in a USES test research report, which analyzed validity differences by sex for 122 validity studies for which validity could be computed separately for males and females (U.S. Department of Labor, 1984a). That report concluded that there are no meaningful differences in GATB validities between males and females.

Date of Study

The committee was concerned about reliance on very old validity studies in drawing general conclusions about GATB validity, as the

TABLE 8-8 Correlations of Validities with Year of Study

Job Family	Number of Studies	GVN	SPQ	KFM
I	23	.22	−.24	.27
II	17	.12	−.08	−.67
III	50	−.25	−.15	.02
IV	235	.03	−.03	−.07
V	217	.00	−.11	−.33

validity studies had been done over a period of four decades. The date of the study was not coded on the data tape containing the summaries of 755 validity studies. But virtually all written reports were also made available to the committee. These contained study dates for more than 400 studies and validity coefficients for 542 independent samples. The date was extracted from each study and added to the data tape.

In the subsequent analysis, date was treated as a continuous variable. Date of study was correlated with GATB composite validity within each job family (Table 8-8). Study date varied from 1945 to 1979, distributed about 10 percent in the 1940s, 40 percent in the 1950s, 40 in the percent 1960s, and 10 percent in the 1970s.

These findings may be artifactual: if, for example, there was a change over time in some study characteristic (e.g., job performance criteria versus training criteria), the true effects of study date would be hidden. Thus partial correlations were computed controlling for criterion type (job performance versus training success) and for study type (predictive versus concurrent), producing the second-order partial correlations shown in Table 8-9.

Only Job Families IV and V offer large enough numbers of studies to merit careful attention. In these two job families, there is no evidence of change over time in the validity of the GVN composite, but there is evidence of a significant decrease in SPQ and KFM validity over time.

Note that this analysis is based on studies for which written reports

TABLE 8-9 Correlations of Validity with Time, Adjusting for Criterion Type and Job Type

Job Family	Number of Studies	GVN	SPQ	KFM
I	19	.24	−.31	.27
II	13	.00	.00	.00
III	45	−.37	−.20	−.07
IV	228	−.04	−.18	−.23
V	210	.04	−.08	−.33

were available. No written reports are available for the most recent 200 or so of the 755 studies in the data base. This means that the decline in GATB validities portrayed in Table 8–1 is not restricted to the newer studies, although it has become more pronounced in the post-1972 data set.

Exploration of Explanations for the Change in Validity Over Time

The decrease in GATB validities over time is puzzling and obviously somewhat worrisome. In trying to find some reasons, we compared the findings from Hunter's analysis of 515 studies, which overlaps closely with the set of studies for which written reports are available, with the 264 more recent studies.

Two procedural issues are worthy of note. First, we can only approximate the data base used by Hunter. We can identify 513 studies as studies that were available to Hunter. These are contrasted with 264 studies added to the tape since Hunter's analysis was done. These total more than 755, because Hunter included a series of studies that later proved to be nonindependent: if two criteria were available in a single study, two validity coefficients were computed and included on the tape as separate studies. These have not been included separately in the analyses based on all 755 studies, but are included here to recreate Hunter's data base as closely as possible. Second, USES has identified and corrected a number of coding errors in the data base. Thus a reanalysis of the same studies Hunter examined will not produce identical results. The 513 Hunter studies have a total N of 37,674; the 264 new studies have a total N of 38,521.

Several hypotheses about possible causes of the mean differences were explored and rejected. One is that the new studies were validated against a different type of criterion. However, 83 percent of both the old and the new studies were validated against on-the-job measures, primarily supervisor ratings, and 17 percent against training measures. A second rejected hypothesis is that the type of job studied changed. A comparison of the job family breakdown between the 515 studies and the present 264 studies appears in Table 8–10. In both data sets, Job Families IV and V predominate, although the old set is evenly divided between the two and the new set has significantly more Family IV studies.

We can rule out the differences in job families as an explanation by considering validities within job family (Table 8–11). Several comments are in order. First, the sample sizes for Families II and III for the job performance criteria are small; thus we focus solely on Families I, IV, and V. Second, only for Job Family IV is the sample size adequate to put any confidence in the findings using the training criterion.

TABLE 8-10   Distribution of Studies Over Job Families

Job Family	Percentage of Studies (N = 515)	Percentage of Studies (N = 264)
I	4	9
II	4	2
III	12	4
IV	40	54
V	40	31

Using the performance criterion, validity is lower in the recent studies for all three composites for all families with meaningful sample sizes (I, IV, and V). With the training criterion, only Family IV has a large sample size; GVN validity actually is slightly higher for the new studies, and the drop in SPQ and KFM in validities is smaller than for the performance criteron for the same family.

TABLE 8-11   Validities for the Two Sets of Studies by Job Family and Type of Criterion

	Performance				Training			
Job Family	Hunter Studies	(N)	New Studies	(N)	Hunter Studies	(N)	New Studies	(N)
				GVN				
I	.31	(1,142)	.15	(3,900)	.41	(180)	.54	(64)
II	.14	(1,155)	.19	(200)	—		—	
III	.30	(2,424)	.25	(630)	.27	(1,800)	.30	(347)
IV	.27	(12,705)	.21	(19,206)	.34	(4,183)	.36	(3,169)
V	.20	(13,367)	.18	(10,862)	.36	(655)	.00	(106)
				SPQ				
I	.32		.13		.47		.40	
II	.17		.16		—		—	
III	.22		.21		.18		.21	
IV	.25		.16		.29		.25	
V	.23		.18		.38		.01	
				KFM				
I	.20		.07		.11		.16	
II	.35		.21		—		—	
III	.17		.17		.11		.02	
IV	.21		.12		.20		.17	
V	.27		.16		.31		.12	

What accounts for this drop in validity? The above analyses have already dealt with two plausible reasons: change over time in the job families studied (from families for which validities are higher to families for which validities are lower) and change over time in the type of criteria used. Both of these factors have been found to moderate GATB validity. However, since analyses reported here present results within job families and within criterion types, this explanation has been ruled out.

Another factor is the role of race. As the next chapter describes in detail, validity for black samples is lower than validity for white samples. The more recent studies contain a heavy minority representation, since many of the studies were undertaken explicitly to build a minority data base. However, even among the recent studies for which separate validities were available by race, total white N is larger than the total black N by a factor of about 5, and the black-white validity difference is substantially smaller than the difference reported here between the earlier and the more recent studies. Thus the inclusion of more minority samples is at best a minor contributor to the validity difference between the earlier and the more recent studies.

Another possible explanation is that the more recent studies exhibit a larger degree of range restriction, thus suppressing validity. Analysis reveals exactly the opposite: the more recent studies show less range restriction (e.g., a slightly larger GATB composite standard deviation).

Some have advanced the argument that the original data base should be trusted and the new studies discounted. The reasoning used is that the new studies were done hurriedly in order to gather data on validity for black workers. In order to obtain minority samples, two things were done: first, data from many organizations were pooled to increase minority sample size and, second, organizations not typical of those usually studied by USES were used because of access to the minority samples. The second of these arguments does not seem compelling on its face. But the hypothesis that pooling across employers could lower validity seemed plausible, because each employer might have an idiosyncratic performance standard (e.g., an employee whose performance is "average" in one organization may be "above average" in another). This would make the criterion less reliable, and thus lower validity.

However, the hypothesis was not borne out when tested empirically. The data tape, containing raw data for 174 studies, included an employer code. Validities were computed two ways: first, pooling data from all employers within a job and, second, computing a separate validity coefficient for each employer within a job. Because many employers contributed only a single case or a handful of cases, separate validity coefficients were computed only for employers contributing 10 or more cases. This reduced the total sample size by about 20 percent. Mean validities were essentially the same whether pooled across employers or computed separately for each employer, thus failing to support the hypothesis that multiple employer samples are an explanation for the validity drop. The Northern Test Development Field Center has since conducted similar analyses and also concluded that only a small part of the decline in validities can be attributed to single- versus multiple-location studies (U.S. Department of Labor, 1988).

We have not been able to derive convincing explanations for the decrease in GATB validities from the data available to us. The drop is especially marked in KFM validities, and one possibility is that jobs on the whole require less psychomotor skill than previously, but this scarcely explains the general decline. One can speculate as to whether there has been some change in the nature of jobs such that the GATB composite abilities are less valid now than had previously been the case. However, if there were such a change, one would expect it to be noted and commented on widely in the personnel testing literature; similar declines in validity have not been observed with the Armed Services Vocational Aptitude Battery, the military selection and classification battery. It is also possible that the explanation lies in some as yet not identified procedural aspects of the validity studies. In short, the validity drop remains a mystery, and the differences between the early and recent studies demand that USES be cautious in projecting validities computed for old jobs to validities for future jobs.

VALIDITY GENERALIZATION ANALYSES

Having looked at the observed mean validities of two sets of studies, and having noted a substantial decrease in validity in the more recent set, we now turn to the issue of correcting the observed validities. In order to demonstrate the full range of available options, we report three validity generalization analyses: one correcting only for the effects of sampling error (what is termed "bare bones" analysis), a second correcting for criterion unreliability, and a third correcting for range restriction as well as criterion unreliability. In each example, analyses are reported first for the sample of studies and then broken down by criterion type (job performance versus training success) and by job family. The chapter ends with our conclusions about the most appropriate estimates of the true validity of the GATB for Employment Service jobs.

Correcting Only for Sampling Error

In this analysis, variance expected due to sampling error is computed: the variance is a function of the mean observed validity and the mean

TABLE 8–12   Validities Corrected for Sampling Error, Based on 264 Studies

Job Family	GVN Mean *r*	Observed SD	Corrected SD	SPQ Mean *r*	Observed SD	Corrected SD	KFM Mean *r*	Observed SD	Corrected SD
					Overall				
	.20	.13	.07	.17	.13	.07	.13	.15	.08
				Job Performance Criterion					
I	.15	.11	.06	.13	.13	.07	.07	.10	.06
II	.19	.13	.07	.16	.14	.08	.21	.18	.10
III	.25	.12	.06	.21	.11	.05	.17	.10	.05
IV	.21	.11	.06	.16	.12	.07	.12	.13	.07
V	.18	.11	.06	.18	.13	.07	.16	.11	.06
				Training Criterion					
I	.54	.12	.05	.40	.08	.00	.16	.05	.00
II	—	—	—	—	—	—	—	—	—
III	.30	.16	.11	.21	.12	.05	.02	.15	.10
IV	.36	.12	.07	.25	.11	.05	.17	.15	.10
V	.00	.16	.12	.01	.15	.10	.12	.11	.04

NOTE: SD = standard deviation.

sample size. What is reported in the tables is the mean observed validity coefficient, the observed standard deviation (SD), and the corrected standard deviation. This corrected SD is found by subtracting variance expected due to sampling error from observed variance: this gives a corrected variance, the square root of which is the corrected standard deviation. Thus, within each job family, the mean observed validity estimates the average true validity of the population of jobs in the family, and, provided the population validities are normally distributed, 90 percent of validities can be expected to fall above the point defined by multiplying 1.28 times the corrected standard deviation (1.28 SD units below the mean is the 10th percentile of a normal distribution) and subtracting the result from the mean validity.

Table 8–12 shows that the observed variability is reduced considerably in virtually all test/job family combinations when the effects of sampling error are removed. If there were no variation in true validities, we would expect the standard deviation of the observed validities to be about 0.10, corresponding to an average sample size of 100; the actual standard deviations are only a little larger than they would be if all variation was due to sampling error. Thus correcting for sampling error produces a marked reduction in the estimated standard deviation of true validities.

TABLE 8–13 Credibility Values for Best Predictors in Each Job Family, Based on 264 Studies

Criterion	Job Family	Test Choice	Mean Validity	90% Credibility Value
Job performance	I	GVN	.15	.06
	II	KFM	.21	.12
	III	GVN	.25	.16
	IV	GVN	.21	.12
	V	GVN	.18	.09
Training	I	GVN	.54	.39
	II	—	—	—
	III	GVN	.30	.16
	IV	GVN	.36	.26
	V	GVN	.12	.05

Credibility values for the preferred test composite for each job family are shown in Table 8–13. We compute credibility values in each job family such that 90 percent of the true validities of jobs in that family will be greater than the given credibility value.

Thus correcting only for sampling error, one finds evidence of modest validity for the GATB for all job families.

Correcting for Criterion Unreliability

Ideally, a good reliability estimate would be available for each study, in which case each validity coefficient could be corrected for unreliability. Unfortunately, reliability data are available only for 285 of the 755 studies. Thus we will revert to the backup strategy of relying on assumed values. One approach is to use the data from the studies for which reliability estimates are available and project that similar reliability values would have been obtained for the rest of the studies.

A problem that researchers in the area of validity generalization have noted is that some methods of reliability estimation are likely to produce inflated reliability measures. For example, a "rate-rerate" method, in which a supervisor is asked to provide a rating of performance on two occasions, typically about two weeks apart, is likely to produce overestimates of reliability, since it is not at all unlikely that the supervisor will remember the previous rating and rate similarly in order to appear consistent. Unfortunately, this method is the most commonly used in the GATB data base, in which it produces a mean reliability value of .86. More appropriate is an interrater reliability method; unfortunately, only four studies in the GATB data base use this method.

On the basis of this lack of meaningful reliability data, Hunter assumed in his validity generalization research for USES that reliability was .60

when job performance was used as the criterion and .80 when training success was used as the criterion. These values were based on a general survey of the criterion measurement literature.

These values have met with some skepticism among industrial/organizational psychologists, many of whom believe that the .60 value is too low, and that interrater reliability is at least on some occasions substantially higher than this. For example, recent research on performance in military jobs, using job sample tests as the criterion, documents interrater reliabilities in the .90s (U.S. Department of Defense, 1989). However, no formal rebuttal of Hunter's position has appeared in print. The .80 for reliability of training success does not appear controversial.

Operationally, we can correct for the effects of criterion unreliability by dividing the mean validity coefficient by the square root of the mean reliability coefficient. Thus, using .60 increases each observed validity by 29 percent and using .80 increases each observed validity by 12 percent. Given the paucity of data, we recommend the more conservative .80 correction.

Correcting for Range Restriction

If the test standard deviation is smaller in the study sample than in the applicant pool, then the validity coefficient for workers will be reduced due to range restriction and will be an underestimate of the true validity of the test for applicants. If the standard deviation for the applicant pool is known, the ratio of study SD to applicant SD is a measure of the degree of range restriction, and the validity coefficient can be corrected to produce the value that would result if the full applicant population had been represented in the study.

In the GATB data base the restricted SD is known for each test; however, no values for the applicant pool SD are available. Hunter dealt with this by making two assumptions: (1) for each job, the applicant pool is the entire U.S. work force and (2) the pooled data from all the studies in the GATB data base can be taken as a representation of the U.S. work force. Thus Hunter computed the GVN, SPQ, and KFM SDs across all 515 jobs that he studied. Then, for each sample, he compared the sample SD with this population SD as the basis for his range-restriction correction.

The notion that the entire work force can be viewed as the applicant pool for each job is troubling. Intuitively we tend to think that people gravitate to jobs for which they are potentially suited: highly educated people tend not to apply for minimum-wage jobs, and young high school graduates tend not to apply for middle-management positions. And indeed there is a large and varied economic literature on educational screening, self-selection, and market-induced sorting of individuals that speaks against the notion that the entire work force can be viewed as the applicant pool for each job (Sueyoshi, 1988).

Some empirical support for the notion that the applicant pool for individual jobs is more restricted than the applicant pool for the entire work force can be found by examining test SDs within job families. Using the logic of Hunter's analysis, if data from all jobs can be pooled to estimate the applicant population SD, then data from jobs in one family can be pooled to estimate the applicant SD for that family. Applying this logic to the GVN subtest produces the following:

GVN SD based on all jobs		53.0
GVN SD based on Job Family	I	45.6
	II	48.6
	III	49.7
	IV	49.2
	V	48.4

Since the mean restricted GVN SD for the 755 studies is 42.2, Hunter's method would produce a ratio of restricted to unrestricted SDs of .80, whereas the family-specific ratios would vary from .85 to .93. Thus there is a suggestion that Hunter's approach may overcorrect. Since the Job Families IV and V that constitute the principal fraction of Employment Service jobs include a very wide range of jobs, we might expect the standard deviation for actual applicant groups to be smaller than that obtained by acting as if all workers in the job family might apply for each job.

Empirical data on test SDs in applicant pools for a variety of jobs filled through the Employment Service are needed to assess whether Hunter's analysis overcorrects for range restriction. In the absence of applicant pool data, the conservative correction for restriction of range would be simply to apply no correction at all.

The effect of Hunter's correction for restriction of range, which assumes a restriction ratio of .80, is to multiply the observed correlations by 1.25 when the observed correlations are modest. The combined effect of his correction for reliability (which assumes average reliabilities of .60) and restriction of range is to increase the observed correlations by 61 percent for job performance and by 40 percent for training success. The more conservative correction recommended by the committee, one that allows for reliability of .80 and no correction for restriction of range in the worker population, would increase each correlation by 12 percent.

Thus sizable differences in estimated validities will occur according to the correction chosen. When the more conservative assumptions are applied to the 264 recent studies, one is left with a very different sense of overall GATB validities than that projected by the USES test research

TABLE 8–14   Validities Corrected for Reliability, Based on 264 Studies, Compared with Hunter's Validities Using His Larger Corrections for Reliability and Restriction of Range, Based on 515 Studies

Job Family	GVN		SPQ		KFM		Counts	
	515	264	515	264	515	264	515	264
				Overall				
	.47	.22	.38	.19	.35	.15	38,620	38,521
			Job Performance Criterion					
I	.56	.17	.52	.15	.30	.08	1,142	3,900
II	.23	.21	.24	.18	.48	.24	1,155	200
III	.58	.28	.35	.24	.21	.19	2,424	630
IV	.51	.23	.40	.18	.32	.13	12,705	19,206
V	.40	.20	.35	.20	.43	.18	13,367	10,862
			Training Criterion					
I	.65	.60	.53	.45	.09	.18	180	64
II	—	—	—	—	—	—	—	—
III	.50	.33	.26	.24	.13	.02	1,800	347
IV	.57	.40	.44	.28	.31	.19	4,183	3,169
V	.54	.00	.53	.01	.40	.13	655	106

reports drafted by Hunter (Table 8–14). Instead of overall GVN validities of .47, they are .22. The KFM validities shrink from .35 to .15 in the recent studies. These differences are not due only to differences in analytic method. The 264 more recent studies simply produce different empirical findings—that is, lower validities—than the earlier 515.

Optimal Predictors Based on the Recent 264 Studies

The corrected correlations in Table 8–14 may be used to develop composite predictors of job performance in the different job families based on the recent 264 studies. These predictors are weighted combinations of GVN, SPQ, and KFM, with the weights chosen to maximize the correlation between predictor and supervisor ratings. Because the composites GVN, SPQ, and KFM are themselves highly intercorrelated (Table 7–1), a wide range of weights will give about the same predictive accuracy. For example, the predictor

$$2 \text{ GVN} + \text{KFM}$$

is very nearly optimal for both Job Family IV and Job Family V.

The optimal predictor in Job Family IV has correlation .24 with supervisor ratings. The optimal predictor in Job Family V has correlation .25 with supervisor ratings. The comparable correlations produced in Hunter's analysis are .53 and .50. The differences are partly due to the lower observed correlations in the recent studies and partly due to our use of more conservative corrections.

FINDINGS: THE GATB DATA BASE

Criterion-Related Validity Prior to 1972

1. Validity studies of the GATB completed prior to 1972 produce a mean observed correlation of about .25 between cognitive, perceptual, or psychomotor aptitude scores and supervisor ratings on the job. The mean observed correlation between cognitive or perceptual scores and training success is about .35.

Criterion-Related Validity Changes Since 1972

2. There are notable differences in the results of GATB validity studies conducted prior to 1972 and the later studies. The mean observed correlation between supervisor ratings and cognitive or perceptual aptitude scores declines to .19, and between supervisor ratings and psychomotor aptitude scores declines to .13.

CONCLUSIONS ON VALIDITY GENERALIZATION FOR THE GATB

1. The general thesis of the theory of validity generalization, that validities established for some jobs are generalizable to other unexamined jobs, is accepted by the committee.

Observed and Adjusted Validities

2. The GATB has modest validities for predicting supervisor ratings of job performance or training success in the 755 validity studies assembled by USES over 45 years. The unexplained marked decrease in validity in recent studies suggests caution in projecting these validities into the future.

3. The average observed validity of GATB aptitude composites for supervisor ratings over the five job families of USES jobs in recent years is about 0.22.

4. In the committee's judgment, plausible adjustments for criterion unreliability might raise the average observed validity of the GATB aptitude composites from .22 to .25 for recent studies. Corresponding

adjustments for the older studies produce a validity of .35, and the average corrected validity across all 755 studies is approximately .30, with about 90 percent of the jobs studied falling in the range of .20 to .40.

These validities are lower than those circulated in USES technical reports, such as Test Research Report No. 45 (U.S. Department of Labor, 1983b), which tend to be .5 or higher. The lower estimates are due to the drop in observed validities in recent studies and to our use of more conservative analytic assumptions. We have made the correction for unreliability based on an assumed value of .80; we have made no correction for restriction of range.

5. In the committee's judgment, two of the three adjustments to observed GATB validities made in the USES analysis—the adjustment for restriction of range and that for criterion unreliability—are not well supported by evidence. We conclude that the corrected validities reported in USES test research reports are inflated.

In particular, we do not accept Hunter's assumption used in correcting for restriction of range, namely that the applicant pool for a particular job consists of all workers in all jobs. This assumption causes the observed correlations to be adjusted upward by 25 percent for small correlations and by 35 percent for observed validities of .50.

Restriction-of-range estimates should be based on data from applicants for homogeneous clusters of jobs. Undoubtedly there is an effect due to restriction of range, but in the absence of data to estimate the effect, no correction should be made.

6. Reliability corrections are based in part on data in the GATB validity data base, and so have more empirical support than the corrections for restriction of range. There remains some question whether a reliability value of .60, which has the effect of increasing correlations by 29 percent, is appropriate for supervisor ratings. Given the weakness of the supporting data, we believe that a conservative correction, based on an estimated reliability of .80, would be appropriate.

Validity Variability

7. Validities vary between jobs. Our calculation is that about 90 percent of the jobs in the GATB studies will have true validities between .2 and .4 for supervisor ratings.

We cannot ascertain how generalizable this distribution is to the remaining jobs in the population. For those jobs in the population that are found to be similar to those in the sample, it seems reasonable to expect roughly the same distribution as in the sample.

8. The GATB is heavily oriented toward the assessment of cognitive abilities. However, the cognitive composite is not equally predictive of

performance in all jobs. Common sense suggests that psychomotor, spatial, and perceptual abilities would be very important in certain types of jobs. But those sorts of abilities are measured much less well. And GATB research has focused more on selection than on classification, with a consequent emphasis on general ability rather than differential abilities.

9. Since GATB validities have a wide range of values over different jobs and have declined over time, introduction of a testing system based on validity generalization does not eliminate the need for continuing criterion-related validity research. The concept of validity generalization does not obviate the need for continuing validity studies for different jobs and for the same job at different times.

9

Differential Validity and Differential Prediction

This chapter addresses the important question of whether the General Aptitude Test Battery (GATB) functions in the same way for different specified groups. Investigations of group differences in the correlations of a test with a criterion measure are commonly referred to as differential validity studies. Such studies can take a variety of forms, including investigations of the possibility that validity coefficients may differ as a function of the setting (e.g., from one job to another or from one location to another) or the group (e.g., demographic group or groups formed on the basis of prior work experience). Investigations of differential prediction, which cover an equally broad range, focus on prediction equations rather than correlation coefficients. A differential prediction study may be used to investigate whether differences in setting or differences among demographic groups (e.g., racial or ethnic groups or gender) affect the predictive meaning of the test scores. We are not concerned here with setting. Our investigation is limited to the possibility that the GATB functions differently for different population groups, and specifically that correlations of GATB scores with on-the-job criterion measures may differ by racial or ethnic group or gender, or that predictions of criterion performance from GATB scores may differ for employees on a given job who are of different racial or ethnic status or gender.

Although questions about differences in correlations and about differential prediction could be raised for groups formed on the basis of a wide range of characteristics, these questions are of particular importance for groups that are known to differ in average test performance. Some of the policy issues regarding the use of tests for selection that are raised by the existence of group differences in average test performance were discussed in the report of the National Research Council's Committee on Ability Testing, from which we quote (Wigdor and Garner, 1982:71–72):

If group differences on tests used for selection do not reflect actual differences in practice—in college or on the job—then using the test for selection may unfairly exclude a disproportionately large number of members of the group with the lower average test scores. Furthermore, even when the groups differ in average performance on the job or in college as well as in average performance on the test, the possible adverse impact on the lower-scoring group should be considered in evaluating the use of the test.

Because the differences in average test scores for some groups are relatively large, and because reliance on the scores without regard to group membership can have substantial adverse impact, "it is important to determine the degree to which the differences reflect differences in performance . . . on the job" (Wigdor and Garner, 1982:73). That is, the results of differential prediction studies are needed.

Studies have been conducted by David J. Synk, David Swarthout, and William Goode, among others, comparing the predictive validities of GATB scores obtained for black employees and white employees (e.g., U.S. Department of Labor, 1987), and for men and women (U.S. Department of Labor, 1984a). Although these comparisons of correlation coefficients for different groups are related to the issue of differential prediction, they do not provide a direct answer to the question of whether group differences in average test scores are reflected in differences in job performance. It is possible, for example, for the correlations between a test and a criterion measure to be identical for two groups when there are substantial differences in the prediction equations for the two groups. Thus, the use of a single prediction equation could lead to predictions that systematically over- or underestimate the job performance of members of one of the groups, even though the validity coefficients are the same. Conversely, it is possible for two groups to have the same prediction equations and the same variability of actual criterion scores about their predicted values, and yet have different validity coefficients.

Prediction equations are usually based on a linear regression model and are influenced by means and standard deviations of the test and criterion measure as well as the correlation. Thus the equations for two groups may differ as the result of differences in means or standard deviations as well as differences in correlations.

Although differential prediction is the more important of the two topics, differences in correlations between scores on the GATB and scores on a criterion measure are also of interest. This is so because there is a common expectation that a test, which may be known to have a useful degree of validity for majority-group employees, may have no useful degree of validity for minority-group employees. Therefore, the results of the committee's investigations of differences in correlations between the GATB and criterion measures are briefly reviewed before turning to a consideration of differential prediction.

GROUP DIFFERENCES IN CORRELATIONS

David J. Synk and David Swarthout compared the validity coefficients obtained for black and for nonminority employees in 113 Specific Aptitude Test Battery validation studies conducted since 1972 for which there were at least 25 people in each of the two groups (U.S. Department of Labor, 1987). For almost all of the 113 studies the criterion measure was based on supervisor ratings, typically "the sum of the scores from two administrations of the Standard Descriptive Rating Scale" (p. 2). The weighted average of the validity coefficients across studies was reported separately by group for each of the nine aptitude scores. Also reported were the weighted average validities for the appropriate composites for each of the five job families. The latter results are of greatest interest here because it is the composites that would be used in the proposed VG-GATB Referral System.

The weighted average job family correlations reported in Table 4 of the Synk and Swarthout report are reproduced in Table 9–1. Also shown are the number of studies and the number of employees on which each of the weighted average correlations is based.

TABLE 9–1   Weighted Average Job Family Correlations for Black and Nonminority Employees

Job Family	Number of Studies	Blacks		Nonminorities	
		N	Average Correlation	N	Average Correlation
I	5	196	−.01	624	.05
II	1	44	.11	81	.07
III	1	66	.19	291	.27
IV	62	3,886	.15	9,938	.19
V	44	3,662	.12	4,834	.20

SOURCE: Based on U.S. Department of Labor. 1987. *Comparison of Black and Nonminority Validities for the General Aptitude Test Battery.* USES Test Research Report No. 51. Prepared by David J. Synk and David Swarthout, Northern Test Development Field Center, Detroit, Mich., for Division of Planning and Operations, Employment and Training Administration. Washington, D.C.: U.S. Department of Labor, Table 4.

As the table shows, the average correlation for black employees is smaller than the corresponding average correlation for nonminority employees for all but Job Family II, in which case the results are based on only one study with a relatively small sample of employees. The difference in the average correlations for black and nonminority employees is statistically significant according to the critical ratio test reported by Synk and Swarthout for Job Families IV and V.

Synk and Swarthout did not present more detailed information about the distributions of the validity coefficients for the two groups within each job family. However, the Northern Test Development Field Center of the U.S. Department of Labor made data available to the committee that we used to compute correlations between the job-specific GATB composite and criterion measures. These correlations were computed separately for each job with at least 50 black *and* 50 nonminority employees with GATB scores and scores on the criterion measure. The data files overlap with those used by Synk and Swarthout, differing mainly in the number of studies, since only studies that included at least 50 people in each group were used in the present analyses. As before, the criterion measure is based on supervisor ratings in most cases, usually the Standard Descriptive Rating Scale.

A total of 72 studies had at least 50 black and 50 nonminority employees. The 72 studies included a total of 6,290 black and 11,923 nonminority employees, for an average of about 87 black and 166 nonminority employees per study. The number of black and nonminority employees per study ranged from 50 to 321 and from 56 to 761, respectively.

The correlation between the GATB composite and the criterion measure was larger for the sample of nonminority employees than for the sample of black employees in 48 of the 72 studies. The average correlation (weighted for sample size) of the job-appropriate GATB composite with the criterion measure was .19 for nonminority employees. The corresponding weighted average for black employees was .12. Thus, the finding of Synk and Swarthout that the average correlation is smaller for blacks than for nonminorities is confirmed in our analysis.

A more detailed comparison of the distributions of correlations between the GATB composite and the criterion measure for the two groups is shown in the stem-and-leaf chart in Table 9–2. The stem-and-leaf chart can be read like a bar chart. The numbers in the center between the brackets give the first digit (i.e., tenths) of the correlation. The numbers to the left give the hundredths digit for each of the 72 correlations based on black employees, and the numbers to the right give the hundredths digit of the 72 correlations based on nonminority employees. For example, in one study the correlation for black employees was .42. That study

TABLE 9–2   Stem-and-Leaf Chart of the Correlations of the Job-Appropriate GATB Composite with the Criterion Measure for Black and Nonminority Employees (stem = .1; leaf = .01)

Leaf for Blacks	Stem	Leaf for Nonminorities
	[.5]	1
	[.4]	
2	[.4]	1
97	[.3]	57778
4430	[.3]	00023
8876665	[.2]	55567788
442200	[.2]	022222333444444
99888776666655	[.1]	55557788889
433222110	[.1]	022234444
98877665	[.0]	5557789
443311111000	[.0]	1133444
300	[−.0]	44
877	[−.0]	7
0	[−.1]	
55	[−.1]	

Median, blacks = .13	Median, nonminorities = .185

is depicted by the leaf of 2 to the left of the [.4]. The 1 to the right of the [.4] represents a study where the correlation for nonminority employees was .41.

As the table shows, there is a general tendency for the distribution of correlations to be higher for nonminorities than for blacks. The difference in medians (.185 versus .13) is similar to the difference in sample-size-weighted means (.19 versus .12). The 25th and 75th percentiles are .11 and .25 for the distribution of correlations based on nonminority employees; the corresponding figures for black employees are .03 and .21. The greater spread in the correlations for blacks compared with nonminorities is to be expected because the average number of black employees per study (87) is smaller than that for nonminorities (166). Hence, the correlations based on data for blacks have greater variability due to sampling error. Nonetheless, for a quarter of the studies, the correlation for blacks is .03 or less.

The above results give only a global picture for one of the minority groups of interest. However, the results raise serious questions about the degree of validity of the job family composites for blacks, especially in Job Families IV and V for which the results are based on a sizable number of studies and large samples of black employees. Not only are the average validity coefficients lower for blacks than for nonminorities, but the level of the correlation for blacks is also quite low.

Comparisons of validity coefficients for other racial or ethnic groups would be of value but data are not presently available. Comparisons of validity coefficients for men and women, however, have been reported by Swarthout, Synk, and Goode (U.S. Department of Labor, 1984a).

Swarthout, Synk, and Goode analyzed the results of 122 Specific Aptitude Test Battery validation studies conducted since 1972 in which there were at least 25 men *or* 25 women. Only 37 of these studies had at least 25 male *and* 25 female employees. For those 37 studies the weighted average validity of the nine aptitude scores for men and women was reported. Except for manual dexterity, for which the average validity was .05 higher for women than for men (.14 versus .09), the average validities for men and women did not differ by more than .02 on the remaining eight aptitudes.

Unfortunately for present purposes, the comparisons of the validities of the job family composites were reported for all studies that had the minimum number of men or 25 women. Thus the averages for men and women are based on overlapping but not identical sets of studies. Since the available studies in Job Families I, II, and III were all single-sex studies, only the results from the Swarthout, Synk, and Goode research for Job Families IV and V are summarized in Table 9–3. As the table (which was taken from Table 6 of the Swarthout, Synk, and Goode research) shows, the weighted average validity for women is quite similar to the corresponding value for men in both job families. Although caution is needed in interpreting these results because the averages for men and women are not based on identical sets of studies, there does not seem to be any indication that the GATB composites for Job Families IV and V are any less valid for women than for men. It might be noted, however, that the average validities reported here are higher for men and women

TABLE 9–3 Weighted Average Job Family Correlations for Male and Female Employees

Job Family	Men			Women		
	Number of Studies	N	Average Validity	Number of Studies	N	Average Validity
IV	51	8,793	.24	37	7,101	.25
V	23	2,365	.20	41	6,262	.22

SOURCE: U.S. Department of Labor. 1984. *The Effect of Sex on General Aptitude Test Battery Validity and Test Scores.* USES Test Research Report No. 49. Prepared by Northern Test Development Field Center, Detroit, Mich., for Division of Counseling and Test Development, Employment and Training Administration. Washington, D.C.: U.S. Department of Labor, Table 6.

than the averages that were presented earlier for blacks and nonminorities. Recall that the average weighted validities reported by Synk and Swarthout for blacks in Job Families IV and V were only .15 (based on 62 studies) and .12 (based on 44 studies), respectively (U.S. Department of Labor, 1987).

DIFFERENTIAL PREDICTION

As has already been noted, differences in validity coefficients are related to differential prediction, but the two are not identical and the latter concept is more relevant to determining if predictions based on test scores are biased against or in favor of members of a particular group. According to *Standards for Educational and Psychological Testing* (American Educational Research Association et al., 1985:12):

There is differential prediction, and there may be selection bias, if different algorithms (e.g., regression lines) are derived for different groups and if the predictions lead to decisions regarding people from the individual groups that are systematically different from those decisions obtained from the algorithm based on the pooled groups.

The *Standards* (p. 12) go on to discuss differential prediction in terms of selection bias:

[In the case of] simple regression analysis for selection using one predictor, selection bias is investigated by judging whether the regressions differ among identifiable groups in the population. If different regression slopes, intercepts, or standard errors of estimate are found among different groups, selection decisions will be biased when the same interpretation is made of a given score without regard to the group from which a person comes. Differing regression slopes or intercepts are taken to indicate that a test is differentially predictive of the groups at hand.

Since the available reports comparing validities do not provide direct evidence regarding the possibility of differential prediction, the committee conducted analyses for this report. Data for these analyses were provided by the Northern Test Development Field Center of the U.S. Department of Labor. The data tape that was provided contained studies used in the Synk and Swarthout comparison of validities for black and nonminority employees (U.S. Department of Labor, 1987).

Although the data tape contains a variety of other information, only one criterion measure and one test-based predictor were used in the analyses reported here. The criterion measure is the same as the one used by Synk and Swarthout. Thus, with the exception of a few studies, the criterion measure is based on supervisor ratings, usually the Standard Descriptive Rating Scale. The predictor is the job family composite appropriate for the job family to which each study is assigned. Group membership was indicated by a variable that identified the individual as black, Native American, Asian, Hispanic, or nonminority. Only individuals identified as either black or nonminority were included in the analyses.

For each of the 72 Specific Aptitude Test Battery validation studies in the data file that had data for 50 or more black and 50 or more nonminority individuals, the following statistics were computed separately for each group and for the total combined group: the mean and standard deviation of the job family composite test score and criterion measure, the correlation between the composite test score and the criterion measure, the slope and intercept of the regression of the criterion measure on the composite test score, and the standard error of prediction. Within each study the regression equations were compared by testing the significance of the difference between the slopes, and if the slopes were not significantly different, the significance of the difference between the intercepts of the regression equations.

Standard Errors of Prediction

The standard error of prediction is based on the spread of the observed scores on the criterion measure around the criterion scores that are predicted from the test scores using the regression line. A larger standard error of prediction indicates that there is more spread around the regression line, and hence the prediction is less precise. If the standard error of prediction was consistently larger for one group than for another, then one could conclude that the errors of prediction were greater for the group with the larger standard error, and hence that the predictor is less useful for that group.

The standard error of prediction was larger for blacks than for nonminorities in 40 of the 72 studies, whereas the converse was true in the remaining 32 studies. Since the standard error of prediction increases as the correlation decreases, one might have expected more of a tendency for the standard error of prediction to be larger for blacks than for nonminorities due to the previously discussed difference in correlations. However, the standard error of prediction also depends on the standard deviation of the criterion scores. Indeed, when the correlations are as low as those typically found between the GATB composite and the criterion measure, the standard error of prediction is dominated by the standard deviation of the criterion scores. Thus, the fact that the standard error of prediction is larger for blacks than for nonminorities only slightly more often (56 percent of the studies) than it is smaller (44 percent) is not inconsistent with the typical difference in correlations.

Slopes

The slopes of the regression of the criterion scores on the job family GATB composite scores were significantly different at the .05 level in only 2 of the 72 studies. The number of significant differences in slopes at the .10 level was 6 of the 72; in 4 of the latter 6 studies, the slope was greater for nonminorities than for blacks, whereas the converse was true in the other 2 studies. Although these results suggest that slope differences are relatively rare, it should be noted that the test for differences in slopes for the two groups in an individual study has relatively little power for the typical sample sizes of the studies.

A more sensitive comparison of the slopes is provided by considering the full distribution of the 72 *t*-ratios computed to test the difference between the slopes obtained for the two groups on a study-by-study basis. A positive *t*-ratio indicates that the slope for nonminority employees is greater than the slope for black employees, albeit not necessarily significantly greater. Conversely, a negative *t*-ratio indicates that the slope for black employees is greater than that for nonminority employees.

The distribution of the *t*-ratios for the tests of differences between slopes for the two groups is shown in the stem-and-leaf chart in Table 9–4. If the pairs of slopes differed only due to sampling error in the 72 studies, positive and negative *t*-ratios would be equally likely and the mean of the 72 *t*-ratios would differ from zero only by chance. As can be seen, positive *t*-ratios outnumber negative ones almost two to one (47 versus 25). The mean of the 72 *t*-ratios is .30, a value that is significantly greater than zero. Thus, there is a tendency for the slope to be greater for

TABLE 9–4   Stem-and-Leaf Chart of the *t*-Ratios for the Tests of Differences Between the Slope of the Regression Based on Data for Black and Nonminority Employees in 72 Studies (stem = 1; leaf = .1)

Stem	Leaf	Count
2	01	2
1	5579	4
1	001112222333444	15
0	555666667888999	15
0	01122233444	11
−0	0012334444	10
−0	56667	5
−1	1233444	7
−1	589	3

NOTE: Median = .45.

nonminorities than for blacks, but the differences are generally not large enough to be detected reliably in an individual study because of relatively small samples of people in each group.

The tendency for the slope to be somewhat greater for nonminorities than for blacks is consistent with the finding that, on average, the correlation between the GATB composite and the criterion measure is higher for nonminorities than for blacks. When slopes are unequal, then the difference between the predictions based on the equations for the two groups will vary depending on the value of the score on the GATB composite.

The practical implication of the difference in slopes depends on the relationship of the two regression lines. When the regression line for nonminorities not only has a steeper slope but also is above the regression line for blacks throughout the range of GATB scores obtained by blacks, then blacks will be predicted to have higher criterion scores if the equation for nonminorities is used than if the equation based on the data for blacks is used. However, the difference will be greater for blacks with relatively high GATB scores than for blacks with relatively low scores. Other combinations are, of course, possible when the slopes differ. However, as we show below, the above pattern is most common.

Intercepts

For the 70 studies in which the slopes were not significantly different at the .05 level, a pooled within-group slope was used and the difference in intercepts for the two groups was tested. In 26 of the 70 studies the intercepts were significantly different at the .05 level. Even with a significance level of .01, 20 of the studies had significantly different intercepts. In all 20 of the latter cases, the intercept for the nonminority employees was greater than the intercept for the black employees. This was also the case for five of the six studies in which the difference was significant at the .05 level but not at the .01 level. Thus, in only 1 of the 26 studies in which the intercepts were significantly different was the intercept greater for black than for nonminority employees.

To get a sense of the magnitude of the difference in intercepts, the intercept for black employees was subtracted from the intercept for nonminority employees and the difference was divided by the standard deviation of the criterion scores based on the sample of black employees. The latter step was taken, in part, to account for differences in the criterion scale from one study to another and, in part, to express the difference in a metric that is defined by the spread of the scores for one of the groups. The distribution of these standardized differences in intercepts is shown in the stem-and-leaf chart in Table 9–5. (Note that all 72

TABLE 9-5   Stem-and-Leaf Chart of Standardized Differences in Intercepts of Regression Lines for Black and Nonminority Employees (stem = .1; leaf = .01)

Stem	Leaf	Count
.8	11	2
.7	1	1
.6	1	1
.5	0122499	7
.4	2233499	7
.3	012233457	9
.2	13455678999	11
.1	1111455999	10
.0	444555777999	12
−.0	0123349	7
−.1	126	3
−.2		0
−.3	04	2

NOTE: Median = .235.

studies are included in the distribution, even though 2 of the studies had significant differences in the slopes, suggesting that a pooled, within-group slope is not entirely appropriate.)

As the table shows, the difference is positive more often than it is negative, with a median value roughly equal to one-quarter of the standard deviation of criterion scores for black employees. Values of these standardized differences in intercepts that are greater than zero indicate that the performance that would be predicted for a given test score would be higher if the equation with the pooled, within-group slope but the intercept for nonminority employees were used than if the equation with the intercept for black employees were used. With positive values the nonminority equation would tend to overestimate the criterion performance of black employees. The converse is true for standardized differences that are less than zero.

Predictions Based on the Total Group

In practice, if a single regression equation were to be used to predict the criterion performance of applicants, presumably it would not be either of the within-group equations that was used to test the differences in intercepts. Rather, a total-group equation based on the combined groups would be used. Therefore, the regression equation based on the combined group of black and nonminority employees was estimated for each study.

TABLE 9–6   Stem-and-Leaf Chart of Standardized Difference in Predicted Criterion Scores Based on the Total-Group and Black-Only Regression Equations: GATB Composite Score = Black Mean Minus One Standard Deviation

Stem	Leaf	Count
.3	01568	5
.2	01112236	8
.1	01244457889	11
.0	0112222333455566677889999	25
−.0	00111111223567788	17
−.1	0015	4
−.2	3	1
−.3	2	1

NOTE: Median = .05.

The potential impact of using a total group regression equation to predict the criterion performance of black employees was evaluated by computing the predicted scores that would be obtained using the total-group equation and comparing those predictions to the values that would be obtained using the corresponding equation based on black employees only. More specifically, at each of three score values on the GATB job family composite, two scores were obtained: the predicted criterion score based on the total-group equation and the predicted criterion score based on the equation for black employees only. The latter predicted value was subtracted from the former and, as before, the difference was divided by the standard deviation of the criterion scores for black employees to take into account between-study differences in the metric of the criterion measure. The three levels of GATB job family composite score that were used were (1) the mean for black employees in the study minus one standard deviation for those employees, (2) the mean for black employees, and (3) the mean plus one standard deviation.

The distributions of these standardized differences in predicted scores are shown in the stem-and-leaf charts in Tables 9–6, 9–7, and 9–8, one for each of the predictor score levels used in the calculations. Analogous to the above intercept comparisons, a positive number indicates that the predicted criterion performance of a black employee with the selected GATB composite score is higher when the total-group equation is used than when the equation for black employees only is used. In this case the total-group equation is said to overpredict or to provide a prediction that is biased in favor of black employees with that GATB composite score. Conversely, negative numbers would be said to underpredict or to yield

TABLE 9–7   Stem-and-Leaf Chart of Standardized Difference in Predicted Criterion Scores Based on the Total-Group and Black-Only Regression Equations: GATB Composite Score = Black Mean

Stem	Leaf	Count
.4	011	3
.3	012358	6
.2	222345588	9
.1	0022223333334555666778999	25
.0	0122223345556666788	18
−.0	12223446	8
−.1	138	3

NOTE: Median = .13.

predictions that are biased against black employees with that GATB composite score.

Although there is substantial variation from study to study, a large amount of which would be expected simply on the basis of sampling variability, there is some tendency for the standardized difference in predicted criterion scores to be positive. The tendency is weakest at the lowest predictor score value (median = .05) and strongest at the highest predictor score value (median = .18). The latter difference is a consequence of the total-group slope typically being slightly greater than the

TABLE 9–8   Stem-and-Leaf Chart of Standardized Difference in Predicted Criterion Scores Based on the Total-Group and Black-Only Regression Equations: GATB Composite Score = Black Mean Plus One Standard Deviation

Stem	Leaf	Count
.6	133	3
.5	011	3
.4	2567	4
.3	01235588	8
.2	00123456788999	14
.1	00244567788889	14
.0	1122233345677	13
−.0	0222445667	10
−.1	27	2
−.2		0
−.3	4	1

NOTE: Median = .18.

slope for black employees only, and it is consistent with the finding noted above that there is a tendency for the slope based on data for nonminorities to be somewhat greater than the slope based on data for blacks.

The above results suggest that the use of a total-group regression equation generally would not give predictions that were biased against black applicants. If the total-group equation does give systematically different predictions than would be provided by the equation based on black employees only, it is somewhat more likely to overpredict than to underpredict. These results are generally consistent with results that have been reported for other tests. As was noted by Wigdor and Garner (1982: 77), for example:

Predictions based on a single equation (either the one for whites or for a combined group of blacks and whites) generally yield predictions that are quite similar to, or somewhat higher than, predictions from an equation based only on data from blacks. In other words, the results do not support the notion that the traditional use of test scores in a prediction yields predictions for blacks that systematically underestimate their performance.

In considering the implications of these results, it is important to note that the criterion measure in most cases consisted of supervisor ratings. Any interpretation of the results depends on the adequacy of the criterion measure, including the lack of bias. In addition, it is important to recall that the correlation of the GATB composite with criterion performance is generally low for black employees (weighted averages of only .15 and .12 for Job Families IV and V, according to the summary reported by U.S. Department of Labor, 1987).

Given the low correlation and the substantial difference in mean scores of blacks and whites on the GATB, use of the test for selection of black applicants without taking the applicant's race into account would yield very modest gains in average criterion scores but would have substantial adverse impact. It is within this context that the differential prediction results need to be evaluated.

Performance Evaluation and the Issue of Bias

It is often demonstrated in the psychological literature that supervisor ratings are fallible indicators of job performance (e.g., Alexander and Wilkins, 1982; Hunter, 1983). In order to combat some of the weaknesses of the genre, a specially developed rating form, the Standard Descriptive Rating Scale, is used for most of the GATB criterion-related validity studies. Raters are told that the information is being elicited only for research purposes, not for any operational decisions.

Nevertheless, the possibility of racial, ethnic, or gender bias contaminating this kind of criterion measure is an issue deserving attention.

Although common sense suggests that evaluations of the performance of blacks or women might well be depressed to some degree by prejudice, it is difficult to quantify this sort of intangible (and perhaps unconscious) effect.

Two recent surveys draw together the efforts to date. Kraiger and Ford (1985) and Ford et al. (1986) provide meta-analyses of the presence of race effects in various types of performance measures. The first review (Kraiger and Ford, 1985) examines the relation between race and (subjective) performance ratings. A total of 74 studies were located, 14 of them using black as well as white raters. The analysis reveals the existence of a suggestive rater-ratee interaction: white raters rated the average white ratee higher than 64 percent of the black ratees, and black raters rated the average black ratee higher than 67 percent of the white ratees.

For white raters, there was sufficient variability and a sufficient number of studies to evaluate the effect of moderator variables. (Although there was more variability for black raters, there were too few studies to perform the moderator analysis.) The authors found a significant ($p < .10$) inverse correlation between the percentage of blacks in a sample and the difference in the average rating. The higher the percentage of blacks, the less the difference. The three remaining moderator effects had nonsignificant effects. Rater training (which may or may not have discussed race) had no impact. The purpose for obtaining the ratings, either for real, administrative reasons or for research only, had no impact. Although there appeared to be a tendency for behaviorally based rating scales to show a greater difference between blacks and whites than did trait scales, it was not significant.

Because the 1985 study was limited to subjective ratings, the authors could not attempt to estimate the relative contributions of ratee performance and rater bias to the differences in ratings found for blacks and whites. The second paper (Ford et al., 1986) represents a preliminary attempt to address the issue of the extent to which race differences in assessments of job performance are the product of meaningful performance differences or the product of rater bias. Ideally, one would have a perfect criterion, one without limitation or bias, that would provide a perfectly accurate measure of job performance for blacks and whites. In the absence of such an ultimate criterion, the authors seek to advance our understanding by looking at the extent of racial differences for objective and subjective ratings of performance.

Ford and colleagues identified 53 studies, published and unpublished, that reported at least one objective performance measure and one subjective rating for a sample of black and white workers. Comparisons are reported for three types or aspects of performance: absenteeism and tardiness; cognitive performance; and direct performance such as units produced, accidents, or customer complaints. The meta-analysis cumulated correlations between race and objective indices of performance and subjective ratings of performance in order to compute mean effect sizes and variances across studies.

For the purposes of the committee's study, Ford and colleagues (1986) make a number of interesting observations. First, they report a relatively high degree of consistency in overall effect sizes across multiple criterion measures; in other words, there are similar magnitudes of difference between blacks and whites no matter what kind of performance is measured or what kind of measurement is used (the effect size ranges from .11 to .34).

Second, contrary to conventional wisdom, they found that the effect sizes for objective and subjective performance criteria were virtually identical. They report (1986:Table 1) for the total sample a mean effect size of the correlation (corrected for unequal sample sizes and attenuation) between ratee race and performance measure of .21 for objective criteria and .20 for subjective criteria. One conclusion that the authors draw from this is that the race effects found in subjective ratings cannot be attributed solely to rater bias.

Interestingly, the biggest reported differences in measured performance between blacks and whites are associated not with the type of criterion measure (objective or subjective) but with the type of performance measured. The biggest mean effect sizes with both objective and subjective measure were for cognitive performance—.34 and .23, respectively. In comparison, the effect sizes for direct performance were .16 for objective measures and .22 for subjective measures. Note that although race differences are smaller when measures of direct performance are used than when cognitive performance measures are used, all measures of on-the-job performance produce much smaller differences in scores between blacks and whites than do predictor tests such as the GATB, on which blacks are typically found to score about one standard deviation below whites. We will return to this subject in Chapter 13.

The studies reported here point up the need for more attention to the matter of performance differences between blacks and whites and the extent to which measured differences reflect meaningful differences in employee performance or are the consequence of bias in the measurement technique.

With regard to the immediate purpose of evaluating the GATB validation research, the possibility of bias in the criterion measure adds further grounds for caution in interpreting the validity of the GATB for minority applicants. The U.S. Employment Service's long-term research agenda should include the task of exploring the influence of bias on supervisor ratings.

CONCLUSIONS

Differential Validity by Race

1. Analysis of the 72 GATB validity studies that had at least 50 black and 50 nonminority employees indicates that correlations are lower for blacks than for whites. The average correlation of the GATB composite with the criterion measure was .12 for black employees and .19 for nonminority employees. Moreover, for a quarter of the studies, the correlation for blacks is .03 or less.

These results raise serious questions about the degree of validity of the job family composites for black applicants. Not only are the average validity coefficients lower for blacks than for nonminorities, but also the level of the correlation for blacks is quite low.

Differential Prediction by Race

2. Are group differences in average test scores reflected in differences in performance? Analysis of the same set of 72 validity studies shows that use of a single prediction equation relating GATB scores to performance criteria for the total group of applicants would not give predictions that were biased against black applicants. That is, the test scores would not systematically underestimate their performance. A total-group equation is somewhat more likely to overpredict than to underpredict the performance of black applicants.

Criterion Bias

3. The results of our differential prediction analysis could be qualified by inadequacies in the criterion measure, including racial or ethnic bias.

Supervisor ratings are susceptible to bias. There is some evidence that supervisors tend to rate employees of their own race higher than they rate employees of another race. Real performance differences could thus be confounded with spurious differences in the performance measure used to judge the accuracy of prediction of GATB scores. This is an issue that should be part of U.S. Employment Service's long-term research agenda.

PART IV

ASSESSMENT OF THE VG-GATB PROGRAM

Part IV contains the committee's appraisal of the VG-GATB Referral System and consideration of the potential effects of its widespread use throughout the Public Employment Service. Chapter 10 lays out the plan for the VG-GATB system as it is envisioned by the U.S. Employment Service for its local office operations; discusses the claims that have been made for the system; and assesses the evidence available on its implementation from a small number of pilot studies. Chapter 11 discusses the likely effects of widespread adoption of the VG-GATB system on the specific groups involved: employers, job seekers, in particular minority job seekers, people with handicapping conditions, and veterans. Chapter 12 is the committee's assessment of the claims of potential economic benefits that have been made for VG-GATB referral, including both gains for individual firms and gains for the economy as a whole.

10

The VG-GATB Program: Concept, Promotion, and Implementation

When the U.S. Employment Service (USES) staff became committed to the VG-GATB idea, they envisioned not just a new role for the General Aptitude Test Battery (GATB), but a whole new regimen that would revitalize the Employment Service system and change its reputation as the referral service of last resort. Building on a shift away from the policy of the 1960s and early 1970s, with its emphasis on the needs of targeted groups of job seekers whom the government wanted to draw into the mainstream economy, those who developed the VG-GATB idea sought to reorient the Employment Service to the needs of employers and of the economy as a whole. Believing that service could be optimized for only one of the Employment Service's three clients—employers, applicants, and the nation (or economy) as a whole—they chose to concentrate on the employer (Hawk et al., 1986:2). They developed a plan for a thorough-going reorganization of the way local offices operate, a plan designed to rationalize the system, improve the quality of people referred to employers, and thereby attract more and better job orders.

In this chapter we present the plan worked out by USES staff for local office operations under the VG-GATB Referral System. We also discuss the sometimes ill-founded claims that have been made for the system and evaluate the results of VG-GATB referral as they have been documented in a handful of pilot studies.

CONCEPTUAL MODEL OF THE VG-GATB REFERRAL SYSTEM

As the details of the plan were worked out with the aid of a number of pilot programs, USES staff put together a conceptual model of the VG-GATB Referral System to assist local offices in transforming their operations. The document is not an official statement of policy, but was used widely in workshops and conferences for state and local Employment Service personnel. Although most of the offices using the VG-GATB Referral System added VG procedures on top of the existing system rather than replace the old procedures, it seems useful to look at the ideal version being promoted by USES. The following discussion is drawn entirely from the document, "Conceptual Model of Full Service Validity Generalization Local Offices" (Hawk et al., 1986).

At the center of the basic principles that inform the conceptual model of a fully implemented VG-GATB Referral System is the idea of high-quality service to employers (and to the economy). Flowing from that overriding goal is the principle that "almost all ES resources" should be devoted to activities designed to provide employers with the most capable available applicants, namely:

1. intake (reception and registration),
2. assessment (testing and evaluation of education, training, and experience),
3. file search, and
4. referral.

It follows in this plan that most applicants should be mainstreamed, that is, they should take the GATB and compete on an equal basis for available job openings. The model recognizes that the standard VG procedures are not applicable to some job seekers, including non-English-speaking and illiterate applicants and those with handicapping conditions. It is suggested that local offices maintain close ties with community organizations that are set up to handle people with such special needs so that they can provide efficient referral to the appropriate agencies. The Job Service itself would be reserved largely for the able-bodied and the competitive.

Figure 10–1 illustrates the full-service VG-GATB office. For convenience, the authors of the document have simplified operations somewhat. For example, file search for veterans, which would usually be a separate operation, is not separate in the figure.

The standard process moves in a straight line from top to bottom of the flow chart. A job seeker entering the VG-GATB Referral System goes first to reception, proceeds to group orientation and registration, and then on to GATB testing. Scores are entered into the (computerized) applicant file. As job orders come in, the best jobs are dealt with first. The files are searched starting with the highest scores so that the best available jobs and the best available applicants are matched. The final stage in the standard process is referral.

At each stage in the process, some individuals would be identified who either cannot participate in the standard process or who are unlikely to benefit from it. Listed at the right of Figure 10–1 are in-house and community services to which the local office can refer such individuals to help make them more competitive. The emphasis is on referring noncompetitive applicants to appropriate external services or assistance—public or private job training organizations, job finding clubs, remedial education, and self-improvement courses—so that, following remediation, they can reenter the standard referral process.

This plan envisions an active role for the Job Service staff in diagnosing the specific problems that prevent applicants from proceeding through the standard process and putting such people in contact with appropriate services. As the diamonds at the left of the figure illustrate, the model also provides counseling services for those in the applicant file who are not being referred because of low scores or lack of marketable skills, or who have a record of multiple unsuccessful referrals. This level of service would require automated file search and so would be possible only in local offices that have computerized files.

Group Orientation and Registration

One notable characteristic of the VG-GATB Referral System is the attempt to streamline the processing of applicants. Under the old procedures, each person entering the local office talks with an interviewer, who assists the individual in filling out an application form. In a busy office, this could entail long waits for the next available counselor. Orientation and application-taking in groups means that one staff member can take care of the preliminaries for many applicants at once and, in the authors' estimation, in about one hour's time. The conceptual plan suggests that orientation sessions be conducted as frequently as the number of people in the reception area warrants, and that the orientation include an overview of the Employment Service, a talk on the benefits of test-based referral, information on other services provided by the local office, and instructions on how to fill out the application form.

Part of the orientation is intended to convince applicants that it is in their interest to take the GATB, since most job orders will be filled using VG-GATB procedures. A brochure, "Doing Your Best on Aptitude Tests," is available, and formal pretesting orientation is suggested for those who seem very apprehensive.

194

SERVICES

A. Remedial Services
1. Vocational Rehabilitation
2. Remedial Education--ABE, ESL
3. Mental Health Clinics
4. Medical Services
5. Drug Rehabilitation Agencies

B. Vocational Skills Training
1. JTPA
2. Public Schools
3. Other Skills Training

C. Supportive Services
1. Day Care
2. Churches
3. Social Service Agencies
4. Eleemosynary Agencies
5. Advocacy Groups
6. Civic Organizations
7. WIN

D. Occupational Information
1. JIS
2. IJB
3. Job-Seeking Skills Workshops
4. Group Counseling
5. AIM/VIP–VG Manual Section C
6. SOICC
7. Test Interpretation Session

E. Attitudinal/Affective
1. Interviewing Skills Workshop
2. Job-Holding Skills Training
3. Job-Finding Clubs
4. Counseling
5. OJT/Work Experience
6. Self-Improvement Courses

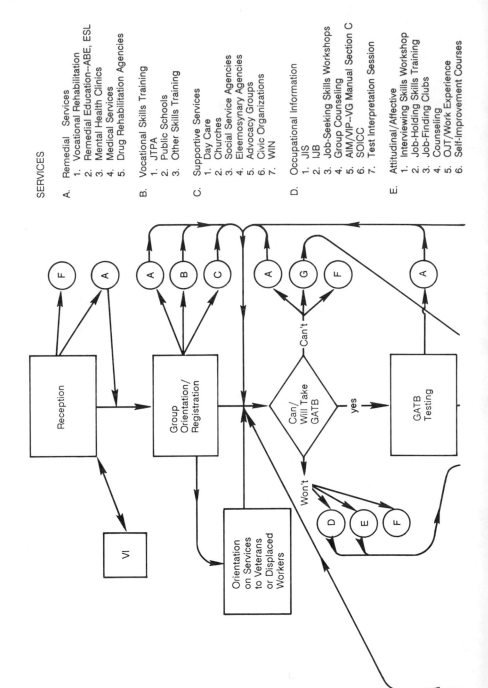

195

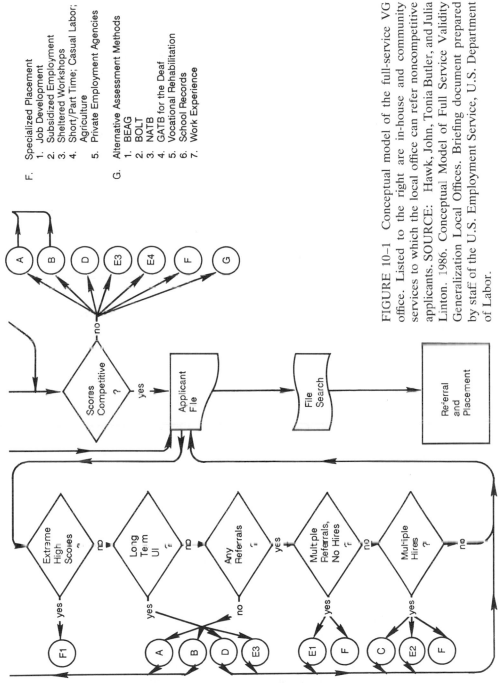

F. Specialized Placement
1. Job Development
2. Subsidized Employment
3. Sheltered Workshops
4. Short/Part Time; Casual Labor; Agriculture
5. Private Employment Agencies

G. Alternative Assessment Methods
1. BEAG
2. BOLT
3. NATB
4. GATB for the Deaf
5. Vocational Rehabilitation
6. School Records
7. Work Experience

FIGURE 10–1 Conceptual model of the full-service VG office. Listed to the right are in-house and community services to which the local office can refer noncompetitive applicants. SOURCE: Hawk, John, Tonia Butler, and Julia Linton. 1986. Conceptual Model of Full Service Validity Generalization Local Offices. Briefing document prepared by staff of the U.S. Employment Service, U.S. Department of Labor.

All applicants who can take the GATB would be scheduled during the orientation session to do so. Local office staff are reminded that special note should be made of any who require a special administration because of a handicapping condition; individuals whose handicap would interfere with performance on the GATB would be referred to a counselor for a personalized assessment and probable referral to a job development program. Such applicants would be exempted from the VG-GATB system.

Applicants who do not take the GATB, the document suggests, should be referred to a counselor for advice on remedial services, alternative assessment methods, or possibly special placement. Their applications would be entered into the file, but they should be informed that file search of tested applicants always precedes search among untested applicants. The files of those who take alternative tests can be placed in the regular VG-GATB file, but they must be flagged to indicate the need for special placement assistance.

GATB Testing

Testing is, of course, the centerpiece of the referral system. Once again, group processing is recommended; testing is by appointment so that the size of the group and the timing of test administration can be suited to local conditions. The conceptual plan emphasizes the importance of good test administration procedures, pointing out that test scores will have a large impact, whether positive or negative, on an applicant's job prospects, possibly over several years.

When the test has been scored, records of applicants with competitive scores are entered into the applicant file; those with very low scores are not likely to be referred under the VG-GATB system and, the document suggests, should probably be sent to a counselor so that the applicant can be directed to remedial services or vocational training available in the community. The counselor might also try a specialized placement such as subsidized employment programs or sheltered workshops.

File Search and Referral

When an employer places a job order, local office staff assign it a code number from the *Dictionary of Occupational Titles* (DOT) and, in the VG-GATB system, one of the five job family designations. The files are then searched for the applicants with the highest test scores in that job family; applicants are selected for call-in from the top down. If the job order imposes an experience requirement, then selection will be from the highest test score on down among those with the appropriate experience.

Veterans enjoy certain rights to priority in file search and/or referral, which must also be built into the file search system.

On the basis of the file search, applicants are called (in rank order of test score save for veterans' priority) and those interested in the job are asked to report to the Job Service office to schedule an interview with the employer and pick up a referral card. It is worthy of note that, whatever the other efficiencies of the VG-GATB Referral System, it does take the job seeker three trips to the local office to get a first referral. And the waiting time for some employers is also extended. Under the old system, most job orders tended to be filled from among those individuals who happened to be in the office. For an employer who needs someone on the job the next day, that system would be preferable. However, employers as well as job seekers who want to increase their options would probably benefit by the file-search and call-in method.

Office Automation

The operational efficiency of the VG-GATB system is heavily dependent on computerization of the applicant files. In describing the conceptual model of the VG-GATB local office, USES devotes a good deal of attention to the experiences of the various states that automated local office operations as part of the VG-GATB experiment. Some have been set up so that a central office receives the answer sheets and maintains the applicant files. In these systems, file search and job matching can be done on a central mainframe computer, and the information can be available across the state. A few states (Arizona, Missouri, Oregon, and South Dakota) have integrated systems; that is, the personal computers in the local office can send test data directly into the mainframe and receive information directly from it. This would seem to offer real advantages in states in which large employers draw from a number of local offices, as is the case with the automobile companies in Michigan. At some time in the future, it could also allow the job seeker to cast a wider net, if job order information for a region or the entire state were available at each local office. An analogy can be drawn to the military selection and classification system, in which 66 Military Entrance Processing Stations (MEPS) across the nation are linked to a central computer. Every potential recruit's test scores and other relevant data are entered directly into the central file, and job counselors at the MEPS have immediate access to information about the jobs available in their Service for which the applicant qualifies.

Many of the local offices that have introduced automation have adopted a decentralized system, with each office doing its own scoring and record keeping. Some have a mainframe, and some work strictly with personal computers. In some states, the local offices have their own scoring equipment but plan to link up with a central mainframe for file maintenance and file search.

The development of software for file maintenance and file search activities has been an important part of the VG-GATB experiment (and, more generally, of the modernization of Employment Service operations). Some states are using system-specific software, but over half the states have adopted a package called the Enhanced National Data System (ENDS) for at least some aspects of file management. And, since 1986, some have been exploring a job-match software package called On-line Data Display System (ODDS).

The conceptual document explains that automated file search, which it calls "job matching," is a key to efficient operation of the VG-GATB Referral System. It allows entry of the employer's selection criteria (e.g., years of experience, education or training requirements, cutoff score on the GATB below which the employer will not accept referrals) and virtually instantaneous identification of the pool of applicants with the highest percentile scores who also meet the employer's criteria. Software systems should be designed to allow keyword matching, the authors point out, so that more precise matching of employers' requirements and applicants' skills can be made than is possible under the very general DOT categories. Within a single DOT code, for example, an applicant's record might specify 46529 secretarial work, 46551 general clerical work, and/or 88595 word processing.

Comment on the Conceptual Model

There can be little doubt that the automation of Job Service operations offers enormous efficiencies when compared with manual file search. This is true whether or not the local office is using the VG-GATB Referral System. What is less clear, however, is how much the principle of top-down selection, which is the fundamental organizing principle of the VG-GATB concept, actually promotes higher quality in the group of applicants sent to an employer in response to a job order. Given the modest validities of the test, which mean that there is a great deal of error in the rank-ordering of applicants, and given the other important selection criteria already used to winnow the pool of applicants (experience, etc.), the increment of greater productivity contributed by test-based selection could be quite small indeed, particularly for jobs that require specialized training or experience.

PROMOTION OF THE VG-GATB REFERRAL SYSTEM

Many of the people involved in developing the VG-GATB system have been very enthusiastic about its potential. USES staff in the central office and in the regional Test Development Field Centers have advertised the merits of the system to the states and to Employers' National Job Service Committees and have worked hard to promote the VG-GATB idea throughout the Employment Service system. The supposed benefits to employers have been written about by a number of satisfied users in magazine and journal articles, both popular and professional.

Although the level of enthusiasm brought to this attempt to improve an important government service cannot but be praised, the committee is concerned by exaggerated and ill-supported claims made for the VG-GATB system, as well as by a noticeable lack of qualifiers and cautions. Our unease begins with the technical reports of the USES test research themselves. Reports No. 43 through No. 47 lay out the scientific basis for the generalizability of the GATB and the estimated economic benefits of the VG-GATB Referral System (U.S. Department of Labor, 1983a,b,c,d,e). These reports, written at a level accessible to the general reader, consistently present the most optimistic interpretation possible. In other chapters of this report we present specific critiques of the various claims made in the technical reports. Here we remark on the tone of the reports because of their influence on Job Service employees and clients who may not be in a good position to judge them critically.

For example, Report No. 43, a summary of John Hunter's research on the GATB, prepared by a private consulting firm, begins with the following claim (U.S. Department of Labor, 1983a):

The U.S. Employment Service can help to improve the productivity of American industry on the order of 50 to 100 billion dollars in the upcoming year. Sound ridiculous? Not at all. In fact, the impact of the Employment Service on the U.S. economy can be accomplished by a new use of an already established and widely accepted Employment Service device for matching people and jobs—the General Aptitude Test Battery—in a way that makes the best use of state-of-the-art research evidence.

The kindest interpretation of this claim is that it is the hyperbole of an enthusiast. Not only is it, as our analysis in Chapter 12 indicates, the product of a theoretical model based on slight empirical evidence; not only does it totally ignore the big difference between theory and likely effects in real-world applications; but it also chooses to express economic gains in a metric (aggregate dollar amounts) that is designed to impress, dazzling all but a small number of macroeconomists who can sensibly interpret numbers of this magnitude.

We cannot claim to have conducted a thorough investigation of the way the VG-GATB system is being advertised to employers and job seekers at the state and local levels. Most committee members have visited at least one local office. We have developed impressions based on information provided by members of our liaison panel. We have during the past 18 months or so received phone calls and letters, both solicited and unsolicited, from employers, job seekers who have taken the GATB, and people who work in the Employment Service system. And we have frequently found ourselves troubled by an overly optimistic assessment of the benefits and a downplaying of the potential legal problems with the VG-GATB Referral System.

For example, a small number of employers told the committee of their shock when the VG-GATB was challenged by the Department of Justice because of its score adjustment procedures. They felt that they had been led to believe that the VG-GATB system would solve potential legal problems by preventing adverse impact in their selection procedures, not make them vulnerable to charges of reverse discrimination. One can see at this distance that this misperception was partly a product of mistaking the Department of Labor's sponsorship of the VG-GATB as a more general stamp of approval by "the Government." But the misperception is also positively encouraged by some of the literature used to promote the system. One state uses a brochure to attract employer-clients that states:

The Legal Implications.

The legality of the General Aptitude Test Battery has been addressed in court cases. The courts have upheld GATB testing as fair and said the testing system conforms to EEOC guidelines.

As a matter of fact, the GATB has been the subject of very little Title VII litigation, too little to talk about "the courts." And the case that was almost certainly the basis for this claim (*Pegues v. Mississippi State Employment Service*, 699 F.2d 760 [1980]) is ambiguous at best. Brought in 1979, it involved a use of the GATB that predates the introduction of the VG-GATB system, with its claim of validity for all 12,000 jobs in the U.S. economy and its use of within-group scoring. In addition, although the trial court accepted arguments for the transportability of validities on the basis of early evidence from the validity generalization research, the appellate court ruled that, in the absence of adverse impact, the testing issue need not be addressed. That record is not sufficient to support the degree of legal acceptability implied by the brochure.

Although in these paragraphs we intend to communicate our very real concern with the way the VG-GATB Referral System has been promoted—and we recommend far more circumspection in the future—we must also take note of the severe budget reductions that have forced deep cuts in both staff and research resources at the national, state, and local levels of the Employment Service system in the past decade. The staff members who have become wedded to the new system have done so partly in response to this serious decline in resources. They have tried to do something about the situation—by reorganizing the system to make local operations more efficient, by attracting better job orders through advertising the presumed benefits of the VG-GATB to employers, and by finding ways to handle more job seekers in a given period of time to alleviate the effects of reduced staffing levels. For this they deserve kudos.

IMPLEMENTATION OF THE VG-GATB REFERRAL SYSTEM: THE PILOT STUDIES

One of the unfortunate consequences of the above-mentioned financial constraints has been that early plans for an ambitious program of pilot studies have gone astray. The empirical evidence of the effects of the VG-GATB Referral System that should have been abuilding in the past eight years has failed for the most part to materialize. States were encouraged to make a gradual implementation, accompanied by careful program evaluation. In most cases, however, these evaluations have been limited to comparing the number of placements made before and after VG-GATB procedures were introduced into an office, a comparison complicated by the downturn of the economy and large staff cuts at the time the experiments were started and by the fact that in most cases there was little disruption of existing practices.

Although 40 states have now introduced the VG-GATB system in one or more local offices, either to supplement or to replace traditional operations, only a few formal studies have been conducted to evaluate the effects of the system. The committee evaluated five pilot studies, two growing out of the very early experience with the new program in local offices in North Carolina and three that look at the effects on job performance in three firms. All the studies purport to show improvements attributable to the introduction of the VG-GATB Referral System in one or more of the following areas:

1. office effectiveness (number of placements made relative to available staff);
2. market penetration (Employment Service placements as a percentage of total new hires in the area); and
3. improved worker performance (measured in terms of absenteeism, quality of workmanship, disciplinary actions, training success, or productivity).

However, of the five studies conducted, only one, that by Madigan et al. (1987), satisfies rigorous research standards; the others can be considered no more than suggestive.

North Carolina Study of Office Effectiveness

The first study, based on data from 1981–1982, is one of two conducted by M.W. McKinney (1984) as part of the very earliest experiment with the VG-GATB Referral System. It is a study of local office effectiveness, comparing offices that did and did not use the new system. Data are presented on indices of effectiveness, work load, and two control variables for three groups of local offices: (1) seven VG-GATB offices in the Raleigh-Durham area; (2) the 48 remaining (non-VG-GATB) offices in North Carolina; and (3) a subset of seven from the second group that were matched on a one-to-one basis with the seven in the first group. Matching was on the basis of office staff numbers and insured unemployment rate.

Means are presented by group for both 1981 (before VG-GATB was implemented in any North Carolina office) and 1982 (after implementation at the seven pilot sites). These data show that between 1981 and 1982, the seven VG-GATB offices improved more than the other local offices with respect to the number of referrals and job placements made; staff "productivity" (number of placements made relative to the number of staff available); and penetration rate (the number of Job Service placements divided by the total number of new hires reported in the area served by the local office). There was no difference among the groups of offices in the mean increase in salary of the new hires.

No data are presented regarding the consistency of effects across the seven matched pairs of sites. Only weighted means are given, without explanation of how the weights were derived.

Although McKinney's findings are suggestive, there are several serious threats to their validity. The seven VG-GATB sites are all from the same part of the state, a design factor that, while convenient for operational reasons, could have influenced the results. At baseline (1981), the seven pilot sites differed substantially from the seven "matched" sites on some key variables. For instance, the seven VG sites were almost one standard deviation lower in productivity, and Raleigh had a disproportionately large demand for secretarial/clerical workers. The interpretability of the results is further blurred by the fact that the VG-GATB system was not even close to fully implemented at the seven VG-GATB sites. Only 18 percent of the applicants at these sites were tested in 1982 instead of the hoped-for 80 percent.

North Carolina Employer Survey

The second study, conducted by McKinney in 1983, was a face-to-face survey of 295 employers who were asked questions about their hiring practices and experiences and their attitudes toward the Employment

Service and the VG-GATB Referral System. The participants were among a larger group of employers who had been briefed on the VG-GATB system a year earlier.

Of the 173 employers who hired anyone during the 18 months of the pilot program, about 52 percent said that the VG-GATB system made the Employment Service more useful to them; 44 percent said applicant quality improved; and 25 percent said VG-GATB selection reduced training and other personnel costs. These variables appeared to interact with each other and with attitude toward the Employment Service.

Again, the results are suggestive, but there are problems with the survey. Employer impressions about hiring experiences were not verified against actual records, although this could have been done with the data base from the first study. Employers who hired hundreds of workers were lumped together with those who hired only one. And employers whose job orders were filled under the VG-GATB procedures were lumped together with those whose referrals may not even have been tested. Above all, the interviews were not neutral. They were conducted by staff working at the pilot study sites who began each session with the following statement:

We have found that Validity Generalization, or VG as we call it, has shown a positive relationship between General Aptitude Test Scores and success on the job.

The Philip Morris Study

D.L. Warmke (1984) conducted a study to assess the impact of VG-GATB hiring on worker performance. From a pool of 32,000 applicants, 1,200 employees were selected at a new Philip Morris plant in Cabarius County, North Carolina, using a four-step screening procedure. At each stage, the percentage of applicants screened out was:

Procedure	Screened Out (%)
Application	40
VG-GATB	51
Interview/physical	2
Noncompensated training	1

The study compared the performance of the 1,200 employees at the new plant to three other groups: (1) the 32 employees who transferred to the new plant from other plants, (2) employees at another Philip Morris plant, and (3) industry-wide averages. There were also comparisons to quality and production goals set by management.

Employees at the new plant performed better than those in the other groups. For instance, compared with the non-VG-GATB plant, the workers at the new plant had: an 81 percent lower lost-workday severity rate; a 59 percent lower quality-defect rate; 58 percent fewer disciplinary actions; and 8 percent greater success in training.

These improvements are attributed primarily to the VG-GATB because that procedure screened out about as many applicants as the other three hurdles combined. The credibility of this interpretation rests on the comparability of the comparison groups; however, there are no data to indicate the comparability. Were the same standards used in making application screening decisions at the VG-GATB plant and the other plant? Did the other plant screen out 40 percent of its applicants on the basis of the application? Did the other plant also have a 1:27 selection ratio?

Conspicuous by their absence are data contrasting the two plants on productivity goals set by management. And no data are provided regarding the correlation between GATB scores and performance measures.

The author recognizes that locational differences could explain the reported results. He argues against this interpretation because the 32 employees not selected by VG-GATB procedures who transferred from other plants did not perform as well in training as the others at the new plant. However, there is no reason to believe that the transfers were similar to the test-selected employees in other relevant characteristics, nor that the training results would carry over to job performance.

The Chrysler Corporation Study

The Northern Test Development Field Center (1987) of the USES conducted a study comparing the performance of 246 employees hired by means of VG-GATB scores with two other groups: transfers from other plants ($N = 422$) and rehires of people from other plants who had used up their recall rights ($N = 468$). Workers in the last group were selected on the basis of previous supervisor performance evaluations.

Five performance measures were used in the study: a supervisor rating of productivity, quality, tool use, job knowledge, adaptability, and overall ability; a supervisor's rank-ordering on overall quality of all of his or her employees; excused and unexcused absences; supervisor's rating of frequency of visits to the medical department; and recommendation to rehire.

On virtually all the measures, the new hires earned better scores than the transfers, who in turn earned better scores than the rehires. However, none of the differences was very large. For example, the VG-GATB group's mean on the first rating scale (productivity, quality, etc.) was only about one-quarter standard deviation above that for all employees. There was almost no variation on the recommendation-to-rehire measure—89 percent of the workers received the highest rating.

This study provides some support for the hypothesis that selection using the VG-GATB can enhance the quality of worker performance, but the magnitude of observed effects is quite small and could have been produced by factors other than the new referral system. (Were the new hires motivated by probationary status?) The study could be improved substantially by analyses that control for some important but unmeasured factors, such as age, sex, and job mix. It would also be useful to know whether the amount of job experience in the two comparison groups is positively correlated with performance.

The Sewing Machine Operator Study

By far the most ambitious and most successful study was that undertaken by the State of Virginia and conducted by Madigan et al. (1987). Its purpose was to assess the validity of VG-GATB selection procedures and to develop estimates of the potential economic benefit to the firm of using such procedures.

The study involved sewing machine operators in five plants owned by a manufacturer of casual wear. A group of 751 of a total of 932 new employees was tested with the GATB prior to hire, but their scores were not used in hiring. Within this group, 27 percent were black and 65 percent had no previous experience; all were women. Their mean VG-GATB Job Family V score was 51, with a standard deviation of 26 and a range of 1 to 99.

Since the job involves piecework, the performance criterion was actual production records plus supervisor ratings of quantity of output, quality of output, flexibility, dependability, receptiveness to instruction, and an overall rating. Turnover and reason for leaving were also recorded.

Employees were paid on a piecework basis and, within the limits of error of industrial engineering studies, employees who worked at the same rate of output but on different operations received the same pay. This allowed the computation of a "time-to-standard" measure (the number of weeks it took the employee to produce at a rate that would earn $3.75 per hour and $4.79 per hour).

An analysis of VG-GATB test scores by quarters of the distribution showed that employees in the higher quarters have generally better performance than those in the lower quarters. For example, the average number of weeks it took employees in each quarter to reach the $4.79 standard was:

Quarter	Weeks to Standard
4 (76–99%)	13.6
3 (51–75%)	14.4
2 (26–50%)	14.1
1 (1–25%)	16.4

The percentage of employees in a quarter who were black increased with quartile number; almost half of those above the third quartile (the highest scores) were black workers.

Comparison of experienced and inexperienced employees showed that they had similar GATB scores and percentages of black workers (29 percent and 24 percent, respectively). However, the experienced workers tended to reach the $4.79 standard faster, averaging 11.1 weeks to standard compared with 15.4 weeks for the inexperienced workers.

Correlations between GATB scores and monthly production averages were statistically significant and ranged from .15 to .24. In addition, turnover rates tended to be higher among those with lower scores.

This study is noteworthy because of the relatively large sample (751 employees), the lack of any restriction in range in that sample (the GATB scores ranged from 1 to 99), and the reliability of the criterion (objective measures of output). The results, since they require no corrections or adjustments, pretty well mean what they say: there is a tendency for sewing machine operators with high VG-GATB Job Family V scores to perform better and have less turnover than those with low scores. However, this relationship is not very strong: the average of all validity coefficients is about .20.

CONCLUSIONS AND RECOMMENDATIONS

Promotion of the VG-GATB Referral System

Conclusions

1. The VG-GATB Referral System is frequently oversold, both at the national and at the state levels. Much of the promotional literature that we have seen overstates the psychometric quality and predictive power of the GATB, underestimates the vulnerability of the referral system to legal challenge, and exaggerates the economic impact of preemployment testing.

2. The overselling of the VG-GATB system in Employment Service advertising is encouraged by the tenor of the technical reports describing the research that undergirds the referral program. They provide optimistic projections of the effects of VG-GATB referral for which the empirical evidence is slight.

Recommendations

1. Given the modest validities of the GATB for the 500 jobs actually studied; given our incomplete knowledge about the relationship between this sample and the remaining 11,500 jobs in the U.S. economy; given the Department of Justice challenge to the legality of within-group scoring and the larger philosophical debates about race-conscious mechanisms and the known problems of using a test with severe adverse impact; given the primitive state of knowledge about the relationship of individual performance and productivity of the firm, we recommend that the claims for the testing program be tempered and that employers as well as job seekers be given a balanced view of the strengths and weaknesses of the GATB and its likely contribution in matching people to jobs.

Implementation of the VG-GATB Referral System: The Pilot Studies

Findings

1. Although 40 states have introduced some form of the VG-GATB Referral System in a number of local offices, and a small number have experimented with the program statewide, only a few formal studies have been conducted to evaluate the effects of the program.

2. The five pilot studies evaluated by the committee showed some improvements resulting from introduction of the VG-GATB Referral System in one or more of the following areas:
   a. office effectiveness (number of placements made relative to available staff);
   b. market penetration (Employment Service placements as a percentage of total new hires in the area); and
   c. improved worker performance (measured in terms of absenteeism, quality of workmanship, disciplinary actions, training success, or productivity).

3. However, of the five pilot studies evaluated, only one satisfied rigorous research or evaluation standards. Although some of the other studies were suggestive, the committee cannot place a great deal of confidence in their favorable assessments of the effects of the VG-GATB Referral System, including the evidence of improved job performance.

Conclusions

1. There is too little evidence based on controlled, rigorous studies of the effects of using the VG-GATB Referral System for the committee to be able to assure policy makers at the Department of Labor that anticipated improvements have indeed occurred. This is not to say that they have not occurred. The evidence simply does not exist to establish the case scientifically. For the moment, policy decisions about the future of the VG-GATB Referral System will have to be made on the basis of more impressionistic and experiential information.

Recommendations

1. If USES decides to continue the VG-GATB Referral System, a series of carefully designed studies should be undertaken to establish more scientifically the efficiencies that are believed to result.

2. This research will need to be a cooperative effort, involving federal and state Employment Service personnel and employers. USES should encourage state Employment Security Agencies that deal with large employers (e.g., Michigan) and states that have fully articulated VG-GATB systems in place (e.g., Virginia, Utah, Oklahoma) to take a leading role in conducting studies to demonstrate the efficacy of the VG-GATB Referral System.

3. We also recommend that the employer community, as a potentially major beneficiary of an improved referral system, take an active part in the effort to evaluate the VG-GATB Referral System. The Employers' National Job Service Committee can help to identify appropriate employers who are willing to commit the resources necessary to study the effects of VG-GATB referral.

11

In Whose Interest: Potential Effects of the VG-GATB Referral System

The previous chapter described the U.S. Employment Service's (USES) conceptual model of local office operations under the VG-GATB Referral System. Although few offices have as yet switched entirely to the new system, most using some combination of old and new procedures, it is reasonable to ask what the effects might be if the full-scale version of the VG-GATB Referral System envisioned in the model were to be widely adopted in the Job Service. Indeed, the Department of Labor did ask the committee to consider the likely impact of widespread adoption on employers, minority job seekers, people with handicapping conditions, and veterans.

Our treatment of the question, covered in this chapter, is necessarily partly conjectural. There is very little systematic evidence available from the pilot studies that speaks to the question of impact on the various Job Service clients. In addition, the national reporting of data each year on aggregate Job Service operations was discontinued in 1985, so there is no longitudinal data base from which to glean any general before-and-after comparisons. Nevertheless, we have ourselves gathered, and we have received from our liaison group members and others in the interested communities, enough information to be able to suggest certain likely effects and to recommend alterations in USES policy in the interest of particular client populations.

EFFECTS ON EMPLOYERS

The VG-GATB Referral System is designed, in the first instance, to serve the interests of employers. Overall, GATB validities support the notion that referral on the basis of rank-ordered GATB scores will, in general, bring modest increases in the estimated job performance of the referred group of job candidates. In other words, using the VG-GATB Referral System as an initial screen will on average provide the employer with a somewhat more productive applicant pool than a nontested population would provide. This effect is, of course, not independent of the wages, benefits, and working conditions offered by the employer; the more competitive workers will actively seek referral to the top employers in a community. Moreover, the potential benefits to any given employer would be diluted as the number of competing employers using the test-based referral program increases.

Empirical support for the finding that top-down referral of tested applicants would in general provide the employer with a set of applicants with better-than-average estimated performance on the job is provided by the Madigan et al. (1987) study of sewing machine operators, described in the previous chapter. Workers with GATB Job Family V scores in the top quarter needed 13.6 weeks on average to reach a given production standard, whereas those in the lowest quarter of the distribution took 16.4 weeks to meet the standard. Correlations between GATB scores and monthly production averages ranged from .15 to .24. In addition, there was somewhat less attrition among the higher scorers. These results indicate that the clothing manufacturer could have had a slightly more productive work force by hiring on the basis of test scores, assuming there were enough job seekers in the area to allow for selectivity. If the job order for some 900 workers absorbed virtually all available labor in the area around the five plants studied, then the test data would be irrelevant.

A number of employers, liaison group members as well as others, contacted the committee about their experiences with the VG-GATB. As might be expected, those who took the effort to write or phone had found the test-based referral system valuable. One large midwestern corporation, which has used the Job Service as its sole supplier of semiskilled labor for many years, was able to compare the traditional and the VG-GATB procedures. With the advent of the VG-GATB system, the company began to look at candidates on the basis of test scores. The director of personnel reported a number of positive effects. First, the tested cohorts were more likely than their predecessors to show up for the entire application process, which involves repeat visits and multiple screens. Supervisors found that the workers selected on the basis of test scores worked out better on the floor, both in terms of performance and reduced absenteeism. One of the most interesting points made was that top-down referral of tested candidates produced a group with better literacy skills, which was considered a great boon in the auto industry because of the need to retrain large segments of the work force every three to five years.

Certain large employers have been attracted to the Job Service because of the introduction of the testing program. The director of the Virginia State Employment Commission and a member of the liaison group, Ralph Cantrell, reported to the committee that the two largest employers in the state list jobs with the Virginia Job Service solely because of its use of the test. Several employers new to the state have required test-based screening, including a major Japanese firm, which indicated that it had chosen to locate there at least in part because of the VG-GATB testing program. Cantrell also notes that a number of Virginia employers who have operations in other states report that the plants that select according to test score outproduce their counterparts.

An Informal Survey of Employers

Thanks to the good offices of the Employers' National Job Service Committee (ENJSC), these impressions can be fleshed out somewhat with information derived from an informal survey of employers who have used the VG-GATB system. A questionnaire, based on a set of questions provided by the committee, was put together by the ENJSC steering committee and sent to the state-level Job Service Employers' Committees for distribution to employers known to be Job Service clients. Some responses were returned to the ENJSC members for forwarding; others came directly to the committee. In all, some 500 employers answered the questionnaire.

Our discussion of the information provided by these employers must be prefaced by a caution about overreliance on the responses. The questionnaire was constructed informally and was not pretested. That some questions were occasionally misunderstood is apparent from the results. Moreover, the respondents cannot be considered representative of Job Service clients since the sample was not scientifically drawn. Within these limitations, however, we can learn a good deal about the practices and attitudes of 500 employers who have experience with their state Employment Service and the VG-GATB procedures.

Most of the employers who took part were medium-sized or small, with 64 percent reporting under 250 employees. The types of jobs they reported filling through the Job Service are largely blue-collar and clerical ones, although nearly a third of the respondents also use it to fill some technical positions.

How Respondents Use the VG-GATB Referral System

Virtually all the respondents reported that they use the VG-GATB system as a preliminary screen only. In all, 99 percent interview the applicants referred by the Employment Service, 94 percent require a written application, 80 percent reported using reference checks, and more than half administer a physical examination. A comparatively small number, about 16 percent, reported administering additional job-specific tests. (This response could be misleading; one suspects that many clerical job orders would require a typing test in addition to the GATB.)

Over half of the 500 employers in the survey said that they include specific selection criteria in their job order. The two most common requirements listed were job experience and the imposition of a minimum cutoff score on the GATB (each criterion used by about 51 percent of respondents), although over a third also reported imposing an education requirement. Some 72 of the 500 respondents said that they have the Job Service interview candidates for them.

One issue of interest to the committee was the number of candidates the employers request per job opening. Among the 500 employers who participated in this informal survey, there was a good deal of variety. Many left the number of referrals up to the Job Service local office. A small number reported that they request just one or two applicants per opening, and an equally small number ask for 11 or more. Most of those who stipulate a referral ratio ask for between 3 and 10 applicants per opening; the median is 5. This information suggests that USES could consider referral models that required two to five people to be referred for each job opening without going beyond the common practice of many employers.

Attitudes Toward the VG-GATB Referral System

A large majority of the respondents were favorably disposed toward the VG-GATB system. It is important to remember that this group cannot be considered representative of Job Service clients in general or of employers who have experience with the VG-GATB. We do not know how many employers received the questionnaire and did not respond, nor have we polled employers who choose to use the Job Service counselors in the traditional way rather than requesting tested applicants. This group of 500 respondents should probably be looked on as predisposed to a positive evaluation of the effectiveness of test-based referral. This does not mean that their judgments should be disregarded, just that they cannot be accepted as definitive.

Close to 90 percent of the respondents felt that the VG-GATB Referral System improved the company's use of human resources. Among the benefits most frequently checked off were decreased training time and reduced interviewing time. Over a third claimed increased productivity and a like number claimed reduced turnover. Only about 7 percent of respondents said that the system did not improve the use of human resources.

At the same time, about 37 percent wrote in disadvantages associated with the VG-GATB system. The most frequent complaint was the increased time lag between the employer's request and the filling of the job order.

Equal Employment Opportunity and Affirmative Action

More than three-quarters of the respondents reported that they have an affirmative action program in place. (Employers with fewer than 15 employees are not subject to Title VII of the Civil Rights Act, so the question would not necessarily be applicable to all who returned the questionnaire. In addition, a small proportion of the questionnaires omitted the question.) This would suggest that the general thrust of the USES policy of adjusting the scores of minority-group candidates is in step with the equal employment opportunity goals of many private-sector employers.

However, the responses to questions about preferred scoring methods suggest that many employers may not be very clear about that aspect of the VG-GATB system. On the questionnaire, the within-group score adjustment used in the VG-GATB system to avoid screening out minority job seekers was explained. The questionnaire then asked which of four scoring methods respondents find most advantageous: within-group percentile scores, total-group percentile scores, a combination of the two, or pass/fail. It provided a very brief explanation of the first two. Some 20 percent of respondents indicated a preference for a pass/fail scoring method, which means they either do not understand the new system or are not involved with it. Only about 10 percent chose the within group option, and a few of the respondents wrote in that they did not realize that the VG-GATB system included such score adjustments. About equal numbers of respondents chose the other two options, with 37 percent of respondents supporting the reporting of total-group scores and 35 percent supporting a system combining total-group and within-group scores.

During the course of its study, the committee heard a good deal of support for within-group scoring, particularly from larger employers. Because large employers of necessity have a trained personnel management staff, often including members with some expertise in tests and measurement, they may well be more aware of the implications of the various scoring procedures than this group of medium-sized and small employers seems to be. These responses appear to show a need for the Employment Service to provide employers with better information about the test scores reported and what they mean. We have specific recommendations on the subject in Chapter 13 on referral and score reporting.

Possible Negative Effects

To this point, the potential effects of further use of the VG-GATB appear to be largely salutary as far as employers are concerned. In general, selecting the group of candidates to refer on the basis of rank-ordered test scores should present the employer with a modestly enriched pool of candidates to choose from. There is theoretical as well as some empirical evidence to support this claim. The main drawback for the individual employer so far mentioned is that in some areas it takes longer for candidates to show up at the employer's door. If computerization of local office operations proceeds apace and if regional job information networks develop, this problem may be eased.

A different sort of problem could well emerge if the Department of Labor decides to support the spread of the VG-GATB system. This problem has to do with jobs that require significant prior preparation. The claim is being made that the GATB predicts performance for all 12,000 jobs in the U.S. economy, and that it predicts best for the cognitively more complex jobs. Although these claims may be true, they could also badly mislead employers. Until now, the preponderance of test-based referrals has been in less-skilled occupations, occupations that do not require extensive prior education and/or training. If for legal, economic, or other reasons employers eliminated more job-specific testing or assessment and depended on this test of general cognitive abilities to fill jobs with more stringent requirements, the more pertinent information about an applicant's qualifications could be lost. This is not merely an academic concern. At least one state is using the VG-GATB to construct the list of eligibles for state merit system jobs, including jobs such as social worker.

EFFECTS ON JOB SEEKERS

Logistics

The most obvious effect of the VG-GATB Referral System on job seekers is that they have to take a three-hour examination in order to be considered for referral. As we have noted, most local offices have implemented the new procedures as a supplement to, not a replacement of, the old counselor-based system. But the conceptual model of a full-scale VG-GATB system would close off the alternate route for most applicants, making the test a necessary hurdle. Since many local offices appear to administer the GATB just once a week, the applicant is likely to be required to make two trips to the Job Service office, once to register and again to take the test.

In contrast to the old system, this is not necessarily inefficient from the applicant's point of view. USES field staff who have helped implement the VG-GATB system argue that it is much less irksome for job seekers. They point out that in large, busy Job Service offices, applicants often have to wait around for hours until a job counselor is available. With the new procedures, applicants are given an appointment for a specific day and time, and thereafter could receive referrals by telephone.

There is some evidence of user attitudes that supports this assessment. K.D. Scott and colleagues (1987), as part of a larger pilot study commissioned by the State of Virginia, surveyed all job applicants who registered with the Roanoke Job Service Office and took the GATB between January and the end of April 1986. Almost 70 percent of the applicants, when presented with six possible reactions from "strongly disagree" to "strongly agree," agreed or strongly agreed that they "did not waste a lot of time at the JS." Over 80 percent found the explanation of the testing and referral process easy to understand, and about 88 percent found the people at the Job Service helpful and courteous. This degree of positive response suggests that, in terms of logistics, the VG-GATB system can work well for job seekers.

Perceptions of Fairness

User perceptions of the more substantive benefits of VG-GATB referral are somewhat less positive. A primary justification for standardized testing, and therefore for VG-GATB referral, is that all applicants are judged by an objective standard—in this case, an objective measure of abilities that are related to job performance. Proponents of the VG-GATB point out that eliminating the subjective judgment of counselors, who may be more or less able to match up suitable workers and jobs, can be particularly important for individuals who incite deep-seated social or cultural prejudices.

We agree that GATB-based referral could have a beneficial impact on job seekers—at least on competitive job seekers—by reducing the possibility of personal prejudice from referral decisions and by giving the Job Service staff a better picture of the relative abilities of all the registrants currently in the files. Particularly in heavy-volume Job Service offices, the identification of prospective candidates could be less hit or miss.

However, there are other aspects to the question. Tests of general ability such as the GATB are particularly valuable in assessing a youth population, people without a lot of life and job experience. The Armed Forces, for example, use a similar test to enlist and classify young men and women, most of whom are between the ages of 17 and 23. Although most have a high school education, few have specialized training or extensive job experience. In that circumstance, it is difficult to propose an alternative method of gauging an applicant's probability of success in the military.

The Job Service deals with a very different clientele. It includes people of all ages, many of whom have years of relevant job experience. For such applicants, GATB scores are not the most important information. The applicant's past record would give an employer a better sense of likely future performance. Exclusive use of VG-GATB referral could well preclude the candidate from being able to present—or the employer from being able to consider—that record. For example, the committee has heard the complaint of a worker who apparently worked successfully for more than 15 years at a semiskilled job in the auto industry. Now, after a period of illness, the worker is trying to get back into the same line of work. But the firm has entered an agreement with the Job Service so that access to the job is solely by test score. The worker is being told that his test scores do not qualify him for the work that he performed for many years. Without getting into the merits of the particular case, the general point is well made that exclusive reliance on the VG-GATB system would deprive some experienced workers of the chance to compete for jobs they have already shown that they can in fact perform.

There appears to be a significant degree of skepticism among job seekers about making testing a necessary prerequisite to referral. Veterans' organizations have protested the requirement on the grounds that many unemployed veterans neither desire nor need to take such a general test of abilities since, with an average age of 50, they have proven work experience and training on which to be judged. Among some population groups, the very existence of the VG-GATB will become a powerful screen; many people simply will not use the Job Service. For example, in one New Jersey office the experiment with the VG-GATB was cut short when the applicant population, a largely minority population, simply stopped using the Job Service.

The Roanoke survey (Scott et al., 1987) provides additional evidence of unease with the test-based approach to job referral. (Although there is less generalized resistance to tests in Roanoke than in the New Jersey community mentioned above, note that the kind of people who aborted the New Jersey experiment would not appear in the Roanoke survey sample, since only those who registered *and* took the GATB during a specified period were given the questionnaire.) The Roanoke applicants were asked to evaluate the following statements on a six-point scale from "strongly disagree" to "strongly agree":

- The GATB was a fair test of my job abilities.
- A test is a fair way to decide which people should be referred to a job.

Of the 1,064 usable questionnaires, some 60 percent of respondents registered at least slight agreement with each of the propositions, and 45 percent agreed or strongly agreed. But put the other way, about 40 percent of applicants did not perceive of the procedure as fair. (This perception of unfairness increased somewhat in a follow-up survey 12 weeks after registration and testing; 50 percent of those who responded had not yet been placed in a job.) There were no significant differences between minority and majority applicants with regard to the fairness questions, but applicants with advanced degrees (beyond high school) were less favorably disposed toward the GATB than others, which has implications for the USES hope that the VG-GATB Referral System will make the Employment Service a more mainline employment agency and help it shed its past reputation as a provider of last resort.

The evidence is far too limited to draw any broad conclusions about the public acceptability of test-based referral. Still, it seems to suggest that the elimination of other routes to referral could narrow the population of job seekers willing to work through the Job Service, and, in some communities, drastically so

Low-Scoring Applicants

For job seekers with very low scores on the GATB, VG-GATB referral will have predictable and completely negative effects. Such applicants will be referred only to the least desirable jobs, if they are referred at all. As we suggest elsewhere, there is a very real possibility that if the VG-GATB system came to dominate the Employment Service system, the effect would be to create a class of perpetually unemployed people, identifiable from early school years as those who are the poor performers on tests of general cognitive ability. Industrial society seems to require less than full employment. It does not require, however, that one category of citizen, low scorers on cognitive tests, be fated to permanent unemployment. Our analysis of GATB validities demonstrates that there is too much error in GATB scores for any argument from economic necessity to be compelling. Even low-scoring applicants have a reasonable chance of performing better than average on the job.

If the conceptual model of the full-service VG-GATB office incorporated special procedures for working with low-scoring applicants, our
concern about the rigidities and limitations of a referral system based on
cognitive test scores would not be as great. But in the VG-GATB system
as it is conceived, with the exception of statutorily mandated special
programs to assist handicapped veterans and perhaps handicapped applicants more generally, those most in need of special assistance in finding
work would be funneled out of the Employment Service system. We
realize that this design is a reflection of the economic stringency that has
descended on the Employment Service both nationally and in the states.
It is, nevertheless, one of the important considerations that leads us to
recommend that VG-GATB referral in no instance be the only set of
procedures used in any local office.

Older Applicants

The evidence presented in Chapter 8 indicates that GATB validities
vary with the mean age of workers in the validation samples. More
specifically, the validity of the cognitive composite (GVN) tended to be
somewhat lower in studies in which the average age of the workers was
higher. The evidence also suggests the possibility that GATB scores
decline with age. The worker samples with higher mean age have notably
lower composite scores, particularly for the spatial (SPQ) and psychomotor (KFM) composites.

This evidence raises the possibility that older workers—workers whose
skills and experience testify to their ability to do the job—will tend to be
excluded by the VG-GATB system.

EFFECTS ON MINORITY JOB SEEKERS

The single most important question with regard to the effects of the
VG-GATB Referral System on minority job seekers is whether the
government—in the near term the Justice Department, ultimately the
courts—find score adjustments a legally and constitutionally acceptable
means of furthering equal employment opportunity goals. Chapter 13, on
referral methods and score reporting, presents some scientific reasons in
support of such a policy. But of course we cannot predict the ultimate
outcome.

Recent experience in the Employment Service system indicates that
minorities have been referred and employed at the same rate as the
majority group, although on the average to somewhat lower-paying jobs.
So long as the VG-GATB Referral System includes within-group score
adjustments, that should continue to be the case. A recent study of the

application of the VG-GATB system in local Job Service offices in Salt Lake City, Provo, and Logan, Utah (Robins, 1988), sustains these expectations: minority applicants (who make up just 7.2 percent of the work force) were placed at a slightly higher rate and in jobs of slightly longer duration than the majority-group applicants. Furthermore, the patterns of service delivery to majority and minority applicants were similar for VG-GATB and regular local offices.

This would not be the case if VG-GATB referral were not accompanied by score adjustments of the magnitude of the within-group percentile scores. Without such adjustments, referral on the basis of rank-ordered test scores would have very severe adverse impact on black and Hispanic applicants. Empirical evidence indicates that the difference in average test scores between majority- and minority-group members ranges from 0.5 to 1 standard deviation. When the average score difference is 1 standard deviation, then referral in order of test score will mean that if 20 percent of an applicant pool is referred to a job, about 20 percent of majority applicants would be referred, compared with 3 percent of minority applicants.

Even if a minimum competency system were used, with all referred at random above a given cutoff score, a cutoff score at the 4th percentile of the majority group would be required for minority applicants to be referred at four-fifths the rate of majority candidates.

We conclude that the VG-GATB Referral System will be viable only if it includes some kind of adjustment of minority scores, so long as the government is committed to a policy of equal employment opportunity that looks to the effects of employment practices on racial and ethnic minority groups.

Assessing Applicants Who Have Marginal English Skills

Foreign-born applicants, whose command of the English (or perhaps any written) language is marginal, cannot be reasonably assessed with the GATB. In some states, particularly in the Southwest and the West, such people constitute a large proportion of the likely Job Service client population.

The problem was well expressed by a professional vocational evaluator working in the state of California (letter from Julia Edgcomb, dated November 23, 1988). Between 40 and 60 percent of this evaluator's clients are non-English-speaking; most of them have a maximum of six years of formal education, with three years being common. Many have been working since the age of 10 and are now trying to find careers outside farmwork. The GATB will portray these job seekers as of very low cognitive abilities because of language difficulties, lack of formal education, and lack of experience with paper-and-pencil tests. Yet many of them, in the writer's experience, are very bright and can demonstrate job-relevant skills in hands-on work simulations. By exclusive use of an instrument that does not permit such people to show their strengths, the Employment Service system would serve neither employers' nor workers' needs as well as it might.

EFFECTS ON PEOPLE WITH HANDICAPS

The populations most at risk of misassessment in a test-based referral system include people with handicapping conditions. Like certain racial and ethnic subgroups, people with many kinds of handicaps have lower scores on average than the majority group. Yet for other population groups, although there are some inconsistencies, the test scores have a fundamental comparability of meaning. No such claim can be made for the scores of people with handicaps. As a consequence, referral based solely on test scores not only would tend to screen out such applicants, but also would do so arbitrarily.

The difficulties of using standardized ability tests to assess people with handicaps were described in an earlier report emanating from the National Research Council (Sherman and Robinson, 1982). The goal of many such people is to participate fully in American life, a goal explicitly recognized as a right in such federal legislation as the Rehabilitation Act of 1973. In order to enter the economic mainstream, people with handicaps need to be able to demonstrate their qualifications. This is more or less difficult depending on the particular handicapping condition. Ability testing poses a quandary. If, on one hand, a test reflects a person's disability rather than the skills actually needed on the job, it becomes a barrier, a vehicle that frustrates that person's attempt to demonstrate job capabilities. If, on the other hand, there is no way for people with disabilities to compete with others for jobs or educational opportunities, they are all too likely to be sidelined.

The most obvious problem is that standardized tests often cannot be administered satisfactorily to people with physical handicaps. Various modifications have been attempted, for example, to provide Braille or oral versions for blind test takers or to modify the response mode for those with motor handicaps. Indeed, the history of nonverbal performance tests began with tests for hearing-impaired people (Anastasi, 1988:290–297). However, such modifications of format and/or content have unknown effects on the construct validity of the instrument and on the meaning of test scores.

The complexities of developing appropriate modifications have emerged gradually over the years. Some are fundamentally logistical, whereas others would have to be called epistemological. In the first category is the following kind of problem: the Employment Service of a northern state recently developed a videotape of a sign language administration of the GATB for use with deaf applicants. Because of its history of aptitude test research for the deaf, the USES Southern Test Development Field Center in North Carolina was asked to review the videotape. One of the things noted by their sign language specialist was the difference between the signing dialects in the two states. The sign that to its Nebraska audience means "exercise" is used in North Carolina to mean "ice cream" or "cold."

Although use of a nonlocal signer could obviously result in some very confused Job Service clients, this kind of problem in redesigning standardized tests for people with handicaps is easy to comprehend, and a good deal of progress has been made over the years in coming up with solutions. The most thorough and detailed documentation of modifications to an employment test was that provided for the Professional and Administrative Career Examination (PACE), a test developed and administered for years to entry-level federal employees by the Office of Personnel Management (OPM) (Nester, 1984). In its modifications for visually and hearing-impaired applicants, for example, OPM developed careful procedures to review item content for appropriateness, deleting items involving color or spatial patterns in tests modified for the blind, and so on. (Unfortunately, much of OPM's work in this area came to an end with the elimination of the PACE in 1981 because of EEO problems.)

The far more difficult issue concerns what is being measured. Are the cognitive processes used by blind test takers the same as those of the sighted? What is the the relation between verbal or linguistic abilities and cognitive abilities? If language is merely a vehicle for such cognitive abilities, is it possible for people who are profoundly hearing impaired to demonstrate cognitive abilities through other vehicles? Does test performance bear the same relationship to job performance for people with visual or hearing impairment as for others? Although research at the Educational Testing Service (ETS) and OPM has brought some interesting insights (Nester, 1984; Willingham et al., 1988), we are a long way from knowing the answers to these questions.

Recent Research Findings

Many of the research issues posed by the earlier National Research Council's Panel on Testing of Handicapped People (Sherman and Robinson, 1982) have been addressed in a four-year research project carried out by ETS and described by Willingham et al. (1988). The study involved two academic entrance examinations, the Scholastic Aptitude Test Battery (SAT) and the Graduate Record Examination (GRE). The subjects were a pool of handicapped applicants and a comparison nonhandicapped group attending the same colleges (for the SAT) and graduate schools (for the GRE). Admittedly, that research based on a college population and using tests designed to predict academic performance is not directly relevant to GATB applications, but its consideration may offer some guidance.

Some general features should be noted here. The handicapping conditions of the students in the study were four: hearing impairment, learning disability, motor handicaps, and visual impairment. These disabilities are listed in the order of the students' disparity from the nonhandicapped group. Clearly the language impairment of the deaf and (to a somewhat lesser extent) the learning disabled represents an extreme, special difficulty with the standard tests, especially the verbal part (U.S. Department of Labor, 1982). For these two groups the SAT-V(erbal) and the SAT-M(ath) are more independent than in the other handicapped groups or the nonhandicapped group. Neither the test scores nor high school grades predicted college performance as well as they did for the nonhandicapped group. Both scores and predictions are better for people with motor handicaps and visual impairment.

The National Research Council panel was especially anxious that research address the issue of comparability, that is, whether the standard and modified tests measure the same abilities and, if so, whether the scores from modified tests could somehow be transformed so as to yield the same scale of measurement as the standardized tests. The experience of the ETS research effort seems to indicate that such a transformation process is not within reach in the present state of the art. Among other things, any such transformations would depend on the availability of some measure of the degree of handicap.

The biggest stumbling block to score comparability is the sheer difficulty of gathering sufficient data to establish comparable scales empirically. Although the SAT is one of the three largest testing programs in the country and is supported by an extensive data base, the ETS research team had great difficulty assembling an "even minimally sufficient" data set to study the validity of scores on the modified versions of the SAT for predicting first-year grade-point average. It was virtually impossible to take account of degree of handicap, and even within type of handicap, the numbers of students for whom all data were available were often small.

Instead, the ETS authors look to more individualized testing procedures to improve the testing of handicapped applicants. In particular they emphasize the importance, in future research, of establishing an appropriate test time for each handicapping condition. Their report suggests that the greatest variable across modifications for the different groups was time—some handicapped groups taking as much as 12 hours for what was a 3-hour test for the nonhandicapped group.

Experience with the GATB

There has not been comparably extensive research on the use of modified GATB tests or test procedures for the handicapped. A series of technical reports from the Employment Security Commission of North Carolina, from the early 1970s to 1980s, does provide, however, considerable information on modified instruction for the deaf.

Several studies by the Employment Security Commission of North Carolina (1971, 1972, 1973) compared scores of high school juniors and seniors from the North Carolina School for the Deaf on the GATB with those on the Nonreading Aptitude Test Battery (NATB) and also compared their scores with nondeaf high school students, regular and educationally deprived. The principal variable in these studies concerned modifications in the instructions—whether through sign language by an expert signer or by newly written instructions that held vocabulary and sentence structures down to lower-grade usage in the elementary schools. Such modifications had a favorable effect on the scores for the deaf, but the scores for abilities G, V, and N still remained significantly lower than those of the nondeaf group. The authors point out that, although the NATB may give a clearer picture of abilities for the educationally deprived group, it does not for the deaf, whose scores on the GATB are either the same or slightly better than on the NATB. Although subsequent Department of Labor memoranda recommended the use of sign language interpreters for deaf applicants, particularly in a regional office where there were many deaf applicants, there was no clear advantage for the signed over the modified written instructions.

The clear disparity between the deaf and the nondeaf on verbal and cognitive factors (G, V, and N) would be especially penalizing in a referral system based on the VG-GATB, since the abilities in which the deaf show more normal scores are less heavily weighted in computing total scores.

We are not aware of validation studies with any of the handicapped groups that relate their GATB score to job performance. Such work, following the pattern of the ETS research cited above, would be useful. We have seen a Technical Assistance Guide from DOL that offers guidance to the local offices in testing the handicapped. The suggestions are quite general and mainly involve careful, patient accommodation to the needs of the applicants—addressed globally without particular suggestions for different handicapped groups. Most of the suggestions, including the use of sign language, having the test administrator record responses for applicants with motor handicaps, and so on, take time. In Chapter 5 we discussed the highly speeded character of the GATB. The time pressure that all applicants encounter would be particularly disconcerting for those with handicaps.

Should Handicapped Applicants Take the GATB?

Given the thin research base on modified forms of the GATB and, more generally, the great uncertainties about the meaning of the scores achieved by many applicants with handicapping conditions, policy makers might wonder if such applicants should be tested at all. The wisest course is to leave the decision to the applicant. If appropriately modified tests are available, and if they are knowledgeably administered, they might provide the applicant with a means of demonstrating skills and capabilities relevant to job performance.

The committee has received communications from a number of job counselors and vocational rehabilitation specialists who have long experience with the GATB and who have found it a useful assessment tool. They also emphasized that it is not always the best method for assessing the capabilities of disabled job seekers and that the imposition of any one instrument could be very damaging to the prospects of such applicants.

The inflexible implementation of VG-GATB procedures would certainly not be in the interest of job seekers with handicaps. Referral by rank-ordered scores would tend to deprive them of the chance even to be in the running for jobs, and, as we said at the beginning, often arbitrarily. The committee was informed of one such instance. A candidate for a state job as an accounting clerk, who has disabilities including a hearing impairment and cerebral palsy, met the requirements, was placed on the list of eligibles, and was sent out on several job interviews. However, before the applicant found a position the VG-GATB system was implemented and all on the list of eligibles had to take the test. On the new list of eligibles, this applicant no longer made the cutoff.

Above all, we recommend that the Employment Service continue to provide the services of job counselors to work with handicapped applicants to find the best means of assessing their skills and of bringing their performance potential to the attention of likely employers. Since state rehabilitation agencies have a wealth of expertise in vocational counseling for people with handicaps, it could well make sense to coordinate their work more closely with that of the Employment Service. One possible option would be to detail state rehabilitation agency counselors to Job Service offices that serve a sizable handicapped clientele.

In any case, handicapped applicants can be served fairly and appropriately only if the Employment Service system remains flexible and responsive to the particular circumstances of each of them.

EFFECTS ON VETERANS

Because the Public Employment Service is a source of benefits for veterans of military service, the introduction of new referral procedures necessarily involves the interests of this constituency. Representatives of military veterans have expressed concern that adoption of the VG-GATB Referral System could conflict with the preference or priority in federal employment and training services granted to most veterans as a matter of law.

Three major veterans' groups have communicated with the committee: the American Legion, the Veterans of Foreign Wars, and the Disabled American Veterans. All have called for the Department of Labor to enunciate a nationally consistent policy for implementing veterans' preference in the Employment Service system. They have also expressed opposition to exclusive use of the VG-GATB system for referral by the Job Service on the grounds that many veterans (average age 50) have no desire to take a written test, preferring instead to be referred on the basis of work experience and training. The American Legion has adopted no official position on the question of using within-group score adjustments to prevent the test-based referral system from adversely affecting the employment opportunities of protected minorities (Rhoades, 1988). The Veterans of Foreign Wars has formally adopted the view that such adjustments represent an abridgement of the entitlements of nonminority veterans since no equivalent adjustments are made to veterans' scores (Veterans of Foreign Wars, 1987).

The History of Veterans' Preference

The first federal law granting employment preference to military veterans was passed at the end of the Civil War. By joint resolution, Congress mandated in March 1865 that persons who had been honorably discharged due to injury or illness incurred in the line of duty should be preferred for appointment to civil jobs, provided that they "possess the business capacity necessary for the proper discharge of the duties of such offices." The hiring preference accorded to disabled veterans was reaffirmed in the act creating the modern civil service in 1883, although the eligibility requirements were sufficiently restrictive in these early years that only a few hundred cases came before the Civil Service Commission annually.

Throughout the years, the operational definition of veterans' preference has varied widely; as policy makers were persuaded at one point in time by those who pursued efficiency in government through merit hiring, and at another by those who considered public employment a rightful reward for military service. For example, in 1881 the Attorney General construed veterans' preference narrowly to mean that a disabled veteran should be granted preference only when his qualifications were equal to those of other candidates—what might be called a tie-breaker rule. This interpretation was overturned in 1910 when the Attorney General ruled that the law required absolute preference for disabled veterans on the list of eligibles (U.S. Civil Service Commission, 1955; Manela, 1976).

In the immediate aftermath of World War I, the scope of veterans' preference was expanded dramatically to include not just disabled veterans, but all honorably discharged soldiers, sailors, and marines, the widows of such servicemen, and the wives of disabled veterans who were not themselves qualified to hold civil service positions. Until 1944, authority to promulgate the rules implementing the Preference Act of 1919 lay with the president. Executive Order 3152 (Aug. 18, 1919) gave absolute preference to all veterans passing competitive examinations with a minimum score of 65. As a consequence, claims to the Civil Service Commission for veterans' preference went from between 600 and 900 per year to 60,000 or 70,000 per year. Questions were rapidly raised about the sacrifice in efficiency in the civil service caused by placing all veterans at the top of the registers of eligibles.

With the support of the American Legion, the Civil Service Commission in 1923 recommended to the president that a system of adding points be instituted—5 points for veterans and 10 points for disabled veterans—in place of absolute priority above a minimum cutoff score. It would, the commission argued, provide a "substantial benefit" without being seriously detrimental to efficiency. Absolute priority was restored to veterans with military service-connected disabilities in 1929 because of complaints that the simple addition of 10 points was not resulting in a sufficient number of appointments for such veterans.

After years of negotiation, the three major veterans' organizations (the American Legion, the Veterans of Foreign Wars, and the Disabled American Veterans), the Civil Service Commission, and the House and Senate Committees on Civil Service reached a compromise arrangement—one that attempted to strike a balance between the principles of merit and reward for military service. This compromise agreement was codified in the Veterans' Preference Act of 1944. In broad outline, the act provided preference for veterans in federal employment as follows:

Civil Service examinations. Disabled veterans are given an additional 10 points on competitive examinations; other veterans receive 5 extra points; and, in certain circumstances, spouses, widows, and mothers receive 10 points above their earned score. (Since 1953, the points have been added only to the scores of veterans who reach a passing score.)

Eligibility lists. The names of 5-point veterans are placed on the list of eligibles in order of their augmented score; in cases of ties with nonveterans, the veteran precedes. Until 1953, disabled veterans continued to be placed at the top of the list of eligibles; since then, the additional preference of absolute priority on the list of eligibles has been restricted to veterans who receive disability compensation or who have a military service-connected disability and is not available for scientific and professional positions of GS-9 or higher.

Civil Service appointments. The 1944 act codified the so-called rule of three, according to which the top three names on the register of eligibles for a particular position are forwarded to the appointing officer for consideration. The selecting officer can pass over a veteran in favor of competing nonveterans only with the approval of the Civil Service Commission.

The Public Employment Service and Veterans' Preference

Since its own creation by the Wagner-Peyser Act of 1933, the Public Employment Service has had major responsibility for promoting veterans' employment. The act provided for veterans' preference and in addition instructed that a federal employee with the title State Veterans' Employment Representative be detailed to every state. The Servicemen's Readjustment Act of 1944 created the position of Local Veterans' Employment Representative so that every full-service local office of the Employment Service has an official in place who oversees local activities to ensure that veterans are accorded all priorities, privileges, and services to which they are entitled by federal law.

The statutory basis for these entitlements is found in Title 38, Chapter 41, of the *United States Code,* which authorizes a national program of job counseling, training, and placement services for eligible veterans and for certain spouses of veterans. Eligibility is defined very broadly to include any person who has served on active duty for at least 180 days and has been discharged other than dishonorably, or who was discharged due to a military service–connected disability. Since 1980, the statute has placed responsibility for veterans' employment and training services with the Assistant Secretary of Labor for Veterans' Employment. The State Directors for Veterans' Employment and, nowadays, the Assistant State Directors (one for every 250,000 eligible veterans and spouses), are administratively responsible to the Assistant Secretary.

From the moment a veteran enters a local Job Service office, special services are made available. The Local Veterans' Employment Representative is to supervise the registration of veterans and provide a special orientation on available training, counseling, and placement services, including federally funded employment and training programs under the Emergency Veterans' Job Training Act of 1983 or the Disabled Veterans' Outreach Program; to promote job development activities such as job fairs; to maintain a data base with information about job opportunities; to encourage employers and labor unions to employ those eligible for veterans' preference and to conduct apprenticeship and on-the-job training programs for them; to supervise job listings of federal contractors to ensure compliance with veterans' set-asides; to identify and assist veterans with readjustment problems; and so on (Fraas, 1983).

Veterans' Priority in Referral

The VG-GATB Referral System, because it would dramatically alter referral procedures in the Employment Service system, has been a topic of concern to the veterans' organizations and to the Assistant Secretary of Labor for Veterans' Employment. Although definitive policies have not yet been enunciated by the agency for the guidance of states that are using VG-GATB referral procedures, some general outlines of Department of Labor policy are visible.

The basic principle of referral priority is that *qualified* veterans shall be referred before qualified nonveterans. Definition of the word qualified is the crux of the matter. In the narrowest interpretation, it would mean that between two applicants with exactly the same test scores, the veteran would be placed ahead of the nonveteran on the referral roster. In the most generous decision rule, all veterans who met the employer-imposed cutoff score (if such there be) would be referred before all nonveterans.

The Department of Labor seems to have decided that a number of alternatives for defining *qualified* are acceptable; neither the Assistant Secretary for Veterans' Employment nor USES has promoted a particular procedure for implementing veterans' priority in the VG-GATB Referral System. And there are dramatic differences in the methods chosen by the states to keep the VG-GATB program in compliance with the statutory requirements. Of the 35 states reporting their procedures in a 1987 survey by the Department of Labor, 24 schedule veterans ahead of others for testing and/or referral. Those that grant veterans referral priority typically put a 24-hour hold on new job orders, during which time only veterans are contacted from the VG-GATB call-in list.

In ranking candidates, 16 states accord veterans absolute priority regardless of test score, ranking all veterans ahead of all nonveterans on the VG-GATB call-in list. One state applies this rule only for those in the 50th to 99th percentiles. Eleven states apply a decile method in which veterans within each decile are referred first from the top down; one state uses a decile variation in which veterans within 10 percentile points are referred first, from the top down. Three states add from 5 to 10 points to veterans' percentile scores and apply veterans' priority in the case of ties. Another three states apply only the tie-breaker rule.

It is noteworthy that the absolute-priority rule adopted by 16 states is far more generous than the preference accorded veterans in traditional federal civil service hiring (procedures for entry-level hiring are currently undergoing change). In that system, test scores are augmented by 5 to 10 points (depending on disability status). Referrals are made from a single list of eligibles three at a time, from the top down. The hiring official has discretion in selecting among the three, except that if a veteran in the group of three is not the one selected, the decision must be approved by the Office of Personnel Management.

Although there has not been uniformity of procedures for extending priority in referral in the past, the veterans' organizations have expressed sharp dissatisfaction with this laissez-faire approach. They are calling for the Department of Labor to issue explicit guidelines or rules for a uniform system of veterans' priority under VG-GATB referral procedures, because the welfare of veterans is a national responsibility and they should therefore be accorded the same treatment in every state. Although they would prefer absolute priority, the veterans' organizations are not pushing for a specific rule. In a formal statement to the committee, Dennis Rhoades, spokesman for the American Legion and member of the committee's liaison group, described two possible approaches to providing veterans' preference in a local office operating under the VG-GATB system: the first would be to continue to rely on the method that times referrals, sending only qualified veterans (in rank order) in response to a job order for the first 24 or 48 hours. The second means would be to apply ordering preference within a range of percentile scores. Although not coming out in favor of a particular approach, Rhoades, like his colleagues in the other veterans' organizations, did reject a simple tie-breaker rule as incompatible with the spirit of the law (Rhoades, 1988).

Veterans and Within-Group Score Adjustments

Questions have been raised about a possible conflict between the VG-GATB within-group scoring procedure and veterans' statutory entitlement to preferential treatment in employment referral. The American Legion maintains a neutral position on score adjustments intended to promote equal employment opportunity for minority-group members "if there is validity established for their use." The Veterans of Foreign Wars, however, has taken the position that the conversion of minority scores is illegal because it deprives nonminority veterans of their legal right to priority in referral. The point was illustrated in a letter (dated May 3, 1988) to the Assistant Secretary of Labor for Veterans' Employment and Training from Robert L. Jones as follows: if a white veteran receives a Job Family IV percentile score of 41, any black applicant with an identical raw score will receive a percentile score of 81; the score for a Hispanic applicant would be 63, and that for a Native American, 59.

There is no doubt that within-group score adjustments would have the effect of drawing minority applicants (veteran and nonveteran alike) into the referral pool while excluding majority-group veterans with the same raw scores. It is also true that government grants of preferential treatment can never be absolute; one person's preference qualifies that of the other. Whether the preference granted by statute to veterans takes precedence over federal attempts to remedy the effects of discrimination against blacks and other protected groups in this case seems to be an open question.

Some have suggested that the way to resolve the issue is to compute adjustments in the scores of veterans as a group. Were there average group differences between veterans and nonveterans, it would be possible to consider such a solution. However, based on admittedly limited data comparing scores in all five job families for two groups defined by veteran status, it appears that veterans and nonveterans have roughly the same mean percentile scores. For example, the 1987–1988 figures for one local office in Michigan show:

	Average Percentile Score	
Job Family	Veterans ($N = 1,100$)	Nonveterans ($N = 3,900$)
IV	54	52
V	53	55

The statewide applicant pool in Utah in early 1988 shows:

	Average Percentile Score	
Job Family	Veterans ($N = 9,958$)	Total ($N = 93,504$)
IV	50.36	52.14
V	47.00	53.82

Unless there are larger average group differences, development of conversion tables for veterans would not significantly change their chances of referral. But a test-based system that does not have some adjustment like the current within-group conversions would seriously reduce the chances of minority veterans.

FINDINGS, CONCLUSIONS, AND RECOMMENDATIONS

Employers

Conclusions

1. Although empirical evidence is sparse, the use of VG-GATB scores top-down to refer applicants appears to offer an employer benefits such as modest improvements in worker performance and reduced training time. Certainly a large majority of the employers who communicated with the committee perceived the VG-GATB system to improve their use of human resources.

2. However, these benefits will tend to attenuate as more employers who compete in the same labor market adopt VG-GATB procedures.

Job Seekers

Conclusions

1. Compared with subjective procedures, test-based referral can potentially reduce the risk that racial or ethnic prejudice will influence referral decisions.

2. At the same time, tests are fallible and they give a narrow reading on human capabilities. To limit all job seekers to a single test-based modality would artificially restrict the opportunities of many applicants.

3. The VG-GATB system has the potential disadvantage for older, experienced workers of basing referral on less relevant information (test score) when more relevant information (past job performance) is available.

4. The VG-GATB Referral System, were it to be the only mode of referral offered through the Employment Service system, would consign the lowest-scoring applicants to receiving little or no assistance in finding work when, in fact, many such applicants could perform satisfactorily on the job.

5. Without the kind of adjustments currently made to the scores of black, Hispanic, and in some cases Native American applicants, the VG-GATB Referral System would have severely adverse impact on

members of these demographic groups. The severity of the adverse impact leads us to conclude that the VG-GATB Referral System is probably not viable without adjustment of minority scores so long as the government is committed to a policy of equal employment opportunity that looks to the effects of employment practices on racial and ethnic minority groups.

6. It is not reasonable to use the GATB to estimate the abilities of foreign-born applicants who have a marginal command of the English language.

Recommendations

1. We recommend that no job seeker be obliged to take the GATB; every local office that uses VG-GATB referral should maintain an alternate referral path for those who choose not to take the test.

2. Because tests provide only partial information about future job performance, we recommend that local Job Service offices that adopt the VG-GATB Referral System continue to use multiple criteria in choosing which applicants to refer.

People with Handicapping Conditions

Findings

1. The central scientific questions concerning the use of standardized tests to estimate the academic or job performance of people with handicaps have revolved around the question of comparability. When such tests are modified to accommodate visual, hearing, motor, or other handicaps, do the modified and regular instruments measure the same abilities? Even if they do, are the resulting scores comparable?

2. Recent research carried out by the Educational Testing Service to investigate these questions in terms of its major cognitive test batteries, particularly the Scholastic Aptitude Test Battery, demonstrates the extreme difficulty of gathering sufficient data to answer these questions empirically. Although the SAT is one of the three largest testing programs in the country and is supported by an extensive data base, the ETS research team had great difficulty assembling an "even minimally sufficient" data set to study the validity of scores on modified versions of the SAT for predicting first-year college grade-point average. It was virtually impossible to take account of degree of handicap, and even within type of handicap the numbers for whom all data were available were often small. Even greater obstacles would confront an effort by USES to establish the comparability of scores on regular and modified forms of the GATB. The

problem of inadequate sample sizes would be even more severe, and the job performance criterion would be more difficult to capture.

Conclusions

1. The GATB cannot play the same role in assessing the qualifications of handicapped and nonhandicapped applicants.

2. Because matching people with handicaps to jobs necessitates consideration both of their abilities and of their particular disabilities in light of specific job requirements, the VG-GATB Referral System, with its emphasis on test scores and automated file search, is not adequate to the situation. Job counselors are essential to the referral process for handicapped applicants.

Recommendations

1. For applicants with handicapping conditions we recommend the continued use of job counselors to make referrals.

2. The GATB should be used when feasible to assess the abilities of handicapped applicants, but as a supplement to decision making, not to take the place of counseling services.

3. Because special expertise in assessing the capabilities of people with handicaps is necessary and available, we recommend that the Department of Labor encourage closer coordination between state rehabilitation agencies and the State Employment Service Agencies. Consideration should be given to placing state rehabilitation counselors in local Employment Service offices that service a sizable handicapped population.

4. Steps should be taken to ensure that no job order is filled automatically and solely through the VG-GATB system. Job counselors who serve handicapped applicants, disabled veterans, or other populations with special needs must have regular access to the daily flow of job orders.

Veterans

Conclusions

1. The language of the legislation and regulations conferring priority or preference in employment on military veterans consistently uses the terminology "qualified veterans." We infer from this that the intent of Congress was to balance considerations of productivity with preferential treatment for veterans.

2. One of the methods of referral priority in use, the tie-breaker method, provides little advantage to veterans.

3. Absolute priority (ranking all veterans before all nonveterans regardless of test score), however, ignores the goal of promoting productivity. It effectively removes the word "qualified" from the implementation of the law.

4. Although two of the methods of referral priority, variants of the decile method, confer quite a bit of advantage on veterans, adding points to percentile scores has the anomalous effect of helping veterans with high scores substantially more than veterans with moderate test scores.

Recommendations

1. If government policy is to strike a balance between maximizing productivity and preference for veterans in employment referral through the VG-GATB Referral System, the Employment Service should adjust veterans' VG-GATB scores by adding a veterans' bonus of some number of points before conversion to percentiles. Unadjusted expectancy scores should also be reported to employers and job seekers.

It should be noted on the referral slip that the percentile score has been adjusted for veterans' preference. If the federal rule were followed, the size of the adjustment would range from one-eighth to one-quarter of a standard deviation corresponding to 5 and 10 percentile points, depending on disability status.

2. The Employment Service should continue to meet the needs of disabled veterans through individualized counseling and placement services.

12

Evaluation of Economic Claims

There is no question that any individual employer who can be selective in hiring workers will benefit. What is problematic is the magnitude of the economic benefits that would accrue to the individual employer or to the economy as a whole if ability testing were more widely used. Part of the Department of Labor's rationale for promoting the VG-GATB Referral System is based on very specific claims of economic benefits. John Hunter, the author of U.S. Employment Service (USES) Test Research Report No. 47, which contains an analysis of the economic benefits of personnel selection using ability tests (U.S. Department of Labor, 1983e), estimates that a "potential increase in work force productivity among the employers who hire through the service would come to $79.36 billion per year." That report also refers the reader to the work of Hunter and Schmidt (1982), in which they estimate productivity gains of between $13 billion and $153 billion in the economy as a whole due to using ability tests for selection. In this chapter we review these claims.

UTILITY ANALYSIS: GAINS FOR THE INDIVIDUAL FIRM

In the first part of the discussion we review the model (known as utility analysis) that Hunter and Schmidt used to estimate how much an individual employer would gain by using ability tests to select workers. The formula that Hunter and Schmidt derive to measure the gains from using ability testing is taken from Brogden (1946):

235

$$G = (r)(s)(A),$$

where

  G = the dollar gain per worker per year due to hiring in order of test score rather than randomly,
  r = the correlation between test score and productivity,
  s = the standard deviation of yearly productivity in dollars among workers in the applicant pool, and
  A = the average test score of those applicants selected, when test scores are standardized to have mean 0 and variance 1 in the applicant pool.

In this formula, the economic benefits to an employer are determined by three parameters. The first is the validity of the test, the extent to which test performance is correlated with productivity. The second and third parameters measure the potential an employer has for improving productivity by selecting better workers. How much productivity could improve depends on the variability of productivity in the employer's applicant pool and on the latitude the employer has in selecting workers. If productivity varies widely, an employer will benefit from using a test that selects the best workers. However, if one worker is about as good as another, the gains from selecting the best will be small. Similarly, if an employer must hire everyone who applies for a job, then it does not help him to know who is best. However, if it is possible to reject 90 or 95 percent of all applicants, it is obviously advantageous to be able to identify the most able workers.

If the selection were random, then the average test score among selected workers would be zero, and there would be no gains in productivity. The gain is derived because the employer can select the top-scoring percentage of those who apply for a job. If the test score distribution is normal, the influence of selectivity, p, on the employer's gains is measured by $M(p)$, a statistical formula that is the inverse of the Mill's ratio.[1] For our purposes, it suffices to note that $M(p)$ calibrates the influence of selectivity, p, on productivity gains. $M(p)$ is a decreasing function of p; the more selective an employer can be, the lower is p and the greater are the potential gains from using ability tests to hire the best workers.

---

[1] The formal definition of $M(p)$ is

$$M(p) = f[H(1 - p)]/p$$

where f and H are, respectively, the density and the inverse of the cumulative distribution function of the standardized normal distribution function.

Potential Benefits of Employment Service Use of the VG-GATB

As a demonstration of the use of the utility formula, we examine the Hunter estimate that optimal test use would have resulted in an estimated benefit of $79.36 billion to employers using the Employment Service system in 1980 (U.S. Department of Labor, 1983e). That figure is widely quoted in promotional literature for the General Aptitude Test Battery (GATB). (The numbers in this discussion relate to 1980. The technique could be applied to contemporary data with corrections for inflation and the scale of Employment Service operations.)

The first number needed for the formula is the *correlation between test score and productivity,* which Hunter takes to be .5, based on USES validity generalization studies connecting test score and supervisor ratings.

The second number is the *standard deviation of worker productivity,* which Hunter estimates to be 40 percent of average wages. This figure is based on six empirical studies that covered clerks, nurse's aides, grocery clerks, adding machine operators, and radial drill-press operators, with estimated standard deviations of 20 percent, 15 percent, 15 percent, 10 percent, 10 percent, and 25 percent (Hunter and Schmidt, 1982: Table 7.1). It is also based on a method of variability assessment developed by Hunter and Schmidt (see U.S. Department of Labor, 1983e) in which supervisors are asked to estimate the dollar value of an average worker and of a worker at the 85th percentile. The ratio of the two estimates is an estimate of the standard deviation of worker productivity (under the assumption that productivity is normally distributed, an assumption that has been supported by Hunter and Schmidt in a study of computer programmers.) Hunter and Schmidt developed values of 60 percent and 55 percent for budget analysts and computer programmers. Combining these estimates with the previous empirical studies produces their overall estimate of the standard deviation of worker productivity as 40 percent of average annual wages.

The final number is the *referral ratio,* the proportion of applicants referred. Hunter takes the value of 10 percent based on an "informal enquiry that the U.S. Employment Service has jobs for only about 1 in 10 of the applicants." The value of $M(p)$ for this referral ratio is 1.76; this means that the average test score over the top 10 percent of scorers is 1.76, when the test is standardized to have mean 0 and standard deviation 1.

Applying Brogden's formula gives a percentage gain, per worker per year, of

$$G = .50 \times 40 \times 1.76 = 35\%.$$

In 1980, the Employment Service placed 4 million applicants in jobs. Average annual wage in the jobs served by the Employment Service is

$16,000. Average job tenure in the United States is 3.6 years. Thus the total wages spent on workers hired in a particular year, over the expected tenure of their jobs, is $230 billion, and, according to Hunter's calculations, the savings if they had been hired top-down in order of test score would be 35 percent × $230 billion = $80.5 billion.

Will VG-GATB Testing Save $80 Billion?

We examine the applicability of Brogden's formula for evaluating gains from the use of the GATB by the Employment Service and reconsider the particular numerical inputs used by Hunter (U.S. Department of Labor, 1983e).

There are two points to consider about the *r* value (correlation between test score and productivity), which Hunter estimates at .5. First, the .5 value is based on corrections for restriction of range and for unreliability in the criterion that the committee does not accept (see Chapter 8) and is significantly larger than is supported by the second wave (post-1972) of GATB validity studies.

Second, Brogden's formula measures the gains to an employer from using ability tests, under the assumption that, without the tests, hiring is random. Hunter asserts that the counseling used by the Employment Service instead of the test "is equivalent to random selection" (U.S. Department of Labor, 1983e). We do not have convincing evidence, however, that the other techniques used by the Employment Service and by employers are of no value. (If, indeed, workers are being selected at random from applicant pools by the alternative methods, how can it be argued, as Hunter does elsewhere, that it is necessary to correct correlations computed on worker groups for restriction of range in order to estimate their values for applicant groups?) In any case, some employers use their own selection methods to screen applicants sent by the Employment Service. In assessing the gains from using ability tests, it would be necessary to understand how ability tests complement existing procedures.

Suppose an employer is using a procedure that has a validity of .10. For example, an employer uses some combination of interviews and biographic information to rank job applicants and hires those who come out best in that ranking. The ranking has a correlation of .10 with productivity.

Now suppose the employer adds an ability test, which in combination with other selection methods has a validity of .3 to select applicants. The gain in productivity can be measured by Brogden's formula, but the validity term in the formula must be replaced by .30 − .10 = .20, the *change in validity* due to adopting the new procedure.

At first glance, it might be thought that the employer's prior procedure with validity .10 could be combined with a cognitive test of validity .30 to produce a combined selection procedure with validity .40, so that the gain in validity due to using the cognitive test is .30. That, however, is not the case. Even if the two are uncorrelated, the correlation of the combined procedures is only .33; if they are positively correlated, it will be somewhat less than this. To discover the improvement due to using a cognitive test, one cannot avoid adjusting for the validity of the prior procedure.

Thus, in place of Hunter's estimate of .5, we suggest that the gain in the validity of an employer's selection procedures from using the GATB is more likely to range from .1 to .3. The .1 corresponds to jobs for which the employer already has a reasonable selection procedure, and the .3 corresponds to jobs for which the current selection procedure is effectively random.

Hunter's estimate of the second value in the Brogden formula is also open to question. The empirical evidence cited for the standard deviation of worker productivity is quite slight—eight studies by five authors (U.S. Department of Labor, 1983e). Six of these studies are for jobs in the Job Families IV and V principally served by the Employment Service, and the standard deviations of output as a percentage of wages average 16 percent. Two of the studies, using a questionnaire of supervisors developed by Hunter and Schmidt, give values of 55 percent and 60 percent for budget analysts and computer programmers, respectively. However, the Employment Service does not see many applicants like budget analyst and computer programmer. It seems overly optimistic to produce a figure of 40 percent as the consensus figure for Employment Service jobs. In Schmidt and Hunter (1983) the low-complexity jobs were estimated to have standard deviations of 20 percent, and in more recent work (Hunter et al., 1988) the estimates have been revised downward to 15 percent. In our judgment, a more appropriate consensus figure for Employment Service jobs would be about 20 percent.

The third figure in Brogden's formula is the selection ratio, which Hunter takes to be 1 in 10 (1 selected for every 10 applicants). In 1980 the Employment Service placed 4 million applicants in jobs. To achieve a selection ratio of 1 in 10, it would have needed 40 million applicants, the top 4 million test scorers being placed. The figures for 1986–1987 were 3.2 million placements of 6.9 million referrals for 19.2 million applicants, a ratio of 1 in 6 (and perhaps 1 in 4 would be more reasonable, because 7 million of the 192 million were unemployment insurance claimants legally obliged to register). The theoretical gains to be reaped from testing come from allocating the top X percent of test scorers to jobs and the bottom $100 - X$ percent to no jobs. Hunter's numbers would mean that 10 percent would be selected and 90 percent would not. For an individual employer who can afford to be highly selective, Brogden's formula may well be applicable. But it cannot apply to the whole economy, for which the prospect of the top-scoring 10 percent working and the bottom 90 percent not working is absurd. And the Employment Service is a microcosm of the economy; of the 16 million applicants not placed during 1986–1987, many will have already had jobs when they applied or will get them through some other route than the Employment Service. Thus, even if they score low on the test, they will get to work, and their productivity must be allowed for.

Suppose there was only one job and all job seekers were tested, and the top 90 percent of test scorers were employed and the rest were unemployed. Ten percent is regarded as a reasonably high rate of unemployment. The gains from testing against random hiring would be computed using a selection ratio of 9 in 10. The corresponding inverse Mill's ratio is .20, which should be compared with an $M(p)$ value of 1.76 when the selection ratio is 1 in 10.

Taking a more optimistic view, let us now assume a selection ratio of 6 to 1 based on the 1986–1987 figures. (This is optimistic in the sense that it supposes that the 16 million workers not placed by the Employment Service did not have or find jobs and so did not lower average productivity.) The corresponding value of $M(p)$ is 1.40. If one accepts the committee's more cautious estimates of the first two values in the Brogden formula, and if the Employment Service referred in order of test score and the employers hired in order of test score, the economic gain by Brogden's rule would be:

$$G = .2 \times 20 \times 1.40 = 5.6\%.$$

This would lead to an estimated dollar gain, in 1980, of $13 billion as opposed to Hunter's $80 billion. However, this is still an overestimate because the average job tenure figure was not discounted for the decreased value of the savings over time. Rather, one year's savings was multiplied by the 3.6-year average tenure figure. A value of 3 would be more appropriate, since next year's savings are not as valuable as this year's.[2] This correction would reduce the dollar gain to about $10.75 billion.

---

[2]To correctly estimate the amount discounted, one would need to know both the appropriate discount rate and the distribution of job tenure (not just its mean). To arrive at the value 3, we took 10 percent as a discount rate. This is probably conservative. The most conservative assumption one could make about the distribution of job tenure would be to suppose that every worker stays on the job for exactly 3.6 years and then quits. Under that assumption, the discounted present value of savings to a firm is 3.15 times annual savings. A less conservative procedure would assume that workers leave jobs at a constant rate. In this case the discounted present value of one year's savings should be multiplied by 2.63. A reasonable compromise value is 3.

The more radical view, with a selection ratio of 9 in 10 (that is, 9 of 10 Job Service applicants get jobs one way or another), would lead to a gain of 0.8 percent. Including the discounted job tenure figure, the dollar gain in this scenario would be on the order of 1.5 billion.

The committee concludes that both the logic and the numbers used in the estimate of $80 billion to be gained from testing are flawed, and that an estimate in the range $1.5 billion to $10 billion is more plausible.

Although we regard this as a plausible estimate of savings, provided both the Employment Service and employers used the GATB optimally, we emphasize that it is not reasonable to conclude that the economy as a whole would save this amount of money or that the gross national product (GNP) could increase by this amount. Employment Service use of the VG-GATB will not improve the quality of the labor force as a whole. If employers using the Employment Service get better workers, employers not using the Employment Service will necessarily have a less competent labor force. One firm's gain is another firm's loss.

With great ambivalence, we have developed alternative computations of the economic gains to be anticipated from widespread use of the VG-GATB system. Such dramatic claims of dollar gains have been proposed—and given a credence perhaps not originally intended—that we feel compelled to demonstrate that a careful critique of the assumptions and the numbers would lead many experts to very different, and much more modest, estimates.

Our ambivalence stems from a reluctance to do anything to encourage further use of dollar estimates in Employment Service literature. Given the paucity of empirical evidence and the state of the art, all estimates of productivity gains from ability testing are highly speculative. The choice of a dollar metric lends a false precision to the analysis. We feel that it is more likely to mislead than to inform policy.

GAINS TO THE ECONOMY AS A WHOLE ARE FROM JOB MATCHING

Several attempts have been made to calculate the gains that would accrue to the economy as a whole if ability testing were used to select all workers in the economy. This calculation cannot be made simply by applying Brogden's formula to the economy as a whole. The reason is that an important source of increased productivity is an employer's ability to select the best-qualified workers and to avoid hiring the least-qualified workers. If there is no selectivity, then an employer gains nothing by identifying the able, since this identification will not affect the hiring decisions.

The economy as a whole is very much like a single employer who must accept all workers. All workers must be employed. Whereas it may be true for an individual firm that more than 10 percent of its workers fit into the top 10 percent of the ability distribution, this can never be true of the entire labor force. The economy as a whole must make do with a labor force that has only 10 percent of the workers who fit into the top 10 percent of the ability distribution. It must somehow reserve 10 percent of its jobs for the least able 10 percent. This situation contrasts with that of the individual employer. If a firm uses tests to identify the able and if the firm can be selective, then it can improve the quality of its work force. The economy as a whole cannot; the economy as a whole must employ the labor force as a whole.[3]

Testing can increase aggregate productivity only if there are gains to be made from matching people to jobs. Estimating those gains requires models and procedures that are different from those used to measure the gains that accrue to an individual employer who uses ability tests. In estimating the effect on the economy as a whole, the model must balance the single employer's gains against the losses of others.

To summarize, utility analysis cannot be applied to the economy as a whole because the economy as a whole cannot have a selection ratio of much less than 100 percent. The economy as a whole must make do with the labor force that it has. It is not possible to assign the best workers to every job.

Economic Gains Based on the Hunter and Schmidt Job-Matching Model

In job matching, individuals are assigned to jobs to maximize overall productivity. In the simplest case, when there is one predictor for each of several jobs, gains over random assignment occur only if the quantity

$$\text{validity} \times \text{standard deviation of productivity}$$

varies over the different jobs. The higher-scoring workers are assigned to the jobs with the higher values of this quantity (Cronbach and Gleser, 1965: Chap. 5).

---

[3] What about the unemployed? One not entirely frivolous answer is that being unemployed is a job; unemployment is essential to the smooth functioning of the economy. If there were no unemployment, then inflation would be unacceptably high. Furthermore, unemployment is necessary if the labor force is to respond to changing economic demands. Without unemployment we would have many blacksmiths and no computer technicians. The fact that the unemployment rate (or at least the unemployment rate that is consistent with reasonable price stability) changes quite slowly is support for this view. If one takes seriously this point of view, then it is clear that productivity can increase if the most able are given the job "work" and the least able remain unemployed. But this conclusion rests on the observation that some jobs are more productive than others and that aggregate productivity increases when the more able are assigned to the more productive jobs. In other words, this is a theory about how good job matching enhances productivity.

Brogden (1955, 1959, 1964) developed algorithms for optimal classification when separate equations are used for predicting success in the different jobs. The assignment part of the problem is mathematically standard. There are m jobs and n workers, and each worker has an expected dollar productivity for each job. Each worker is assigned to a job to maximize expected total productivity. This is a problem in the field of linear programming called the assignment problem. It will take a while to do the calculation when m and n are large, but it is clear what needs to be done. The hard problem is developing a plausible estimate of dollar productivity for each worker for each job, then assessing the gain in using optimal assignment versus random assignment.

Under some simplifying assumptions, Brogden (1959) showed that the gain from optimal assignment was proportional to $(1 - c)$, where c is the correlation between the predictors used in the different jobs. Under these assumptions, it is thus important to classify jobs so that different prediction equations are appropriate for the different jobs.

Schmidt and Hunter (1983) present two job-matching models that assign workers optimally. In the first of these, the univariate model, they divide jobs into four types: management-professional, skilled trade, clerical, and semiskilled and unskilled labor. Productivity is predicted by a single predictor, cognitive ability, with correlation .4 in all jobs. The standard deviation of productivity is assumed proportional to average productivity in the job. Thus the optimal classification assigns higher-ability workers to the higher-wage jobs, for which their expected productivity is higher because the standard deviation of productivity in dollars is higher.

If there is a single predictor, then Brogden (1959) would predict no gains from the use of testing. Hunter and Schmidt's different conclusion is based on a different assumption about the way in which:

$$\text{validity} \times \text{standard deviation of productivity}$$

varies across jobs. Hunter and Schmidt argue that the higher the average productivity of a job, the greater is the influence of a worker's ability on the output of the job. Some fragmentary confirming evidence that supports this point of view can be found in Hunter et al. (1988). Brogden implicitly assumes that the effect of ability on job output is the same for all jobs. We regard the Hunter and Schmidt assumption as plausible but note that there is very little evidence about the nature of the relationship of ability to output.

In the second of Hunter and Schmidt's models, the multivariate model, different predictors are used for the different job types. Cognitive ability is used for managerial-professional and for semiskilled-unskilled, with an assumed correlation of .4 for each. Cognitive ability and spatial ability predict productivity in skilled trades, and the three correlations between the two abilities and productivity are assumed to be .4. Cognitive ability and perceptual ability predict productivity in clerical work, and the three correlations between the two abilities and productivity are assumed to be .4. Finally, the correlation between spatial and perceptual ability is assumed to be .16.

The workers are assigned in the second model as follows: first, those scoring highest on cognitive ability are assigned to the management-professional group; then, of those remaining, the highest scorers on spatial plus cognitive ability are assigned to the skilled trades; of those remaining, the highest scorers on perceptual plus cognitive ability are assigned to clerical work; and the remainder go to semiskilled-unskilled labor. (Although it is a minor academic point, this assignment does not maximize productivity; despite their high cognitive ability, some prodigious scorers on spatial ability should be assigned to skilled trades.)

Hunter and Schmidt use their models to estimate the amount by which the GNP would increase if testing were used to place all workers optimally in jobs. Under the assumption that validity is .4, their estimates range from 1.7 percent of the GNP for the univariate model (using a low— 16 percent of average output—estimate of the standard deviation of productivity) to 8.1 percent of GNP for the multivariate model (using a high— 40 percent of average output—estimate of the standard deviation of productivity).

Using our preferred parameters—validity is .2 and the standard deviation of productivity on a job is 20 percent of output on that job—their univariate model suggests that improved job matching would increase the GNP by about 1.1 percent; the multivariate model suggests an increase of 2.1 percent.

These percentage increases should be compared with the 35 percent increase estimated by Hunter for Employment Service jobs (U.S. Department of Labor, 1983e). Hunter and Schmidt argue that their multivariate model overestimates the potential gain from a testing program because it does not take into account that placement is not now at random. They suggest that a reasonable way to correct this estimate of the potential gains is to take the difference between the multivariate and univariate models. Under their assumptions, these gains would range from 1.6 percent to 4 percent of the GNP; under our preferred assumptions, this technique puts potential gains at 1 percent of the GNP.

How do these economy-wide models relate to Employment Service use of the GATB? This is an important question, because a policy that would increase the GNP by just 1 percent would be of enormous value to the country (1 percent of the GNP in 1987 was $45 billion). In answering this question it is important to remember that only a small fraction of those who find jobs each year do so through the Employment Service system. The gains that Hunter and Schmidt calculate would be realized only if *all* employers used tests optimally. It is also important to remember that the most important assumptions of the Hunter-Schmidt models rest on a very slim empirical foundation.

Nevertheless, the committee views the economy-wide matching models as a promising way to assess the economic effects of testing. By looking beyond a single job, they offer the Employment Service a device for balancing the demands of all employers and all applicants. In particular, if they are to be taken seriously, they would require a job classification scheme that as much as possible reduces the correlation between predictors in different job classes. The present five-family classification scheme is not adequate for effective multivariate matching.

Few economists have tried to answer the question of how productivity is affected by the way in which workers are matched to jobs. Those who have approached this problem have used models and procedures that are very different from those used by Hunter and Schmidt. Most economic models assume that workers choose the job for which they are best fitted. With this maintained assumption it is not possible to address the question that Hunter and Schmidt ask. Some economic models (notably those of Heckman and Sedlacek, 1985, and Willis and Rosen, 1979) have been tested in the sense that they have been successfully fitted to data about the U.S. economy. In this weak sense they have a firmer empirical base than the Hunter-Schmidt models. However, on the issue of how much output would go up if people were better fitted to their jobs, they are, at present, silent.

Hunter and Schmidt's economy-wide models are based on simple assumptions for which the empirical evidence is slight. The most important one is that the standard deviation of productivity is proportional to average wage of the job. That assumption is supported by only a very few studies. Without that effect there would be no gains in placing higher-scoring workers in the more highly paid jobs. The second set of assumptions concerns the correlation of various aptitudes with productivity. Although there are many more data on which to base these correlations, there is much variation in the data and considerable disagreement about what the correlations should be. The general concept of the models is promising, but the particular numerical values used can be regarded as only illustrative. We do not know how well employers and workers match themselves already. We do not have a classification of jobs that lends itself to job matching, so the gains from the multivariate model are only theoretical.

SUPERVISOR RATINGS AND TRUE PRODUCTIVITY

Proponents of the VG-GATB claim that its use will lead to increased productivity. The scientific base of GATB research does not support such an inference directly. This is because the GATB validity studies do not report correlations between test performance and productivity; instead they report correlations between test performance and a surrogate for productivity, supervisor ratings. (A number of studies report correlations between test scores and performance in training programs. In analysis of the economic benefits of using the GATB, the data on training are largely ignored.) A small number of studies, discussed in Chapter 10, have attempted to measure the economic benefits of using the GATB directly. The small number and mixed quality of these studies make it difficult to draw inferences that can be generalized to other settings.

The correlation between test scores and true productivity could well be either higher or lower than the correlation between test scores and supervisor's ratings. *If* the GATB measures productivity, and *if* supervisor ratings are imperfect measures of productivity, then the correlation between productivity and test scores will be higher than the reported correlation between test scores and supervisor ratings. For an elaboration of this point see the discussion of criterion unreliability in Chapter 6.

If, however, the GATB measures well what supervisors regard highly and if supervisor ratings tend to ignore or overlook significant contributions to productivity, contributions that are not well measured by the GATB, then the correlation between supervisor ratings and GATB scores will exceed the correlation between productivity and GATB scores.

Which is the case? In the absence of direct data on the joint distribution of test scores, supervisor ratings, and productivity, we cannot say with confidence whether reported validity coefficients overstate or underestimate the true correlation between test scores and productivity.

It seems highly unlikely that data that will resolve this problem will exist in the near future (or ever). What then is to be done? The most reasonable course would seem to be to regard correlation with supervisor ratings as the best available estimate of the correlation between test scores and productivity. However, those who use these numbers to evaluate potential economic gains should be aware of the uncertain scientific base on which their estimates rest.

FINDINGS, CONCLUSIONS, AND RECOMMENDATIONS

A major attraction of the VG-GATB system is the anticipation of substantial economic gains. USES Test Research Report No. 47 (U.S. Department of Labor, 1983e), written by John Hunter, contends that a potential increase in work force productivity of $79.36 billion per year would accrue if the 4 million placements made by the Employment Service system were based on top-down referral from GATB test scores.

Our evaluation of the potential economic effects of the VG-GATB Referral System included study of the work of labor economists as well as the utility analysis developed in recent years by psychologists. We have looked carefully at Hunter's work with GATB data as well as the more elaborate models proposed by Hunter and Schmidt in other contexts.

Findings

Benefits to the Individual Employer

1. There is evidence in the economics and industrial/organizational psychology research literature that people who score higher on ability tests tend to produce more and make fewer errors, as well as to complete training somewhat faster and stay on the job longer.

2. How selective an individual firm can be depends on the people available and how much the firm can offer its employees in pay and other benefits. Selection can operate only within those conditions, and the potential gains are commensurately constrained.

Aggregate Economic Effects

1. There is no well-developed body of evidence from which to estimate the aggregate effects of better personnel selection. A number of theoretical models have been developed that imply various estimates of productivity gains from improved selection and placement. But we have seen no empirical evidence that any of them provides an adequate basis for estimating the aggregate economic effects of implementing the VG-GATB on a nationwide basis.

The Hunter-Schmidt Models

1. The Hunter-Schmidt univariate and multivariate models for estimating the aggregate economic gain of optimal selection are potentially valuable. However, we have seen no empirical evidence that supports

their estimates of dollar gains in the GNP if employment testing with top-down scoring were widely used.

Conclusions

1. Our review of the economics literature and our analysis of the Hunter-Schmidt theoretical models lead us to reject their estimates of specific dollar gains from test-based selection.

2. Furthermore, given the state of scientific knowledge, we do not believe that realistic dollar estimates of aggregate gains from improved selection are even possible. They lend a spurious certainty to the argument for the VG-GATB Referral System that can only mislead policy makers, employers, and those who administer the referral system.

3. We agree that better selection of workers would be likely to benefit individual employers and that a better matching of people to jobs according to their particular abilities or other work-related characteristics would tend to foster the economic health of the community, all other things being equal. But the current state of economic knowledge does not permit estimation of the overall economic effects of widespread testing.

Recommendation

1. Given the primitive state of knowledge about the aggregate economic effects of better personnel selection, we recommend that Employment Service officials refrain from making dollar estimates of the gains that would result from test-based selection.

PART V

CONCLUSIONS AND RECOMMENDATIONS

Whereas the committee's specific conclusions and recommendations appear at the end of each chapter, Part V highlights the committee's most important recommendations. Chapter 13 presents the committee's recommendations on the use of score adjustments for black and Hispanic job seekers in the VG-GATB Referral System and its recommendations on what scores to report to test takers and employers. Chapter 14 is a summary of the committee's central recommendations: it recapitulates the committee's statements on operational use of the VG-GATB system, methods of referring applicants to jobs, options for reporting GATB scores to employers and to job seekers, promotion of the VG-GATB system, research on its effects, and action with regard to veterans and people with handicapping conditions.

13

Recommendations for Referral and Score Reporting

A particular charge of the committee is to review the use of within-group scoring in the VG-GATB Referral System. This method of scoring transforms raw scores into percentile scores referenced to particular subpopulations (black, Hispanic, and other). It was adopted to prevent the test-based referral system from adversely affecting the employment opportunities of minority applicants. The adjustments made by computing percentile scores within the specified subpopulations have the effect of erasing average group differences in reported test performance.

There are several steps in the production of within-group percentile scores. First, the raw test scores for each applicant are converted into five job family scores, based on predetermined weightings of the cognitive, perceptual, and psychomotor composites. Then each of the applicant's five job family scores is converted to a percentile score, which shows the applicant's ranking with respect to others in the same ethnic or racial subgroup on a scale of 1 to 100. That ranking is derived from norm groups constructed from samples of blacks, Hispanics, and majority-group job incumbents who took the test in a number of General Aptitude Test Battery (GATB) validity studies.

In the VG-GATB system, applicants are referred to jobs in order of their percentile scores, and the scores are reported to employers without designations of the applicant's group identity. Hence a black applicant with a Job Family IV within-group score of 70 percent will have the same referral status as a white ("other") applicant with a within-group score of 70 percent, although their raw scores would be 283 and 327, respectively.

251

Within-group scoring is without question race-conscious. It is an example of what some commentators describe as an inclusionary or benign racial classification, because it was adopted by the U.S. Employment Service (USES) in order to enrich the employment opportunities of black and Hispanic job seekers (while at the same time promoting the overall quality of applicants referred to an employer). Others, chief among them the former Assistant Attorney General for Civil Rights, Wm. Bradford Reynolds, view within-group scoring as intentional racial discrimination, an abridgment of the equal protection clause of the Constitution and illegal under Title VII of the Civil Rights Act of 1964.

In its interim report (Wigdor and Hartigan, 1988) the committee concluded that, as an instrument of public policy, the "within-group referral procedure is an effective way to balance the conflicting goals of productivity and racial equity," at least as far as the individual employer is concerned. Nevertheless, the committee refrained from endorsing the way within-group percentile scores are being used in the VG-GATB Referral System because of concerns about its legal status, about the representativeness of the norm groups used in score conversions, and about potential misunderstanding by employers and applicants in interpreting the reported scores. The sole use of group-based percentile scores, in the absence of any information about the applicant's self-reported group membership or about the size of the adjustments made to minority scores, would encourage two kinds of misinterpretation on the part of employers:

1. The employer could easily assume that all individuals with the same reported score achieved the same raw score on the GATB.

2. The employer might also be led to assume that all candidates with the same percentile score on the test would have the same expected performance on the job.

We could have added a third reservation, for, if the VG-GATB Referral System became a very important route to employment, policy makers would have to anticipate that at least some applicants might claim minority status at the local Job Service office in order to get the benefit of preferential score adjustments and make no such claim at the workplace, so that the meaning of the reported score would be interpreted with reference to the majority group.

Despite these reservations, we conclude this chapter with the recommendation that score adjustments, possibly within-group percentile score adjustments, continue to play a role, albeit a somewhat different role, in the VG-GATB Referral System for reasons that emerge from our technical analyses of GATB data as well as considerations of social policy.

The analysis in the committee's interim report was based on theoretical comparisons of within-group scoring and a number of alternative referral and reporting options. It was taken as given that referral would be based on a test in which minority average scores were substantially lower than majority average scores. The assumptions that allowed the theoretical comparisons were chosen to match, as best we knew, the circumstances of Employment Service referrals. The comparisons also depended on assumptions about the validity of the test and its predictive behavior for different racial groups.

We are now in a position to look again at alternative score reporting and referral models, but at this time many of the earlier assumptions can be replaced by empirical statements. Evidence presented earlier in this report establishes that the average scores of black Job Service clients are substantially lower than those of majority clients, although the difference varies somewhat by job family.

Our earlier assumption that the GATB does not predict differently for different racial groups needs some qualification in light of the analyses presented in Chapter 9. There is evidence that the GATB has somewhat lower correlations with supervisor ratings of job performance for blacks compared with whites. Nevertheless, the use of a regression equation based on the combined group of black and nonminority workers would generally not give predictions that are biased against blacks. Insofar as the total-group equation gives systematically different predictions, it is somewhat more likely to overpredict the performance of blacks than to underpredict. The degree of overprediction is slight at the lower score ranges, and somewhat larger at higher score levels.

We have now made independent estimates of GATB validities (presented in Chapter 8), taking account of recent (post-1972) validity studies. The modest relationship between GATB scores and ratings of performance on the job—our estimate is an average corrected validity of .30 with about 90 percent of the jobs studied falling in the range of .20 to .40— is one important factor for policy makers to consider in assessing various referral alternatives.

PERSPECTIVES ON TEST FAIRNESS

What makes the use of a test fair? Like most Americans, testing specialists have wrestled with questions of equity and fairness in the past two decades. A number of models for the fair use of tests have been proposed in the psychometric literature. The following discussion of fairness draws on this literature as well as more popular sources to build a framework for the analysis of score reporting and referral methods.

To illustrate various perspectives on fairness, we take as given the conditions that would apply in the proposed VG-GATB system:

1. Applicants meeting other criteria set by the employer will be referred in order of their scores on the test.

2. The test is modestly predictive of job performance, so expected performance increases with test score.

3. The applicants represent several population subgroups.

4. There are substantial subgroup differences in average scores on the test.

When can the use of a test be said to be fair to the various subgroups? The perspectives offered by psychometricians are derived from quantitative analysis of the joint distributions of group status, test score, and job performance (as indicated by a criterion measure such as supervisor ratings of performance). Since only group status and test scores are known for applicants, information about future job performance must be extrapolated from validity studies of job incumbents who have taken the test.

The many definitions of fairness that have grown out of concern about the use of employment tests can be distilled for our purposes into two general approaches: fairness in predicting job performance from test score and fairness in selection, given job performance.

Fairness in Predicting Job Performance from Test Score

It can be argued that selection is fair if the predicted distribution of job performance for people with a given test score does not vary by population subgroup. We expect a white person with a test score of 70 to perform about the same as a black or Hispanic person with a test score of 70. In this conception of fairness, the focus is on prediction and whether the test predicts differently for different groups. If there is no evidence of differential prediction by group, then knowing any individual's test score is sufficient to predict job performance; the employer can make the same inferences about future job performance for all applicants. If, however, a test is found to predict differentially (as the GATB appears to for white and black applicants), then information about group status would be necessary to make appropriate inferences from test scores.

In this definition, fairness consists of the evenhandedness with which the test predicts the future job performance of various subgroups. If a given test score can be associated with the same level of future job performance for black and white applicants, that is to say, if there is no predictive bias, then the test is fair and, to the extent that one feels that selection should be based solely on predicted performance, the selection system is fair. Note that this definition of test fairness does not address group differences in average test scores or the legal problem of adverse impact.

This definition is the classical one (Cleary, 1968) and the conception of fairness most widely accepted in the psychometric literature, at least as a minimum requirement (e.g., Petersen and Novick, 1976; American Educational Research Association et al., 1985). When testing professionals refer to test bias, it is differential prediction that they have in mind (contrary to certain popular usage, in which the claim of bias refers to group differences in average scores). The general approach also appears in the fair pay literature. In that context, fairness requires that the formula best predicting pay as a function of legally compensable factors (qualifications, experience, seniority) be the same for all groups.

Because of the existence of substantial group differences in average test scores, particularly differences between black and majority-group job applicants, many now find this definition of fairness insufficient, at least as it pertains to allotting employment opportunity. A test may be fair in predicting performance, but nevertheless predict performance rather poorly. When that is so, many able workers will be rejected by the test, including a disproportionately large number of able minority workers.

Fairness in Selection, Given Job Performance

An alternative approach to fairness focuses not on prediction equations, but on realized job performance (e.g., Darlington, 1971; Cole, 1973). Selection can be considered "performance fair" if people with a given level of performance on the job have the same distribution of test scores, no matter what population subgroup they belong to. In that case, a rule that selects workers in order of test score will select the same proportion of good workers in each population subgroup. The question asked from this perspective is, Do workers of equal job proficiency in the several groups have the same chance of selection?

At first glance, it would seem that if the use of a test is fair in the first sense, it would also be fair in the second. But it is possible to satisfy both definitions of fairness only if prediction of job performance from test score is perfect, or if all groups have the same joint distribution of test score and performance. Neither of these conditions is met in the GATB. Tests are at best only moderately good predictors of job performance. Human performance is far too complex to expect anything approaching perfect prediction. One of the consequences of prediction error is that some people who could perform well on the job but who score in the lower ranges on the test are screened out, whereas

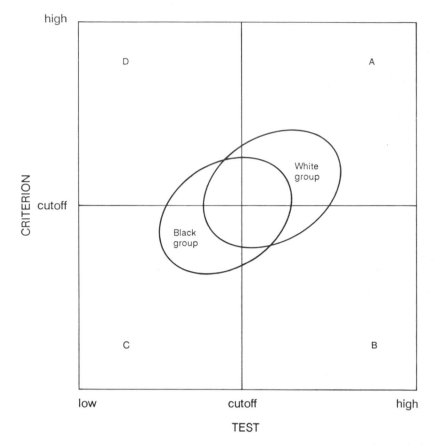

FIGURE 13–1   Effects of imperfect prediction when there are subpopulation differences in average test scores.

some others who do well on the test, and hence are selected, will perform inadequately on the job. So long as there are average group differences in test scores—and these are likely to manifest themselves whenever racially or ethnically identifiable subgroups live in circumstances of comparative disadvantage—the effects of imperfect prediction will fall more heavily on these disadvantaged minorities than on other social groups.

Figure 13–1 shows why the effects of imperfect prediction fall disproportionately on groups that have lower average test scores than the majority group. It should be remembered, however, that the phenomenon is not the result of some racial or ethnic bias inherent in the test; the impact is the same for all low-scoring individuals, regardless of group identity. Not only do low scorers have a greater likelihood of being erroneously rejected, but high scorers also have a greater likelihood of being erroneously accepted.

In the figure the horizontal line labeled "criterion cutoff" distinguishes adequate from unsatisfactory performance on the job. The vertical line labeled "test cutoff" represents the score below which no applicant will be selected. Ellipses representing the joint distribution of job and test performance for majority and minority groups are superimposed, one upon the other. Note that the white group has higher job performance and test scores on average, although there is also a good deal of overlap between the two groups. The intersection of the criterion cutoff and test cutoff creates four sectors: Sector A = successful performance on both test and criterion; Sector B = successful test performance, unsuccessful job performance; Sector C = unsuccessful performance on both test and criterion; and Sector D = successful job performance and unsuccessful test performance. Sectors B and D represent prediction error.

Because the average test and performance scores are higher for the majority group than for the minority group, more of the majority ellipse falls in Sector A (successful performance on both test and criterion). Conversely, more of the minority ellipse falls in Sector C (unsuccessful performance on both test and criterion). Now observe Sectors B and D. A larger segment of the majority ellipse than the minority ellipse can be seen to fall in B, which means that proportionally greater numbers of majority applicants will be selected but will perform unsuccessfully. And a larger segment of the minority ellipse falls in Sector D, which means that minority applicants who could have performed adequately on the job will be screened out in greater numbers. It is the Sector B and D effects that violate the conception of fairness that we have called "performance fair." They occur despite the absence of any predictive bias in the test itself.

Richard T. Seymour, representing the Lawyers' Committee for Civil Rights Under Law at a meeting of the committee and its liaison group, made a forceful statement of this view of fairness as a function of performance (Seymour, 1988). His analysis, which is based on GATB validity data for 47 jobs, illustrates the effects of rejection errors and acceptance errors: many more of the successful black job incumbents in the validity studies would not have been referred had the test scores been the basis of referral; conversely, of the marginal job incumbents (those who received low supervisor ratings), a greater proportion of whites than blacks would have been referred had test scores been used. These effects of prediction error led him to conclude that the GATB produces "an extreme degree of racial unfairness" (Seymour, 1988):

The evidence is overwhelming that tests work differently for blacks and for whites, and that they both systematically under-predict black job performance and over-predict white job performance. [Reliance on cognitive ability tests] can only be justified as an affirmative-action program for whites, to ensure that whites are represented in desirable jobs at rates beyond the natural limits of their abilities.

As a consequence, he strongly recommends against further use of the VG-GATB Referral System.

Mr. Seymour seems not to acknowledge the two types of fairness analysis we have described when he claims (erroneously) that the GATB underpredicts black job performance and overpredicts white performance. We must reemphasize the point that the effects he describes are not inherently bound up with race or ethnicity, but rather with high and low scores. Nevertheless, the undoubted effect of imperfect prediction when social groups have different average test scores is to place the greater burden of prediction error on the shoulders of the lower-scoring group. Is this fair? In the final analysis, we think not. But there are complexities to the question that require explication.

An Example Comparing Different Concepts of Fairness

As a more concrete way of illustrating the effects pictured in Figure 13–1, we present the results of a GATB validity study on carpenters that included 91 whites and 45 blacks. The individuals in the study were already on the job. They took the GATB test and were rated by their supervisor. Arbitrary cutoffs were used to divide the groups into high and low test scorers and high and low performers on the job. The frequency counts showing joint distributions of job and test performance for each group are shown in the table below:

Frequency Counts Showing the Joint Distributions of Test Performance and Job Performance for 91 White and 45 Black Workers:

| | Test Performance | | | |
| | Whites ($N = 91$) | | Blacks ($N = 45$) | |
Job Performance	Fail	Pass	Fail	Pass
Good	11	60	8	8
Poor	11	9	24	5

There are three different ways to convert these frequency counts to percentages, and each presents a different perspective on fairness. The first method evaluates predictive fairness. The raw data are converted to percentages so that the columns sum to 100, as shown in the table below.

Column Percentages Computed to Elucidate the Conception of Predictive Fairness:

| | Test Performance | | | |
| | Whites | | Blacks | |
Job Performance	Fail (%)	Pass (%)	Fail (%)	Pass (%)
Good	50	87	25	62
Poor	50	13	75	38
	(100)	(100)	(100)	(100)

Now we can see that 50 percent of white carpenters (11 of 22) who fail the test do well on the job, whereas only 25 percent of black carpenters (8 of 32) do so. And whereas only 13 percent of whites who pass the test do poorly on the job, the figure for blacks is 38 percent. When analyzed this way, the data reveal that more white test failers than black ones would do satisfactory work if given the chance, and more blacks than whites are passing the test and proving to be unsatisfactory workers. Thus the test overpredicts black job performance and is predictively unfair to whites.

The second method of converting the frequency counts illustrates performance fairness. It creates percentages in such a way that the row percentages sum to 100, as shown in the table below.

Row Percentages Computed to Elucidate the Conception of Performance-Based Fairness:

| | Test Performance | | | | | |
| | Whites | | | Blacks | | |
Job Performance	Fail (%)	Pass (%)		Fail (%)	Pass (%)	
Good	15	85	(100%)	50	50	(100%)
Poor	55	45	(100%)	83	17	(100%)

Look first at good workers who fail the test and would therefore never have been referred to the employer had a test-based system been in place (sector D in Figure 13–1). The numbers are 15 percent for white carpenters (11 of 71) and 50 percent for black carpenters (8 of 16). For the poor workers, 45 percent of white workers who are poor performers (9 of 20) pass the test and thus are among those who would have been referred for employment (sector B in Figure 13–1). By comparison, only 17 percent of blacks (5 of 29) who are poor workers passed the test. Viewed this way, the percentages say that good black workers will be disproportionately screened out in a test-based referral system, and unsatisfactory white workers disproportionately screened in. The test is performance-biased against black workers.

There is a third way to look at the frequency data, and that is to compute percentages within each racial group. The effect is to show what the numbers in each cell would be for blacks and for whites if the sample size was 100 for each group, as shown in the table below.

Proportional Percentages of White and Black Workers in Each Test Performance by Job Performance Category:

Job Performance	Test Performance				
	Whites		Blacks		
	Fail (%)	Pass (%)	Fail (%)	Pass (%)	
Good	12	66	18	18	
Poor	12	10	53	11	
		(100%)		(100%)	

This presentation of the data also tells an important story. First, group differences in test performance and job performance are a reality. Black carpenters score substantially lower on the test, so any system of top-down referral will find proportionally more blacks below the cutoff score than whites, 71 percent compared with 24 percent. Black carpenters also perform poorly on the job in substantially greater proportions, or, put the other way, a larger percentage of whites perform satisfactorily on the job, 78 percent compared with 36 percent of black carpenters. (This numerical demonstration assumes that the supervisor ratings of performance are themselves valid.)

Second, the proportion of correct classifications is reasonably similar for the two groups; 78 percent of white carpenters were correctly classified compared with 71 percent of blacks. But the damaging prediction errors fall more heavily on the black carpenters. Of the 36 percent who performed well on the job, 18 percent—fully one-half—would not have been referred for employment under a straight rank-ordering of applicants.

Each way of looking at the data provides insights about the effects of using a test to screen job applicants. Which truth is the most important truth? At this point in our history, it is certain that the use of the GATB without some sort of score adjustments would systematically screen out blacks, some of whom could have performed satisfactorily on the job. Fair test use would seem to require at the very least that the inadequacies of the technology should not fall more heavily on the social groups already burdened by the effects of past and present discrimination.

EQUITY AND EFFICIENCY:
COMPARISON OF FOUR REFERRAL MODELS

The question of fair use of the GATB is not one that can be settled by psychometric considerations alone—but neither can referral policy be decided on the basis of equity concerns alone. If there is a strong federal commitment to helping blacks, women, and certain other minority groups move into the economic mainstream, there is also a compelling interest in improving productivity and strengthening the competitive position of the country in the world market. The underlying principle of the VG-GATB system is to make the maximization of performance the basis of the person-job match. It is a productivity-oriented referral procedure that, through the addition of score adjustments, has been made responsive to equal employment opportunity policy.

In our interim report, we evaluated six possible referral rules for their effect on estimated job performance and on the proportion of minority-group members who would be referred. In the following discussion we look at four rules, including one new variant, that most clearly illustrate the available policy options. Two of the rules use linear adjustments to minority scores, different for each group, to increase minority referral rates. The four rules presented for consideration are: (1) raw-score, top-down referral; (2) within-group percentile score, top-down referral; (3) performance-based score, top-down referral; and (4) minimum competency referral.

Raw-score, top-down referral is referral made from the total group of applicants in order of unmodified test score. This rule complements the conception of fairness as lack of differential prediction. If the predicted job performance for a given test score is the same for all population groups, then the set of applicants with highest expected productivity is obtained by referring in order of test score. However, given current average group score differences, the rule would produce substantial adverse impact on the lower-scoring groups. The question that policy makers must ask of the VG-GATB system is whether the gains in expected performance are sufficient to justify this impact.

Within-group percentile score, top-down referral is referral in which a percentile score is computed for each applicant by comparing the raw score for that applicant with the scores obtained by a norm group of the same racial or ethnic identity. (Equivalently, a different linear transformation is applied to the raw test score for the different groups so that the mean and the variance of test scores are the same for all groups. In the simplest case, the quantity m is added to each minority score, where m is the difference between majority and minority means.) Referral is made from the total group of applicants in order of modified test score. Given average GATB validities of about .3, this referral rule would eliminate the disproportionate rates of false rejections of able black workers and false acceptances of inadequte white workers described in the discussion of performance fairness. If GATB validities were substantially higher, the rule would overcompensate.

Performance-based score, top-down referral, a variant of the previous rule, is referral by test scores that are adjusted for group membership in such a way that the distribution of test scores at a given level of performance is the same for all groups. In the simplest case, a different linear transformation is applied to the raw test score for the different groups so that the mean and the variance of test scores for a given performance score are the same for all groups. That is, the score adjustment adds $(1 - r^2)m$ to each minority score, where r is the correlation between test score and job performance, and m is the difference between majority- and minority-group means. Although conceptually attractive, this approach requires that the test's validity for the job be estimated.

Although this rule will be seen (Tables 13–1, 13–2) to function essentially the same as the within-group percentile rule when test validities are modest (as they currently are for the GATB), we treat it separately because it is more specifically a remedy for imperfect prediction. Were there a test with perfect or nearly perfect predictive power, this rule would function like the raw-score, top-down rule.

Minimum competency referral is the system used before the introduction of VG-GATB procedures in which applicants who score above some minimum cutoff score, set perpahs by the employer, are referred at random. We may view selection under this rule as being determined by an adjusted test score that is obtained from the original by randomly reassigning test score values above the cutoff to all examinees who initially score above the cutoff and randomly reassigning test score values below the cutoff to all examinees who score initially below the cutoff.

Analysis of the Referral Rules

There are two statistical computations used to assess both the gains in expected performance from using the GATB and its adverse impact on groups that tend to score low on the test. The first is the correlation between the test score and job performance. The gain in expected performance, under certain assumptions about the distribution of test scores and job performance measures when workers are selected in order of their test scores, is proportional to the correlation between test score and job performance (Brogden's formula, see Chapter 12, this volume). The second is the proportion of minorities referred. These proportions are determined by the distributions of test scores for the different population groups.

Our analysis compares the four referral rules by computing the correlations of test scores with job performance, as well as the means and standard deviations of the test scores for minority and majority groups. The majority-group scores are assumed to have a mean of 0 and a standard deviation of 1.

We present the analysis in two scenarios. The first assumes that the GATB predicts job performance equally well for black and white groups. The second assumes that predictions of job performance from GATB scores differ somewhat, with the effect that use of a single prediction equation will slightly overpredict the performance of blacks. Our analysis of the subset of GATB validity studies that report results separately by race indicates that such differential prediction may exist, but the small sample sizes and the possibility of bias in the criterion (supervisor ratings) make us reluctant to place too much emphasis on the results.

For convenience in comparing the performance of the various referral rules with and without the effects of differential prediction, both analyses are based on the small number of studies that report validities separately by race. The average validity coefficient for this set of 72 studies is substantially lower than the mean value of .3 for all 755 GATB validity studies used elsewhere in the report.

Scenario A: No Differential Prediction, Applicant Groups Are Like the Norm Group (Table 13–1)

1. The raw test score and job performance have correlation .2 for the majority group and for the minority group, and the same regression line predicts mean job performance for a given test score in both groups. The uncorrected correlation of .2 is based on the set of 72 validity studies that contain at least 50 black and 50 nonminority workers (see Chapter 9). Note that the average value for these studies is at the lower end of the range of validities (.2 to .4) found for the entire set of 755 studies undertaken by USES.

2. The mean test score for the minority group is .9 standard deviations below the mean test score for the majority group, and the minority group and majority group have equal test score standard deviations. These assumptions are taken from the USES norm groups for Job Families IV and V, which include almost all jobs typically filled through the Employment Service. (The norm-group differences in average test scores between "other" and black are 1 standard deviation for Job Family IV and 0.8 standard deviation for Job Family V; since jobs are divided nearly evenly between the two families, an overall figure of .9 is assumed.)

TABLE 13–1   Scenario A: No Differential Prediction. Correlations with Job Performance, Minority Group Means, and Standard Deviations,[a] and Percentage of Minority Group Referred When 20 Percent of the Majority Group Are Referred, for Different Referral Rules

Referral Rule	Correlation	Minority Mean	Minority Standard Deviation	Percentage of Minority Group Referred
Raw score	.22	−0.90	1.0	4
Within-group	.20	0.00	1.0	20
Performance-based	.20	−0.04	1.0	19
Minimum competency (10% cutoff)	.09	−0.49	1.2	13
Minimum competency (30% cutoff)	.13	−0.58	1.1	8

[a]Taking majority-group means to be 0 and standard deviations to be 1.

3. Thirty percent of the applicant group is minority. This figure corresponds to recent Employment Service national registrations. This fraction may vary markedly from job to job and from locality to locality.

As Table 13–1 illustrates, the two referral models that incorporate score adjustments dramatically increase the percentage of minority applicants referred and yet show only small decreases in predictive power compared with the raw-score, top-down referral rule. The minimum competency model does not compare favorably on either dimension of interest, expected performance or minority presence in the referral pool.

Scenario B: Differential Prediction, Applicant Groups Are Like Worker Groups (Table 13–2)

1. The correlation between test score and job performance for the majority group is .20. The correlation between test score and job performance for the minority group is .15. The difference between expected job performance of majority and minority groups is 0.20 standard deviations (in units of majority job performance) when the test score is at the majority average.

These assumptions are drawn from the analysis in Chapter 9 of 72 GATB studies that contained at least 50 black and 50 nonminority workers. (The correlations have not been corrected for reliability or restriction of range.) First, the correlation of test score and job performance is somewhat lower for blacks than for whites. Second, at any given test score, blacks with that test score have lower average job performance than whites with the test score. This effect appears in the regression

TABLE 13–2   Scenario B: Differential Prediction. Correlations with Job Performance, Minority Group Means, and Standard Deviations,[a] and Percentages of Minority Group Referred When 20 Percent of the Majority Group Are Referred, for Different Referral Rules

Referral Rule	Correlation	Minority Mean	Standard Deviation	Percentage of Minority Group Referred
Raw score	.23	−0.90	0.9	3
Within-group	.18	0.00	0.9	18
Performance-based	.19	−0.05	0.9	16

[a]Taking majority-group means to be 0 and standard deviations to be 1.

equations as differences in the regression intercepts. The correlations obtained from the 72 studies are substantially lower than those obtained in the 755 studies, and they are based on relatively few workers, so that we cannot confidently extend the corresponding regression equations to all workers. Nevertheless, it seems prudent to consider these assumptions as an alternative scenario allowing for differential prediction.

2. The mean test score for the minority group is 0.9 standard deviations below the mean test score for the majority group, and the minority-group standard deviation is 0.9 that of the majority group. These assumptions are based on 72 GATB studies, each of which each contained at least 50 black and 50 nonminority workers, all from Job Families IV and V; the median difference in average test scores (with the majority-group standard deviation in each study set equal to 1) is 0.88; the median ratio of minority standard deviation to majority standard deviation is .90.

These assumptions disagree with the USES norm groups only in the minority-group standard deviations being .9 rather than 1. (It might be argued that the lower minority standard deviations are due to restriction in range operating differently for the minority group and the majority group. The same argument would justify correcting the observed minority correlation by 10 percent to .165; but, in the absence of data on plausible applicant groups, we here accept the numbers as given.) The median majority-group standard deviation for the 72 jobs agrees quite closely with the standard deviations used in the USES norm group, so that within-group scoring is equivalent to increasing minority scores by 0.9 majority-group standard deviations.

3. Thirty percent of the applicant group is minority, in agreement with the observed proportion in the 72 studies.

From Table 13–2, we see the same general pattern of large gains in the percentage of minority applicants who would be referred under the models that incorporate score adjustments at some cost to expected performance. The principal difference between the two scenarios lies in the effect on the validity coefficient of using the referral rules that incorporate score adjustments. For the example with no differential prediction, using the within-group and performance-based rules causes a drop of 10 percent in the correlation; for the model with differential prediction, using these rules causes a drop of about 20 percent in the correlation. The larger reduction in correlation observed under the assumption of differential prediction is due principally to the difference in mean scores of the two groups, not to the lower validities found in this data set.

The effect on productivity of the drop in correlation from .22 to .20 in Scenario A or from .23 to .18 in Scenario B depends on a number of unconsidered variables, including selection ratio. When the selection ratio is high—say 1 in 3—such a decline in correlation is trivial. However, if a great deal of choice is available—say 10 or 20 viable candidates for every job opening—such a drop in correlation will result in a much larger difference in expected productivity. In that case, the additional 10 percent reduction in correlation due to differential production makes it of considerable practical interest to know which of the two scenarios is more likely to be applicable.

Effects of the Referral Rules

Raw-Score, Top-Down Referral

This rule results in the highest expected performance in the referred group and the lowest minority-group proportion referred. The effect is extreme when the referral ratio is low. If the referral ratio is 1 in 5 for the majority group and the applicant group is 30 percent minority, only 4 percent of the minority applicants will be referred, one-seventh of the majority-group rate. Yet, when the validity is modest, as it is here, many of the minority applicants excluded would have performed better than many of the majority workers included.

Conclusion This rule has an adverse impact on minority applicants that, in our judgment, is out of all proportion to the gains in expected job performance (as measured by supervisor ratings).

Within-Group Percentile Score, Top-Down Referral

This rule achieves the highest proportions of minority referrals, with some loss in correlation with job performance. When the applicant group has the same distribution of minority and majority scores as the norm group, the proportion of minorities referred is the same as the proportion of minorities in the applicant group, and the goal of eliminating adverse impact is achieved. For the 72 worker groups in the differential validity studies, the rule appears to refer nearly proportionately overall, although there are substantial deviations in particular worker groups.

Conclusion The within-group referral rule is race-conscious. There is negligible difference between this rule and the performance-based rule that is designed to refer workers at the same level of job performance in the same proportion for each group. Thus the within-group referral rule is an effective way to achieve proportionate referrals of workers at the same level of job performance. Admittedly it will increase somewhat the rate of false acceptances, but the loss in overall expected job performance is small.

Performance-Based Score, Top-Down Referral

As Tables 13–1 and 13–2 illustrate, this rule is very similar in application to the previous one. When the correlation expressing validity between test score and job performance is .3, and the minority-group average test score is 1 standard deviation less than the majority-group average test score, then this score adjustment adds approximately $(1 - .09) = 0.91$ standard deviation to each minority score. Referral is then in order of the adjusted score. In comparison, the within-group percentile score adjustment would add 1 standard deviation to each minority score. The difference between the two rules is negligible for the modest validities observed for the GATB.

Conclusion The slight drop in correlation that occurs for each of the score adjustment strategies suggests that the choice between the raw score, top-down rule and either of the rules that incorporates a score adjustment cannot be based principally on efficiency grounds, at least not for the range of (corrected) validities of .2 to .4 that we have calculated for Employment Service jobs. In choosing between within-group and performance-based score adjustments, there is no reason to prefer one to the other by its correlation with job performance. In terms of legal admissibility, both are race-conscious, both would virtually eliminate the adverse impact of the GATB on black and Hispanic applicants, and both can be seen as counteracting prediction error for minority groups. Because the performance-based score adjustment is responsive to changes in test validities (with high validities, smaller score adjustments would be made and the proportion of minorities referred would be reduced), policy makers at the Department of Labor will want to consider whether the performance-based referral rule might be legally more defensible. For the same reason, if policy makers choose this rule, special caution should be exercised to ensure that test validities are not overstated.

Minimum Competency Referral

Note from Table 13–2 that this referral rule is inferior to both of the score adjustment strategies because it reduces the correlation quite dramatically without much increasing minority referrals. Minimum competency referral is the only alternative to raw-score, top-down referral examined here that is not race-conscious, but it might well open the Employment Service to a Title VII challenge, since it would produce markedly unequal referral rates for majority and minority applicants.

The So-Called Golden Rule Procedure

Thus far we have explored two basic conceptions of fairness in testing, one of which focuses on prediction and the other on job performance. We have also examined four systems for assembling the pool of applicants to be referred to an employer. The first, raw-score, top-down referral, corresponds to the idea that the use of a test is fair if a given score predicts about the same level of criterion performance regardless of group identity. Two of the referral models, those involving score adjustments, complement the conception of fairness that focuses on realized job performance. Minimum competency referral, the fourth option discussed, does not advance either idea of fairness and is the least attractive model in terms of maximizing expected performance.

There is another approach to the issue of fairness in testing that has gained some currency in the past few years. It is based on the premise that a test can be considered fair only if it produces the same distribution of scores for all population subgroups. Called the Golden Rule procedure (after the insurance company, not the maxim), it is a strategy for selecting test items with the goal of eliminating group differences in test scores. Using this procedure, items are field-tested with minority- and majority-group members and, whenever possible, items are selected that show the least difference in the proportions correct obtained by each group. Because items are selected explicitly to reduce the difference between minority- and majority-group performance, this procedure should in theory yield tests in which the overall difference between minority and majority performance is reduced.

Since 1985 the Golden Rule procedure has been used in assembling the tests used in the licensing of life, property, and casualty insurance agents in the State of Illinois. It is the consequence of a lawsuit against the State of Illinois and the Educational Testing Service filed by the Golden Rule Insurance Company on behalf of five black examinees who failed the licensing examination in 1976.

In an out-of-court settlement, the parties agreed to assembling tests using the following system. Racial status of candidates taking the test would be recorded and used on an ongoing basis with test performance data to sort items into two types: Type I items are those in which (1) the difference in proportions correct between black and white examinees is not significantly greater than 0.15, and (2) the overall proportion correct is not significantly less than 0.40 (thus eliminating the very difficult items). Type II items are those that fail to meet the above criteria for between-group differences or item difficulty. Tests were to be assembled by selecting Type I items whenever possible. Whenever Type I items were not available or when their use was inappropriate according to generally accepted principles of test construction, Type II items could be used. In either case, items with the smallest between-group differences were to be used first.

For a number of reasons, theoretical and practical, the Golden Rule procedure has been greeted with skepticism by the psychometric profession. And in fact, its first systematic application has not been promising. As part of the consent decree, an advisory committee of academic and insurance professionals was established to advise the State of Illinois on the use and effects of the new tests for insurance agents. Statistics on the performance of black and white examinees were studied by the advisory committee over a three-year period. A member of the GATB committee who served on the Golden Rule advisory committee reports that the general consensus was that the procedure resulted in only a modest decrease in test performance differences between black and white examinees.

The reasons for the failure of the procedure to bring substantial reductions in group differences in test scores stem in part from the requirements of a large-scale testing program. The item pool was not stable over time, in part because test forms were periodically made public as part of the settlement. New items were constantly being introduced and old ones retired. Consequently, the number of test items on which statistics were available was never large compared with the number of different test forms needed both to maintain test security and to have alternate forms available for those who wished to retake the exam. This problem was exacerbated by the very detailed content specifications for the insurance agent test. In some content areas, the number of items available did not permit much selection based on between-group differences.

Obtaining large numbers of effectively interchangeable items is always a difficult practical problem. But the problems with the procedure are more than logistical. A number of scholars have pointed out that the two rules of exclusion (the overall minimum correct response rate, 0.40, and the differential correct response rate, 0.15) work at cross purposes, with the result that the procedure will not necessarily reduce the between-group difference in means. This is so because the items with the smallest between-group difference in proportion correct are the very easy and the very difficult items. The minimum 0.40 rule eliminates the difficult items (Linn and Drasgow, 1987; Marco, 1988). Moreover, even without the minimum 0.40 rule, the reductions in group differences in item scores would not come close to eliminating the degree of adverse impact associated with top-down, total-group selection (Marco, 1988). In other words, if the policy goal is to eliminate adverse impact, the Golden Rule procedure, although also race-conscious, is not nearly as effective as either of the score adjustment strategies discussed above.

The Golden Rule procedure's effects on the quality of tests, however, would be detrimental. The construct validity of a test would be altered if items were selected primarily on a basis other than optimal measurement. Moreover, the predictive value of the test would be reduced for majority and minority examinees. Test reliability would also be reduced. Items of middle difficulty and items most closely associated with total score would tend to be eliminated more than easy items. As a result, the reliability of the test might be increased for lower-scoring examinees, but for middle- and high-scoring examinees, the opposite result is more likely (Marco, 1988).

We do not see the Golden Rule procedure as a viable alternative for the Department of Labor to consider. For technical and practical reasons it does not rival score adjustment strategies. Moreover, the losses in test validity incurred are not offset by the marginally improved legal attractions it offers.

An Alternative Referral Rule

From the perspective of fairness to all Employment Service applicants, the major drawback of the two rules that require score adjustments is that white applicants will be referred to employers in somewhat smaller numbers than they otherwise would have been. In other words, increasing the referral rates of racial and ethnic minorities will produce a concomitant reduction in the referral chances of some white applicants with higher raw test scores and somewhat greater predicted success on the job.

In order to avoid that diminution in the prospects of majority-group applicants while at the same time enhancing the competitive position of minority applicants, the committee recommends the consideration of a referral rule that combines the essential features of both the raw-score, top-down and the within-group score, top-down rules.[1] To achieve both kinds of fairness, all applicants who would have been chosen by a straight ranking of unadjusted scores will be referred, and, in addition, all applicants whose adjusted scores qualify them will also be referred. Thus, no job seeker will be denied an opportunity that would have been available under either fairness model. Since the score adjustment is commensurate with the effects on minority groups of imperfect prediction and since no group is greatly damaged by the combined-rules approach, the legal objections raised by the Assistant Attorney General for Civil Rights to the VG-GATB testing program may be assuaged.

Although we recommend the Combined Rules Referral Plan to the serious consideration of the Department of Labor and other federal authorities in the fair employment practices area, we cannot claim that it is a panacea for the legal stalemate in which many employers find themselves. It is a compromise and as such may fail to satisfy advocates on either side of the fairness question. Depending on an employer's selection decisions, the total procedure could produce some degree of adverse impact on minority groups, although of far lesser severity than would a referral system based on unadjusted scores. At the same time, majority job seekers could claim that enrichment of the referral pool by definition dilutes their chances for selection. Policy makers at the Department of Labor will need to consider the potential legal risks of this referral strategy just as they do the risks of other referral plans.

On a practical level, if there is a burden imposed by the Combined Rules Referral Plan, it is that the local Job Service office must deal with a somewhat larger number of people to fill a job order and the employer must consider more applicants than is absolutely necessary under either rule alone. There is some concern that this necessity might make the strategy impractical for small, low-volume offices.

Operationalizing the Combined Rules Referral Plan

For illustrative purposes, the plan is presented as it might work in a local office that has a sufficiently large number of otherwise qualified job seekers on hand to allow selectivity. The thrust of the plan is to increase the flexibility of the employer by referring either more high scorers or more minority applicants than would otherwise have been seen.

An employer sends a job order for 10 job openings and asks to see 20 applicants. Twenty becomes the base number. The referral group is

---

[1]Although we phrase our recommendation in terms of within-group score adjustments, performance-based adjustments could be substituted with virtually identical results. Our slight preference for the within-group strategy is that it is easier to put into practice.

TABLE 13–3   Applicants Referred Under Total-Group, Within-Group, and a Combined Rules Referral Plan

| | | Percentile Score | | Referral Method | | |
| | | Total-Group | Within-Group | Total-Score | Within-Group | Combined-Rules |
Applicant	Race	Total-Group	Within-Group	Total-Score	Within-Group	Combined-Rules
1	W	71		X	X	X
2	W	65		X	—	X
3	W	63		X	—	X
4	B	60	82	X	X	X
5	W	58		—	—	—
6	W	57		—	—	—
7	W	54		—	—	—
8	B	51	73	—	X	X
9	B	48	70	—	X	X
10	B	38	60	—	—	—

NOTE: X = Referred; — = Not referred.

assembled in two stages. First, a list of all otherwise eligible candidates in the files is compiled on the basis of rank-ordered, total-group scores. The top 20 scorers are identified; they will be placed in the referral group. Second, the same list of candidates is reordered with minority scores converted to within-group percentile scores. Again, the top 20 scorers are identified for placement in the referral group. Thus an applicant is placed in the referral group by having a high total-group percentile score, a high within-group percentile score, or both. There will be a good deal of overlap between the stage-one and stage-two selections, so the total referral group will be less than double the baseline figure.

Under the Combined Rules Referral Plan no applicant is excluded who would have been referred if the Employment Service had made the baseline 20 referrals on just total-group or just within-group percentile scores.

To illustrate, Table 13–3 describes a situation in which the employer has two job openings and has asked for a referral ratio of 2:1. The baseline referral figure is 4. On the basis of file search there are 10 applicants who meet the employer's initial requirements (education, minimum cutoff score, and so on). The 10 are listed in order of total-group percentile score. A total-group referral procedure would refer the first four candidates listed. The within-group method would in this example refer three black applicants, two of whom had lower total-group scores than competing majority candidates. With this set of scores, the combined rules would result in a referral group augmented by two for a total of six applicants who will be referred to the employer.

Not the least of the attractions of the Combined Rules Referral Plan, in the committee's judgment, is that it places responsibility for the composition of the work force with the employer. It gives the employer the flexibility to emphasize predicted performance, racial and ethnic representativeness, or a combination of these policies according to the job in question, the affirmative action posture of the firm, or other situational factors. The Job Service is not placed in the position of appearing to relieve the employer of these decisions, an implication that some employers seem to have drawn from the VG-GATB system of referral based only on within-group scores.

Norm Groups for Within-Group Scoring

If any referral plan that incorporates the within-group score adjustment strategy is adopted, USES will need to undertake the construction of more satisfactory norm groups on which to base the score adjustments. In practice, there will be considerable variation in the applicant groups for different jobs in different localities. There is evidence from the data supporting the within-group percentile tables, from employer representatives in the committee's liaison group, and from some applicant data obtained by the committee, of noticeable differences between the national norm group currently used by the Employment Service for score conversions and applicant groups.

Differences in means or standard deviations of the applicant groups from the norm group could cause quite different referral rates and validities of the within-group score for particular jobs. If, for example, an employer set qualifications for a job that are correlated with test score, then the applicants for the job would be expected to have a smaller standard deviation in test score than the norm group, and the differences between majority-group and minority-group mean score would be expected to be lower. The effect of using within-group scoring based on national norms would be to refer minorities in larger fractions than in the applicant pool, and to significantly reduce the validity of the test, because of overestimates of standard deviations.

It obviously is not practical for the Employment Service to devise a different additive factor for every job in every locality. But we do recommend that norm groups be developed by job family and, if possible, by smaller, more homogeneous clusters of jobs.

In addition, the score adjustment factor should be computed differently than is currently done. Currently the adjustment factor is computed as the difference between the mean scores in a given job family composite of all majority- and minority-group workers in the national norm group. The correct factor is the mean score difference between majority-group and minority-group applicants for the same job, averaged over all jobs. Similarly, standard deviations should be computed for applicants to a particular job, and then averaged over jobs. The current computation does not properly allow for differences between jobs.

Suppose, for example, that there are two jobs, and applicants for the jobs scored as follows:

Job	Minority	Majority
1	7 12 17 20	18 22
2	15 19	19 23 25 25

The Employment Service calculation pools the scores for all jobs to obtain a difference of 7 between majority- and minority-group average scores. The difference between average scores for each job is 6.

In order to assess the effect of the current within-group referral norm groups on actual jobs, we used 72 jobs from David Synk and David Swarthout's research (U.S. Department of Labor, 1987). The differences between minority and nonminority mean test scores expressed in majority standard deviations showed wide variation, with a median of 0.85 and quartiles of 0.65 and 1.10. (The quartiles would be 0.74 and 0.96 if the variation were due only to sampling error; thus there is evidence of substantial real variation in the standardized population differences.)

We applied the within-group referral rule to the incumbents in each job, with a selection ratio set so that 50 percent of the nonminority workers would be accepted. The median acceptance rate for minority workers was 55 percent. There is thus some evidence that the referral rule accepts minority workers at a slightly higher rate than nonminority workers. However, these are workers on the job, not applicants, and if there were greater differences between mean scores for applicants than for workers, the referral rates for minority and nonminority workers might be about the same.

THE PROBLEM OF REPORTING SCORES

The general principle that should guide policy on reporting test scores is that the employer and the applicants should be given sufficient information to make correct inferences about a candidate's likely job performance from the test score. This information should include one or more scores, a description of the method of computing the scores, and information about the validity of the test.

We have suggested the possibility of using two scores in creating the group of applicants to be referred on a job order, a total-group percentile score and a within-group percentile score. For score reporting purposes we again find merit in a combination of scores because neither the total-group nor the within-group percentile score is an entirely satisfactory means of communicating information about job applicants.

Reporting Within-Group Percentile Scores

In the VG-GATB Referral System as it now operates, the Employment Service reports the candidate's within-group percentile score to the employer with an explanation of the scoring method, but without information about which adjustment, if any, has be made to the score.

The within-group percentile scores reported to the employer are potentially misleading. The purpose of the scoring method is to indicate an individual's predicted job performance with reference to other applicants *within* his or her own ethnic or racial group. But employers may mistakenly infer that two applicants with the same percentile score did equally well on the test, no matter what their racial or ethnic identity. Employers are not given the conversion tables and so have no way of determining the correspondence between scores obtained within different groups. On one hand, this could lead employers to underestimate the magnitude of group differences in raw scores (for example, on certain GATB composites a raw score that places an applicant at the 50th percentile among blacks would place an applicant at the 16th percentile among whites). On the other hand, it could lead employers to underestimate the amount of overlap in test scores that exists between the groups.

The within-group percentile scores have been reported to applicants without their being informed that the percentile scores are based on different norm groups for different racial and ethnic groups. That practice is deceptive.

Reporting Total-Group Percentile Scores

Reporting total-group percentile scores is also potentially misleading, because the employer has no information about the levels of job performance that can be expected from a particular score. It is tempting for the employer to infer that a person at the 16th percentile of whatever norm group on the test score will be at the 16th percentile of the norm group in job performance; Employment Service literature promoting the VG-GATB Referral System indicates that the most able workers within each ethnic group are being referred. But the correspondence between test score percentile and job performance percentile depends on the correlation between test score and job performance. For example, if that correlation is .3, a person at the 16th percentile on the test score is expected to be at the 38th percentile on job performance. Finally,

TABLE 13-4   Total Group Percentiles and Corresponding Expectancy of Above-Average Job Performance (Test Score and Job Performance Are Jointly Normal with Correlation .3)

Percentiles	Expectancies of Above-Average Performance (%)
2.5	27
16.0	38
50.0	50
84.0	62
97.5	73

providing a score referenced to the total group without qualifying its relevance to a particular job could have a harmful effect on minority applicants, who, on the average, score lower on the GATB. They will appear to be unqualified for the job, but their scores may have only a modest relationship to performance on the job.

Expectancy Reporting

There are methods of reporting information to employers that directly incorporate the degree of predictability of job performance from test score. One such method uses expectancies specifying the probability that a worker with a given test score will be above average in job performance. Whereas percentile scores show where an applicant is located on the test with reference to all other applicants in the relevant population, an expectancy score tells the likelihood of above-average performance given the validity of the test.

The real value of this approach to scoring is that it gives the employer a much more realistic basis for comparing candidates than is possible with raw scores or percentile scores. When a test has only modest validity for predicting job performance, score differences that look enormous when expressed as percentiles are shown to predict a much closer likelihood of above-average performance on the job. Suppose we take the average GATB validity of .3. As Table 13-4 shows, extreme scores on the test distribution correspond to modest scores on the expectancy distribution, reflecting the modest predictability of job performance from test score.

Proposed Protocol for Reporting Scores

In the committee's judgment, a combination of percentile and expectancy scores will provide job applicants and prospective employers with the best picture of the applicant's comparative suitability for the job. Our proposal is that two scores be reported for each applicant:

1. A within-group percentile score with the corresponding norm group identified.

2. An expectancy score (derived from the total-group score) equal to the probability that an applicant will have above-average job performance.

The first score indicates how the applicant fared on the test in comparison with others in the same ethnic or racial group. This information is particularly useful to employers who are actively working to increase the representation of minority groups in their work force. The second score gives the employer a better means of comparing applicants against the criterion of job performance. And in general it will show applicants and employers alike that low scorers on the test have a reasonable chance of being above-average workers.

Examples of such a reporting protocol using a validity of .3 would look as follows:

Name	Within-Group Percentile Computed for "Black" Group[*]	Total-Group Expectancy Score: Chance of Being Better-Than-Average Worker
Grace Birley	16	25
James Jones	50	40
Shelton Pike	84	50

Name	Within-Group Percentile Computed for "Other" Group[*]	Total-Group Expectancy Score: Chance of Being Better-Than-Average Worker
Nancy Rathouse	16	40
William Cole	50	50
Theresa Brewer	84	60

Name	Within-Group Percentile Computed for "Hispanic" Group[*]	Total-Group Expectancy Score: Chance of Being Better-Than-Average Worker
Juan Gomez	16	33
Chester Alverez	50	44
Olivia Gerber	84	56

[*]GATB subpopulation norms exist for "black," "Hispanic," and "other" groups.

CONCLUSIONS

Fair Use of the GATB

1. Use of GATB scores in strict top-down, rank-ordered fashion is fair in the sense that a given test score predicts about the same level of job

performance for majority-group and minority-group applicants. However, it would have severe adverse impact on minority job seekers.

2. This adverse effect on minority job seekers cannot be justified on the grounds of efficiency, for at the levels of validity typical of the GATB, the efficiency losses from adjusting minority scores are slight.

3. Although the GATB does not appear to be inherently biased against minority-group test takers, the undoubted effect of imperfect prediction when social groups have different average test scores is to place the greater burden of measurement error on the shoulders of the lower-scoring group. Since black, Hispanic, and Native American minority groups have lower group means on the GATB, able workers in these groups will experience higher rejection rates than workers having the same level of job performance in the majority group when referral is based on a rank-ordering of all test scores.

4. In the judgment of the committee, fair test use requires at the very least that the inadequacies of the technology should not fall more heavily on the social groups already burdened by the effects of past and present discrimination.

5. The so-called Golden Rule procedure, a strategy for reducing group differences in test scores through the selection of test items, does not appear to be defensible technically and does not provide the intended practical remedy.

6. The committee therefore concludes that, for purposes of referral, equity and productivity will be best served by a policy of adjusting the GATB test scores of black, Hispanic, and Native American job seekers served by the Employment Service system.

Referral Rules

7. Raw-score, top-down referral gives the highest expected performance in the referred group and the lowest proportion of minority-group members referred. At the levels of validity we find for the GATB, this referral method has an adverse impact on minority applicants that is out of all proportion to the productivity gains.

8. Within-group score, top-down referral achieves the highest proportions of minority referrals, with slight overall losses in estimated job performance. Given present GATB validities, this score adjustment strategy is an efficient way of referring workers at a given level of job performance in about the same proportion, whatever their racial or ethnic group.

9. Performance-referenced score, top-down referral (adjustments to minority scores based on the predictive validity of the test) produces results virtually identical to within-group score, top-down referral at the

validities observed for the GATB. It demonstrates similarly slight losses in efficiency and large gains in the proportion of minorities referred. However, this method is responsive to changes in test validities; with high validities, smaller score adjustments would be made and the proportion of minorities referred would be reduced. This may make it legally the more acceptable of the score adjustment strategies.

10. Both score adjustment strategies are race-conscious; both would virtually eliminate the adverse impact of the GATB on black and Hispanic subpopulations, and both adjustments would be commensurate with the far less than perfect relation between the GATB test score and job performance.

11. Minimum competency referral results in significant losses in expected job performance and would still produce markedly unequal referral rates for majority and minority applicants.

Reporting Test Scores

12. The test scores reported to employers and job seekers should allow them to make the most accurate possible judgments about likely job performance.

13. Neither the within-group percentile scores currently reported under the VG-GATB Referral System nor total-group percentile scores convey sufficient information, and both are potentially misleading.

RECOMMENDATIONS

If the Department of Labor continues to promote a test-based referral system for filling job orders, we recommend the following alterations to the current VG-GATB Referral Program.

Referral Rule

1. The committee recommends the continued use of score adjustments for black and Hispanic applicants in choosing which applicants to refer to an employer, because the effects of imperfect prediction fall more heavily on minority applicants as a group due to their lower mean test scores. We endorse the adoption of score adjustments that give approximately equal chances of referral to *able* minority applicants and *able* majority applicants: for example, within-group percentile scores, performance-based scores, or other adjustments.

Given current GATB validities, such adjustments are necessary to ensure that able black and Hispanic workers will not experience higher rejection rates than workers of the same level of job performance in the majority group. Referral in order of within-group percentile scores is one effective way to balance the dual goals of productivity and racial equity, given the modest levels of GATB validities. Should these validities increase dramatically as testing technology improves, the performance-based rule would warrant consideration.

2. We also recommend that USES study the feasibility of what we call a Combined Rules Referral Plan, under which the referral group is composed of all those who would have been referred by the total-group or by the within-group ranking method.

Score Reporting

3. The committee recommends that two scores be reported to employers and applicants:
  a. A within-group percentile score with the corresponding norm group identified.
  b. An expectancy score (derived from the total-group percentile score) equal to the probability that an applicant will have above-average job performance.

This combination of scores indicates how well an applicant performed on the test with reference to others of the same subpopulation, information that is useful to employers who are actively seeking to increase the representation of minorities in their work force under an affirmative action program. The expectancy score shows that even low scorers have a reasonable chance of success on the job and will help employers avoid placing totally unwarranted weight on small score differences.

Norm Groups

4. If the within-group score adjustment strategy is chosen, we recommend that USES undertake research to develop more adequate norming tables.

The data on Native Americans is particularly weak, but all of the norming samples are idiosyncratic convenience samples. As a consequence, there is reason to doubt that the particular constant factors added to minority scores are the most appropriate ones.

5. An attempt should be made to develop norms for homogeneous groups of jobs, at the least by job family, but if possible by more cohesive clusters of jobs in Job Families IV and V if possible.

6. The adjustment factor that should be computed is the mean score difference between majority-group and minority-group applicants for the same job, averaged over all jobs.

14

Central Recommendations

In this chapter the committee presents a core set of recommendations that emerge from the earlier discussions throughout the report. Chapter 14 is not a comprehensive list of all recommendations in Chapters 4 through 13, but is limited to those that bear most directly on the design and implementation of the VG-GATB Referral System. Although a thorough understanding of the committee's statements here depends on the discussions in Chapters 4 through 13, policy makers will find here a summation of the most essential points. The findings and conclusions on which these recommendations are based appear at the ends of the appropriate chapters, as do further recommendations for research.

OPERATIONAL USE OF THE VG-GATB REFERRAL SYSTEM

A thorough evaluation of the General Aptitude Test Battery (GATB) leads us to conclude that the test has modest levels of validity for predicting job performance, and that these predictive validities are strong enough to produce some enhancement of worker performance for individual employers who use test information in selecting employees.

We accept, as a general approach, the theory of validity generalization, whereby validities estimated for some jobs may reasonably be expected to hold for similar jobs not studied. We conclude that the range of GATB validities found in the 500 jobs studied would roughly generalize to the kinds of jobs typically handled by the U.S. Employment Service (USES). At the same time, we note that the GATB was not designed to function as

281

the centerpiece of a widely used referral system, and it is not currently supported by a research and development program that would justify its use in this way.

1. *On the basis of these findings, the committee recommends that any expansion of the VG-GATB Referral System be accompanied by a vigorous program of research and development. Two inadequacies in the testing program must be corrected:*
   a. *Test Security:* It is essential that measures be taken to provide for test security to ensure fairness to examinees. Most important is the regular development of alternate forms of the test and frequent replacement of old forms. (As a point of comparison, the Department of Defense develops three new forms of the Armed Services Vocational Aptitude Battery every four years.) In addition, USES must produce, and the states must enforce, clearly specified security procedures of the kind used to maintain the confidentiality of other large-scale test batteries.
   b. *Test Speededness:* A research and development project should be put in place to reduce the speededness of the GATB. A highly speeded test, one that no one can hope to complete, is vulnerable to distortion from coaching. For example, scores can be improved by teaching test takers to fill in all remaining blanks in the last minute of the test period. In addition, preliminary evidence suggests the possibility of differential impact by race of highly speeded tests. If this characteristic of the GATB is not altered, the test will not retain its validity when given a gatekeeping function that is widely recognized.
2. *We recommend that no job seeker be obliged to take the GATB; every local office that uses VG-GATB referral should maintain an alternative referral path for those who choose not to take the test.*
There are dangers in instituting a single, uniform testing system throughout the Public Employment Service—and such dangers would exist even if the test instrument were far superior to anything available today. Tests are not only fallible, but they also give a narrow reading on human capabilities. To permit only one route into the work force would result in its impoverishment. Giving the sort of primacy envisioned to a single instrument would also unnecessarily burden certain job seekers, for some people are simply not well served by cognitive tests because of test anxiety, certain kinds of handicapping conditions, or language problems. Overreliance on testing could also tend to create an underclass of low-scoring registrants who never get referred to jobs.

In addition, there are large classes of jobs for which the test is not needed for various reasons. For example, employers with openings for unskilled labor will usually consider all applicants; testing the applicants would be an unnecessary burden. Nor is it appropriate to encourage employers to use the GATB if able workers can be better identified by other, more job-specific methods, as would be the case with jobs such as musician or master electrician that require special skills or training.

3. *Because tests provide only partial information about future job performance, we recommend that Job Service offices that adopt the VG-GATB Referral System continue to use multiple criteria in choosing which applicants to refer.*

Employment Service personnel should help employers who elect to use the VG-GATB system decide how test scores and other job-related information, such as experience, skills, or education, should be used in establishing a referral decision rule. The employer should also be encouraged to consider able applicants who have not taken the test. The best service to employer and job seeker alike will be obtained by using multiple criteria, tailored as much as possible to each job situation.

REFERRAL METHODS

Our examination of USES validity studies confirms that there are sizable differences in mean scores on the GATB, ranging from one-half to one standard deviation, between blacks or Hispanics and the majority group. As a consequence, referrals made in the order of unmodified GATB scores would adversely affect the employment chances of minority job seekers. Furthermore, because the GATB has only modest predictive validity correlations (our conservative estimate is that they average .3, corrected), low-scoring applicants who could have been successful performers will be screened out (see Chapter 13). Because greater proportions of minority applicants fall in the low-scoring group, exclusive use of unadjusted GATB scores would result in referring able minority workers in much lower proportions than majority workers at the same level of job performance.

4. *The committee recommends the continued use of score adjustments for black and Hispanic applicants in choosing which applicants to refer to an employer, because the effects of imperfect prediction fall more heavily on minority applicants as a group due to their lower mean test scores. We endorse the adoption of score adjustments that give approximately equal chances of referral to* able *minority applicants and* able *majority applicants: for example, within-group percentile scores, performance-based scores, or other adjustments.*

Given the modest current levels of GATB validities, such adjustments are necessary to ensure that able black and Hispanic workers will not experience higher rejection rates than workers of the same level of performance in the majority group. Referral by within-group percentile scores is one effective way to balance the dual goals of productivity and racial equity.

 5. *If the within-group score adjustment strategy is chosen,*
   a. *we recommend that USES undertake research to develop more adequate norming tables.*

The data on Native Americans are particularly weak, but all the norming samples are idiosyncratic convenience samples. As a consequence, there is reason to doubt that the particular constant factors added to minority scores are the most appropriate ones.

   b. *An attempt should be made to develop norms for homogeneous groups of jobs, at the least by job family, but if possible by more cohesive clusters of jobs in Job Families IV and V.*
   c. *To correctly compute within-group percentiles, USES must estimate the average difference between the majority group scores and minority group scores in applicants for homogeneous groups of jobs.*

 6. *We also recommend that USES study the feasibility of what we call a Combined Rules Referral Plan, under which the referral group is composed of all those who would have been referred either by the total-group or by the within-group ranking method.*

This method of referral is attractive because it does not curtail the chances of any majority group applicants in order to increase the opportunities of minority applicants. In addition, when combined with a complementary score reporting system, it gives employers a choice. Depending on their affirmative action posture, they can choose to ignore race entirely and select solely on the basis of predicted performance, or to select from an enriched pool that includes the highest-scoring minority-group members available. The method does require referring a somewhat larger number of applicants for each job order, and so increases the selection task for the employer.

SCORE REPORTING

The uppermost concern in reporting GATB scores should be to provide the most accurate and informative estimate of future job performance possible. Used in isolation, percentile scores (whether computed for the whole population or by specified subgroups) can be misleading when test validities are modest, because they appear to say much more about expected job performance than is warranted. The sole use of total-group percentile scores would compound the problem vis-à-vis minority groups by encouraging the incorrect inference that differences in job performance between high and low scorers will be as great as the differences in test scores. Reporting only scores that have been adjusted to reflect standing within a racial or ethnic group, however, is also deceptive—the more so as test validity increases—since it masks group differences in predicted performance.

7. *The committee recommends that two scores be reported to employers and applicants:*
   a. *a within-group percentile score with the corresponding norm group identified and*
   b. *an expectancy score (derived from the total-group percentile score) equal to the probability that an applicant's job performance will be better than average.*

This combination of scores provides information on how well an applicant performed on the test with reference to others of the same subpopulation while also indicating the probability of above-average performance irrespective of group. In other words, it provides both a within-group and a total group comparison.

In addition, the expectancy score is more informative than other scoring methods because it reflects the predictive accuracy of the test as well as the performance of the applicant. With a test of modest validities like the GATB, this scoring method helps to prevent the incorrect inference that large differences in test scores reflect similarly large differences in performance on the job; employers and applicants are informed that even low scorers on the test have a reasonable chance of being above-average workers.

An example of our recommended scoring protocol, using a test validity of .3, follows. (For some classes of jobs different validities might be appropriate.)

Name	Within-Group Percentile Computed for "Black" Group*	Total-Group Expectancy Score: Chance of Being Better-Than-Average Worker
Grace Birley	16	25
James Jones	50	40
Shelton Pike	84	50

Name	Within-Group Percentile Computed for "Other" Group*	Total-Group Expectancy Score: Chance of Being Better-Than-Average Worker
Nancy Rathouse	16	40
William Cole	50	50
Theresa Brewer	84	60

Name	Within-Group Percentile Computed for "Hispanic" Group*	Total-Group Expectancy Score: Chance of Being Better-Than-Average Worker
Juan Gomez	16	33
Chester Alverez	50	44
Olivia Gerber	84	56

*GATB subpopulation norms exist for "black," "Hispanic," and "other" groups.

PROMOTION OF THE VG-GATB REFERRAL PROGRAM

USES technical reports make overly optimistic projections of the effects of VG-GATB referral. Perhaps as a consequence, much of the promotional literature that we have seen overstates the psychometric quality and predictive power of the GATB, underestimates the vulnerability of the referral system to legal challenge, and exaggerates the economic impact of preemployment testing.

8. *Given the modest validities of the GATB for the 500 jobs actually studied; given our incomplete knowledge about the relationship between this sample and the remaining 11,500 jobs in the U.S. economy, given the Department of Justice challenge to the legality of within-group scoring and the larger philosophical debates about race-conscious mechanisms and the known problems of using a test with severe adverse impact, given the primitive state of knowledge about the relationship of individual performance and productivity of the firm, we recommend that the claims for the testing program be tempered and that employers as well as job seekers be given a balanced view of the strengths and weaknesses of the GATB and its likely contribution in matching people to jobs.*

9. *Given the primitive state of knowledge about the aggregate economic effects of better personnel selection, we recommend that Employment Service officials refrain from making any dollar estimates of the gains that would result from test-based selection.*

10. *The Employment Service should make clear to employers using the VG-GATB Referral System that responsibility for the relevance of selection criteria and the effects of selection on the composition of their work force lies directly with the employer. Use of tests approved by the U.S. Employment Service does not alter this allocation of responsibility under federal civil rights law.*

We have seen Employment Service literature that could be understood to say that use of the VG-GATB protects employers from legal challenge of their employee selection procedures. We have heard from a number of employers that they believed this to be the case because the VG-GATB has been promoted by the federal government. USES should take pains to correct this misapprehension and to inform employers routinely that they are not relieved of their responsibility for maintaining nondiscriminatory selection procedures by using the U.S. Employment Service.

EFFECTS OF THE VG-GATB SYSTEM

There is too little evidence based on controlled, rigorous studies of the effects of using the VG-GATB Referral System for the committee to be able to assure policy makers at the Department of Labor that anticipated improvements have indeed occurred. This is not to say that they have not occurred. The evidence simply does not exist to establish the case scientifically. For the moment, policy decisions about the future of the VG-GATB Referral System will have to be made on the basis of more impressionistic and experiential information.

11. *If USES decides to continue the VG-GATB Referral System, it should undertake a series of carefully designed studies to establish more solidly the efficiencies that are believed to result.*

12. *This research will need to be a cooperative effort, involving federal and State Employment Service personnel and employers. USES should encourage state Employment Security Agencies that deal with large employers (e.g., Michigan) and states that have fully articulated VG systems in place (e.g., Virginia, Utah, Oklahoma) to take a leading role in conducting studies to demonstrate the efficacy of the VG-GATB Referral System.*

13. *We also recommend that the employer community, as a potentially major beneficiary of an improved referral system, take an active part in the effort to evaluate the VG-GATB Referral System. The Employers' National Job Service Committee can help to identify appropriate employers who are willing to commit the resources necessary to study the effects of VG-GATB referral.*

SPECIAL POPULATIONS

Veterans

Like members of protected minority groups, military veterans have been the object of federal law and policy intended to increase their participation in the work force. The Wagner-Peyser Act creating the Public Employment Service in 1933 placed responsibility for veterans' employment with this system. The act also stipulated that qualified veterans should have priority over qualified nonveterans in employment and training services. The language of the legislation and regulations conferring preference or priority on military veterans consistently uses the terminology "qualified veterans." We infer from this wording that the intent of Congress was to balance considerations of productivity with preferential treatment for veterans.

14. *If government policy is to strike a balance between maximizing productivity and preference for veterans in employment referral through the VG-GATB Referral System, the Employment Service should adjust veterans' VG-GATB scores by adding a veterans' bonus of some number of points before conversion to percentiles. Unadjusted expectancy scores should also be reported to employers and job seekers.*

It should be noted on the referral slip that the percentile score has been adjusted for veterans' preference. If the federal rule is followed, the size of the adjustment would range from one-eighth to one-quarter of a standard deviation, corresponding to 5 and 10 percentile points, depending on disability status.

15. *The Employment Service should continue to meet the needs of disabled veterans through individualized counseling and placement services.*

People with Handicapping Conditions

When tests are modified to accommodate visual, hearing, motor, or other handicaps, questions are raised about the comparability of the modified and regular instruments and about the meaning of the resulting scores. Even in the best of circumstances, very few data exist to answer these questions empirically; for the GATB, the research base is meager when it exists at all. Special administrations are offered for people with hearing problems, but the test has not been modified for people with visual handicaps. Extreme caution is clearly required in interpreting test results from special administrations or regular administrations to people with handicapping conditions.

16. *For applicants with handicapping conditions, we recommend the continued use of job counselors to make referrals.*

17. *Measures should be taken to ensure that no job order is filled automatically and solely through the VG-GATB system. Job counselors who serve handicapped applicants, disabled veterans, or other populations with special needs must have regular access to the daily flow of job orders.*

18. *To ensure that handicapped applicants who can compete with tested applicants are given that opportunity, the GATB should be used when feasible to assess the abilities of handicapped applicants. But the*

test should be used to supplement decision making, not to take the place of counseling services.

19. *Because special expertise in assessing the capabilities of people with handicaps is necessary and available, we recommend that the Department of Labor encourage closer coordination between state rehabilitation agencies and the State Employment Service Agencies. States should consider placing state rehabilitation counselors in local employment service offices that serve a sizable population of handicapped people.*

References

Alexander, E.R., and R.D. Wilkins
  1982 Performance rating validity: the relationship of objective and subjective measures of performance. *Group and Organization Studies* 7:485–496.
American Educational Research Association, American Psychological Association, and National Council on Measurement in Education
  1985 *Standards for Educational and Psychological Testing.* Washington, D.C.: American Psychological Association.
Anastasi, Anne
  1988 *Psychological Testing,* 6th ed. New York: MacMillan.
Angoff, W.H.
  1971 Scales, norms, and equivalent scores. In R.L. Thorndike, ed., *Educational Measurement,* 2d ed. Washington, D.C.: American Council on Education.
Baxter, B.
  1941 An experimental analysis of the contributions of speed and level in an intelligence test. *Journal of Educational Psychology* 32:285–296.
Bell, Derrick
  1984 *Race, Racism, and American Law.* New York: Little, Brown.
Bemis, Stephen
  1968 Occupational validity of the GATB. *Journal of Applied Psychology* 52:240–244.
Boag, A.K., and M. Neild
  1962 The influence of the time factor on the scores on the Triggs Diagnostic Reading Test as reflected in the performance of secondary school pupils. *Journal of Educational Research* 55:181–183.
Boger, J.H.
  1952 An experimental study of the effects of perceptual training on group IQ test scores of elementary pupils in rural ungraded schools. *Journal of Educational Research* 46:42–52.

291

Brigham, Carl C.
   1923   *A Study of American Intelligence.* Princeton, N.J.: Princeton University Press.
   1930   Intelligence tests of immigrant groups. *Psychological Review* 37(2):158–165.
Briscoe, C.D., W. Muelder, and W. Michael
   1981   Concurrent validity of self-estimates of abilities relative to criteria provided by standardized test measures of the same abilities for a sample of high school students eligible for participation in the CETA program. *Educational and Psychological Measurement* 41:1285–1294.
Brogden, H.E.
   1946   On the interpretation of the correlation coefficient as a measure of predictive efficiency. *Journal of Educational Psychology* 2:171–183.
   1955   Least squares estimates and optimal classification. *Psychometrika* 20:249–252.
   1959   Efficiency of classification as a function of number of jobs, percent rejected, and the validity and intercorrelation of job performance estimates. *Educational and Psychological Measurement* 19:181–190.
   1964   Simplified regression patterns for classification. *Psychometrika* 29:393–396.
Bureau of National Affairs, Inc.
   1988   *Recruiting and Selection Procedures.* Personnel Policies Forum Survey No. 146. Washington, D.C.: Bureau of National Affairs. May.
Buros, O.K., editor
   1972   *The Seventh Mental Measurements Yearbook.* Highland Park, N.J.: Gryphon Press.
Callender, John C., and H.G. Osburn
   1980   Development and test of a new model for validity generalization. *Journal of Applied Psychology* 65:543–558.
Cassel, R.N., and G.W. Reier
   1971   Comparative analysis of concurrent and predictive validity for the GATB Clerical Aptitude Test Battery. *Journal of Psychology* 79:135–140.
Cleary, T.A.
   1968   Test bias: prediction of grades for Negro and white students in integrated colleges. *Journal of Educational Measurement* 5:115–124.
Cole, Nancy S.
   1973   Bias in selection. *Journal of Educational Measurement* 10:237–255.
Cooley, W.W.
   1965   Further relationships with the TALENT battery. *Personnel and Guidance Journal* 44:295–303.
Cronbach, Lee J.
   1984   *Essentials of Psychological Testing,* 4th ed. New York: Harper & Row.
Cronbach, Lee J., and G.C. Gleser
   1965   *Psychological Tests and Personnel Decisions,* 2d ed. Urbana: University of Illinois Press.
Daly, J.L., and R.F. Stahmann
   1968   The effect of time limits on a university placement test. *Journal of Educational Research* 62:103–104.
Darlington, Richard B.
   1971   Another look at "cultural fairness." *Journal of Educational Measurement* 8:71–82.
Davidson, W.M., and J.B. Carroll
   1945   Speed and level components in time limit scores: a factor analysis. *Educational and Psychological Measurement* 5:411–427.
Delahunty, Robert J.
   1988   Legal and Policy Issues in Employment Testing. Statement by the Special Assistant to the Assistant Attorney General for Civil Rights, Department of

Justice. Prepared at the request of the Committee on the General Aptitude Test Battery, Commission on Behavioral and Social Sciences and Education, National Research Council, Washington, D.C. May 23.

Dong, H., Y. Sung, and S. Goldman
1986 The validity of the Ball Aptitude Test Battery (BAB) III: relationship to the CAB, DAT, and GATB. *Educational and Psychological Measurement* 46:245–250.

Draper, Norman R., and Harry Smith
1981 *Applied Regression Analysis,* 2d ed. New York: John Wiley & Sons, Inc.

Dubin, J.A., H. Osburn, and D.M. Winick
1969 Speed and practice: effects on Negro and white test performances. *Journal of Applied Psychology* 53:19–23.

Eagleson, O.W.
1937 Comparative studies of white and Negro subjects in learning to discriminate visual magnitude. *Journal of Psychology* 4:167–197.

Edel, Abraham
1977 Preferential consideration and justice. Pp. 111–133 in William T. Blackstone and Robert D. Heslep, eds., *Social Justice and Preferential Treatment: Women and Racial Minorities in Education and Business.* Athens, Ga.: The University of Georgia Press.

Ehrenberg, Ronald G., and Robert S. Smith
1987 *Modern Labor Economics: Theory and Policy.* Glenview, Ill.: Scott, Foresman.

Employment Security Commission of North Carolina
1971 Technical Report on Aptitude Test Scores of Deaf High School Students on the General Aptitude Test Battery and the Nonreading Aptitude Test Battery.
1972 Technical Report on Aptitude Test Scores of Deaf High School Students on the General Aptitude Test Battery and the Nonreading Aptitude Test Battery.
1973 Technical Report on the Development of Revised GATB Instructions for the Deaf.

Fishkin, James S.
1983 *Justice, Equal Opportunity, and the Family.* New Haven, Conn.: Yale University Press.

Flaugher, Ronald L., and L.W. Pike
1970 Reactions to a Very Difficult Test by an Inner City High School Population: A Test and Item Analysis. Research Memorandum 70–11. Princeton, N.J.: Educational Testing Service.

Ford, J. Kevin, Susan L. Schechtman, and Kurt Kraiger
1986 Study of race effects in objective indices and subjective evaluations of performance: a meta-analysis of performance criteria. *Psychological Bulletin* 99(3):330–337.

Fozard, J.L., R.L. Nuttall, and N.C. Waugh
1972 Age-related differences in mental performance. *Aging and Human Development* 3: 19–24.

Fraas, Charlotte Jones
1983 *Federal Veterans' Employment Assistance Programs.* Washington, D.C.: Congressional Research Service, Education and Public Welfare Division, Library of Congress.

Glass, Gene V., and Julian C. Stanley
1970 Statistical methods in education and psychology. In Gene V. Glass, ed., *Prentice-Hall Series in Educational Measurement, Research, and Statistics.* Englewood Cliffs, N.J.: Prentice-Hall, Inc.

Gulliksen, H.A.
1950a The reliability of speeded tests. *Psychometrika* 15:259–260.
1950b *Theory of Mental Tests.* New York: Wiley.

Hakstian, A.R., and R. Bennett
1978 Validity studies using the Comprehensive Ability Battery (CAB): II. Relationship with the DAT and GATB. *Educational and Psychological Measurement* 38:1003–1015.

Hart, Bernard, and Charles D. Spearman
1914 Mental tests of dementia. *Journal of Abnormal Psychology* 9:217–264.

Hawk, John, Tonia Butler, and Julia Linton
1986 Conceptual Model of Full Service Validity Generalization Local Offices. Briefing document prepared by staff of the U.S. Employment Service, U.S. Department of Labor.

Heckman, James J., and Guilherme Sedlacek
1985 Heterogeneity, aggregation, and market wage functions: an empirical model of self-selection in the labor market. *Journal of Political Economy* 93(6):1077–1125.

Hedges, Larry V., and Ingram Olkin
1985 *Statistical Methods for Meta-Analysis*. New York: Academic Press.

Helmstadter, G.C., and D.H. Ortmeyer
1953 Some techniques for determining the relative magnitude of speed and power components of a test. *Educational and Psychological Measurement* 12:280–287.

Hoogenboom, Ari
1961 *Outlawing the Spoils: A History of the Civil Service Reform Movement, 1865–1883*. Urbana: University of Illinois Press.

Howe, M.A.
1975 General Aptitude Test Battery Q: an Australian empirical study. *Australian Psychologist* 10:32–44.

Hull, C.L.
1928 *Aptitude Testing*. Yonkers-on-Hudson, N.Y.: World Book.

Hunter, John E.
1983 A causal analysis of cognitive ability, job knowledge, job performance, and supervisor ratings. Pp. 257–266 in F.J. Landy, S. Zedeck, and J. Cleveland, eds., *Performance Measurement and Theory*. Hillsdale, N.J.: Lawrence Erlbaum.
1986 Cognitive ability, cognitive aptitudes, job knowledge, and job performance. *Journal of Vocational Behavior* 29:340–362.

Hunter, John E., and Frank L. Schmidt
1976 Critical analysis of the statistical and ethical implications of various definitions of "test bias." *Psychological Bulletin* 83(6):1053–1071.
1982 Fitting people to jobs: the impact of personnel selection on national productivity. Ch. 7 in Marvin D. Dunnette and Edwin A. Fleishman, eds., *Human Performance and Productivity: Vol. 1, Human Capability Assessment*. Hillsdale, N.J.: Lawrence Erlbaum Associates.

Hunter, John E., Frank L. Schmidt, and Michael K. Judiesch
1988 Individual differences in output as a function of job complexity. Michigan State University. Submitted to *Journal of Applied Psychology*.

James, Lawrence R., Robert G. Demaree, and Stanley A. Mulaik
1986 A note on validity generalization procedures. *Journal of Applied Psychology* 71:440–450.
1988 Validity generalization: rejoinder to Schmidt, Hunter and Raju. *Journal of Applied Psychology* 73:673–678.

Jensen, A.R.
1986 *g*: artifact or reality. *Journal of Vocational Behavior* 29:301–331.

Katzenmeyer, W.G.
1962 Social Interaction and Differences in Intelligence Test Performance of Negro and White Elementary School Pupils. Doctoral dissertation, Duke University.

Kendall, L.M.
1964 The effects of varying time limits on test validity. *Educational and Psychological Measurement* 24:789–800.

Kettner, N.
1976 Armed Services Vocational Aptitude Battery (ASVAB Form 5): Comparison with GATB and DAT Tests. Final report, May 1975–October 1976. Armed Services Human Resources Laboratory, Brooks Air Force Base, Texas.

Kevles, Daniel J.
1968 Testing the Army's intelligence: psychologists and the military in World War I. *Journal of American History* 55:565–581.
1985 *In the Name of Eugenics*. New York: Alfred A. Knopf.

Kish, G.B.
1970 Alcoholics' GATB and Shipley profiles and their interrelationships. *Journal of Clinical Psychology* 26:482–484.

Klineberg, O.
1928 An experimental study of speed and other factors in racial differences. *Archives of Psychology* 15:109–123.

Knapp, R., L. Knapp, and W. Michael
1977 Stability and concurrent validity of the Career Ability Placement Survey (CAPS) against the DAT and the GATB. *Educational and Psychological Measurement* 37:1081–1085.

Kraiger, Kurt, and J. Kevin Ford
1985 A meta-analysis of ratee race effects in performance ratings. *Journal of Applied Psychology* 70(1):56–65.

Linn, Robert L., and Fritz Drasgow
1987 Implications of the Golden Rule settlement for test construction. *Educational Measurement: Issues and Practice* (Summer):13–17.

Linn, Robert L., D.L. Harnisch, and Stephen B. Dunbar
1981 Corrections for range restriction: an empirical investigation of conditions resulting in conservation corrections. *Journal of Applied Psychology* 66:655–663.

Lippmann, Walter
1922 A future for tests. *The New Republic* 33(November 29):9.
1923 The great confusion. *The New Republic* 33(January 3):146.

Louis, Thomas A., Harvey V. Fineberg, and Frederick Mosteller
1985 Finding for public health from meta-analysis. *Annual Review of Public Health* 6:1–20.

Madigan, Robert M., Diana L. Deadrick, and K. Dow Scott
1987 A Validation Study of the VG Testing Procedure for Selection of Sewing Machine Operators. Prepared for Virginia Employment Commission by the Barringer Center, R.B. Pamplin College of Business. Virginia Polytechnic Institute and State University, Blacksburg.

Manela, Stewart S.
1976 Veterans' preference in public employment: the history, constitutionality, and effect on federal personnel practices of veterans' preference legislation. *The George Washington University Law Review* 441:623–641.

Marco, Gary L.
1988 Does the use of test assembly procedures proposed in legislation make any difference in test properties and in the test performance of black and white test takers? *Applied Measurement in Education* 1(2):109–133.

Marshall, Burke
    1984   A comment on the nondiscrimination principle in a "nation of minorities." *The Yale Law Journal* 93:1006–1012.
McCormick, Ernest J., P.R. Jeanneret, and Robert C. Meacham
    1972   A study of job characteristics and job dimensions as based on the Position Analysis Questionnaire (PAQ). *Journal of Applied Psychology Monograph* 56: 347–368.
McKinney, Michael W.
    1984   Final Report: Validity Generalization Pilot Study. Southern Test Development Field Center, Raleigh, N.C.
McLaughlin, Donald H., Paul G. Rossmeissl, Lauress L. Wise, David A. Brandt, and Ming-mei Wang
    1984   Validation of Current and Alternative Armed Services Vocational Aptitude Battery (ASVAB) Area Composites: Based on Training and Skill Qualification Test (SQT) Information on Fiscal Year 1981 and 1982 Enlisted Accessions. Technical Report 651. Alexandria, Va.: U.S. Army Research Institute for the Behavioral and Social Sciences.
Mollenkopf, W.G.
    1960   Time limits and the behavior of test takers. *Educational and Psychological Measurement* 20:223–230.
Moore, R., and J. Davies
    1984   Predicting GED scores on the basis of expectancy, valence, intelligence, and pretest skill levels with the disadvantaged. *Educational and Psychological Measurement* 44:483–489.
National Commission on Civil Disorders
    1968   *Report of National Advisory Commission on Civil Disorders.* New York: Bantam Books.
Nester, Mary Anne
    1984   Employment testing for handicapped people. *Public Personnel Management* 13: 417–434.
Newton, Lisa H.
    1973   Reverse discrimination as unjustified. *Ethics* 83:312. [Quoted in Husak, Douglas N. 1978. Preferential hiring and reverse discrimination in favor of blacks: a moral analysis. *The American Journal of Jurisprudence* 23:143–168.]
Northern Test Development Field Center
    1987   A Comparison of Validity Generalization with Other Selection Techniques Used at Chrysler Corporation. Annual Work Plan Project No. 4403. Northern Test Development Field Center, Detroit, Mich.
O'Malley, P., and J. Bachman
    1976   Longitudinal evidence for the validity of the Quick Test. *Psychological Reports* 38: 1247–1252.
Perry, Michael J.
    1977   The disproportionate impact theory of racial discrimination. *University of Pennsylvania Law Review* 125:540–589.
Petersen, Nancy S., and Melvin R. Novick
    1976   An evaluation of some models for culture-fair selection. In *On Bias in Selection. Journal of Educational Measurement* 13(Spring):3–29.
Petersen, Nancy S., Michael J. Kolen, and H.D. Hoover
    1989   Scaling, norming, and equating. In Robert L. Linn, ed., *Educational Measurement,* 3d ed. New York: Macmillan.

Rawls, John
  1971   *A Theory of Justice*. Cambridge, Mass.: Belknap Press of Harvard University.
Reed, James
  1987   Robert M. Yerkes and the mental testing movement. In Michael M. Sokal, ed., *Psychological Testing and American Society, 1890-1930*. New Brunswick, N.J.: Rutgers University Press.
Rhoades, Dennis K.
  1988   Statement submitted to the Committee on the General Aptitude Test Battery, National Research Council, Annapolis, Md. August 3.
Robertson, Peter C.
  1976   EEOC Guidelines on Employment Discrimination: A Staff Analysis of the History of the EEOC Guidelines on Employee Selection Procedures. Memo submitted to the General Accounting Office.
Robins, Hal B.
  1988   Pre-Employment Testing in Utah. Technical report. Labor Market Information Services, Utah Department of Employment Security, Salt Lake City.
Rotman, C.B.
  1963   A Study of the Effect of Practice Upon Motor Skills of the Mentally Retarded. Doctoral dissertation, Boston College.
Sakalosky, J.C.
  1970   A Study of the Relationship Between the Differential Aptitude Test Battery and the General Aptitude Test Battery Scores of Ninth Graders. Master's thesis, Millersville State College.
Schmidt, Frank L., and John Hunter
  1977   Development of a general solution to the problem of validity generalization. *Journal of Applied Psychology* 62:529–540.
  1981   Employment testing: Old theories and new research findings. American Psychologist 36:1128–1137.
  1983   Individual differences in productivity: an empirical test of estimates derived from studies of selection procedure utility. *Journal of Applied Psychology* 68:407–414.
Schmidt, Frank L., John E. Hunter, Alice N. Outerbridge, and M.H. Trattner
  1985   The impact of job selection methods on size, productivity, and payroll cost of the federal work force: an empirically based demonstration. *Personnel Psychology* 39:1–29.
Schmidt, Frank L., John E. Hunter, and Kenneth Pearlman
  1982   Progress in validity generalization: comments on Callender and Osburn and future developments. *Journal of Applied Psychology* 67:835–845.
Schmidt, Frank L., John E. Hunter, and Nambury S. Raju
  1988   Validity generalization and situational specificity: a second look at the 75% rule and Fisher's z transformation. *Journal of Applied Psychology* 73:665–672.
Scott, K. Dow, Jil A. Stoddard, Robert M. Madigan, and Diana L. Deadrick
  1987   An Examination of Job Applicant Attitudes Toward the VG Screening Procedure. Prepared for the Virginia Employment Commission by the Barringer Center, R.B. Pamplin College of Business. Virginia Polytechnic Institute and State University, Blacksburg.
Seymour, Richard T.
  1988   Tests Which Work Differently Between Blacks and Whites: The Achilles' Heel of "Validity Generalization." Prepared for National Commission on Testing and Public Policy. Lawyers' Committee for Civil Rights Under Law, Washington, D.C. [presented at meeting of Committee on the General Aptitude Test Battery,

Commission on Behavioral and Social Sciences and Education, National Research Council, Annapolis, Md., August 3].

Sherman, Susan W., and Nancy M. Robinson, editors
1982   *Ability Testing of Handicapped People: Dilemma for Government, Science, and the Public.* Panel on Testing of Handicapped People, Committee on Ability Testing, Assembly of Behavioral and Social Sciences, National Research Council. Washington, D.C.: National Academy Press.

Spearman, Charles
1927   *The Abilities of Man.* New York: Macmillan.

Stigler, Stephen M.
1986   *History of Statistics.* Cambridge, Mass.: Belknap Press of Harvard University.

Sueyoshi, Glenn T.
1988   An Appraisal of the Economic Evidence on the Equilibrium Effects of Ability Testing. Paper prepared for Committee on the General Aptitude Test Battery, Commission on Behavioral and Social Sciences and Education, National Research Council, Washington, D.C.

Terranova, C.
1972   The relationship between test scores and test time. *Journal of Experimental Education* 40:81–83.

Thorndike, E.L.
1913   Educational diagnosis. *Science* 37(January 24):141.

Thorndike, R.L.
1986   The role of general ability in prediction. *Journal of Vocational Behavior* 29:332–339.

Tribe, Laurence H.
1988   *American Constitutional Law,* 2d ed. New York: The Foundation Press, Inc.

Tyack, D.B.
1974   *The One Best System: A History of American Urban Education.* Cambridge, Mass.: Harvard University Press.

Uhlaner, J.E., and Daniel J. Bolanovich
1952   Development of Armed Forces Qualification Test and Predecessor Army Screening Tests, 1946–1950. PRS Report 976. Personnel Research Section, Department of the Army, Washington, D.C.

U.S. Civil Service Commission
1955   History of Veteran Preference in Federal Employment: 1865–1955. Washington, D.C.: U.S. Civil Service Commission.

U.S. Department of Defense
1982   *Profile of American Youth: 1980 Nationwide Administration of the Armed Services Vocational Aptitude Battery.* Washington, D.C.: Office of the Assistant Secretary of Defense (Manpower, Reserve Affairs, and Logistics), U.S. Department of Defense.

1984a   Counselor's Manual for the Armed Services Vocational Aptitude Battery Form 14. DOD 1304.12X. North Chicago, Ill.: U.S. Military Entrance Processing Command.

1984b   Technical Supplement to the Counselor's Manual for the Armed Services Vocational Aptitude Battery Form-14. DOD 1304.12x1. North Chicago, Ill.: U.S. Military Entrance Processing Command.

1984c   Test Manual for the Armed Services Vocational Aptitude Battery. DOD 1304.12AA. North Chicago, Ill.: U.S. Military Entrance Processing Command.

1989   Joint-Service Efforts to Link Enlistment Standards to Job Performance: Recruit Quality and Military Readiness. Report to the House Committee on Appropriations. Office of the Assistant Secretary of Defense (Force Management and Personnel), U.S. Department of Defense.

U.S. Department of Labor
  1970 *Manual for the USES General Aptitude Test Battery. Section III: Development.* Washington, D.C.: Manpower Administration, U.S. Department of Labor.
  1979 *Manual for the USES General Aptitude Test Battery. Section II: Occupational Aptitude Pattern Structure.* U.S. Employment Service, Employment and Training Administration. Washington, D.C.: U.S. Department of Labor.
  1980 *Manual for the USES General Aptitude Test Battery. Section II-A: Development of the Occupational Aptitude Pattern Structure.* U.S. Employment Service, Employment and Training Administration. Washington, D.C.: U.S. Department of Labor.
  1982 *Special Technical Report on Aptitude Research for the Deaf.* Washington, D.C.: U.S. Department of Labor.
  1983a *Overview of Validity Generalization for the U.S. Employment Service.* USES Test Research Report No. 43. Division of Counseling and Test Development, Employment and Training Administration. Washington, D.C.: U.S. Department of Labor.
  1983b *The Dimensionality of the General Aptitude Test Battery (GATB) and the Dominance of General Factors Over Specific Factors in the Prediction of Job Performance for the U.S. Employment Service.* USES Test Research Report No. 44. Division of Counseling and Test Development, Employment and Training Administration. Washington, D.C.: U.S. Department of Labor.
  1983c *Test Validation for 12,000 Jobs: An Application of Job Classification and Validity Generalization Analysis to the General Aptitude Test Battery.* USES Test Research Report No. 45. Division of Counseling and Test Development, Employment and Training Administration. Washington, D.C.: U.S. Department of Labor.
  1983d *Fairness of the General Aptitude Test Battery: Ability Differences and Their Impact on Minority Hiring Rates.* USES Test Research Report No. 46. Division of Counseling and Test Development, Employment and Training Administration. Washington, D.C.: U.S. Department of Labor.
  1983e *The Economic Benefits of Personnel Selection Using Ability Tests: A State of the Art Review Including a Detailed Analysis of the Dollar Benefit of U.S. Employment Service Placements and a Critique of the Low-Cutoff Method of Test Use.* USES Test Research Report No. 47. Division of Counseling and Test Development, Employment and Training Administration. Washington, D.C.: U.S. Department of Labor.
  1984a *The Effect of Sex on General Aptitude Test Battery Validity and Test Scores.* USES Test Research Report No. 49. Prepared by Northern Test Development Field Center, Detroit, Mich., for Division of Counseling and Test Development, Employment and Training Administration. Washington, D.C.: U.S. Department of Labor.
  1984b Forms C and D of the General Aptitude Test Battery: An Historical Review of Development. Division of Counseling and Test Development, Employment and Training Administration, U.S. Department of Labor, Washington, D.C.
  1984c *Validity Generalization Manual. Section A: Job Family Scoring.* For USES General Aptitude Test Battery. U.S. Employment Service, Employment and Training Administration. Washington, D.C.: U.S. Department of Labor.
  1986 *Reliability and Comparability: Forms C and D. Addendum to Manual for the USTES General Aptitude Test Battery. Section III: Development.* U.S. Employment Service, Employment and Training Administration. Washington, D.C.: U.S. Department of Labor.
  1987 *Comparison of Black and Nonminority Validities for the General Aptitude Test Battery.* USES Test Research Report No. 51. Prepared by David J. Synk and David Swarthout, Northern Test Development Field Center, Detroit, Mich., for

Division of Planning and Operations, Employment and Training Administration. Washington, D.C.: U.S. Department of Labor.

1988   *Cross Validation of Job Families Using an Expanded Data Set.* USES Test Research Report No. 53. Prepared by David Swarthout, Northern Test Development Field Center, Detroit, Mich., for Division of Planning and Operations, Employment and Training Administration. Washington, D.C.: U.S. Department of Labor.

Vane, J.R., and R.T. Kessler
1964   The Goodenough Draw-a-Man Test: long-term reliability and validity. *Journal of Clinical Psychology* 20:487–488.

Veterans of Foreign Wars
1987   Resolution No. 611: Validity generalization (VG). Adopted by the 88th National Convention of the Veterans of Foreign Wars of the United States, held in New Orleans, Louisiana, August 14–21, 1987.

Warmke, Dennis L.
1984   Successful Implementation of the "New" GATB in Entry-Level Selection. Paper presented at Region IV Conference of American Society for Personnel Administration, October 15.

Wesman, A.G.
1960   Some effects of speed in test use. *Educational and Psychological Measurement* 20: 267–274.

Wigdor, Alexandra K., and Wendell R. Garner, editors
1982   *Ability Testing: Uses, Consequences, and Controversies. Part I: Report of the Committee.* Committee on Ability Testing, Assembly of Behavioral and Social Sciences, National Research Council. Washington, D.C.: National Academy Press.

Wigdor, Alexandra K., and John A. Hartigan, editors
1988   *Interim Report: Within-Group Scoring of the General Aptitude Test Battery.* Committee on the General Aptitude Test Battery, Commission on Behavioral and Social Sciences and Education, National Research Council. Washington, D.C.: National Academy Press.

Wilbourn, James M., Lonnie D. Valentine, Jr., and Malcolm J. Ree
1984   Relationships of the Armed Services Vocational Aptitude Battery (ASVAB) Forms 8, 9, and 10 to Air Force Technical School Final Grades. AFHRL Technical Paper 84–08. Working paper. Manpower and Personnel Division, Brooks Air Force Base, Texas.

Willingham, Warren W., Marjorie Ragosta, R.E. Bennett, H. Braun, D.A. Rock, and D.E. Powers
1988   *Testing Handicapped People.* Boston, Mass.: Allyn & Bacon.

Willis, Robert J., and Sherwin Rosen
1979   Education and self-selection. *Journal of Political Economy* 87(5):57–536.

Yerkes, Robert, editor
1921   Psychological examining in the United States Army. Vol. XV in *Memoirs of the National Academy of Sciences.* Washington, D.C.: U.S. Government Printing Office.

APPENDIXES

A

A Synthesis of Research on Some Psychometric Properties of the GATB

Richard M. Jaeger, Robert L. Linn, and *Anita S. Tesh*

This paper provides a detailed evaluation of three topics that bear on the overall quality of the General Aptitude Test Battery (GATB): its construct validity as supported by convergent validity evidence; its reliability; and the interchangeability of its forms. The first section presents the results of an exhaustive literature search for evidence that the GATB aptitude composites measure the same characteristics as other similarly named aptitude tests. The second section brings together the research on the stability of GATB aptitude scores over time and among forms of the test battery. And finally, the paper addresses the comparability of the GATB subtests from one form to another.

CONSTRUCT VALIDITY ISSUES

According to the *Standards for Educational and Psychological Testing,* a statement of standards for the development and use of tests that is adhered to by the major professional societies in the testing field, validity is of paramount concern in assessing the use of tests (American Educational Research Association et al., 1985:9):

Validity is the most important consideration in test evaluation. The concept refers to the appropriateness, meaningfulness, and usefulness of the specific inferences made from test scores. Test validation is the process of accumulating evidence to support such inferences. . . . Although evidence may be accumulated in many ways, validity always refers to the degree to which that evidence supports the

303

inferences that are made from the scores. The inferences regarding specific uses of a test are validated, not the test itself.

We are concerned here with a particular category of validity evidence involving construct-related evidence. According to the *Standards* (p. 9), "evidence classed in the construct-related category focuses primarily on the test score as a measure of the psychological characteristic of interest." The *Standards* also provide examples of the types of evidence that can be used to support construct validity claims (p. 10):

Evidence for the construct interpretation of a test may be obtained from a variety of sources. Intercorrelations among items may be used to support the assertion that a test measures primarily a single construct. Substantial relationships of a test to other measures that are purportedly of the same construct and the weaknesses of relationships to measures that are purportedly of different constructs support both the identification of constructs and distinctions among them. Relationships among different methods of measurement and among various non-test variables similarly sharpen and elaborate the meaning and interpretation of constructs.

In this section we examine evidence that bears on claims that the subtests of the GATB measure the aptitudes with which they are identified in the GATB *Manual* (U.S. Department of Labor, 1970), and nothing more. We provide a summary of correlations between subtests or aptitudes of the GATB and correspondingly labeled subtests or aptitudes of other test batteries.

Convergent Validity Evidence

The psychometric literature contains a substantial number of studies of the strength of relationships between subtests of the GATB and corresponding subtests of other batteries. As noted above, evidence of strong positive relationships between purported measures of the same construct is supportive of construct validity claims for all related measurement instruments. Thus the claim that the subtests of the GATB measure the aptitudes attributed to them would be enhanced by data of this sort and weakened if small to moderate correlations between corresponding subtests were to be found.

Chapter 14 of Section III of the GATB *Manual* (U.S. Department of Labor, 1970) is entitled "Correlations with Other Tests." The chapter contains correlation matrices resulting from studies of the GATB and a variety of other aptitude tests and vocational interest measures. Results from 64 studies are reported, including several involving the initial edition of the GATB (B-1001). In this summary, we restrict attention to studies involving the current version of the GATB (B-1002, Forms A–D) and appropriate aptitude tests. Since the publication of the GATB *Manual,* correlations between various GATB aptitudes or subtests and corresponding subtests of other test batteries have been provided in studies by Briscoe et al. (1981); Cassel and Reier (1971); Cooley (1965); Dong et al. (1986); Hakstian and Bennett (1978); Howe (1975); Kettner (1976); Kish (1970); Knapp et al. (1977); Moore and Davies (1984); O'Malley and Bachman (1976); and Sakalosky (1970). The sizes and compositions of examinee samples used in these studies are diverse, as are the aptitude batteries with which GATB subtests and aptitudes were correlated. They range from 40 ninth-grade students who completed both the GATB and the Differential Aptitude Test Battery (DAT), to 1,355 Australian army enlistees who completed the GATB and the Australian Army General Classification Test. However, in 8 of 13 studies (many of which examined several independent samples of examinees), the samples consisted of high school students.

Three rules were followed in selecting appropriate studies of the convergent validity of the GATB aptitudes with other, corresponding aptitude measures. First, only correlations between GATB aptitudes or subtests and corresponding components of other aptitude batteries were included. Thus, correlations with self-reports of aptitude or with achievement measures or performance scores were purposefully omitted. Second, only correlations with aptitude battery components having titles similar to the GATB measure of interest were retained; for example, a correlation between GATB Aptitude G and the abstract reasoning score on the DAT was included; a correlation between GATB Aptitude G and the numerical reasoning score on the DAT was excluded. Third, in studies that reported correlations between all possible pairs of measures composed of a GATB aptitude and an aptitude from another battery, only the largest correlation between any GATB aptitude and an aptitude from the other battery was retained. When rules two and three were applied simultaneously, a correlation was included only if it reflected a relationship between a GATB aptitude and the appropriate aptitude from another battery *and* only if it exceeded the correlations between that GATB aptitude and any other aptitude assessed by the other battery.

Data on the convergent validity of the GATB aptitudes were tabulated for each aptitude (Table A-1). Distributions of convergent validity coefficients for the three cognitive aptitudes (G, V, and N) and the three perceptual aptitudes (S, P, and Q) are displayed in pictorial form in Figure 4–2, and in tabular form in Table A-2.

Convergent Validity of GATB Aptitude G (General Intelligence)

The 51 convergent validity coefficients that were reported for the GATB-G aptitude ranged from .45 to .89, with a median value of .75. Since G is a broadly defined construct that is assessed through the

TABLE A-1   Stem-and-Leaf Displays of Convergent Validity Coefficients for the GATB Aptitudes

a. G, General Intelligence		b. V, Verbal Ability		c. N, Numerical Ability	
Stem	Leaf	Stem	Leaf	Stem	Leaf
8	001112244579	8	5	8	5
7	778888889999	8	0001133	8	01
7	0112334555	7	5566788889999	7	5556666678
6	777899	7	00000011222223334444	7	0111222224
6	0135	6	55678889999	6	55667778999
5	66799	6	0024	6	00222233
5	0	5	79	5	6777888
4	5	2	2	5	134
				4	3

d. S, Spatial Aptitude		e. P, Form Perception		f. Q, Clerical Perception	
Stem	Leaf	Stem	Leaf	Stem	Leaf
7	01123	6	5	7	6
6	689	5	8	6	59
6	0223	5	3	6	1
5	7899	4	59	5	558
5	1	4	44	5	00
4	5	3	8	4	77
3	0			4	4
				3	6
				3	23
				2	4

g. K, Motor Coordination		h. F, Finger Dexterity		i. M, Manual Dexterity	
Stem	Leaf	Stem	Leaf	Stem	Leaf
5	8	4	1	5	0
		3	7		

NOTE: The stem unit is .1. Therefore, the stem entry 8 followed by a leaf entry of 0 indicates a correlation coefficient of .80; each digit in a sequence of "leaves" indicates a different correlation coefficient.

TABLE A-2 Summary Statistics for Distributions of Convergent Validity Coefficients for the Cognitive GATB Aptitudes (G, V, and N) and the Perceptual GATB Aptitudes (S, P, and Q)

Aptitude	Number of Studies	Validity Coefficients				
		Minimum	First Quartile	Median	Third Quartile	Maximum
G	51	.45	.67	.75	.79	.89
V	59	.22	.69	.72	.78	.85
N	53	.43	.61	.68	.75	.85
S	19	.30	.58	.62	.70	.73
P	8	.38	.44	.47	.57	.65
Q	16	.24	.38	.50	.60	.76
K	1	.58	.58	.58	.58	.58
F	2	.37	.37	.39	.41	.41
M	1	.50	.50	.50	.50	.50

arithmetic, vocabulary, and spatial subtests of the GATB, a median convergent validity coefficient of .75 does provide adequate evidence of the convergent validity of the GATB intelligence aptitude. Data on the convergent validity of GATB-G are presented in Table A-1a.

Convergent Validity of GATB Aptitude V (Verbal Ability)

The 59 convergent validity coefficients that were reported for the GATB-V aptitude ranged from .22 to .85, with a median value of .72. Considering the variety of measures with which GATB-V was correlated, and the less-than-perfect reliabilities of the GATB subtests that contribute to V and the tests with which it was correlated, a median validity coefficient of .72 provides adequate evidence of convergent validity for the GATB verbal ability measure. Although the minimum observed validity coefficient of .22 is discomforting, it is not at all representative of validity coefficients in the lowest fourth of the distribution for V; the next-lowest observed coefficient was .57. Data on the convergent validity of GATB-V are presented in Table A-1b.

Convergent Validity of GATB Aptitude N (Numerical Ability)

The 53 convergent validity coefficients that were found for the GATB-N aptitude ranged from .43 to .85, with a median value of .68. A median convergent validity coefficient of .68 is somewhat smaller than would be desired for a measure of numerical ability. However, a claim to convergent validation for GATB-N is reasonably well supported by the data at hand, since three-fourths of the coefficients exceed .61 and a fourth are larger than .75. It should also be noted that, in several of the studies reviewed, correlations were provided for GATB subtests rather than GATB aptitudes. Such correlations will be attenuated by smaller reliabilities than would be found for the GATB aptitudes. Data on the convergent validity of GATB-N are presented in Table A-1c.

Convergent Validity of GATB Aptitude S (Spatial Aptitude)

The 19 convergent validity coefficients that were found for the GATB-S aptitude ranged from .30 to .73, with a median value of .62. The GATB spatial ability aptitude (S) is somewhat less highly correlated with its counterpart measures in other test batteries than is the verbal ability aptitude. A median concurrent validity coefficient of .62 with a range from .30 to .73 and a fourth of the coefficients below .58 suggests that somewhat different spatial perception constructs are measured in various batteries, or that the reliabilities of spatial ability measures are somewhat lower than those of corresponding verbal ability measures. Although these data do not cast serious doubt on the construct validity of the spatial ability aptitude, they are not as supportive as the evidence amassed for the verbal ability measure. Data on the convergent validity of GATB-S are presented in Table A-1d.

Convergent Validity of GATB Aptitude P (Form Perception)

The eight convergent validity coefficients that were found for the GATB-P aptitude ranged from .38 to .65, with a median value of .47. The convergent validity of the GATB form perception aptitude (P) is thus not well supported by the evidence compiled in this review. As measured by the GATB, form perception depends on examinees' abilities to discriminate among detailed patterns shown on common tools and to match the outlines of two-dimensional geometric forms represented by line drawings. Both tests are somewhat speeded, perhaps adding an ability component that is not as prevalent in the other test batteries used to generate the validity coefficients. Whatever the basis for these results, it would seem prudent to undertake a comparative content analysis of the tool matching and form matching subtests of the GATB and the supposedly corresponding measures in the test batteries used to generate these convergent validity coefficients. Data on the convergent validity of GATB-P are presented in Table A-1e.

Convergent Validity of GATB Aptitude Q (Clerical Perception)

The 16 convergent validity coefficients that were reported for the GATB-Q aptitude ranged from .24 to .76, with a median value of .50. The literature reviewed provided fewer convergent validity coefficients for the GATB clerical perception aptitude (Q) than for a number of other GATB aptitudes. Although many of the validity coefficients found for clerical perception were larger than those found for the form perception aptitude (P), evidence supporting the convergent validity of clerical perception was not as compelling as that found for the three cognitive aptitudes (G, V, and N). Even when somewhat smaller reliabilities are considered, a median validity coefficient of .50 (uncorrected for unreliability) suggests that the GATB name comparison subtest might measure a somewhat different construct than do the subtests that contribute to clerical perception measures in other test batteries. Indeed, the description of the clerical perception aptitude provided in the GATB *Manual* suggests a somewhat broader aptitude (including arithmetic perception) than does the description of the name comparison subtest on which it is based. Data on the convergent validity of GATB-Q are presented in Table A-1f.

Convergent Validity of the Psychomotor Aptitudes—K (Motor Coordination), F (Finger Dexterity), and M (Manual Dexterity)

Unfortunately, review of the literature since publication of the GATB *Manual* produced very few studies of the convergent validity of subtests underlying the psychomotor aptitudes (K, F, and M) of the GATB. There was one correlation for K, motor coordination (.58), two for F, finger dexterity (.37, .41), and one for M, manual dexterity (.50). And the correlations reported for these aptitudes in the *Manual* cannot be regarded as convergent validity coefficients. Data on the convergent validity of aptitudes K, F, and M are presented in Table A-1g, h, and i, respectively.

Summary of Convergent Validity Results

Distributions of convergent validity coefficients for the cognitive aptitudes of the GATB (G, V, and N) provide moderately strong support for claims that these aptitudes are appropriately named and measured. Corresponding results for the perceptual aptitudes of the GATB (S, P, and Q) are less convincing. Data for the psychomotor aptitudes are so meager that judgment on their convergent validity must be withheld.

Although the median convergent validity coefficient observed for the spatial aptitude (S) was respectably large, the corresponding median values for the form perception (P) and clerical perception (Q) aptitudes were smaller than would be desired. The three-dimensional space subtest is said to measure both intelligence and spatial aptitude and might therefore require greater reasoning ability and inferential skill than is typical of measures of spatial aptitude found in other batteries. As has already been noted, the name comparison subtest of the GATB appears to tap only a subset of the skills typically associated with clerical perception.

Distributions of convergent validity coefficients for the cognitive and perceptual GATB aptitudes are summarized in Table A-2 and for ease of visual comparison, in Figure 4-2.

RELIABILITY OF THE GATB APTITUDE SCORES

Aptitude tests such as the GATB are intended to measure stable characteristics of individuals, rather than transient or ephemeral qualities. Such tests must measure these characteristics consistently, if they are to be useful. *Reliability* is the term used to describe the degree to which a test measures consistently. The *Standards* define reliability as follows (American Educational Research Association et al., 1985:19):

Reliability refers to the degree to which test scores are free from errors of measurement. A test taker may perform differently on one occasion than on another for reasons that may or may not be related to the purpose of measurement. A person may try harder, be more fatigued or anxious, have greater familiarity with the content of questions on one test form than another, or simply guess correctly on more questions on one occasion than another. For these and other reasons, a person's score will not be perfectly consistent from one occasion to the next. . . . Differences between scores from one form to another or from one occasion to another may be attributable to what is commonly called *errors of measurement*. . . . Measurement errors reduce the reliability (and therefore the generalizability) of the score obtained for a person from a single measurement.

Fundamental to the proper evaluation of a test are the identification of major sources of measurement error, the size of the errors resulting from these sources, the indication of the degree of reliability to be expected between pairs of scores under particular circumstances, and the generalizability of scores across items, forms, raters, administrations, and other measurement facets.

The *Standards* further state (p. 19) that test developers are primarily responsible for assessing a test's reliability and for identifying major sources of measurement error. When a test is composed of subtests, the reliability of each must be investigated and reported in adequate detail, so that test users can determine whether the test and subtests are sufficiently reliable to be used for the purposes intended.

The reliability coefficient of a test is defined technically as the square of the correlation between a hypothetical true score and the score actually observed. The reliability coefficient represents the degree to which differences among test takers' scores represent actual differences in their abilities, rather than errors of measurement. If a test had a reliability coefficient of 1.0, all of the differences among test takers' scores (i.e., variation in their scores) would represent differences in their abilities, and none would represent errors of measurement. We would describe such a test as being "perfectly reliable." If a test had a reliability coefficient of zero, differences among test takers' scores would be due solely to errors of measurement, and the test would be termed "totally unreliable." In practice, tests of human abilities and aptitudes are neither perfectly reliable nor totally unreliable; some variation in test scores reflects true differences among test takers' abilities and some reflects errors of measurement.

Because test reliability generally increases as test length increases, and subtests are shorter than the test they compose, reliability coefficients for subtests are typically smaller than corresponding coefficients for the test as a whole. When the adequacy of a test's reliability is judged, it is therefore important to consider the reliability of every score that is separately reported and interpreted. In the case of the GATB, reliabilities of aptitude scores are of central interest.

The psychometric literature includes a variety of methods for estimating test reliability. Popular methods differ in their sensitivity to various sources of measurement error, in their applicability to different types of tests, and in their usefulness for particular purposes. When tests are used to assess aptitudes or other traits that are expected to be stable across weeks, months, or years, the most appropriate reliability estimation procedures will reflect the stability of measurements across time. Such reliability estimates are termed *stability coefficients* or *indices of temporal stability*. Stability coefficients are based on the consistency of examinees' performances during two test administrations and might be spuriously inflated because of examinees' memories of their initial responses. Risks of distortion due to memory effects can be avoided if reliability estimates are based on the administration of two forms of the same test, separated by the amount of time the aptitudes measured are assumed to remain stable. Such reliability estimates are termed "equivalent-forms reliability coefficients." A number of studies of the temporal stability and equivalent-forms reliability of the GATB aptitude scores are summarized below.

Temporal Stability of the GATB Aptitude Scores

Studies of the temporal stability of GATB aptitude scores have examined a variety of time periods between test administrations, ranging from one day to four years. These studies of the consistency of GATB aptitude scores have used samples of examinees that vary widely in age and level of education, including employed adults, junior high school students, high school students, and college students. Estimates of the temporal stability of GATB aptitude scores have also been computed for examinees of different races. Table A-3 contains a summary of indices of the temporal stability of GATB aptitude scores reported by Senior (1952), Showler and Droege (1969), and the U.S. Department of Labor (1970, 1986). The estimates presented below were based on sequential administration of either the same or different GATB test forms.

Temporal Stability by Age

As shown in Table A-3, coefficients of stability for the GATB cognitive aptitudes G, V, and N consistently exceed .80 when samples are composed of adults and time intervals between successive test administrations are no more than three years. For corresponding examinee samples and time periods, coefficients of stability for the GATB perceptual aptitudes S, P, and Q are at least 0.70. Aptitude K showed similar stability in all but one study. The other GATB psychomotor aptitudes, F and M, which are measured by subtests that require manipulation of objects, were found to have somewhat lower coefficients of stability than did aptitudes measured by pencil-and-paper subtests. Coefficients of stability for GATB aptitudes F and M were reported to be at least .57 when estimated for samples of adult examinees over time periods up to three years. The temporal stabilities of the GATB psychomotor aptitudes are not as well estimated as are those of the cognitive and spatial aptitudes, since fewer studies have included the GATB subtests that require manipulation of objects.

All of the GATB aptitude scores are less stable for samples of ninth- and tenth-graders than for samples of adults. A portion of this instability might be attributed to the maturation of these younger examinees during the period between successive administrations of the GATB, and might therefore reflect valid changes in the relative ordering of the examinees on the aptitudes assessed, rather than instability due to measurement error.

Temporal Stability by Time Interval

The range of stability coefficients for GATB aptitude scores across test-retest intervals from one day to four years varied from .51 to .94. For specific time intervals, stability coefficients also varied greatly across aptitudes. Stability coefficients tended to be largest for the cognitive aptitudes (G, V, and N) and smallest for the psychomotor aptitudes (K, F, and M).

For GATB cognitive aptitudes G, V, and N, an increase of more than seven weeks in the time interval between successive test administrations is necessary to reduce the average stability coefficient by .01. For the

TABLE A-3 Coefficients of Stability for the GATB, by Aptitude Score

Study	Forms Administered	Interval	Number of Subjects	G	V	N	S	P	Q	K	F	M
Showler and Droege (1969)	A,B	1 day	409	.93	.87	.93	.85	.85	.85	.91	.78	.84
USES Manual (1986)	A,C,D	1 week	3,344 high	.92	.91	.92	.86	.87	.88	.88		
			low	.82	.84	.84	.72	.75	.73	.70		
	A,C,D	1 week	533 high								.71	.74
			low								.57	.65
Showler and Droege (1969)	A,B	2 weeks	354	.92	.89	.92	.82	.85	.81	.91	.75	.78
USES Manual (1970)	1001	2 weeks	156	.89	.90	.93	.87	.82	.88	.90	.81	.86
	A	2 weeks	276 males	.94	.94	.93	.88	.88	.86	.88		
			246 females	.94	.94	.87	.83	.86	.89	.91		
	B	2 weeks	168 males	.94	.91	.91	.89	.86	.86	.89		
			155 females	.94	.93	.92	.88	.84	.85	.88		
Showler and Droege (1969)	A,B	6 weeks	324	.91	.88	.93	.84	.82	.86	.76	.70	.80
USES Manual (1970)	A	3 months	605 males	.85	.86	.82	.81	.72	.74	.86	.65	.73
			554 females	.89	.86	.86	.80	.74	.77	.69	.69	.72
	B	3 months	212 males	.87	.89	.87	.81	.70	.76	.51		
			231 females	.87	.89	.85	.87	.72	.77	.91		
Showler and Droege (1969)	A,B	13 weeks	325	.90	.87	.92	.82	.80	.84	.91	.68	.79
	A,B	26 weeks	293	.94	.89	.93	.85	.83	.79	.85	.70	.73
	A,B	1 year	302	.90	.85	.83	.83	.78	.74	.79	.76	.76
USES Manual (1970) (11th graders)	A,B	1 year	6,624	.83	.82	.81	.74	.67.	.71	.75	.65	.73
			3,229 boys	.84	.82	.83	.75	.67	.73	.82	.64	.71
			3,028 girls	.83	.82	.80	.72	.68	.68	.85	.67	.74
Showler and Droege (1969)	A,B	2 years	288	.85	.87	.87	.79	.74	.77	.74	.69	.72
USES Manual (1970) (10th graders)	A,B	2 years	6,839	.82	.81	.79	.73	.65	.68	.72	.62	.69
			3,348 boys	.82	.82	.80	.76	.65	.70	.76	.62	.68
			3491 girls	.83	.81	.78	.71	.70	.66	.84	.62	.69
Showler and Droege (1969)	A,B	3 years	306	.90	.85	.88	.84	.76	.74	.70	.73	.79
USES Manual (1970) (9th graders)	A,B	3 years	7,078	.79	.79	.77	.70	.62	.63	.68	.57	.64
			3,398 boys	.78	.79	.78	.72	.63	.66	.72	.56	.63
			3,680 girls	.80	.79	.76	.69	.62	.60		.58	.65
Noel Senior (1952)	B-1001	4 years	146	.77	.77	.79	.77		.62			
			76 males	.69	.68	.80	.71		.77			
			70 females	.80	.80	.69	.75		.69			

GATB perceptual aptitudes S, P, and Q, estimates are, on average, initially smaller than for the GATB cognitive aptitudes (G, V, and N) and also vary more widely at specific test-retest time intervals. The relationship between average stability coefficient and test-retest time interval is modeled less well (by ordinary least-squares linear regression) for these aptitudes than for the GATB cognitive aptitudes.

The GATB psychomotor aptitudes, K, F, and M, have still lower estimated stability coefficient intercepts of .84, .70, and .76, respectively. Aptitude K, which is measured with a pencil-and-paper subtest, has an initial stability coefficient that is in the same range as those of the GATB perceptual aptitudes. The two psychomotor aptitudes that are measured with subtests requiring the manipulation of objects, F and M, have somewhat lower average initial stability coefficients. It also appears to be the case that the stabilities of these two psychomotor aptitudes degrade at a faster rate as a function of time interval than is true of GATB aptitudes that are measured with pencil-and-paper subtests.

Data on coefficients of stability of the GATB aptitudes were summarized by computing simple linear regressions of stability coefficients as a function of the time interval between the initial administration and the second administration of the GATB. A scatter diagram that illustrates this relationship for the GATB-G aptitude is shown in Figure 4–1. From the data in the figure we can conclude that stability coefficients for the GATB-G are large (approximating .91, on average) for very small time intervals and degrade slowly as the time interval is increased. Similar patterns were observed for the other GATB aptitudes, although initial values of the stability coefficient were smaller for the spatial aptitudes than for the cognitive aptitudes, and smaller still for the psychomotor aptitudes. These data are summarized in Table A-4, which contains initial values of stability coefficients, the degradation of stability coefficients (amount by which they decrease from initial values) for a 100-day interval between the initial administration of the GATB and the second administration, and the proportion of variance in GATB stability coefficients that is explained by a linear regression on the time interval between the initial and the second GATB administration. The relationship is well explained by a linear relationship for the cognitive and spatial aptitudes, but not for the psychomotor aptitudes.

Equivalent Forms Reliability

Stability coefficients that are based on two administrations of the same test form such as those discussed above are subject to spurious inflation because examinees might remember, and merely duplicate, their initial responses to test items. To avoid this problem, test reliability is some-

TABLE A-4   Initial Values and Degradation of GATB Stability
Coefficients, and Proportion of Variance Explained by Linear
Relationship, by GATB Aptitude

GATB Aptitude	Initial Value of Stability Coefficient	Degradation of Stability Coefficient (100-day interval)	Proportion of Variance Explained
G	.9089	.0099	.58
V	.8936	.0094	.64
N	.8943	.0099	.56
S	.8323	.0082	.42
P	.8074	.0153	.49
Q	.8108	.0106	.44
K	.8390	.0088	.11
F	.6994	.0069	.19
M	.7572	.0068	.24

times estimated by correlating examinees' scores on two different forms of a test. The forms are designed to be psychometrically parallel; that is, equivalent in format, in length, and in the distribution of difficulties and correlations of their items. Parallel test forms are sometimes administered at the same time and are sometimes administered with an intervening time interval. In the former case, correlations between examinees' scores are most sensitive to differences in their performances on the two samples of items that compose the parallel forms. Such estimates of reliability are called "coefficients of equivalence." In the latter case, the temporal instability of examinees' performances also attenuates correlations. These estimates of reliability are called "test-retest parallel-forms estimates" and reflect temporal stability as well as equivalence of performance across parallel test forms.

Four operational forms of the GATB, labeled A, B, C, and D, are currently in use. Forms A and B have been used since 1947 and are now restricted to retesting of initially tested examinees and other low-incidence uses. Forms C and D were normed in 1983 and are currently the primary operational forms of the GATB. Many of the estimates of temporal stability discussed above were based on the administration of parallel forms of the GATB. Results of these studies, as well as other studies of the equivalence of alternate forms of the GATB, are summarized in Table A-5.

The coefficients of equivalence reported in the table are similar in pattern to the coefficients of stability described earlier. Form A and B coefficients tend to be a bit larger than Form A and C coefficients or Form A and D coefficients. Although conclusions must be tentative because the

TABLE A-5 Coefficients of Equivalence for the GATB, by Aptitude Score

Study	Order of Form Administration	Interval	Number of Samples	G	V	N	S	P	Q	K	F	M
Showler and Droege (1969)	A,B	1 day	409	.93	.87	.93	.85	.85	.85	.91	.78	.84
USES *Manual* (1970)	A,B	1 week	95 males	.92	.93	.92	.80	.84	.85			
			85 females	.90	.89	.90	.78	.84	.81			
Showler and Droege (1969)	A,B	2 weeks	354	.92	.89	.92	.82	.85	.81	.91	.75	.78
	A,B	6 weeks	324	.91	.88	.93	.84	.82	.86	.88	.70	.80
	A,B	13 weeks	325	.90	.87	.92	.82	.80	.84	.91	.68	.79
	A,B	26 weeks	293	.94	.89	.93	.85	.83	.79	.91	.70	.73
USES *Manual* (1970)	A,B	1 year	302	.90	.85	.83	.83	.78	.74	.85	.76	.76
	A,B	1 year	6,624 (11th graders)	.83	.82	.81	.74	.67	.71	.79	.65	.73
Showler and Droege (1969)	A,B	2 years	288	.85	.87	.87	.79	.74	.77	.85	.69	.72
USES *Manual* (1970)	A,B	2 years	6,839 (10th graders)	.82	.81	.79	.73	.65	.68	.74	.62	.69
Showler and Droege (1969)	A,B	3 years	306	.90	.85	.88	.84	.76	.74	.84	.73	.79
USES *Manual* (1970)	A,B	3 years	7,078 (9th graders)	.79	.79	.77	.70	.62	.63	.70	.57	.64
USES *Manual* (1986)	A,C	1 week	562	.90	.89	.89	.82	.80	.83	.74		
	C,A	1 week	564	.88	.88	.89	.80	.81	.84	.78		
	A,C	1 week	273								.57	.65
	A,D	1 week	562	.88	.88	.88	.81	.82	.83	.80		
	D,A	1 week	556	.88	.87	.87	.81	.81	.79	.82		
	A,D	1 week	260								.71	.74
	C,D	1 week	543	.90	.89	.89	.84	.81	.84	.78		
	D,C	1 week	543	.89	.90	.90	.82	.84	.80	.80		

number of studies is small, coefficients of equivalence between Forms C and D appear to be of about the same magnitude as Form A and B coefficients. As was true of coefficients of stability for the GATB aptitudes, the cognitive aptitudes (G, V, and N) appear to be the most reliable. In addition, the coefficients of equivalence of the psychomotor aptitudes that are assessed by tests that require manipulation of objects (F and M) tend to be smallest. With the exception of these latter two aptitudes, scores on the GATB aptitudes appear to be assessed with acceptably large interform equivalence and stability for time intervals of one year or less.

It is also possible to estimate the reliability of a test using data collected in a single test administration. Such reliability estimates are called "internal consistency coefficients" since they are effectively correlations of two or more subtests with each other. Internal consistency estimates are not appropriate for assessing the reliability of speeded tests because the consistency actually measured is the consistency of the speed of response, not the consistency of correct answers or of ability.

No estimates of the internal consistency of the GATB subtests or aptitudes are provided in the GATB *Manual* (U.S. Department of Labor, 1970) or in more recent literature that was reviewed in preparing this appendix. Since all subtests of the GATB are administered under conditions that impose severe time limits on examinees, estimates of the internal consistency of the GATB subtests are likely to be spuriously high (Anastasi and Drake, 1954; Cronbach and Warrington, 1951; Gulliksen, 1950a,b; Helmstadter and Ortmeyer, 1953; Lord and Novick, 1968; Mollenkopf, 1960; Morrison, 1960; Rindler, 1979; Stafford, 1971; Wesman, 1960). It is therefore appropriate that Employment Service publications on the GATB and other psychometric literature be devoid of estimates of internal consistency for the GATB.

EQUATING ALTERNATE FORMS OF THE GATB

The *Standards* describe the goal for equated forms of a test (American Educational Research Association et al., 1985:31):

Ideally, alternate forms of a test are interchangeable in use. That is, it should be a matter of indifference to anyone taking the test or to anyone using the test results whether form A or form B of the test was used. Of course, such an ideal cannot be attained fully in practice. Even minor variations in content from one form to the next can prevent the forms from being interchangeable since one form may favor individuals with particular strengths, whereas the other form may favor those with slightly different strengths.

Although considerable care may be taken to make two forms of a test as similar as possible in terms of content and format, the forms cannot be expected to be precisely equal in difficulty. Consequently, the use of simple number-right scores without regard to form is generally inappropriate because such scores would place the people taking the more difficult of the two forms at a disadvantage. To take the unintended differences in difficulty into account, "it is usually necessary to convert the scores of one form to the units of the other, a process called test equating" (American Educational Research Association et al., 1985:31).

There are a number of data collection designs and analytical techniques that may be used to equate forms of a test. Detailed descriptions of the various approaches can be found in Angoff (1971) and in Petersen et al. (1989). Regardless of the approach, however, there are two major issues that need to be considered in judging the adequacy of the equating: (1) the degree to which the forms measure the same characteristic or construct and (2) the magnitude of the errors in the equating due to the procedure and sampling.

Comparability of Constructs Measured

Although the analytical techniques used in equating could be applied to scores from any pair of tests, it makes sense to consider scores to be interchangeable only when forms measure essentially the same characteristics. For example, equating techniques could be used to convert scores on an achievement test in, say, biology such that the distribution of converted biology scores had the same mean and standard deviation as scores on a physics achievement test for some large sample of test takers. Clearly, however, it would not be a matter of indifference to most test takers whether they were administered the biology test or the physics test. Those with greater strengths in biology would prefer the biology test, whereas the converse would be true for those with greater strengths in physics.

In practice, of course, the differences between forms that are to be equated are not so obvious or extreme as the difference between a biology and a physics test. However, subtle differences in test content or the format of the test items can sometimes lead to important shifts in what the test forms measure and therefore to conversions that can give an unintended advantage or disadvantage to particular test takers.

If alternate forms of a test measure the same characteristics, one would expect scores on the two forms to be highly correlated. In the case of a battery of tests, such as the GATB, one would also expect the pattern of correlations among the parts of the tests to be similar for different forms. Evidence regarding both of these issues is provided in an addendum to the 1970 *Manual for USES General Aptitude Test Battery, Section III: Development,* titled "Reliability and Comparability: Forms C and D" (U.S. Department of Labor, 1986).

Pairs of three forms of Subtests 1 through 8 of the GATB were administered to a sample of 3,344 people in 20 participating states. A total of six subsamples ranging in size from 545 to 567 were administered pairs of Forms A, C, and D in counterbalanced order. That is, one subsample (AC) was administered Form A first and then Form C a week later, a second subsample (CA) was administered Form C first and Form A a week later. The remaining four subsamples (AD, DA, CD, and DC) were defined in an analogous fashion.

The correlations between the scores on the alternate forms for each of Subtests 1 through 8 and for the seven aptitude scores that are based on the first eight subtests of the GATB provide estimates of the alternate form reliabilities of the subtests and of the aptitude scores. The alternate-form reliabilities of the first three aptitudes (intelligence, verbal, and numerical) are close to .90, a level that is consistent with alternate-form reliabilities of aptitude tests of high technical quality that are provided by major test publishers. The reliabilities of the remaining four aptitudes (spatial, form perception, clerical, and motor coordination) are lower, close to .80.

The alternate-form reliabilities of the subtests are in the .80s for Subtests 1 through 4 (name comparison, computation, three-dimensional space, and vocabulary) and the high .70s to .80 for Subtests 5, 6, and 8 (tool matching, arithmetic reasoning, and mark making). The lowest reliabilities were obtained for Subtest 7, form matching, where two of the correlations, both involving the relationship between Forms A and C, fall below .70.

In addition to providing alternate-form reliabilities for the first eight subtests of the GATB, the addendum to the *Manual* (U.S. Department of Labor, 1986) also reports matrices of intercorrelations among the eight scores for each of the three forms involved in the reliability and comparability study. Correlations for each pair of subtests show that the three forms of the GATB are virtually indistinguishable in terms of the pattern of correlations among the subtests. The similarity in the patterns of intercorrelations coupled with the reasonably high alternate-form reliabilities suggest that, with the possible exception of Subtest 7, form matching, the forms are measuring sufficiently similar characteristics to equate the forms and use the equated scores interchangeably.

Much less evidence is provided regarding the comparability of Subtests 9 through 12 of the GATB than was provided for Subtests 1 through 8. The evidence that is available is based on smaller samples of test takers and provides less support for concluding that the subtest scores can be treated as being interchangeable after equating.

Subtests 9 through 12 of Form A were administered to 273 test takers followed by Form C one week later. Another sample of 260 test takers was administered Forms A and D in the same pattern (Table A-6). The

TABLE A-6   Alternate-Form Reliabilities of Subtests 9 Through 12 of the GATB and of the Aptitudes Based on Those Subtests, Based on Samples of Sizes 266 and 273

	Reliabilities	
	Forms A,C	Forms A,D
Subtest		
9. Place	.62	.72
10. Turn	.52	.56
11. Assemble	.45	.60
12. Disassemble	.54	.70
Aptitude		
Manual Dexterity	.65	.74
Finger Dexterity	.57	.71

alternate-form reliabilities for both the subtest scores and for the two aptitudes that are based on Subtests 9 through 12 are lower than were obtained for Subtests 1 through 8. The correlations of the Form C with Form A scores are particularly low.

In addition to having low alternate form reliabilities, the degree to which the alternate forms measure the same skills is brought into question by the differences in the patterns of correlations among the subtests. The intercorrelations for each pair of subtest scores are listed in Table A-7. Two correlations for each pair of subtests are shown for Form A. The first is based on the subsample that also took Form C; the second correlation is based on the subsample that also took Form D.

These correlations are subject to greater sampling error than the ones that were summarized above for Subtests 1 through 8 because of their smaller sample sizes. In addition, there are no replications for Forms C and D. Nonetheless, the pattern of correlations for Form C seems to differ from that of Form D. Indeed, considering the Form C versus Form D

TABLE A-7   Correlations Between Subtest Scores by Form

Subtest Pairs	Correlations		
	Form A	Form C	Form D
9 with 10	.66 and .62	.73	.53
9 with 11	.40 and .42	.50	.32
9 with 12	.50 and .52	.44	.49
10 with 11	.44 and .40	.50	.27
10 with 12	.56 and .56	.50	.35
11 with 12	.57 and .46	.50	.49

correlation between subtests, one pair of subtests at a time, four of the six pairs of correlations are significantly different at the .05 level.

In summary, the alternate-form reliabilities and patterns of correlations do not provide sufficient evidence that Subtests 9 through 12 of Forms A, C, and D measure essentially the same characteristics. Hence, the scores from different forms for these subtests should not be considered to be interchangeable.

Equating Procedure and Sampling Errors

The first GATB equating was to place B-1002 (Form A and Form B) on the scale developed for B-1001. To equate Form A, four groups of high school students were administered the old and one of the two new forms, in counterbalanced order. The representativeness of these groups is questionable. One group had to be dropped because test scores were not comparable; the remaining total sample size was 585. The conversion of Form B was similar, but was based on 412 high school students. These are very small samples on which to base equating. The equating procedures, while not specified, appeared to be linear.

The information that is available in the 1984 and 1986 addenda to the *Manual* (U.S. Department of Labor, 1984, 1986) is inadequate for a complete evaluation of the equating of Forms C and D. Thus, the comments on this aspect of the equating are brief and inconclusive.

The design used to investigate the reliability and comparability of Subtests 1 through 8 of Forms A, C, and D is a standard equating design. It is referred to as "Design II: Random groups—both tests administered to each group, counterbalanced" by Angoff (1971). This design provides equating results that have much greater precision, i.e., smaller standard errors of equating, than the more commonly used designs in which only one of the forms is administered to each group. Given this design, the sample sizes were consistent with accepted practice for test equating.

Details of the equating of Subtests 1 through 8 of Forms C and D to Form A are not reported. The data from the reliability and comparability study could have been used with one of the analytical procedures described by Angoff (1971) for Design II. However, information about the specific procedure that was used is not provided. No evidence regarding the adequacy of the equating (e.g., comparisons of linear and equipercentile equating results or estimates of standard errors of equating at different score levels) is presented. Hence, an independent evaluation is not possible.

For Subtests 9 through 12, reservations about equating have already been expressed because of questions about the comparability of the characteristics measured by the different forms. The order of administration was not counterbalanced in the design that was used to investigate the alternate-form reliability and comparability of Subtests 9 through 12; consequently, a separate standardization sample was obtained for purposes of equating.

The standardization sample (for Subtests 9 through 12) consisted of a total of 2,092 persons from 11 states. Form C was administered to 981 people and Form D to 1,111 people in the standardization sample. Although details of assignment to the two subsamples are not presented, they were apparently considered to be random samples from the same population as the Form A standardization sample to which Forms C and D were equated. Random assignment is a critical part of Angoff's (1971: 569) "Design I: Random groups—one test administered to each group." Hence, it seems important to understand the basis for considering the Form C and D standardization samples to be randomly equivalent to the Form A standardization sample.

The 1986 addendum to the *Manual* indicates that both linear and equipercentile equating procedures were obtained for the equating of Subtests 9 through 12, but because the two procedures produced very similar results it was decided that the linear equating would be used (U.S. Department of Labor, 1986). Such a decision is consistent with accepted practice. However, no information comparing the results of the two procedures is provided. Hence it is not possible to provide an independent evaluation of this decision.

REFERENCES

American Educational Research Association, American Psychological Association, and National Council on Measurement in Education
   1985   *Standards for Educational and Psychological Testing.* Washington, D.C.: American Psychological Association.
Anastasi, A., and R. Drake
   1954   An empirical comparison of certain techniques for estimating the reliability of speeded tests. *Educational and Psychological Measurement* 14:529–540.
Angoff, W.H.
   1971   Scales, norms, and equivalent scores. In R.L. Thorndike, ed., *Educational Measurement,* 2d ed. Washington, D.C.: American Council on Education.
Briscoe, C.D., W. Muelder, and W. Michael
   1981   Concurrent validity of self-estimates of abilities relative to criteria provided by standardized test measures of the same abilities for a sample of high school students eligible for participation in the CETA program. *Educational and Psychological Measurement* 41:1285–1294.
Cassel, R.N., and G.W. Reier
   1971   Comparative analysis of concurrent and predictive validity for the GATB Clerical Aptitude Test Battery. *Journal of Psychology* 79:135–140.
Cooley, W.W.
   1965   Further relationships with the TALENT battery. *Personnel and Guidance Journal* 44:295–303.

Cronbach, Lee J., and W.G. Warrington
 1951 Time limit tests: estimating their reliability and degree of speeding. *Psychometrika* 14:167–188.
Dong, H., Y. Sung, and S. Goldman
 1986 The validity of the Ball Aptitude Test Battery (BAB) III: relationship to the CAB, DAT, and GATB. *Educational and Psychological Measurement* 46:245–250.
Gulliksen, H.A.
 1950a The reliability of speeded tests. *Psychometrika* 15:259–260.
 1950b *Theory of Mental Tests*. New York: Wiley.
Hakstian, A.R., and R. Bennett
 1978 Validity studies using the Comprehensive Ability Battery (CAB) II: Relationship with the DAT and GATB. *Educational and Psychological Measurement* 38:1003–1015.
Helmstadter, G.C., and D.H. Ortmeyer
 1953 Some techniques for determining the relative magnitude of speed and power components of a test. *Educational and Psychological Measurement* 12:280–287.
Howe, M.A.
 1975 General Aptitude Test Battery Q: an Australian empirical study. *Australian Psychologist* 10:32–44.
Kettner, N.
 1976 Armed Services Vocational Aptitude Battery (ASVAB Form 5): Comparison with GATB and DAT Tests. Final report, May 1975–October 1976. Armed Services Human Resources Laboratory, Brooks Air Force Base, Texas.
Kish, G.B.
 1970 Alcoholics' GATB and Shipley profiles and their interrelationships. *Journal of Clinical Psychology* 26:482–484.
Knapp, R., L. Knapp, and W. Michael
 1977 Stability and concurrent validity of the Career Ability Placement Survey (CAPS) against the DAT and the GATB. *Educational and Psychological Measurement* 37:1081–1085.
Lord, F.M., and Melvin R. Novick
 1968 *Statistical Theories of Mental Test Scores*. Reading, Mass.: Addison-Wesley.
Mollenkopf, W.G.
 1960 Time limits and the behavior of test takers. *Educational and Psychological Measurement* 20:223–230.
Moore, R., and J. Davies
 1984 Predicting GED scores on the basis of expectancy, valence, intelligence, and pretest skill levels with the disadvantaged. *Educational and Psychological Measurement* 44:483–489.
Morrison, E.J.
 1960 On test variance and the dimensions of the measurement situation. *Educational and Psychological Measurement* 20:231–250.
O'Malley, P., and J. Bachman
 1976 Longitudinal evidence for the validity of the Quick Test. *Psychological Reports* 38:1247–1252.
Petersen, Nancy S., Michael J. Kolen, and H.D. Hoover
 1989 Scaling, norming, and equating. Chap. 6 in Robert L. Linn, ed., *Educational Measurement*, 3d ed. New York: Macmillan.
Rindler, S.E.
 1979 Pitfalls in assessing test speededness. *Journal of Educational Measurement* 16:261–270.

Sakalosky, J.C.
  1970   A Study of the Relationship Between the Differential Aptitude Test Battery and the General Aptitude Test Battery Scores of Ninth Graders. Master's thesis, Millersville State College.
Senior, N.
  1952   An Analysis of the Effect of Four Years of College Training on General Aptitude Test Battery Scores. Unpublished master's thesis, University of Utah, Provo.
Showler, W.K., and R.C. Droege
  1969   Stability of aptitude scores for adults. *Educational and Psychological Measurement* 29:681–686.
Stafford, R.E.
  1971   The speededness quotient: A new descriptive statistic for tests. *Journal of Educational Measurement* 8:275–278.
U.S. Department of Labor
  1970   *Manual for the USTES General Aptitude Test Battery. Section III: Development.* Washington, D.C.: Manpower Administration, U.S. Department of Labor.
  1984   Forms C and D of the General Aptitude Test Battery: An Historical Review of Development. Division of Counseling and Test Development, Employment and Training Administration, U.S. Department of Labor, Washington, D.C.
  1986   *Reliability and Comparability: Forms C and D.* Addendum to *Manual for the USTES General Aptitude Test Battery. Section III: Development.* U.S. Employment Service, Employment and Training Administration. Washington, D.C.: U.S. Department of Labor.
Wesman, A.G.
  1960   Some effects of speed in test use. *Educational and Psychological Measurement* 20:267–274.

B

Tables Summarizing GATB Reliabilities

TABLE B-1 Effect Sizes for GATB Aptitude Scores, from Initial Testing to Retesting[a] for GATB Cognitive Aptitudes: Studies with Same-Form Retesting

Study	Form Administered	Interval	Number of Samples	G	V	N
Buckner (1962)		4 years	214	0.91	0.83	0.53
USES *Manual* (1970)	A	2 weeks	276 males	0.43	0.32	0.34
	A	2 weeks	246 females	0.48	0.43	0.45
	B	2 weeks	168 males	0.46	0.34	0.41
	B	2 weeks	155 females	0.40	0.35	0.41
	B	2 weeks	212 males	0.43	0.28	0.29
	B	2 weeks	231 females	0.42	0.29	0.36
	A	3 weeks	605 males	0.48	0.33	0.37
	A	3 weeks	554 females	0.50	0.35	0.41

[a]Mean changes expressed in standard deviations of the initial-testing distribution.

TABLE B-2   Effect Sizes for GATB Aptitude Scores, from Initial Testing to Retesting[a] for GATB Cognitive Aptitudes: Studies with Alternate-Form Retesting

Study	Form Administration Order	Interval	Number of Samples	G	V	N
USES *Manual* (1970)	A,B	1 week	95 males	0.26	0.17	0.20
	A,B	1 week	85 females	0.19	0.24	0.22
USES *Manual* Addendum (1986)	A,C	1 week	562	0.24	0.05	0.19
	A,D	1 week	562	0.20	0.07	0.10
	C,A	1 week	563	0.19	0.14	0.13
	C,D	1 week	544	0.19	0.12	0.08
	D,A	1 week	556	0.27	0.16	0.24
	D,C	1 week	543	0.25	0.07	0.21
Showler and Droege (1969)	A,B	1 day	409	0.24	0.17	0.26
	A,B	2 weeks	354	0.15	0.14	0.16
	A,B	6 weeks	324	0.02	0.03	0.06
	A,B	13 weeks	325	0.15	0.14	0.16
	A,B	26 weeks	293	0.09	0.05	0.04
	A,B	1 year	302	0.21	0.19	0.21
	A,B	2 year	288	0.21.	0.18	0.20
	A,B	3 years	306	0.23	0.30	0.18

[a]Mean changes expressed in standard deviations of the initial-testing distribution.

TABLE B-3   Effect Sizes for GATB Aptitude Scores, from Initial Testing to Retesting[a] for GATB Perceptual Aptitudes: Studies with Same-Form Retesting

Study	Form Administered	Interval	Number of Samples	S	P	Q
Buckner (1962)		4 years	214	0.85	0.73	1.00
USES *Manual* (1970)	A	2 weeks	276 males	0.55	0.46	0.64
	A	2 weeks	246 females	0.63	0.59	0.72
	B	2 weeks	168 males	0.52	0.48	0.62
	B	2 weeks	155 females	0.60	0.60	0.73
	B	2 weeks	212 males	0.67	0.55	0.76
	B	2 weeks	231 females	0.60	0.64	0.83
	B	3 weeks	605 males	0.56	0.51	0.80
	A	3 weeks	554 females	0.67	0.55	0.77

[a]Mean changes expressed in standard deviations of the initial-testing distribution.

TABLE B-4 Effect Sizes for GATB Aptitude Scores, from Initial Testing to Retesting[a] for GATB Perceptual Aptitudes: Studies with Alternate-Form Retesting

Study	Form Administration Order	Interval	Number of Samples	S	P	Q
USES *Manual* (1970)	A,B	1 week	95 males	0.40	0.33	0.44
	A,B	1 week	85 females	0.28	0.36	0.49
USES *Manual* Addendum (1986)	A,C	1 week	562	0.39	0.41	0.35
	A,D	1 week	562	0.39	0.24	0.38
	C,A	1 week	563	0.41	0.18	0.48
	C,D	1 week	544	0.46	0.30	0.41
	D,A	1 week	556	0.38	0.25	0.44
	D,C	1 week	543	0.36	0.34	0.35
Showler and Droege (1969)	A,B	1 day	409	0.38	0.53	0.55
	A,B	2 weeks	354	0.32	0.40	0.54
	A,B	6 weeks	324	0.21	0.27	0.43
	A,B	13 weeks	325	0.29	0.34	0.46
	A,B	26 weeks	293	0.17	0.30	0.36
	A,B	1 year	302	0.23	0.13	0.38
	A,B	2 year	288	0.21	0.17	0.29
	A,B	3 years	306	0.19	0.20	0.23

[a]Mean changes expressed in standard deviations of the initial-testing distribution.

TABLE B-5 Effect Sizes for GATB Aptitude Scores, from Initial Testing to Retesting[a] for GATB Psychomotor Aptitudes: Studies with Same-Form Retesting

Study	Form Administered	Interval	Number of Samples	K	F	M
Buckner (1962)		4 years	214	1.08		
Rotman (1963) (Mentally retarded subjects with an average of 4.55 days' practice)		4.6 days (avg)	40	0.94	0.43	1.23
Rotman (1963) (Mentally retarded subjects retested without practice)		4.6 days (avg)	40	0.52	0.38	0.04
USES *Manual* (1970)	A	2 weeks	276 males	0.43		
	A	2 weeks	246 females	0.57		
	B	2 weeks	168 males	0.51		
	B	2 weeks	155 females	0.63		
	B	2 weeks	212 males	0.83		
	B	2 weeks	231 females	0.85		
	A	3 weeks	605 males	0.60	0.80	0.92
	A	3 weeks	554 females	0.56	0.86	0.96

[a]Mean changes expressed in standard deviations of the initial-testing distribution.

TABLE B-6   Effect Sizes for GATB Aptitude Scores, from Initial Testing to Retesting[a] for GATB Psychomotor Aptitudes: Studies with Alternate-Form Retesting

Study	Form Administration Order	Interval	Number of Samples	K	F	M
Showler and Droege (1969)	A,B	1 day	409	0.44	0.64	0.61
	A,B	2 weeks	354	0.42	0.53	0.52
	A,B	6 weeks	324	0.42	0.62	0.44
	A,B	13 weeks	325	0.31	0.41	0.31
	A,B	26 weeks	293	0.26	0.36	0.34
	A,B	1 year	302	0.41	0.40	0.28
	A,B	2 year	288	0.38	0.44	0.50
	A,B	3 years	306	0.23	0.27	0.34
USES *Manual* Addendum (1986)	A,C	1 week	273		−.26	−.13
	A,D	1 week	260		−.19	0.64
	A,C	1 week	562	0.08		
	A,D	1 week	562	0.33		
	C,A	1 week	563	0.22		
	C,D	1 week	544	0.17		
	D,A	1 week	556	0.34		
	D,C	1 week	543	0.09		

[a]Mean changes expressed in standard deviations of the initial-testing distribution.

C

Biographical Sketches

JOHN A. HARTIGAN (*Chair*) is the Eugene Higgins professor of statistics and director of the Statistical Computing Laboratory at Yale University. His teaching and research interests center on the foundations of probability and statistics, Bayes theory, classification, statistical computing, and graphical methods. He is an elected fellow of the American Statistical Association and the Institute of Mathematical Statistics and an elected member of the International Statistical Institute and the Royal Statistical Society. He received BSc and MSc degrees in mathematics from the University of Sydney and a PhD degree in mathematical statistics from Princeton University.

LORRIE A. SHEPARD (*Vice Chair*) is professor and chair of research and evaluation methodology in the School of Education at the University of Colorado, Boulder. She is past president of the National Council on Measurement in Education and past editor of both the *Journal of Educational Measurement* and the *American Educational Research Journal*. Her research includes applied psychometric studies, aimed at topics such as standard setting and bias detection, and policy studies addressing issues of test use. She received a BA degree in history from Pomona College and an MA degree in counseling and a PhD degree in educational research from the University of Colorado.

MARCUS ALEXIS is dean of the College of Business Administration at the University of Illinois, Chicago. An expert on decision making, marketing, and the economic role of minorities, he has taught at Macal-

329

ester College, De Paul University, the University of Rochester, and Northwestern University and has been a Ford Foundation faculty study fellow at Harvard University and the Massachusetts Institute of Technology. He was a commissioner of the Interstate Commerce Commission from 1979 to 1981. He is currently deputy chairman of the Federal Reserve Bank of Chicago, a trustee of the Teachers Insurance & Annuity Association (TIAA), and a member of the board of directors of the Metropolitan Planning Council for the City of Chicago. He is a member of the board of governors of the Beta Gamma Sigma society, a member of the American Economic Association, the National Economic Association, and the Econometric Society, and a past member of the board of the Caucus of Black Economists. He is on the editorial board of the *Review of Black Political Economy* and has served on the board of economists of *Black Enterprise*. He received AB and honorary Doctor of Humane Letters degrees from Brooklyn College, an MA degree from Michigan State University, and a PhD degree in economics from the University of Minnesota.

MANFRED EMMRICH is director of the North Carolina State Employment Service Division of the Employment Security Commission of North Carolina, responsible for the operation of employment services provided by 84 local Job Service centers and branch offices across the state. From 1978 to 1985, Emmrich served as a senior associate with MDC, Inc., a nonprofit research and development group with special interests in productivity and employment and training issues. Emmrich was chair of the Employment Security Commission of North Carolina from 1973 to 1978, responsible for the state's employment service, unemployment insurance, and labor market information programs. From 1962 to 1973, Emmrich held various management and executive positions in the Macke Company. Prior to entering the private sector, Emmrich served in the U.S. Army as an officer in Army Intelligence and Security. A former president of the Interstate Conference of Employment Security Agencies, Inc., Emmrich currently serves on that organization's Employment and Training Committee. Emmrich has a BA degree in economics from Davidson College.

LARRY V. HEDGES is chairman of the Measurement Evaluation and Statistical Analysis Program and of the Department of Education at the University of Chicago. His research is concerned with statistical methods for combining evidence from replicated research studies, statistical models in cognitive psychology, and the social psychology of scientific research. He is the coauthor (with Ingram Olkin) of *Statistical Methods for Meta-Analysis* and is the associate editor of the *Journal of Educational Statistics* and *Psychological Bulletin*. He received a BA degree from the University of California, San Diego, and MS and PhD degrees from Stanford University, all in statistics.

IRA J. HIRSH is Edward Mallinckrodt distinguished university professor of psychology and audiology at Washington University, where he has also been chair of the Department of Psychology and dean of the Faculty of Arts and Sciences. His research on speech, hearing, and deafness has been carried out at the Central Institute for the Deaf, where he was formerly director of research and is currently senior research scientist. He is a member of the National Academy of Sciences and a fellow of the Acoustical Society of America (past president), the American Psychological Association, and the American Speech and Hearing Association. From 1982 to 1987 he was chair of the Commission on Behavioral and Social Sciences and Education of the National Research Council. He has an AB degree from the New York State College for Teachers at Albany, an MA degree from Northwestern University, and a PhD degree in experimental psychology from Harvard University.

RICHARD M. JAEGER is professor of education and director of the Center for Educational Research and Evaluation at the University of North Carolina, Greensboro. His research is concerned with educational measurement and applied statistics. He is coeditor of *Minimum Competency Achievement Testing* (1980), author of *Statistics: A Spectator Sport* (1983) and *Sampling in Education and the Social Sciences* (1984), and editor of *Complementary Methods for Research in Education* (1987). He is past editor of the *Journal of Educational Measurement* and is on the editorial boards of several journals. He is past president of the National Council on Measurement in Education and a member of the American Statistical Association, the American Educational Research Association, and the American Evaluation Association. He received a BA degree in mathematics from Pepperdine College and MS and PhD degrees in mathematical statistics and educational research methodology, respectively, from Stanford University.

STEPHEN P. KLEIN is a senior research scientist with the RAND Corporation where he directs policy research studies in the fields of education, health, and criminal justice. He also serves as a consultant to several professional licensing boards on matters relating to testing. He is a member of the American Psychological Association, the American Educational Research Association, and the National Council on Measurement in Education. He received a BS degree from Tufts University and MS and PhD degrees in industrial psychology from Purdue University.

ROBERT L. LINN is professor of education at the University of Colorado, Boulder. His research is directed at applied and theoretical problems in educational and psychological measurement. He is a former president of the Division of Evaluation, Measurement, and Statistics of the American Psychological Association, former president of the National Council on Measurement in Education, and former vice president of the American Educational Research Association for the Division of Measurement and Research Methodology. He has served as editor of the *Journal of Educational Measurement* and was vice chair of the committee that developed the 1985 *Standards for Educational and Psychological Testing*. He received an AB degree in psychology from the University of California, Los Angeles, and an MA degree in psychology and a PhD degree in psychological measurement from the University of Illinois, Urbana-Champaign.

JOHN M. RAUSCHENBERGER is a personnel research consultant in the Workforce Research and Selection Systems Section of the Employee Development Office at the Ford Motor Company. He is a member of the American Psychological Association, the Society for Industrial and Organizational Psychology, the Academy of Management, and the Equal Employment Advisory Council's Subcommittee on Employee Selection Procedures. He serves as a special reviewer for the *Journal of Applied Psychology* and is on the editorial board of *Personnel Psychology* journal. He received a BS degree in psychology and MA and PhD degrees in industrial psychology, all from Michigan State University.

MICHAEL ROTHSCHILD is professor of economics and dean of social sciences, University of California, San Diego. His research concerns the economics of information, financial economics, law and economics, and industrial organization. He is a member and fellow of the Econometric Society and a member of the American Economic Association. He received a BA degree from Reed College, an MA degree from Yale University, and a PhD degree in economics from the Massachusetts Institute of Technology.

PAUL R. SACKETT is associate professor at the Industrial Relations Center of the University of Minnesota. He was previously associate professor of psychology at the University of Illinois, Chicago, and on the faculty of the School of Business at the University of Kansas. He has published extensively in the areas of assessment of managerial potential, job analysis, honesty in the workplace, and psychometric issues in employee selection. He is coauthor (with George F. Dreher) of *Perspectives on Employee Staffing and Selection* (1983), editor of *Personnel Psychology,* and serves on the editorial board of the *Journal of Applied Psychology*. He received a PhD degree in psychology from the Ohio State University.

O. PETER SHERWOOD is solicitor general of New York State. A litigator, he has tried cases and argued appeals in many state and federal courts, including several cases involving challenges to employment testing practices under Title VII. Before joining the Office of the New York Attorney General, he was an assistant counsel at the NAACP Legal Defense and Educational Fund, Inc., where his practice was focused on fair employment practices litigation. Until 1987 he was an adjunct assistant professor of law at the New York University School of Law, where he taught constitutional law and fair employment practices law. He received a BA degree from Brooklyn College of the City University of New York and a JD degree from New York University School of Law.

HOWARD F. TAYLOR is professor of sociology at Princeton University. His research interests encompass the methodology of test score heritability estimation, social psychology, and race and ethnic relations. His books include *The IQ Game: A Methodological Inquiry into the Heredity-Environment Controversy* (1980) and *Balance in Small Groups* (1978). He is a member of the American Sociological Association, a fellow of the Sociological Research Association, and vice president of the Eastern Sociological Society and has been a member of the editorial boards of several journals. He received a BA degree from Hiram College and MA and PhD degrees in sociology from Yale University.

ALEXANDRA K. WIGDOR is study director of the Committee on the General Aptitude Test Battery and also serves as study director of the Committee on the Performance of Military Personnel. Previously, as study director of the Committee on Ability Testing, she coedited (with Wendell R. Garner) *Ability Testing: Uses, Consequences, and Controversies* (1982). Trained as an historian, her research interests now include human performance assessment, the legal and social dimensions of psychological testing, and the development of governmental policy on testing and selection. A member of Phi Beta Kappa, she received BA and MA degrees from the University of Missouri and studied further at the Free University of Berlin, the University of Maryland, and the Institute for Historical Research, University of London.

HILDA WING, currently a research psychologist with the Federal Aviation Administration, served as research associate for the Committee on the General Aptitude Test Battery and the Committee on the Performance of Military Personnel. Previously she was with the Psychological Corporation, served as chief of the predictor development team at the U.S. Army Research Institute for the Behavioral and Social Sciences, and was research psychologist at the U.S. Office of Personnel Management. Her primary area of expertise is personnel testing. She is a member of the

American Psychological Association and has served as chair of its Committee on Employment and Human Resources, and of its Committee on Psychological Tests and Assessment. She received an AB degree in mathematics from Middlebury College and MA and PhD degrees in experimental psychology from the Johns Hopkins University.

Index

R